CU00701640

The Origins of Sectarianism in Early Modern Ireland

Ireland is riven by sectarian hatred. This simple assumption provides a powerful explanation for the bitterness and violence which has so dominated Irish history. Most notably, the troubles in Northern Ireland have provided fertile ground for scholars from all disciplines to argue about and explore ways in which religious division fuelled the descent into hostility and disorder. In much of this literature, however, sectarianism is seen as, somehow, a 'given' in Irish history, an inevitable product of the clash of the Reformation and Counter-Reformation, something which sprang fully formed into existence in the sixteenth century. In this book, leading historians provide the first detailed analysis of the ways in which rival confessions were developed in early modern Ireland, the extent to which the Irish people were indeed divided into two religious camps by the mid seventeenth century, and also their surprising ability to transcend such stark divisions.

ALAN FORD is Professor of Theology at the University of Nottingham. He is the author of *The Protestant Reformation* (1997) and editor, with James Maguire and Kenneth Milne, of *As by Law Established: The Church of Ireland since the Reformation* (1995).

JOHN MCCAFFERTY is Director of the Mícheál Ó Cléirigh Institute at University College Dublin. He has published articles on late medieval and early modern Ireland.

The Origins of Sectarianism in Early Modern Ireland

Edited by

Alan Ford and John McCafferty

CAMBRIDGE
UNIVERSITY PRESS

CAMBRIDGE UNIVERSITY PRESS
Cambridge, New York, Melbourne, Madrid, Cape Town, Singapore, São Paulo

Cambridge University Press
The Edinburgh Building, Cambridge CB2 2RU, UK

Published in the United States of America by Cambridge University Press,
New York

www.cambridge.org
Information on this title: www.cambridge.org/9780521837552

First published 2005

Printed in the United Kingdom at the University Press, Cambridge

A catalogue record for this book is available from the British Library

ISBN-13 978-0-521-837-552 hardback
ISBN-10 0-521-837-553 hardback

Contents

Preface   *page* vii
List of contributors   viii
List of abbreviations   ix

1   Living together, living apart: sectarianism in
    early modern Ireland   1
    ALAN FORD

2   Confessionalisation in Ireland: periodisation
    and character, 1534–1649   24
    UTE LOTZ-HEUMANN

3   Protestant prelates or godly pastors? The dilemma
    of the early Stuart episcopate   54
    JOHN McCAFFERTY

4   'In imitation of that holy patron of prelates the
    blessed St Charles': episcopal activity in Ireland and
    the formation of a confessional identity, 1618–1653   73
    TADHG Ó HANNRACHÁIN

5   A haven of popery: English Catholic migration to
    Ireland in the age of plantations   95
    DAVID EDWARDS

6   The Irish historical renaissance and the shaping
    of Protestant history   127
    ALAN FORD

7   Religion, culture and the bardic elite in early
    modern Ireland   158
    MARC CABALL

8   The political and religious thought of Florence
    Conry and Hugh McCaughwell   183
    MÍCHEÁL MacCRAITH

9   Sectarianism: division and dissent in Irish Catholicism   203
    BRIAN JACKSON

10 Purity of blood and purity of faith in early modern Ireland 216
    DECLAN DOWNEY

11 Concluding reflection: confronting the violence
    of the Irish reformations   229
    JOHN MORRILL

Index   240

Preface

This book is a product of a symposium on sectarianism in early modern Ireland, held in University College Dublin in April 1998. Organising such an event is dependent upon two things: gaining sufficient financial support to gather everyone together; and securing participants who can contribute creatively both in formal presentations and the informal discussions which are such an essential part of these meetings. We have been fortunate in both respects. We are grateful for the support provided by the Arts Faculty and the School of History in University College Dublin, without which neither the symposium nor the book would have been possible. But we would also like to thank our contributors, who, in the course of the two days, worked significantly towards expanding and, in our cases, revising, the way in which we envisioned sectarianism.

The process of transforming these insights into a book was, inevitably, a longer one than we had perhaps originally envisaged. But the final product has been considerably enriched by the advice and encouragement of Bill Davies and Michael Watson at Cambridge University Press, and of Professor John Morrill, that universal factotum of early modern British and Irish history.

ALAN FORD
JOHN MCCAFFERTY

Contributors

MARC CABALL is the Director of the Irish Research Council for the Humanities and Social Sciences, Dublin

DECLAN DOWNEY is Lecturer in the School of History, University College Dublin

DAVID EDWARDS is Lecturer in the Department of History, University College Cork

ALAN FORD is Professor of Theology, University of Nottingham

BRIAN JACKSON is Managing Director of the Abbey Theatre, Dublin

UTE LOTZ-HEUMANN is Wissenschaftliche Assistentin in the Department of History, Humboldt-University in Berlin

JOHN MCCAFFERTY is Lecturer in the School of History, University College Dublin and Director of the Micheál Ó Cléirigh Institute

MÍCHEÁL MACCRAITH is Professor of Modern Irish at University College Galway

JOHN MORRILL is Professor of British and Irish History at the University of Cambridge

TADHG Ó HANNRACHÁIN is Lecturer in the School of History, University College Dublin

Abbreviations

ARSI	*Archivum Romanum Societas Iesu, Rome*
Bodl.	Bodleian Library, Oxford
Cregan, 'Episcopate'	D. F. Cregan, 'The social and cultural background of a counter-reformation episcopate, 1618–60', in Art Cosgrove and Donal McCartney (eds.), *Studies in Irish history* (Dublin: University College Dublin, 1979), pp. 85–117
CRS	Catholic Record Society
CSPI	Calendar of state papers relating to Ireland (London: Public Record Office, 1860–1912)
EHS	English Historical Studies
IHS	Irish Historical Studies
Wadding papers	Brendan Jennings (ed.), *Wadding papers 1614–38* (Dublin: Irish Manuscripts Commission, 1953)
NHI	T. W. Moody, F. X. Martin and F. J. Byrne (eds.), *A new history of Ireland, vol. III: early modern Ireland, 1534–1691* (Oxford: Clarendon Press, 1976)
UW	C. R. Elrington and J. H. Todd (eds.), *The whole works of the Most Rev. James Ussher*, 17 vols. (Dublin, London, 1829–64)

1 Living together, living apart: sectarianism in early modern Ireland

Alan Ford

In 1615 Richard Stanihurst gave an account of the torture and death of the Catholic archbishop of Cashel, Dermot O'Hurley at the hands of his Protestant gaolers in 1584:

The officials put the archbishop's bare feet in boots which they filled with oil, tied his legs to the uprights of the stocks, and then lit a fire underneath. The boiling-hot oil worked its way up from his feet to his shins and other parts, torturing him unbearably, so that bits of skin fell away from the flesh, and pieces of flesh from the bare bones. The official in charge of the torture, unaccustomed to such bizarre mutilation, rushed suddenly from the room not wanting to continue looking at such monstrous barbarity, worse than that of wild beasts, nor to hear any longer in his fleeing ears the cries of the innocent archbishop which re-sounded in the vicinity. The Calvinist torturers feasted for a while on these extraordinary cruelties, but were clearly not satisfied. Accordingly after a few days they took the mangled archbishop early in the morning, almost dying from his continual torture . . . to a field not far away from Dublin Castle . . . and there hanged the innocent man from the gallows with a noose roughly made from brushwood. . .[1]

In 1646 Sir William Temple described Catholic atrocities in the 1641 rising:

Others they buried alive, a manner of death they used to severall British in severall places: and at Clownis within the Countie of Fermanagh, there were seventeen persons, having been hanged till they were halfe dead, cast together into a pit, and being covered over with a little earth, lay pittifully, sending out the most lament-able groanes for a good time after. Some were deadly wounded and so hanged up on tenterhooks. Some had ropes put about their necks and so drawn thorow water . . . others were hanged up and taken down and hanged up againe severall tmies . . . Others were hanged up by the armes, and with many slashes and cutts they made the experiment with their swords how many blows an Englishman would endure before he dyed. Some had their bellies ript up, and so left with their guts running about their heels. But this horrid kind of cruelty was principally

[1] Richard Stanihurst, *Brevis praemunitio pro futura concertatione cum Jacobo Usserio* (Douai, 1615), p. 29.

reserved by these inhumane monsters for women, whose sex they neither pitied nor spared, hanging up severall women, many of them great with childe, whose bellies they ripped up as they hung, and so let the little infants fall out.[2]

Over 350 years later, the pattern was little different:

On the night of 14 August 1994, Seán Monaghan, a young Catholic man, was abducted in West Belfast by a member of a Loyalist paramilitary organisation, the Ulster Freedom Fighters. He was taken to a house on the Shankill Road and tortured. He managed to escape through a window and appealed for help to a woman in a house across the street. The woman phoned her daughter who came with her boyfriend and took him to her home.

Others then took possession of Mr Monaghan who was bound and gagged with black tape. He was taken out of the house and murdered a short distance away.[3]

Such stories of sectarian cruelty provide a constant backdrop to Irish history. To the casual observer, the temptation is, simply, to despair, as the hopeless cycle of violence and revenge, begetting still further brutality and bloodshed, is repeated down the centuries. To politicians, concerned with building a more tolerant society, reminders of the sectarian past can be seen as an embarassment, a negative model for a forward-looking, modern country.[4] To those of a more scholarly bent, however, stories such as these constitute a standing challenge – to explore this undercurrent of hatred and violence in Irish history, identify its roots and the driving forces behind it, and trace how it has developed and changed over time. Traditionally, answers to these kinds of questions are provided by anthropologists, geographers, historians, sociologists – those academics who are involved in analysing the functioning (and malfunctioning) of societies across the ages. And, indeed, there are a number of such studies, ranging from general historical treatments which begin in the sixteenth century, to detailed sociological studies of sectarianism in Northern Ireland in the latter part of the twentieth century.[5] Yet, for all

---

[2] John Temple, *The Irish rebellion* (London, 1646), pp. 95–6.

[3] R. K. McVeigh, 'Cherishing the children of the nation unequally: sectarianism in Ireland', in Patrick Clancy *et al.* (eds.), *Irish Society: sociological perspectives* (Dublin: Institute of Public Administration, 1995), p. 620; the final quotation is from *The Irish News*, 27 August 1994.

[4] McVeigh, 'Sectarianism in Ireland', pp. 623–4; R. F. Foster, 'Remembering 1798', in R. F. Foster, *The Irish story: telling tales and making it up in Ireland* (London: Penguin, 2002), pp. 228–30.

[5] Joseph Liechty, 'The problem of sectarianism and the Church of Ireland', in Alan Ford, James McGuire and Kenneth Milne (eds.), *Principle and pragmatism: towards a history of the Church of Ireland'* (Dublin: Lilliput Press, 1993), pp. 204–22; Joseph Liechty, *Roots of sectarianism in Ireland: chronology and reflections* (Belfast: Joseph Liechty, 1993); Joseph Liechty and Cecelia Clegg, *Moving beyond sectarianism: religion, conflict, and reconciliation in Northern Ireland* (Dublin: Columba Press, 2001); J. D. Brewer and G. I. Higgins,

the scholarly activity, there is a certain mismatch between the vast volume of material on modern Irish history and the equally large out-pouring of work on the Northern Ireland problem on the one hand, and the rather scant literature on sectarian hatred in Ireland on the other.[6] Sectarianism is, according to a sociologist, 'undertheorised', whereas to a historian it is, more simply, 'under-researched'.[7]

The purpose of this volume is to make a contribution to tackling that neglect. Not, of course, to cover the full sweep of post-reformation Irish history or offer a comprehensive account of the origins of Irish sectarianism – that would be premature. But rather to examine the emergence of separate structures and attitudes in early modern Ireland, that period when Protestants and Catholics began to live apart and create parallel communities, institutions, cultures and histories. Each chapter constitutes an analysis of a part of this phenomenon. Ute Lotz-Heumann places Ireland in the wider European context of confession building. John McCafferty's and Tadhg Ó hAnnracháin's twin chapters explore how the rival bishops coped with the difficult relationship between episcopal ideals and the rather more messy and complicated realities which sprang from the existence of two religions in Ireland. David Edwards' ground-breaking examination of the interaction between Catholicism and plantation reveals the previously unsuspected scale of Catholic settlement in Ireland. Alan Ford, Marc Caball and Mícheál MacCraith each analyse a different aspect of the cultural and ideological developments and readjustments which were required by the development of separate churches. And finally Brian Jackson and Declan Downey look at how Irish Catholics reacted at home and in exile to the identification of Irish nation and Catholic church.

But the purpose of this introduction is not to summarise the later chapters. Rather it seeks to explore some of the wider issues relating to the nature and context of sectarianism in early modern Ireland, such

---

Anti-Catholicism in Northern Ireland, 1600–1998: the mote and the beam (Basingstoke: Macmillan, 1998); Brian Lambkin, *Opposite religions still? Interpreting Northern Ireland after the conflict* (Aldershot: Ashgate, 1996); Catherine Hirst, *Religion, politics and violence in nineteenth-century Belfast: the Pound and Sandy Row* (Dublin: Four Courts, 2002); E. Cairns, 'The object of sectarianism: the material reality of sectarianism in Ulster Loyalism', *Journal of the Royal Anthropological Institute*, new series 6 (2000), 437–52; Sean Farrell, *Rituals and riots: sectarian violence and political culture in Ulster, 1784–1886* (Lexington: University Press of Kentucky, 2000); and see further references in McVeigh, 'Sectarianism in Ireland', pp. 622–3.

[6] A search for 'sectarian' or 'sectarianism' in April 2004 produced a total of 52 hits from the 5,550 records on the CAIN bibliography of the Northern Ireland conflict: http://cain.ulst.ac.uk/bibdbs/cainbib.htm.

[7] McVeigh, 'Sectarianism in Ireland', pp. 622–5; Marianne Elliott, *The long road to peace in Northern Ireland* (Liverpool: Liverpool University Press, 2002), p. 178.

as periodisation and terminology, and, in order to assess its grip on Irish society, it analyses the significance of the contrary evidence of coexistence and cooperation.

Periodisation

Where do the roots of sectarianism lie? Ireland, it has been suggested, is 'frozen in the pre-modern', one of those pardonable exaggerations which point to an essential truth – that the roots of modern Irish problems lie deep in the past.[8] In the case of sectarianism, this would clearly point to the reformation as the *fons et origo*. After all, on the European mainland it was the reformation that created, almost immediately, the fundamental religious bitterness and those fateful competing claims to religious truth which provided the breeding-ground for sectarianism. Luther called the pope Antichrist (and worse), whilst Johannes Cochlaeus, the chief defender of Catholic orthodoxy, labelled Luther as a child of the devil, fornicator, adulterer and pervert. The mutual hatred translated effortlessly to Ireland. Catholics in Munster were advised in 1592 that worship in the Church of Ireland was 'the devil's service, and the professors thereof, devils'; in 1613 the warning was repeated in Ulster – Protestant clergy spoke 'the devil's words'; 'all should be damned that hear them'.[9] The main duty of Protestant theologians was, according to the professor of theology at Trinity, to 'love God, and hate the Pope'.[10] The two rival episcopates saw themselves as engaged in a 'struggle between good and evil or between truth and lies'.[11]

In 1618 Hugh McCaughwell, who briefly served as Catholic archbishop of Armagh before his death in 1626, published his *Scáthán Shacramuinte na hAithridhe*, a treatise on the sacrament of penance, designed to defend Catholic doctrine and attack Protestant heresy, which included an attack on 'Luteir mac Lucifer', Luther son of Lucifer, largely derived from Cochlaeus.[12] His counterpart, James Ussher, Protestant archbishop of Armagh from 1625, returned the compliment, drawing

---

[8] Kieran Flanagan, 'Sociology and religious difference – limits of understanding anti-Catholicism in Northern Ireland', *Studies* 89 (2000), consulted online: URL: http://www.jesuit.ie/studies/articles/2000/000907.htm.

[9] *CSPI, 1592–6*, p. 15; *CSPI, 1611–14*, p. 429; Brian MacCuarta, 'Catholicism in the province of Armagh, 1603–1641', unpublished Ph.D. dissertation, University of Dublin, 2004, p. 92.

[10] Joshua Hoyle, *A rejoinder to Master Malone's reply concerning the real presence* (Dublin, 1641), sig (a4v).

[11] Below, p. 65.

[12] Aodh Mac Aingil, *Scáthán shacramuinte na haithridhe* (ed.), Cainneach Ó Maonaigh (Dublin: Institute for Advanced Studies, 1952); see below, ch. 8, p. 197.

up with his fellow bishops in 1626 an uncompromising attack upon the Roman Catholic church declaring it to be superstitious, idolatrous, erroneous, heretical and apostatical.[13]

Ireland, then, was bedevilled by sectarian divisions and religious violence from the beginning of the reformation. For centuries that was certainly what many historians and commentators believed. David Rothe and Philip O'Sullivan Beare, two of the leading historians of the early seventeenth century, painted a portrait of an island which, from the beginning, had consistently resisted the efforts of the English to impose Protestantism: Rothe told how the reformation legislation had only been railroaded through Elizabeth's parliament in 1560 by force; whilst that other distinguished historian, Philip O'Sullivan Beare, recounted the slaughter of the Trinitarian order under Henry VIII for resisting royal supremacy.[14] The religious struggle, as Mary Hayden pointed out in 1935, was seen as lasting 'from 1534 to almost our own day'.[15]

But the casual assumption that sectarianism began with the reformation and lived unhappily ever after has not stood up to closer historical investigation. Both O'Sullivan and Rothe were reading back into the past the depths of contemporary early seventeenth century sectarian bitterness. Evidence for continuous sectarian strife between Protestant and Catholic is largely missing from the early decades of the Irish reformation and even, arguably, from Elizabeth's first parliament.[16] It is therefore not coincidental that the examples of Irish sectarian hostility cited above come from the later sixteenth and early seventeenth centuries. For this is the period which historians, for various reasons, have begun to focus upon when seeking the origins of sectarianism in Ireland.

Thus discussions about the failure of the reformation and the success of the counter-reformation, which also began initially with quite broad time-frames, have tended to home in upon the period from the 1580s through to the early decades of the seventeenth century. That, it has been suggested, was when rival Catholic and Protestant churches were established, and conflict and controversy became a normal part of religious life. This did not of course preclude the subsequent failure or

---

[13] Richard Parr, *The life of . . . James Usher* (London, 1686), p. 28.

[14] Alan Ford, 'Martyrdom, history and memory in early modern Ireland', in Ian McBride (ed.), *History and memory in modern Ireland* (Cambridge: Cambridge University Press, 2001), pp. 64–5.; H. A. Jefferies, 'The Irish parliament of 1560: the Anglican reforms authorised', *IHS* 26 (1988), 128–41.

[15] R. D. Edwards, *Church and state in Tudor Ireland: a history of the penal laws against Irish Catholics 1534–1603* (Dublin: Talbot Press, 1935), p. vii.

[16] Jefferies, 'Irish parliament of 1560', pp. 128–41; there are in fact remarkably few martyrdoms in Ireland during the 1530s and 1540s: see the graph in Ford, 'Martyrdom, history and memory', p. 54.

success of the counter-reformation or reformation: the future is not immutably fixed by the past. But this period did see the construction of some of the fundamental building blocks for the creation of what turned out to be decidedly persistent separate communities.[17]

This focus on the decades after the 1580s has gained further support from an unexpected quarter. Whereas traditionally historians have tended to compare Irish developments with those in England, in recent decades research on the German reformation and counter-reformation has produced a new explanatory framework – the process of confessionalisation, a movement identified in Catholic, Lutheran and Calvinist territories alike, which saw the creation of distinct denominational ideologies, identities and structures during the later sixteenth and early seventeenth centuries. Ute Lotz-Heumann and Karl Bottigheimer in particular have sought to broaden the geographic (not to mention linguistic) scope of Irish historians by pointing to the experience of Germany and using some of the models and techniques derived from the study of confessionalisation to analyse what was happening in Ireland.[18] Far from being unique, as is often fondly imagined, Ireland is rather to be seen as part of broader European trends. The result of this approach is the most comprehensive treatment yet of the development of two separate denominations which identifies the period after 1580 as the crucial one in the double confessionalisation of Ireland.[19]

Terminology

If we are agreed that the seminal period in the growth of distinct Irish religious denominations is the latter part of the sixteenth and the early seventeenth centuries, what terms are we going to use to describe that process of differentiation? We have, so far, used the words sectarianism and confessionalisation as if they were self-explanatory. But of course there are fundamental philosophical questions about how universal

[17] B. I. Bradshaw, 'Sword, word and strategy in the reformation in Ireland', *Historical Journal* 21 (1978), 475–502; N. P. Canny, 'Why the reformation failed in Ireland: *une question mal posée*', *Journal of Ecclesiastical History* 30 (1979), 423–50; K. S. Bottigheimer, 'The failure of the reformation in Ireland: *une question bien posée*', *Journal of Ecclesiastical History* 36 (1985), 196–207; Aidan Clarke, 'Varieties of uniformity: the first century of the Church of Ireland', in W. J. Shiels and Diana Wood (eds.), *The churches, Ireland and the Irish*, Studies in Church History 25 (1985), pp. 105–22.

[18] K. S. Bottigheimer and Ute Lotz-Heumann, 'Ireland & the European Reformation', *History Ireland* 6 (1998), 13–16; K. S. Bottigheimer and Ute Lotz-Heumann, 'The Irish Reformation in European perspective', *Archiv für Reformationsgeschichte* 89 (1998), 268–309.

[19] Ute Lotz-Heumann, *Die doppelte Konfessionalisierung in Irland: Konflikt und Koexistenz in 16. und in der ersten Hälfte des 17. Jahrhunderts* (Tübingen: Mohr Siebeck, 2000).

terms relate to the particular entities they supposedly describe, and there are further historiographical issues about the assumptions which lurk behind such 'isms', and the way in which the very process of labelling can impose an artificial or inappropriate model on disparate data. It is possible that the three examples of sectarian brutality with which we opened have very little in common in terms of motivation and are, in fact, just three disjointed, unrelated events in Irish history. The process of labelling, in short, is not neutral or 'purely' descriptive: it also involves judgements about the existence, nature and similarity of what is being described.

There are, as a result, drawbacks as well as advantages to using terms such as confessionalisation and sectarianism. The former is useful because it offers historians a heuristic tool, which helpfully links the processes of change between Catholic and Protestant denominations, and offers a model for the process of parallel church-building in early modern Ireland. It also seeks to break down the compartmentalisation between religious and secular forces by linking religious change to state-building, arguably an asset in the early modern period. Equally, however, it is not without its disadvantages. There is the obvious query about how a concept which is derived from the distinctive experience of early modern Germany can usefully provide an interpretative framework for other countries. Historians have explored its usefulness in the Netherlands, France, eastern Europe and Italy and the results have not always been positive.[20] The concern to establish common patterns and structures, and to apply them across European early modern history can be constraining as well as enlightening, and may result in the distinctive experience of individual countries being shoehorned into an overly prescriptive and not particularly helpful model. It has, in addition, a teleological thrust, seeking to trace the development of the modern state out of the confessional territories of early modern Germany, which may not be wholly appropriate for Ireland. A further limitation of confessionalisation as a concept is that its focus is primarily on the early modern period, especially the hundred years before the Treaty of Westphalia in 1648. This can, of course, be seen as a helpful way of offsetting the Irish obsession with lengthy time-frames; on the other hand, it also distracts

---

[20] J. I. Israel, *The Dutch Republic: its rise, greatness and fall, 1477–1806* (Oxford, 1995), ch. 11; R. Po-chia Hsia, *Social discipline in the reformation: central Europe, 1550–1750* (London: Routledge, 1989); Bruce Gordon, 'Konfessionalisierung, Stände und Staat in Ostmitteleuropa (1550–1650)', *German History* 17 (1999), 90–4; cf. further references in Philip Benedict, 'Confessionalisation in France?' Critical reflections and new evidence', in R. A. Mentzer and Andrew Spicer, *Society and culture in the Huguenot world, 1559–1685* (Cambridge: Cambridge University Press, 2002), p. 44.

from the *longue durée* which, as our opening stories suggest, remains an important part of the study of sectarianism.[21] There is ultimately here a difference in historical styles and methodologies; more pragmatic Irish historians may not always view 'the undeniable inventiveness of German historians in forging ideal-typical interpretative constructs, as well as their high degree of theoretical self-consciousness' as entirely an asset.[22]

What, then, of the alternative term? Sectarianism has certain advantages over confessionalisation. It shifts the focus away from the horizontal, pan-European comparative perspective, confined within the narrow time-frame of the early modern period, towards a more vertical and largely Irish historical development, stretching from the early modern period to the present day. The term itself has two meanings. The founding fathers of religious sociology, Max Weber and Ernst Troeltsch, first used it to describe a particular form of church polity. In contrast to the large-scale, universalist-minded church type organisation which sought an alliance with the state and which included all citizens, the sect saw itself as a small group of dedicated Christians, converts to the one truth, separate from society.[23] Developed by sociologists of religion into a sophisticated tool to analyse church types, this approach has occasionally been applied to Ireland.[24] Much more influential, though, is the older, more negative seventeenth-century use of the word sectarian to describe narrow-minded and bigoted members of fringe religious groups. The study of sectarianism in the Irish context is, as a result, less concerned with the first aproach, delineating the ways in which sects, strictly defined, have developed, or their relation to churches and denominations, but rather looks at the ways in which religious groups in Ireland have adopted some of the more negative attributes of sectarian behaviour.

This, then, is the concept which has been applied by a number of disciplines to the study of Irish history and society. The definitions of the

---

[21] See H. H. W. Robinson-Hammerstein, 'The confessionalisation of Ireland? Assessment of a paradigm', *IHS* 32 (2001), 567–78; and other reviews of Lotz-Heuman, *Doppelte Konfessionalizierung*, by Steven Ellis in *JEH* 53 (2002), 607–8 and Ole Grell in *EHR* 118 (2003), 782–3.

[22] Benedict, 'Confessionalisation in France?' p. 45.

[23] Some pointers to a vast literature: H. R. Niebuhr, *The social sources of denominationalism* (New York: New American Library, 1975); B. R. Wilson, *The social dimensions of sectarianism: sects and new religious movements in contemporary society* (Oxford: Clarendon, 1990); Roland Robertson, *The sociological interpretation of religion* (Oxford: Basil Blackwell, 1970).

[24] Steve Bruce, *God save Ulster: the religion and politics of Paisleyism* (Oxford: Clarendon Press, 1986), pp. 184ff.; and see below, ch. 9.

term vary, with the main division arising over the way in which religion is viewed, some seeing it as a primary motivating force, others more reductively as part of a 'symbolic labelling process', or 'boundary marker', which really reflects more fundamental social, political or ethnic divisions.[25] All are agreed, however, on its usefulness as a means of explaining and analysing the twentieth-century Northern Irish problem. But less attention has been paid to its roots. Only two extended treatments have been produced. A sociologist, John Brewer, has examined one side of the sectarian coin, anti-Catholicism, and traced it back to the early seventeenth century, whilst an historian, Joseph Liechty, has offered a broad sketch of the development of sectarianism in Ireland from the reformation, as a preliminary to a broader analysis of modern Irish sectarianism.[26]

For Brewer, sectarianism is 'the determination of actions, attitudes and practices by beliefs about religious difference, which results in their being invoked as the boundary marker to represent social stratification and conflict'.[27] Brewer does, though, allow for religion to be more than 'merely' a marker. Anti-Catholicism, one of the 'tap roots' of sectarianism, occurs at three levels: ideas, the individual and social structures.[28] Theology is clearly an important source for such views, and here Brewer argues that there is considerable historical continuity, with many of the objections to the Roman Catholic church first raised by the reformers echoing down the ages to the present day. But sectarianism also has distinct socio-economic and political elements, which can fuse with the theological objections to Catholicism in such a way that the latter are almost forgotten, leaving us with religion as a boundary-marker.[29] Ultimately, Brewer sees sectarianism as a sociological process, used as means of defending Protestant interests by creating and maintaining social and political divisions.[30] There is thus a balance to be struck between the role played by religion and the impact of other forces in dividing Irish society.[31]

---

[25] For other definitions of sectarianism: Report of Church of Ireland General Synod Standing Committee, Sub Committee on Sectarianism, April 1999, URL: http://www.ireland.anglican.org/archives/issues/issarchive/subcomsect.html; John Sugden and Alan Bairner, *Sport, sectarianism and society in a divided Ireland* (Leicester: Leicester University Press, 1993), p. 15; Paul Connolly, *Sectarianism, children and community relations in Northern Ireland* (Coleraine: University of Ulster, Centre for the Study of Conflict, 1999), p. 7.

[26] Liechty, *Roots of sectarianism*; Brewer and Higgins, *Anti-Catholicism.*

[27] J. D. Brewer, 'Sectarianism and racism, and their parallels and differences', *Ethnic and Racial Studies* 15 (1992), 358–9.

[28] Brewer and Higgins, *Anti-Catholicism*, p. 2.   [29] *Ibid.*, pp. 4–5.

[30] *Ibid.*, pp. 11–12.   [31] *Ibid.*, p. 15.

Liechty's definition of sectarianism is similarly nuanced:

a series of attitudes, actions, beliefs and structures, at personal communal and institutional levels, which always involves religion, and typically involves a negative mixing of religion and politics . . . which arises as a distorted expression of positive human needs, especially for belonging, identity and the free expression of difference . . . and is expressed in destructive patterns of relating: hardening the boundaries between groups; overlooking others; belittling, dehumanising, or demonising others; justifying or collaborating in the domination of others; physically intimidating or attacking others.[32]

Though shorter, Liechty's historical accounts of sectarianism are in one sense more comprehensive, since they sketch both sides of the process. Sectarianism in Northern Ireland he sees as not a product of recent events, such as partition, or the Troubles, rather it dates back to the early modern period, or even beyond to the Anglo-Norman invasion.[33] He identifies three fatal religious principles as underpinning its growth: that of *nulla salus extra ecclesia* (no salvation outside the church), which leads to an exclusive sense of righteousness; the fateful Augustinian dictum that error has no right, which throughout history has been used to persecute and punish religious opponents; and finally the sense of divine providence – the belief that God operates in and through history – which, when combined with the first two principles can produce a heady sectarian cocktail which offers the firm assurance that God is on your side and that the punishments and disasters suffered by one's opponents are both just and heaven-sent. These definitions and analyses of sectarianism provide a useful starting point for our inquiry into its early modern manifestations, alerting us in particular to the interaction between social, political and religious divisions, and the question of whether religion is a primary or merely a secondary motivating force.

But the concept of sectarianism is not without its problems. There is also an element of moral judgement involved in the use of the term. Those who use it in relation to Northern Ireland see it as essentially destructive, an evil akin to racism or anti-Semitism, which has to be combated and condemned as well as analysed. The best general treatment of the topic derives from a project which sought to help people in Northern Ireland transcend religious differences and 'move beyond' sectarianism.[34] Whilst not denying the destructive capacity of sectarianism in Irish history, it is not *necessarily* a negative phenomenon – at one

---

[32] Liechty and Clegg, *Moving beyond sectarianism*, pp. 102–3.
[33] *Ibid.*, pp. 63–7; Liechty, *Roots of sectarianism*, pp. 2–3.
[34] Liechty and Clegg, *Moving beyond sectarianism*.

moderate extreme it shades off into pride in one's own identity. As Richard English has pointed out, it is possible to argue that 'self-segmentation is normal and necessary within society and that it is seen in many innocuous forms everywhere (self-segmentation according to family, friends, social and sexual groups, musical taste, sporting preferences and so on)'.[35] It is possible that the blanket use of the concept as a term of abuse may import negative judgements which are not necessarily applicable to all the aspects being studied and which would be missing from a more value-neutral term such as confessionalisation.

Living together, living apart

Irish history, it appears, is riven by sectarian hatred. Ian Paisley can happily quote Martin Luther across a span of almost half a millennium:

I can hardly pray when I think on them [the Papists] without cursing. I cannot say, Hallowed be thy name, without adding, Cursed be the name of the Papists, and of all those who blaspheme God! If I say, Thy kingdom come, I add, Cursed be the Popedom, and all kingdoms that are opposed to Thine! If I say, Thy will be done, I add, Cursed be the designs of the Papists, and of all those – may they perish! – who fight against Thee![36]

Yet how dominant is this thread of sectarianism? Without wishing to airbrush away the sectarian horrors of Irish history, there is nevertheless counter-evidence of the ability of Catholic and Protestant to coexist and create a society with political, economic and religious institutions that, with certain exceptions, functioned relatively effectively. For all the mayhem and savagery of the 1580s and 1590s, Irish society in the early decades of the seventeenth century seemed to have adjusted to the unusual situation of having two rival churches. Despite persecution, Catholics erected an effective institutional framework.[37] As Brian Jackson has shown in his study of Drogheda in the early 1620s, their structures were not all that dissimilar from Protestant ones: the Catholic church 'existed in a curious "through the looking glass" world where the actions of Catholic institutions mirrored their official Protestant counterparts'.[38] Protestant bishops competed, without much noticeable

---

[35] Richard English, 'Sectarianism and politics in modern Ireland', in Dennis Kennedy (ed.), *Nothing but trouble? Religion and the Irish Problem* (Belfast: Irish Association for Cultural, Economic and Social Relations, 2004).

[36] *Extracts from the great reformer's writings as selected by Dr. Ian R. K. Paisley*, European Institute for Protestant Studies. URL: http://www.ianpaisley.org/article. asp?ArtKey= Luther-speak; accessed 31/8/2003.

[37] See below, Chapter 4.   [38] See below, Chapter 9.

success, with their counterparts to pursue the apostolic episcopal ideal.[39] Catholic and Protestant political theorists struggled to find common ground between their contradictory assumptions to enable mutual accommodation between the Protestant state and the majority Catholic population.[40]

The contrast, even contradiction, between hostility and coexistence is part of a general historical problem, the tendency of historians to focus upon the large and dramatic events – or the 'vortex of antagonism', as Frank Wright termed it – at the expense of the everyday, to think in term of sharp divisions when the reality may be both more messy and more accommodating.[41] This brings us back to the tyranny of terminology: the very label used helps to create the reality by leading us to corral the variety of Irish history within the distorting sectarian lens of Protestant versus Catholic: 'Diversity may defy collective labelling, but collective labelling in turn suppresses diversity and encourages stereotyping. Consequently such stereotypical portrayal of two traditions in Northern Ireland – "them and us" – fails . . . to do justice to reality, however analytically convenient or politically expedient such a rudimentary dualistic taxonomy may appear to be.'[42] And indeed there are facts which do not fit the historians neat explanatory frameworks and which therefore risk being ignored, both in Ireland and elsewhere in Europe. Even at the height of the French wars of religion with their headline massacres, 'complicities and compromises' can be observed at the local level.[43] As two historians of nineteenth-century Germany have put it:

Historians have often overlooked this rich world of give and take, knowledge and ignorance, living together and apart. The large questions of history, and the analytical tools we use to examine the past, all too often push us to see difference where commonality also existed, conflict where there was also neighbourliness.[44]

---

[39] See below, Chapter 3.

[40] See below, Chapter 8; Alan Ford, '"Firm Catholics" or "loyal subjects"? Religious and political allegiance in early-seventeenth-century Ireland', in D. G. Boyce, Robert Eccleshall and Vincent Geoghegan (ed.), *Political discourse in seventeenth- and eighteenth-century Ireland* (London: Palgrave, 2001), pp. 1–31.

[41] Frank Wright, 'Reconciling the histories: Protestant and Catholic in Northern Ireland', in Alan Falconer and Joseph Liechty (eds.), *Reconciling memories*, 2nd edn. (Dublin: Columba Press, 1998), p. 71.

[42] F. W. Boal, M. C. Keane and D. N. Livingstone, *Them and us? Attitudinal variation among churchgoers in Belfast* (Belfast: Institute of Irish Studies, 1997), p. 172.

[43] Gregory Hanlon, *Confession and community in seventeenth-century France: Catholic and Protestant coexistence in Aquitaine* (Philadelphia: University of Pennsylvania Press, 1993), p. 5.

[44] Helmut Walser Smith and Chris Clark, 'The fate of Nathan', in Helmut Walser Smith (ed.), *Protestants, Catholics and Jews in Germany, 1800–1914* (Oxford: Berg, 2001), p. 19.

This tension between living together and living apart – and the fascinating ability of people to do both at the same time – creates a real challenge for those who wish to focus solely upon just one of these apparently contradictory aspects of Irish history. Thus, attempts to study the emergence of sectarianism, or to trace its continuity across the centuries are continually questioned, contradicted and undermined by the evidence of peaceful coexistence and the ability of Protestants and Catholics to live together; while, on the other hand, efforts to emphasise coexistence are confronted with the familiar litany of violent outbreaks, from 1641 down to the twentieth-century 'Troubles'.

The fact that this book focuses upon the confessionalisation of Ireland – the living apart – requires, as an antidote or counter-balance, an initial exploration of the other side of the coin – living together. The task confronting historians is to put side by side, both at the micro- and macro-historical level, the evidence both for hostility and for coexistence, and analyse the interdependence of the two, so that key questions can be answered about the relationship between Catholic and Protestant in early modern Ireland and the balance between everyday intercourse and shared cultural, social and political allegiances on the one hand, and religious and sectarian hostility on the other.

Part of the difficulty facing such an investigation is the sheer complexity of the problem, both theoretically and practically. A number of interpretative models for the interaction between confessionalisation and coexistence can be constructed, but they produce markedly different results. It is possible, for instance, to stress the pacific nature of the relationship between the two religious traditions, seeing the outbreaks of violence as exceptional. And indeed, in everyday terms, it is difficult to maintain a high level of sectarian hostility. As Seamus Heaney describes his own upbringing in Northern Ireland: 'You can't really fall out. You can't live two lives. You can't live a life of sectarian resentment and, at the same time, neighbourly cooperation. I suppose it is possible – but we didn't anyway.'[45] Thus in modern studies of ethnic conflicts the functioning of mixed communities has been seen as dependent upon an underlying pragmatic ability to 'get on', whatever the supposed imperatives of their leaders.[46] More directly relevant, the ability of James Ussher and other Protestant Irish historians to cooperate with their Catholic colleagues and fellow-countrymen has frequently been

---

[45] M. J. Richtarik, *Acting between the lines: The Field Day Theatre Company and Irish cultural politics 1980–1984* (Oxford: Clarendon Press, 1994), p. 95.
[46] Yehuda Amir, 'Contact hypothesis in ethnic relations', in Eugene Weiner (ed.), *Handbook of interethnic coexistence* (New York: Continuum, 1998), pp. 162–81.

documented.[47] Analysis of the 1641 depositions has produced the interesting suggestion that 'animosity towards the settlers depended on the extent of contact with English culture before the rebellion; where contact had been close, behaviour was generally restrained'.[48] On a more prosaic level, it is evident that planters and natives managed to overcome sixteenth-century linguistic barriers and develop a pragmatic bilingualism.[49] The Scottish traveller, William Lithgow, provided a fascinating vignette of how Protestant ministers, nominally in charge of churches in largely Irish parishes, related to the Catholic priests:

> The alehouse is their church, the Irish priests their consorts, their auditors be fill, and fetch more, their text Spanish sacke, their prayers carrousing, their singing of Psalmes the whiffing of tobacco, their last blessing *aqua vitae*, and all their doctrine sound drunkennesse. And whensoever these parties meet, their pairing is Dane-like from a Dutch pot, and the minister still purse bearer, defrayeth all charges for the priest: arguments of religion, like Podolian Polonians they succumbe; their conference onely pleading mutuall forbearance; the minister afraid of the priests wood-carnes, and the priests as fearefull of the ministers apprehending, or denoting them, contracting thereby a Gibeonized covenant, yea, and for more submissions sake, hee will give way to the priest to mumble masse in his church, where he in all his life never made prayer nor sermon.[50]

Yet it is painfully clear that interaction between religiously divided communities does not inevitably breed famliarity and mutual understanding. Much depends upon the context, frequency and depth of their contacts. It is perfectly possible that the necessity for everyday, outward cooperation can simply cloak deep underlying hostility, offering a neat explanation for the familiar pattern in Irish history of lengthy periods of relative sectarian peace, followed by major outbreaks of violence. The superficially convivial relations between the minister and the priest in Lithgow's account are, after all, underpinned on both sides by the threat of violence. As one nineteenth-century Catholic commentator put it, whilst there was 'a community of necessity, and sometimes of courtesy', this was only superficial: 'seeming friends and neighbours could in a moment take their places in opposite hosts, and join in deadly

---

[47] See below, p. 151.

[48] Michael Perceval-Maxwell, *The outbreak of the Irish rebellion of 1641* (Dublin: Gill & Macmillan, 1994), p. 228.

[49] Compare Patricia Palmer, 'Interpreters and the politics of translation and traduction in sixteenth-century Ireland', *IHS* 33 (2003), 257–77, with N. P. Canny, *Making Ireland British, 1580–1650* (Oxford, 2001), pp. 452ff.

[50] William Lithgow, *The totall discourse, of the rare adventures, and painefull peregrinations of long nineteene years travailes from Scotland, to the most famous kingdomes in Europe, Asia, and Affrica* ([London], 1640), pp. 439–40.

combat'.[51] One could go further and argue that the very process of interaction between the communities played a major role in creating their mutually exclusive identities, as group solidarity was strengthened by defining itself in opposition to the dreaded 'other'.

Alternatively, one can question the extent of interaction itself. Some historians have suggested that Protestants in early modern Ireland sought to create a system of apartheid in order to ensure that they gained and maintained a monopoly on power, land and influence. In response Catholics were forced to develop their own separate structures.[52] This increasing tendency of religious groups to form distinct communities, with their own schools, universities and political groupings, and their own kin and marriage networks, naturally reduced the necessity and opportunity for cooperation and familiarisation, enabling sectarian assumptions and hostility to flourish unchecked behind the tightly controlled and limited formal interchanges.[53] A distinction can be made between the public and private spheres, the latter allowing, even requiring, at least some level of interaction, whilst at home, amongst friends and kin, the two communities lived separate lives.

But models such as these have one obvious flaw – they assume a large degree of both group solidarity and religious self-awareness. More sophisticated approaches have to explore the fissiparous tendencies within the religious or ethnic communities themselves – the tensions between Old English and native Irish Catholics, or Presbyterian and Church of Ireland Protestants, say – and examine the bonds that linked particular subsets of those groups across the religious divide. It may prove to be the case that common aspects of culture, social status, group identity, wealth or interest could create ties between the separate communities; or that commitment to higher ideals could transcend religious boundaries and actually fulfil Tone's dream of substituting the common name of Irishman for Protestant, Catholic and dissenter.

---

[51] John O'Driscol, *Views of Ireland, moral, political, and religious* (London, 1823), I, p. vi, quoted in Desmond Bowen, *The Protestant crusade in Ireland, 1800–70* (Dublin: Gill & Macmillan, 1978), p. 141.

[52] Bradshaw, 'Sword, word and strategy', 502; N. P. Canny, 'Protestant planters and apartheid in early modern Ireland', *IHS* 25 (1986), p. 107.

[53] Cf. the suggestion that the Catholic minority in England engaged in a similar policy of apartheid: Lawrence Stone, *The crisis of the aristocracy, 1558–1641* (Oxford: Clarendon Press, 1965), p. 614; and the idea of a 'columnised' Dutch society 'divided into comprehensive, largely self-contained religious blocks, each one endogamous, with its own norms and values, charitable systems, educational institutions, and business networks': B. J. Kaplan, '"Dutch" religious tolerance: celebration and revision', in Henk van Nierop and R. Po-Chia Hsia (eds.), *Calvinism and religious toleration in the Dutch Golden Age* (Cambridge: Cambridge University Press, 2002), p. 26.

A similar result could be achieved by lack of popular awareness of the significance, or even existence, of boundary markers. Recent studies of the microhistory of religious cosmologies show the many ways in which central commands and religious orthodoxies can be understood, misunderstood and interpreted by individuals.[54] Similar lessons about the varieties of popular responses to pressure from above can be derived from the ways in which some modern German historians have stressed the significance of everyday personal life in contrast to the assumption of some historians of the dominance of political forces or movements.[55] What this means when applied to Ireland is that the sharp distinctions drawn by the Jesuit or puritan preacher could simply have been ignored by their audiences. A recent survey of early modern Irish religion stresses that at the popular level Protestant and Catholic had much in common.[56] Marc Caball suggests that, far from being in the vanguard of the counter-reformation, the bardic elite remained 'largely aloof' from sectarian controversy in the sixteenth century.[57]

There are, then, significant questions, in Ireland as in other European countries, about the relationship between sectarian violence on the one hand, and 'coexistence and complicity' on the other hand. In particular, to what extent is the latter secondary to the former – was coexistence an accident, or a product of a set of unusually favourable circumstances, or, alternatively, was it 'structurally plausible and widespread'? Was conflict basic to Irish society, or a result of the malfunction of essentially peaceable social relations? Was there an invisible line between Protestants and Catholics, which could of course be crossed, but was nevertheless recognised by all as fundamental? Ultimately, answers to these questions depend both on the assumptions which historians bring to the study of societies and on the way that society functioned in early modern Ireland. Do they see social relations as inherently discordant and violent, as innately peaceful and cooperative, or all these at the same time?[58] The only way to investigate the question is to perform the scholarly tasks of research, analysis and self-analysis.

[54] Carlo Ginsburg, 'Microhistory: two or three things that I know about it', *Critical Inquiry* 20 (1993), 10–35; Carlo Ginzburg, *The cheese and the worms: the cosmos of a sixteenth-century miller* (Baltimore: Johns Hopkins University Press, 1992).

[55] Alf Lüdtke (ed.), *The history of everyday life: reconstructing historical experiences and ways of life* (Princeton: Princeton University Press, 1995).

[56] Raymond Gillespie, *Devoted people: belief and religion in early modern Ireland* (Manchester: Manchester University Press, 1997).

[57] Below, Chapter 7.

[58] For this discussion, I am dependent on Hanlon, *Confession and community*, Introduction (quotations are from p. 6); and Philip Benedict, *Christ's churches purely reformed: a social history of Calvinism* (New Haven: Yale University Press, 2003), ch. 11.

This is, obviously, a massive challenge. Even to trace the ways that Irish people constructed communities which operated both within and across the fault lines of Protestant and Catholic would require a lengthy investigation of early modern Irish society at local and national levels. For our purposes here, though, it is still possible to look, very briefly, beyond our concentration on the forces seeking to create separate communities, and instead to identify just two possible areas of interaction – Eltonian 'points of contact' – to see how far they illustrate the extent to and the ways in which Irish Catholics and Protestants were brought together, or pushed apart, in the early seventeenth century.

Sacraments

The sacraments were one of the fundamental sources of theological division at the reformation: Catholics and Protestants disagreed over both their number and their nature. Arcane arguments over Christ's presence in the bread, even whether he was physically confined to the right hand of God, split not just Catholics and Protestants, but the Protestants themselves.[59] Interestingly, these arguments often penetrated to the popular level, producing Protestant disgust at the idolatry of the mass, and Catholic rejection of the heretical Protestant eucharist. But attitudes towards other sacraments – particularly rites of passage – were more flexible and ambiguous. Marriage provides the obvious test case. Endogamy could, it is true, reinforce group solidarity; but marriage could also be used to forge alliances across religious and political divides. Both churches, not surprisingly, sought to control marriage by insisting that it was subject to religious rules and sanctions. 'Hope of commodity makes many a man marry his children to papists . . . a thing forbidden in the seventh of Deuteronomy', complained George Andrewes, later Bishop of Ferns and Leighlin, in a sermon at Limerick in 1624.[60] The leaders of the state church often commented negatively on the unfortunate habit which native clergy had of marrying Catholic wives.[61] The Synod of Tuam in 1658 was the first of a number on the Catholic side to ban mixed marriages.[62] Further efforts were made to ensure purity by

---

[59] Hermann Sasse, *This is my body: Luther's contention for the real presence in the sacrament of the altar* (Adelaide: Lutheran Publishing House, 1977); B. A. Gerrish, *Grace and gratitude: the eucharistic theology of John Calvin* (Edinburgh: T&T Clark, 1993).
[60] George Andrewe, *A quaternion of sermons preached in Ireland* (Dublin, 1625), p. 36.
[61] Alan Ford, *The Protestant reformation in Ireland*, 2nd edn (Dublin: Four Courts, 1997), p. 45.
[62] Alison Forrestal, *Catholic Synods in Ireland, 1600–1690* (Dublin, 1998), p. 105.

forbidding Catholics from marrying before or having their children baptized by a Protestant minister, and by banning Catholics from acting as godparents in Protestant baptisms, and Protestants from being godparents at Catholic baptisms.[63]

The results of this can be traced in early modern Ireland in the increasing segregation of the two religious groupings. The most thorough investigation of this issue, by Colm Lennon, suggests that during the later sixteenth century there was indeed a significant shift in marriage patterns amongst the Dublin aldermen, as religion became a decisive factor.[64] Evidence of the attitudes of the most prominent Irish Protestant landowner, the earl of Cork, suggests that he was much less concerned with whether his children and relations married into the English, Anglo-Irish or native Irish nobility, than with their partner's religion – 'For Cork, religion was far more important than ethnicity.'[65] Similarly, as David Edwards demonstrates, the choice of marriage partners made by Catholic English colonists in Ireland suggests that when faced with the choice between racial and religious loyalty, the latter prevailed.[66] The conclusion is, then, plain: 'The confessional division of society manifested itself in marriage alliances.'[67]

But did it always? First, it must be noted that native Irish marriage practices were notoriously idiosyncratic and markedly resistant to the imposition of ecclesiastical norms.[68] Second, the repeated clerical fulminations against intermarriage – like clerical condemnation of sin – can be interpreted in two markedly different ways: if one emphasises their firm and unequivocal nature, they can be seen as evidence for the strict church control over the laity; alternatively, though, a focus upon the evident need for regular repetition suggests that the injunctions may not have been always as effective as the church would have wished. Rather than the rather tardy ban on mixed marriages, perhaps normal practice

[63] *Ibid.*, pp. 106–7.

[64] Colm Lennon, *The lords of Dublin in the age of reformation* (Dublin: Irish Academic Press, 1989), pp. 87–9, 160–1.; Colm Lennon, 'The shaping of a lay community in the Church of Ireland, 1558–1641', in Raymond Gillespie and W. G. Neely (eds.), *The laity and the Church of Ireland, 1000–2000: all sorts and conditions* (Dublin: Four Courts, 2002), pp. 55–7.

[65] Patrick Little, 'The Geraldine ambitions of the first earl of Cork', *IHS* 33 (2002), 163; Michael MacCarthy-Morrogh, *The Munster plantation: English migration to southern Ireland 1583–1641* (Oxford: Clarendon Press, 1986), p. 276.

[66] Below, p. 121; MacCarthy-Morrogh, *Munster plantation*, p. 277.

[67] Lotz-Heumann, *Doppelte Konfessionalizierung*, p. 132.

[68] Kenneth Nicholls, *Gaelic and Gaelicised Ireland in the middle ages* (Dublin: Gill & Macmillan, 1972), pp. 73–7; Art Cosgrove, 'Marriage in medieval Ireland', in Art Cosgrove (ed.), *Marriage in Ireland* (Dublin: College Press, 1985), pp. 28–34.

was represented by the rather more pragmatic synodal legislation which ordained that where a mixed marriage did occur, the Catholic partner must be allowed to keep up their faith and the children should be brought up as Catholics.[69] As late as 1639 the Catholic bishop of Down and Connor, Hugh Magennis, complained about the long-established abuse in his dioceses where Catholics participated in Protestant sacraments of baptism and marriage and *vice versa*.[70] Since baptism was one sacrament which was recognised as valid across the churches, it provided obvious scope for cooperation. One of the first things which William Bedell attempted to do when he arrived in his diocese of Kilmore in 1630 was to reach an arrangement with the local Catholic population about baptism.[71] The earl of Cork was happy to invite two prominent local Catholic gentry to act as godparents to his younger children.[72] Catholic synodal legislation, however, tried to prevent such interaction, banning Catholics from serving as godparents in heretical baptisms, and preventing Protestants from serving as godparents in Catholic baptisms.[73]

Similar ambiguities arise in relation to that other rite of passage, funerals. Here there were inevitable tensions about sacred space, as Catholics sought to continue to bury their dead in the churches, monasteries and abbeys which they had traditionally used, but which were now under the control of the state church or, sometimes, Protestant settlers.[74] The established church in Ireland tried to maintain Protestant control over such space, by limiting Catholic access to Protestant churches and banning burials in abbeys, priories and other places.[75] But there is no doubt that Catholics continued to bury their dead, especially in those monasteries which had come into the possession of Catholic families, but even in churches and graveyards which were now under the control of Protestant ministers, throughout our period.[76]

---

[69] Forrestal, *Catholic Synods*, p. 105.
[70] J. Hagan (ed.), 'Miscellanea Vaticano-Hibernica', *Archivium Hibernicum* 5 (1916), 106.
[71] *UW*, XV, pp. 470–1.
[72] MacCarthy-Morrogh, *Munster plantation*, p. 278.
[73] Forrestal, *Catholic synods*, pp. 105–6.
[74] Cf. the similar tensions in France: K. P. Luria, 'Separated by death? Burials, cemeteries, and confessional boundaries in seventeenth-century France', *French Historical Studies* 24 (2001), 185–222.
[75] Chetham's Library, Manchester, MS A.6.77 (National Library of Ireland, Microfilm P1924), p. 362; N. P. Canny, *Making Ireland British, 1580–1650* (Oxford: Oxford University Press, 2001), pp. 446ff.; D. L. Edwards, *The Ormond lordship in County Kilkenny, 1515–1642: the rise and fall of Butler feudal power* (Dublin: Four Courts Press, 2003), pp. 289–90.
[76] Clodagh Tait, *Death, burial and commemoration in Ireland, 1550–1650* (Basingstoke: Palgrave, 2002), pp. 73, 77ff.

Obviously Catholic funerary monuments and symbols were even erected
in St Patrick's cathedral in Dublin as late as 1618, while Catholics
during the same period regularly added mortuary chapels to Protestant
places of worship.[77] There is, of course, a perfectly mundane reason for
such an accommodation on the part of the state church – such burials
were a source of income.[78] But quite how this kind of compromise
should be interpreted is, again, complex. The already classic recent
study of early modern Irish burial practices points to a three-fold model
derived from French experience: first, bonds of rank and privilege could
transcend religious boundaries resulting in shared burial places; second,
despite evident awareness of religious difference, compromises could be
reached which allowed both sides to preserve traditional practices; and
third, there lurked the desire of the church authorities to impose a rigid
distinction along confessional lines, which shattered the possibility of
compromise.[79] Though, during the early seventeenth century, accom-
modations were clearly reached, sectarian sentiments remained beneath
the surface. Matthew Archbold of Westmeath asked in 1618 that he be
buried in Multyfarnham Abbey, providing it had not been 'polluted' by
Protestants.[80] As the 1641 rising revealed, Catholic resentment of Protestant appropriation of sacred space could result in violent attacks on
Protestant graves and corpses.[81]

Education

The leading Irish Jesuit, Henry Fitzsimon, recounted how, in the early
seventeenth century, he had insisted not only that his flock should not
marry Protestants, but that they should not attend Protestant educational institutions. In particular, he sought to ensure that the children of
Catholics were taken away from Trinity College, the state university
founded in 1592.[82] In the diocese of Leighlin in 1612, according to
the Protestant bishop, a Catholic priest taught the people that 'whoso-
ever did send their children or pupils to be taught by a schoolmaster of
our religion, they were excommunicated *ipso facto* and should certainly
be damned without they did undergoe great penance'.[83] And on the
Protestant side, one of the ambitions of the Dublin administration was to
replicate in Ireland the post-reformation experience of England, where

[77] *Ibid.*, pp. 79–80.   [78] *Ibid.*, pp. 79.
[79] *Ibid.*, p. 81.   [80] *Ibid.*, p. 77.
[81] Canny, *Making Ireland British*, pp. 514ff.
[82] Henry Fitzsimon, *Words of comfort . . . letters from a cell . . . and diary of the Bohemian war of 1620*, Edmund Hogan (ed.) (Dublin, 1881), pp. 56, 68–9.
[83] Trinity College, Dublin, MS 1066, pp. 141–2.

the strict policing of the teaching profession had ensured that new generations were brought up as Protestants. Thus the repeated official attempts to create and police an effective system of state education at diocesan and parish levels and prevent the Irish from having access to Catholic education abroad.

There is little doubt that from the 1580s onwards separate Protestant and Catholic systems began to emerge.[84] In her path-breaking analysis of changing educational patterns, Helga Robinson-Hammerstein traced the way in which Irish Catholics switched from English to continental counter-reformation universities towards the end of the sixteenth century.[85] On the other side of the confessional divide, Trinity's foundation in 1592 provided an unquestionably Protestant alternative that served as a seminary for the state church.[86] Evidence can also be found for Catholic schools in Ireland parallel to the state system of grammar schools: in 1595 Sir John Dowdall complained that each town has schools presided over by a 'superstitious or idolatrous schoolmaster' 'whereby the youth of the whole kingdom are corrupted and poisoned with more gross superstition and disobedience than all the rest of the Popish crew in all Europe'.[87] Most notably, in 1615 regal visitation of the Church of Ireland a flourishing Catholic grammar school was discovered in Galway which the state tried to close down.[88] The diocesan school in Meath can be seen as symbolic of this separate educational development: in 1604 the Protestant bishop, Thomas Jones, reported on his efforts in Trim, where he had placed three university graduates who had kept a free school. But they only attracted six scholars, and even these departed as soon as the masters sought to bring them to church.[89] The problems persisted; the diocesan schoolmaster in Ossory in 1634 complained that he could not secure financial support for the school from the inhabitants of the diocese 'because they would rather maintain the popish schoolmasters to whom they send their children'.[90] If, as Robinson-Hammerstein puts it, 'The real key to . . . confessional formation of . . . separated societies . . . was education', then this would

[84] Lotz-Heumann, *Doppelte Konfessionalisierung*, 317ff.
[85] H. H. W. Hammerstein, 'Aspects of the continental education of Irish students in the reign of Queen Elizabeth', *Historical Studies* 8 (1971), 137–54.
[86] Ford, *Protestant reformation*, 77ff.
[87] C. E. Maxwell, *Irish history from contemporary sources, 1509–1610* (London: George Allen & Unwin, 1923), pp. 146–7.
[88] British Library MS 19,836, fol. 109; John Lynch, *De praesulibus Hiberniae* (Dublin: Irish Manuscripts Commission, 1944), II, p. 184.
[89] Public Record Office SP 63/216/8, *CSPI, 1603–6*, pp. 152–3.
[90] British Library, Harleian MS 4297, fol. 2r.

suggest that by the early seventeenth century confessionalisation was well established in Ireland.[91]

Yet, on the other hand, Catholics and Protestants *were* educated together in early seventeenth century Ireland. In 1622, the free school in Dublin had 122 pupils, 43 of whom were noted as not attending church; and though it had sent 100 scholars to Trinity College over the previous dozen or so years, the school had also sent 160 to complete their education overseas.[92] Other state schools also sent pupils on to Jesuit colleges on the continent.[93] Similarly, detailed investigation of the composition of the student body at Trinity College suggests that it was more diverse than has often been presumed in the early seventeenth century, though increasingly dominated by Protestants and New English by the 1630s.[94] Interpreting these scattered examples of ecumenical education is not easy. On the one hand, there is clear evidence of separate systems of schooling in Ireland leading on to alternative Protestant and Catholic university institutions. There were, though, clearly areas where the otherwise separate Catholic and Protestant systems overlapped, offering a space for coexistence. How extensive this overlap was, and whether it increased or diminished over time, whether it was simply a product of a shortage of suitable teachers, and how significant the experience of joint education was for Catholics and Protestants, are all essential topics for further research.

Conclusion

It is clear then that between the late sixteenth century and the middle of the seventeenth century rival Protestant and Catholic churches emerged in Ireland. Each laid claim to the exclusive religious loyalty of the Irish people and, in an ideal world, desired the support of the state to enforce this. Each sought to build up the necessary structures to translate its claim into reality. Obviously, each failed. The resultant parallel structures and rival claims provided the institutional framework within which sectarianism could grow and flourish in Ireland not just in the early modern period but right down to the present century.

But sectarianism was moderated by pragmatism. Religious divisions could be transcended and transformed by social, political and economic

---

[91] Robinson-Hammerstein, 'Confessionalisation of Ireland?', 577.
[92] Ford, *Protestant reformation*, p. 92.
[93] *Ibid.*, p. 114.
[94] Alan Ford, 'Who went to Trinity? The early students of Dublin University', in H. H. W. Robinson-Hammerstein (ed.), *European universities in the age of the reformation* (Dublin: Four Courts Press, 1998), pp. 53–75.

interaction in what was, after all, a rather small country. The normal bonds of society could thus offset the formal division between Protestant and Catholic. There was, in fine, a tension between custom and pragmatism on the one hand and doctrine and dogma on the other. At different times, in different political or military circumstances, one or the other could gain the upper hand. By the 1630s, as the country seemed to be moving away from the disruption and division of the later sixteenth century into a period of peace and stability, James Ware could hail the birth of a new Ireland in which all were now one people. There is, though, a world of difference between the optimism of the 1630s and the grim realities of the early 1640s, when, on both sides, normal civil society disintegrated in the face of sectarian hatred and savagery. It was not just that servants and tenants attacked their masters, it was trusted neighbours who robbed and pillaged their former friends: one rebel in Co. Kildare, when challenged about breaking the tenth commandment, 'said that the Protestants were not neighbours of theirs but they were heretics and therefore no breach of conscience to take away their goods'.[95] It is this mysterious transition from peaceful coexistence to brutal hostility which poses a standing challenge to all scholars who seek to explain the origins and nature of Irish sectarianism.

[95] Quoted by N. P. Canny, 'Religion, politics and the Irish rising of 1641', in Judith Devlin and Ronan Fanning (eds.), *Religion and rebellion* (Dublin: University College Dublin Press, 1997), p. 64.

2   Confessionalisation in Ireland: periodisation
     and character, 1534–1649

Ute Lotz-Heumann

This chapter offers an interpretation of Irish history in the sixteenth and seventeenth centuries by a historian who was trained in the German historiographical tradition. This is a tradition which is in many respects different from that of Ireland, Britain and North America: 'German historians have an industry they call 'Periodisierung' (periodisation) and they take it very seriously' – thus the English historian C. H. Williams in 1967.[1] 'Periodisation', the definition of historical periods and the discussion of their usefulness in historiographical debate, has a long tradition in German historiography. In order to justify their interest in periodisation German historians argue that, as Wolfgang Reinhard has put it, 'even the most pragmatic and rather arbitrary selection of two years to identify a portion of history could result in the smuggling of some theoretical concept into apparently factual statements'.[2] For example, choosing dynastic dates as limits for a book on the history of any European country in the early modern period implies different things: that the rule of a certain dynasty constitutes a unified epoch in this country's history or, more generally, 'that crown and dynasty are the factors which really matter'.[3] Consequently, German historians

This chapter was originally submitted in spring 1999. Only a limited number of monographs published after that date could be included in the notes when the chapter was minimally revised in 2003. The chapter is based on my *Die doppelte Konfessionalisierung in Irland: Konflikt und Koexistenz im 16. und in der ersten Hälfte des 17. Jahrhunderts* (Tübingen: Mohr Siebeck, 2000). For reviews of this book in English see H. Robinson-Hammerstein, 'The confessionalisation of Ireland? Assessment of a paradigm', *IHS* 32 (2001), 567–78; S. Ellis, *Journal of Ecclesiastical History* 53 (2002), 607–8; Raingard Esser, *History Ireland* 10 (2002), 52; Regina Pörtner in Regina Pörtner (ed.), *Research on British history in the Federal Republic of Germany 1998–2000: an annotated bibliography* (London: German Historical Institute, 2002), pp. 46–7. I should like to thank Professor Karl S. Bottigheimer and Professor Alan Ford for making helpful stylistic suggestions, and I am grateful to the *Gottlieb Daimler- und Karl Benz-Stiftung* for a research fellowship in 1995.
[1] Wolfgang Reinhard, 'The idea of early-modern history', in Michael Bentley (ed.), *Companion to historiography* (London: Routledge, 1997), p. 281.
[2] *Ibid.*   [3] *Ibid.*

argue, periodisations and their underlying concepts and interpretations have to be constantly discussed and, if necessary, revised. This is the other 'industry' of German historiography: the development of theoretical concepts in order to explain and categorise historical phenomena and processes, which is often closely connected with discussions on periodisation.

One such theoretical concept is the paradigm of confessionalisation (*Konfessionalisierung*) which was developed by the two German early modernists Wolfgang Reinhard and Heinz Schilling in order to interpret the period of increasing religious and political conflicts in the Holy Roman Empire between the Peace of Augsburg in 1555 and the beginning of the Thirty Years War in 1618. This period was, however, an age of religious polarisation and conflict not only in the empire, but all over Europe. As a consequence of the Protestant reformation of the first half of the sixteenth century, most conflicts in Europe in the second half of the sixteenth and the first half of the seventeenth century had a religious as well as a political dimension.[4] Therefore, Reinhard and Schilling have always understood the concept of confessionalisation as a heuristic instrument which can also be applied to the history of other European countries in the early modern period.[5]

This chapter is divided into three parts. First, I will describe the concept of confessionalisation as it was developed in German historiography. Second, I will explain why I suggest the application of this paradigm to Irish history; why it can, in my opinion, provide early modern Irish history with a terminology and periodisation in line with the results of recent research. Third, I will propose a periodisation for Irish history between 1534 and 1649 from the point of view of the concept of 'confessionalisation'.

The concept of confessionalisation

Like Irish historiography, German historiography in the nineteenth century was confessionally divided and this was connected with the question of nation-building: there were the Prussian and Protestant

---

[4] One needs only to think of the civil wars in sixteenth-century France or the revolt of the Netherlands.

[5] H. Schilling, 'Die Konfessionalisierung von Kirche, Staat und Gesellschaft: Profil, Leistung, Defizite und Perspektiven eines geschichtswissenschaftlichen Paradigmas', in W. Reinhard and H. Schilling (eds.), *Die katholische Konfessionalisierung* (Gütersloh: Gütersloher Verlaghaus, 1995), p. 4; see also W. Reinhard, 'Konfession und Konfessionalisierung in Europa', in W. Reinhard (ed.), *Bekenntnis und Geschichte: Die Confessio Augustana im historischen Zusammenhang* (Munich: Vögel, 1981), pp. 165–89.

historians who were protagonists of a Lesser Germany (*Kleindeutschland*) on the one hand and the Catholic historians, oriented towards a Greater Germany (*Großdeutschland*) on the other hand.[6] It was in the nineteenth century that the usefulness of the term counter-reformation was first discussed in German historiography, and it is therefore my starting point for an explanation of the concept of confessionalisation, which German historians see as a replacement for the term 'counter-reformation'.

From the later eighteenth century, the term 'counter-reformations' (in the plural) had been used in German scholarship 'for the purpose of describing any local reversal of the Reformation, any particular instance, for example in Germany, of the regaining of a territory formerly Protestant, or of the extinction of Protestantism within a certain area'.[7] It was the Protestant historian Leopold von Ranke who introduced counter-reformation (in the singular) 'into the terminology of historical periodisation',[8] seeing a continuous movement and process instead of only individual events.[9] This periodisation was quickly accepted in historiography, and the Catholic historian Moriz Ritter gave it wide currency by using it in the title of his book *Deutsche Geschichte im Zeitalter der Gegenreformation und des dreißigjährigen Krieges, 1555–1648.*[10] The term *Gegenreformation* was also adopted by other European historiographies as 'counter-reformation', *contre-réforme* etc., and the periodisation of the sixteenth century into 'the reformation' followed by 'the counter-reformation' gained wide currency.[11]

However, counter-reformation as a concept as well as a periodisation is one-dimensional because it stresses the aspect of reaction and resistance to Protestantism and neglects that of reform within Catholicism.[12] This was the point made by the Protestant historian, Wilhelm Maurenbrecher, whose research into Catholic reform movements before

---

[6] On the interpretation of the early modern period, particularly the Protestant reformation, by these historiographical traditions see H.Th. Gräf, 'Reich, Nation und Kirche in der groß- und kleindeutschen Historiographie', *Historisches Jahrbuch* 116 (1996), 367–94; and T. A. Brady, 'The Protestant reformation in German history' (Washington: German Historical Institute, 1998), 9–34.

[7] H. O. Evennett, *The spirit of the counter-reformation* (Cambridge: Cambridge University Press, 1968), p. 4, see also pp. 4–22; for the history of the term see H. Jedin, *Katholische Reformation oder Gegenreformation?* (Luzern, 1946), pp. 10–25.

[8] Evennett, *Counter-reformation*, p. 5.

[9] *Ibid.*, pp. 5–6; Jedin, *Reformation oder Gegenreformation*, p. 10.

[10] 3 vols. (Stuttgart: Cotta, 1889–1908).

[11] E.g., A. G. Dickens, *The counter reformation* (London: Thames & Hudson, 1968).

[12] W. Reinhard, 'Gegenreformation als Modernisierung? Prolegomena zu einer Theorie des konfessionellen Zeitalters', *Archiv für Reformationsgeschichte* 68 (1977), 226–9; W. Reinhard, 'Reformation, counter-reformation, and the early-modern state: a reassessment', *Catholic Historical Review* 75 (1989), 383–4.

the Protestant reformation convinced him that Catholicism not only reacted to Luther, but that there was a Catholic reformation before, and independent of, the Protestant movement. Accordingly, in 1880 Maurenbrecher published a book entitled *Geschichte der katholischen Reformation* – thereby introducing the concept of a 'Catholic reformation'.[13] This concept was taken up and given wider currency by the Catholic historian Ludwig von Pastor in his *Geschichte der Päpste*.[14]

This new terminology, although it was not confessionally determined at its inception, did not escape the confessional division in German historiography. Maurenbrecher's term Catholic reformation appealed to Catholic historians because it offered them the possibility of avoiding the term counter-reformation with its problematic connotation of a mere reaction to Protestantism. Catholic historians started to use terms like 'Catholic reformation and restoration' in order to replace 'counter-reformation'. On the other hand, the term 'Catholic reformation' was rejected by Protestant historians – largely because they did not want the term 'reformation' to be used for anything other than the *Protestant* reformation. Protestant historians therefore continued to use the term 'counter-reformation'.[15]

As a consequence, German historiography remained confessionally divided on the question. Responding to this state of affairs, Hubert Jedin, a scholar of Catholic background, wrote a short treatise in 1946, in which he described the conceptual and terminological problems of the terms 'counter-reformation' and 'Catholic reformation' and suggested the compromise terminology 'Catholic reform and counter-reformation'.[16] In 1958 the emphasis of historical research was changed fundamentally by the Catholic historian Ernst Walter Zeeden. In an article in the *Historische Zeitschrift* he suggested a new concept and terminology. Zeeden stressed that in the second half of the sixteenth century Catholicism, Lutheranism and Calvinism started to build modern, clearly defined confessional churches each of which centred on a confession of faith. He called this process 'confession-building' (*Konfessionsbildung*), a neutral term which could be applied to all

---

[13] (Nördlingen: C. H. Beck); see Evennett, *Counter-reformation*, p. 7; H. Jedin, 'Katholische Reformation oder Gegenreformation?', in E. W. Zeeden (ed.), *Gegenreformation* (Darmstadt: Wissenschaftliche Buchgesellschaft, 1973), pp. 11–12.

[14] *Geschichte der Päpste seit dem Ausgang des Mittelalters*, 16 vols. (Freiburg im Breisgau: Herder, 1886–1933), V, *Geschichte der Päpste im Zeitalter der katholischen Reformation und Restauration*.

[15] Jedin, *Reformation oder Gegenreformation*, pp. 7–9, 12–15.

[16] *Ibid.*; see also Jedin, 'Katholische Reformation oder Gegenreformation?', pp. 79–81.

churches.[17] Two scholars of the next generation, Wolfgang Reinhard and Heinz Schilling, from, respectively, Catholic and Protestant backgrounds, developed Zeeden's approach. Reinhard and Schilling introduced the paradigm of 'confessionalisation', which widened confession-building into a concept of societal history.[18]

The concept of confessionalisation proceeds from the general observation that in the Middle Ages and in the early modern period the religious and the secular – church and state – were closely linked. Consequently, the confessional divisions and conflicts of the early modern period affected not only the area of religion and church, but the entire social and political system. 'The concept confessionalization contains this political and societal dimension.'[19] It stresses the connections between confession-building and early modern state-formation and integrates these two processes into one historiographical concept.

---

[17] E. W. Zeeden, 'Grundlagen und Wege der Konfessionsbildung im Zeitalter der Glaubenskämpfe', *Historische Zeitschrift*, 185 (1958), 249–99; see also E. W. Zeeden, *Die Entstehung der Konfessionen: Grundlagen und Formen der Konfessionsbildung im Zeitalter der Glaubenskämpfe* (Munich: Oldenbourg, 1965) E. W. Zeeden, *Konfessionsbildung: Studien zur Reformation, Gegenreformation und katholischen Reform* (Stuttgart: Klett-Cotta, 1985). Zeeden suggested two general terms for the period between 1500 and 1650: 'Zeitalter der Glaubensspaltung und Konfessionsbildung' (age of religious division and confession-building) and 'Zeitalter der Glaubenskämpfe: Reformation und katholische Reform' (age of religious conflicts: reformation and Catholic reform). E. W. Zeeden, 'Zur Periodisierung und Terminologie des Zeitalters der Reformation und Gegenreformation: Ein Diskussionsbeitrag', in Zeeden, *Konfessionsbildung*, p. 65 (reprint of article from *Geschichte in Wissenschaft und Unterricht* 7 (1956), 433–7). Neither suggestion was near as influential as his term *Konfessionsbildung* (confession-building).

[18] The most important articles on the concept of confessionalisation by Reinhard and Schilling are: Reinhard, 'Konfession und Konfessionalisierung'; W. Reinhard, 'Zwang zur Konfessionalisierung? Prolegomena zu einer Theorie des konfessionellen Zeitalters', *Zeitschrift für historische Forschung* 10 (1983), 257–77; Reinhard, 'Reformation, counterreformation', pp. 383–404; W. Reinhard, 'Was ist katholische Konfessionalisierung?', in Reinhard and Schilling (eds.), *Die katholische Konfessionalisierung*, pp. 419–52; H. Schilling, 'Die Konfessionalisierung im Reich: Religiöser und gesellschaftlicher Wandel in Deutschland zwischen 1555 und 1620', *Historische Zeitschrift* 246 (1988), 1–45 (translated as 'Confessionalization in the empire: religious and societal change in Germany between 1555 and 1620', in H. Schilling, *Religion, political culture and the emergence of early-modern society* (Leiden: Brill, 1992), pp. 205–45); H. Schilling, 'Confessional Europe', in T. A. Brady, H. A. Oberman and J. D. Tracy (eds.), *Handbook of European history 1400–1600*, 2 vols. (Leiden: E. J. Brill, 1995), II, pp. 641–75; Schilling, 'Die Konfessionalisierung von Kirche, Staat und Gesellschaft'. See also the proceedings of three conferences on confessionalisation: H. Schilling (ed.), *Die reformierte Konfessionalisierung in Deutschland – Das Problem der 'Zweiten Reformation'* (Gütersloh: Gütersloher Verlaghaus, 1986); H.-C. Rublack (ed.), *Die lutherische Konfessionalisierung in Deutschland* (Gütersloh: Gütersloher Verlaghaus, 1992); Reinhard and Schilling (eds.), *Die katholische Konfessionalisierung*; and R. P. Hsia, *Social discipline in the reformation: central Europe, 1550–1750* (London: Routledge, 1989), somewhat mistitled since it describes the process of confessionalisation in early modern Germany.

[19] Schilling, 'Confessionalization in the empire' p. 208.

Confession-building and state-formation could interact in opposite ways; in many cases confessionalisation 'enabled states and societies to integrate more tightly'.[20] This was the case if the principle of *cuius regio, eius religio* was successfully enforced. But 'confessionalization could also provoke confrontation with religious and political groups fundamentally opposed to this . . . integration of state and society. The process of confessionalization took place between the two poles of state-building and confessional conflict.'[21]

The paradigm of confessionalisation has shifted historians' approach to the confessional divide of the sixteenth and seventeenth centuries. The confessional churches are seen not only from the traditional point of view which stresses differences in doctrine and ritual, but also from a comparative point of view which looks at parallel developments and 'functional similarities'[22] between the confessional churches. This has also led to new terminology. The terms which were used by German historians to describe the development of the three confessional churches – Catholic reform/counter-reformation, second reformation (for Calvinism) and Lutheran orthodoxy – have been replaced by the parallel terms Catholic/Calvinist/Lutheran confessionalisation and the term 'age of confessionalisation'.[23]

Reinhard has identified seven mechanisms which led to successful confessionalisation, i.e., the successful implementation of the *cuius regio, eius religio* principle and a politico-religious integration of society. First, the establishment of 'pure doctrine' and its formulation in a confession of faith: this meant distinguishing one confessional church from other churches and eliminating possible sources of confusion. Second, the distribution and enforcement of these new norms, for example, through confessional oaths and subscription. In this way, the religious orthodoxy of personnel in strategic positions – for instance, theologians, priests, teachers and secular officials – was to be ensured and dissidents were to be removed. Third, propaganda and censure; this meant making use of the printing press for propaganda purposes on the one hand, and preventing rival churches from using the printing press on the other hand. Fourth, internalisation of the new norms through, above all, education, but also through catechising, sermons and pilgrimages. Fifth,

---

[20] *Ibid.*, p. 209.   [21] *Ibid.*   [22] *Ibid.*, p. 210.

[23] Reinhard and Schilling have also used the alternative terms 'confessional age' and 'confessional Europe'. W. Reinhard, 'Gegenreformation als Modernisierung? Prolegomena zu einer Theorie des konfessionellen Zeitalters', *Archiv für Reformationsgeschichte* 68 (1977), 251–2; Schilling, 'Confessional Europe'.

disciplining the population; visitations and the expulsion of confessional minorities were to ensure that the confessional group remained as homogeneous as possible. Sixth, rites and the control of participation in rites such as baptism and marriage through the keeping of registers. Seventh and lastly, Reinhard refers to the confessional regulation even of language. For example, while names of saints were particularly appealing to Catholics, they were forbidden in Geneva.[24] Confessionalisation also resulted in long-term social and mental changes. One of the long-term consequences of successful, i.e., integrative confessionalisation was confessional homogenisation, that is, the repression of forms of worship not authorised by the respective churches. Another long-term consequence was the development of confessionalised cultural and political – often national – identities.[25]

In recent years the paradigm of confessionalisation has proven its worth as a research tool by inspiring many articles and Ph.D. theses.[26] And even if authors like Olaf Mörke or Benjamin Kaplan who have worked on the Netherlands came to the conclusion that confessionalisation was not a national phenomenon, but a phenomenon restricted to localities and individual churches, they nevertheless used the paradigm as an heuristic instrument.[27] In the following, the concept of confessionalisation will be

[24] Reinhard, 'Zwang zur Konfessionalisierung?', p. 263; Reinhard, 'Was ist katholische Konfessionalisierung?', p. 426; Reinhard, 'Reformation, counter-reformation', pp. 391–5.

[25] H. Schilling, 'Nationale Identität und Konfession in der europäischen Neuzeit', in B. Giesen, (ed.), *Nationale und kulturelle Identität: Studien zur Entwicklung des kollektiven Bewußtseins in der Neuzeit* (Frankfurt a. M.: Suhrkamp, 1991), pp. 192–252.

[26] For an overview of the historiography see: Ute Lotz-Heumann, 'The concept of "Confessionalization" a historiographical paradigm in dispute', *Memoria y Civilización: Anuario de Historia* 4 (2001), 93–114; and also Heinz Schilling, Literaturbericht, 'Konfessionelles Zeitalter', parts I–IV, *Geschichte in Wissenschaft und Unterricht* 48 (1997), pp. 350–69 (part I), pp. 618–27 (part II), pp. 682–94 (part III), pp. 748–66 (part IV). Although the concept of confessionalisation is now widely accepted in German historiography, it has also been challenged. See, e.g., H. R. Schmidt, *Konfessionalisierung im 16. Jahrhundert* (Munich: Oldenbourg, 1992). Two aspects of the paradigm have been criticised: its alleged 'etatistic focus' and its alleged neglect of 'the people' and their cooperation with or resistance to confessionalisation. This criticism has to be taken seriously, but it also has to be made clear that the etatistic focus of confessionalisation was not part of the original definition of the concept by Schilling which stressed the possibility of fundamental opposition to state-sponsored confessionalisation. Above, note 21; see also H. Schilling, *Konfessionskonflikt und Staatsbildung* (Gütersloh: Gütersloher Verlaghaus, 1981).

[27] B. J. Kaplan, *Calvinists and libertines: confession and community in Utrecht, 1578–1620* (Oxford: Clarendon Press, 1995); O. Mörke, 'Die politische Bedeutung des Konfessionellen im Deutschen Reich und in der Republik der Vereinigten Niederlande. Oder: War die Konfessionalisierung ein "Fundamentalvorgang?"', in R. G. Asch and H. Duchhardt (eds.), *Der Absolutismus – ein Mythos? Strukturwandel monarchischer*

used as a research tool in order to suggest a periodisation for Irish history between 1534 and 1649.

Application of the confessionalisation paradigm to Ireland

The application of this concept to Ireland is useful in several respects: *first*, with regard to method and approach, *second*, from a historiographical viewpoint, and *third*, not least with regard to periodisation. *First*, the close connection between religion and politics is at the heart of the concept of confessionalisation. It draws attention to the fact that almost all early modern governments strove to enforce the *cuius regio, eius religio* principle. In consequence, the problem at the root of the religio-political conflicts in early modern Ireland – the English government's continuous insistence on enforcing Protestantism and suppressing Catholicism – can be seen first of all as a normal European phenomenon of the period and does not have to be seen as a colonial or 'unique' characteristic.[28]

Second, the concept of confessionalisation focuses attention on those areas of life and historical processes where the interconnection and interdependence of religion and politics was particularly close. This also has important historiographical consequences. For, it is these processes which modern historians often try to subdivide into 'religious' and 'political' factors. In the eyes of contemporaries, however, religious and political motives were in practice inseparable. Therefore, the application of the paradigm of confessionalisation helps to overcome the frequent division of labour between historians of religion and historians of political history, who of course do not see religion and politics isolated from each other, but tend to stress one over the other.[29]

Herrschaft in West- und Mitteleuropa, ca. 1550–1700 (Cologne: Böhlau, 1996), pp. 125–64.

[28] It has to be emphasised that this is meant only with regard to the early modern period. When considering the fact that confessional conflicts remained such a persistent force in Irish history up to the late twentieth century, one will have to discuss unique turning-points in Irish history which brought this about. But during the early modern period the close interaction between confession-building and state-building was a universal phenomenon in Europe, leading either to politico-religious integration, or to conflicts, as in Ireland.

[29] See, e.g., the different emphasis given to the political and religious aspects of the estrangement of the Old English elite in Ciaran Brady, *The chief governors: the rise and fall of reform government in Tudor Ireland, 1536–1588* (Cambridge: Cambridge University Press, 1994), pp. 209–44; and Colm Lennon, *The lords of Dublin in the age of reformation* (Dublin: Irish Academic Press, 1989).

Similarly, there has traditionally been a confessional division of labour between religious and church historians.[30] Recent historiography is beginning to bridge this gap. Raymond Gillespie's book, *Devoted People*, is an interconfessional study of popular religion in early modern Ireland.[31] This is without doubt an important historiographical development: horizontality is a new integrative approach of religious history, shedding the old vertical church history and focusing on religion as a social phenomenon instead of the churches as institutions.[32] The paradigm of confessionalisation, on the other hand, aims at overcoming confessional division of labour in historiography by employing a comparative approach. If one looks at the rival confessional churches in a single conceptual framework, their interaction can be analysed and their developments can be compared to reveal similarities as well as fundamental differences.

Third, the application of the concept of confessionalisation to Ireland offers new possibilities of periodisation. Currently, there are basically two different periodisations of Irish history in the sixteenth and the first half of the seventeenth centuries, neither of which reflects the results of recent research. The first and more traditional periodisation is derived from the reformation/counter-reformation paradigm. In this periodisation, the age of the reformation is followed by the age of the counter-reformation. We find this approach, for example, in Robert Dudley Edwards' *Church and state in Tudor Ireland*,[33] Hayes-McCoy's passages in volume III of the *New history of Ireland*,[34] the writings of Brendan

---

[30] As Alan Ford and John McCafferty put it in the unpublished prospectus for the symposium 'Catholics and Protestants: the origins of sectarianism in Ireland' (Dublin, 1998): 'Even in the twentieth century, as scholars have jettisoned overt religious allegiances, the requirements of research and specialisation have ensured that they have focused almost exclusively upon one or other of the churches in Ireland' (p. 1).

[31] Raymond Gillespie, *Devoted people: belief and religion in early-modern Ireland* (Manchester: Manchester University Press, 1997); see also Raymond Gillespie, *The sacred in the secular: religious change in Catholic Ireland, 1500–1700* (Vermont: St Michael's College, 1993); Raymond Gillespie, 'The religion of Protestants: a view from the laity, 1580–1700', in Alan Ford, James McGuire and Kenneth Milne (eds.), *As by law established; the Church of Ireland since the reformation* (Dublin: Lilliput Press, 1995), pp. 89–99.

[32] Patrick Collinson, 'The vertical and the horizontal in religious history: internal and external integration of the subject', in Ford, McGuire and Milne (eds.), *As by law established*, pp. 15–32.

[33] R. D. Edwards, *Church and state in Tudor Ireland* (Dublin: Talbot Press, 1935). Edwards uses the term 'Anglican schism' for the establishment of the state church under Henry VIII; ch. 10 is entitled 'The Edwardian reformation'; ch. 11, 'The Catholic reaction,' describes Mary's reign and ch. 16 is entitled 'The counter-reformation in Ireland'.

[34] G. A. Hayes-McCoy, 'Conciliation, coercion, and the Protestant Reformation, 1547–71: the completion of the Tudor conquest and the advance of the counter-reformation, 1571–1603', *NHI*, pp. 69–141.

Bradshaw[35] and still, albeit implicitly, in Colm Lennon's overview of sixteenth-century Ireland.[36]

There are two difficulties with this periodisation.

1. As I have already mentioned, the term 'counter-reformation' has problematic connotations, expressing Catholic *reaction* to the Protestant reformation, but no independent movement of church reform. It could of course be argued that for today's historians the term counter-reformation implicitly also carries the meaning of Catholic reform and that there is therefore no need to replace the term. However, in the new *Oxford companion to Irish history* Hiram Morgan explains the term counter-reformation as 'The revival of Catholicism in Ireland, as elsewhere in western Europe, was not just a reaction to Protestantism, but the continuation of a movement already visible before the Reformation.'[37] Obviously, the term counter-reformation does not adequately represent all aspects of Catholicism in Ireland in the second half of the sixteenth century and beyond.

2. The course of Irish history in the sixteenth and seventeenth centuries does not match the reformation–counter-reformation periodisation. The term reformation (without an adjective) is usually associated with a popular movement like the Lutheran reformation in Germany, but there was no popular Protestant reformation in Ireland in the first half of the sixteenth century. And, what is more important, ever since Alan Ford's detailed investigation of the Church of Ireland[38] we know that the end of the sixteenth and the beginning of the seventeenth century was not only the period of 'Catholic reform', i.e., the regeneration of the Catholic church, but also the essential

---

[35] E.g., Brendan Bradshaw, 'The reformation in the cities: Cork, Limerick and Galway, 1534–1603', in J. Bradley (ed.), *Settlement and society in medieval Ireland* (Kilkenny: Boethius, 1988), pp. 445–76.

[36] Colm Lennon, *Sixteenth-century Ireland: the incomplete conquest* (Dublin: Gill & Macmillan, 1994), ch. 11 is entitled 'From reformation to counter-reformation'.

[37] In S. J. Connolly (ed.), *The Oxford companion to Irish history* (Oxford: Oxford University Press, 1998), p. 120. See also the discussion of the term 'counter-reformation' and the problems of its definition in Colm Lennon, 'The counter-reformation in Ireland, 1542–1641', in Ciaran Brady and Raymond Gillespie (eds.), *Natives and newcomers: essays on the making of Irish colonial society, 1534–1641* (Dublin: Irish Academic Press, 1986), pp. 75–7. Lennon favours a very broad definition of the term: 'I wish to take the counter-reformation in Ireland as encompassing the elements of native response to the reformation, the preservation of older forms of practice and devotion, some reform impulses already manifest in the pre-reformation period and the spiritual force of the Tridentine reforms fusing with or transmuting native Catholicism' (pp. 77–8).

[38] Alan Ford, *The Protestant reformation in Ireland, 1590–1641*, 2nd edn (Dublin: Four Courts Press, 1997).

formative period of the Church of Ireland as a Protestant church, i.e., of the Protestant reformation, which in Ireland was not a popular reformation.

The second approach with regard to periodisation and terminology which is currently applied to Irish history tries to take this fact into account and therefore uses the term reformation in the plural. Two of the latest books on early modern Irish religious history employ this term: Samantha Meigs' *The Reformations in Ireland: Tradition and Confessionalism, 1400–1690* and Henry Jefferies' *Priests and Prelates of Armagh in the Age of Reformations, 1518–1558*.[39] The term reformations, which seems so handy and useful at first glance, nevertheless poses considerable problems of definition and periodisation. It is a vague term and means different things in the works mentioned above.

Henry Jefferies uses the term with reference to the Henrician and the Edwardian reformations.[40] His usage is the same as Christopher Haigh's in his book *English reformations*, where he employs the term 'reformations' in order to refer to the different phases and forms of the English reformation, that is, the political reformations under Henry VIII and Edward VI as opposed to what he calls the Protestant reformation under Elizabeth I.[41] Meigs, in contrast, seems to use the term reformations in a different sense;[42] the usage in her book, which describes the development of Irish Catholicism from 1400 onwards, seems to be derived from the model of a 'late medieval-to-early modern era'[43] between *c.* 1400 and *c.* 1600, which is prominent in North American historiography[44]

---

[39] S. A. Meigs, *The reformations in Ireland: tradition and confessionalism, 1400–1690* (London: Macmillan, 1997); H. A. Jefferies, *Priests and prelates of Armagh in the age of reformations, 1518–1558* (Dublin: Four Courts Press, 1997).

[40] The last chapter of Jefferies, *Priests and prelates of Armagh* is entitled 'The early Tudor reformations and Marian restoration'.

[41] Christopher Haigh, *English reformations* (Oxford: Clarendon Press, 1993). Part II is entitled 'Two political reformations, 1530–1553', and part III 'Political reformation and Protestant reformation'.

[42] Unfortunately, Meigs does not explain the use of the term 'reformations' in the title of her book except by adding the date '1400–1690'. The term does not reappear in her table of contents.

[43] T. A. Brady, 'Introduction: renaissance and reformation, late middle ages and early-modern era', in Brady, Oberman and Tracy (eds.), *Handbook of European history*, I, p. xvii.

[44] E.g., Steven Ozment, *The age of reform 1250–1550* (New Haven: Yale University Press, 1980); and the two volumes of the *Handbook of European history* edited by Brady, Oberman and Tracy, and the review of this handbook by H. Lehmann in *Archiv für Reformationsgeschichte* 88 (1997), 412–14. German historians have also applied this periodisation to European history: see, above all, E. Hassinger, *Das Werden des neuzeitlichen Europa 1300–1600* (Braunschweig: Georg Westermann, 1959).

and – as *temps des réformes* – in French historiography.[45] In this sense the term reformations or the age of reformations denotes a reform period spanning the fifteenth to seventeenth centuries and including not only the Protestant and Catholic reformations but also late medieval church reform.[46]

Thus, the terms reformation and reformations, particularly without an adjective, do not provide us with a useful terminology and periodisation because they have been given so many different meanings. I am not denying that it might be useful to see a *temps des réformes* in European history, but I doubt that it makes sense with regard to Irish history. Periodisation is, after all, about identifying deep-rooted changes in history. And the first half of the sixteenth century, especially the years 1534–41 with the introduction of direct rule to Ireland and Henry VIII's break with Rome, was clearly a period of deep-rooted changes and constitutes the beginning of the early modern period in Ireland.[47] All in all, a different terminology and periodisation are called for. This has also been expressed in recent historiography on the religious history of Ireland and the terms confessionalisation and confessionalism have been introduced in this context. While Ford draws his use of the term confessionalisation from the concept developed by Reinhard and Schilling, Bradshaw and Meigs, though they employ the term confessionalism, have not defined it or explained how they are using it.[48]

The term confessionalism may be derived from Ronny Po-Chia Hsia's *Social discipline in the Reformation*,[49] in which he introduces the concepts of *Konfessionsbildung* and *Konfessionalisierung* and translates them as 'the

[45] E.g., Pierre Chaunu, *Le temps des réformes: histoire religieuse et système de civilisation – la crise de la chrétienté – l'éclatement (1250–1550)* (Paris: Fayard, 1975); Marc Venard (ed.), *Histoire du Christianisme des origines à nos jours, tome VII: De la réforme à la réformation (1450–1530)* (Paris: Desclée, 1994).

[46] For example, in a collection of essays edited by Beat Kümin, the term is used with regard to a European 'age of reformations' between 1470 and 1630. Beat Kümin (ed.), *Reformations old and new: essays on the socio-economic impact of religious change, c. 1470–1630* (Aldershot: Ashgate, 1996).

[47] In this I follow most accounts of sixteenth-century Ireland: e.g., Lennon, *Sixteenth-century Ireland*; N. P. Canny, *From reformation to restoration: Ireland, 1534–1660* (Dublin: Helicon, 1987); *NHI*. But see S. G. Ellis, *Ireland in the age of the Tudors 1447–1603: English expansion and the end of Gaelic rule* (London: Longman, 1998), esp. p. xv, who argues for a 'Tudor age' in Irish history.

[48] Ford uses the term confessionalisation in Alan Ford and Kenneth Milne (eds.), The Church of Ireland: a critical bibliography, 1536–1992, *IHS* 28 (1993), 358; Ford, *Protestant reformation*, pp. 18, 20. Bradshaw uses the term confessionalism in Brendan Bradshaw, 'The English reformation and identity formation in Ireland and Wales', in Brendan Bradshaw and Peter Roberts (eds.), *British consciousness and identity: the making of Britain, 1533–1707* (Cambridge: Cambridge University Press, 1998), e.g., p. 51. Meigs uses the term in the subtitle of her book *The reformations in Ireland*.

[49] Hsia, *Social discipline*.

formation of confessions' and 'confessionalization'.[50] Later, however, he uses the term confessionalism for 'the formation of religious ideologies and institutions in Lutheranism, Calvinism, and Catholicism' and stresses explicitly that 'confessionalization refers to the interrelated *processes* by which the consolidation of the early-modern state, the imposition of social discipline, and the formation of confessional churches transformed society'.[51] There is a contradiction in these definitions; the word confessionalism does not imply a 'process' or 'formation', but either a fixed ideology ('-ism') or a condition, a state of affairs which is static and unchanging. This is, however, not what the two concepts of confession-building (or, as Hsia also calls it, 'formation of confessions') and confessionalisation express; they stress the aspect of gradual development, of a process leading towards confessionalism. In this context, it remains an open question whether confessionalism in the strict sense of the word, that is, the complete permeation of politics and society by the different confessional ideologies and cultures, was the consequence of the processes of confession-building and confessionalisation. Judging from the results of recent research, confessionalism was never absolute, and certain areas of life (like popular religion or the *res publica litteraria*) were to a high degree 'immune' to complete confessionalisation.[52]

Nevertheless, the confessional division between Catholic and Protestant has been a major force in Irish history since the sixteenth century. However, this division did not spring into being immediately after 1536, as the older – confessionally determined – historiography held.[53] Recent scholars have agreed that the 'political reformation' of Henry VIII in Ireland, i.e., the establishment of the royal supremacy, was above all a legal and administrative act. In contrast to the Protestant reformation of the first half of the sixteenth century in Germany, it was not a reformation of doctrine and/or a popular reformation.[54] Historians are also largely agreed that neither of the two confessional churches that were already forming on the continent had a decisive influence on the religious history of Ireland before the 1580s.[55] Then, both churches

---

[50] *Ibid.*, pp. 2–3.

[51] *Ibid.*, pp. 4–5 (the italics are in the original text).

[52] E.g., Gillespie, *Devoted people*. The question of confessionalisation as a 'fundamental process' is also discussed with respect to different areas of life in Lotz-Heumann, *Die doppelte Konfessionalisierung*, pp. 306–16.

[53] Introduction, above, p. 5.

[54] E.g., P. J. Corish, *The Catholic community in the seventeenth and eighteenth centuries* (Dublin: Helicon, 1981), p. 3; Ellis, *Age of the Tudors*, pp. 205–9; Lennon, *Sixteenth-century Ireland*, pp. 134–43.

[55] E.g. Ellis, *Age of the Tudors*, p. 205; Ford, *Protestant reformation*, p. 23; Lennon, *Sixteenth-century Ireland*, pp. 315–24. In contrast, Bradshaw maintains the thesis that

entered a process of confession-building. The increasing significance of confessional conflicts in Irish history from the late sixteenth century onwards makes clear that the formation of two rival confessional churches led to the confessionalisation of society and politics. In Ireland, where the *cuius regio, eius religio* principle did not succeed, the process of confessionalisation resulted in religious confrontation and political opposition to state-building.[56] In this respect, Ireland can be said to have experienced a process of dual confessionalisation; two processes of confessionalisation, one Catholic and one Protestant, confronted each other in the realms of religion, politics and society, but neither of them was 'successful' in terms of enforcing the *cuius regio, eius religio* principle.[57] In contrast, the two confessionalisations were defeated by one another. In the following, a periodisation of this process of dual confessionalisation will be offered which is based on the results of recent research on the religious, political and social developments in early modern Ireland.

Periodisation

I suggest dividing Irish history from the early sixteenth to the middle of the seventeenth century into five phases: the *first* phase from 1534 to 1558/60 was one of political and legal reformation on the one hand and religious uncertainty on the other. The *second* phase from 1558/60 to *c.* 1580 can be called the preparatory phase of confessionalisation, with the final establishment of a Protestant state church in Ireland and with political conflict being for the first time defined as 'religious war'. The *third* phase from *c.* 1580 to 1603 saw the gradual formation of confessional churches in Ireland as well as the gradual confessionalisation of Irish politics and society. Ireland changed from a preconfessional to a confessionalised society. After 1603, two further phases of confessionalisation can be identified: the *fourth* phase from 1603 to 1632 can be characterised as 'confessionalisation *inside* Irish society' because the confessional conflicts

---

the majority of the population in Ireland became consciously Catholic during Mary's reign: Bradshaw, 'English reformation and identity formation', p. 4: 'the so-called mid-Tudor crisis marked a shift in attitude'.

[56] However, this failure of the principle of *cuius regio, eius religio* in Ireland was not unique in Europe. On this question see K. S. Bottigheimer and U. Lotz-Heumann, 'The Irish reformation in European perspective', *Archiv für Reformationsgeschichte* 89 (1998), 268–309.

[57] It should not be forgotten that the establishment of the *cuius regio, eius religio* principle was not only an aim of the English crown. Catholic 'rebels' in Ireland in the early modern period fought for the same objective – a state in which Catholicism, not Protestantism would be the religion 'by law established'.

visible during this outwardly peaceful era developed within Irish society, particularly between the Protestant New English and the Catholic Old English.[58] This was also a phase of intensified confession-building for both churches in Ireland. The *fifth* phase which starts with the deputyship of Thomas Wentworth in 1632 and ends with the Cromwellian conquest of 1649 can be characterised as 'confessionalisation *from outside*'. During this phase, the religious and political development of Ireland was decisively influenced by the British and European contexts of Irish history, personified by Lord Deputy Wentworth, on the one hand, and the papal nuncio Rinuccini on the other.

The first phase from 1534 to 1558/60 brought political and legal – but not religious – reformation through Henry VIII's break with Rome legalised by the Irish parliament in 1536 and the Act declaring him king of Ireland in 1541. It was also the period of new and increased attempts at establishing English political control over Ireland:[59] early modern state-formation in a dependent territory.[60] The Kildare Rebellion of 1534 can be regarded as the first incidence of resistance against this process of state-building.[61] The policy of surrender and regrant, aiming at the political integration of the Gaelic lords into the Irish kingdom, as well as the more severe policies of military conquest and plantation during the mid-Tudor period, were all manifestations of this process.[62]

From the point of view of confession-building and confessionalisation, the period was clearly preconfessional. Henry's reformation was political, dynastic and legal, and the two subsequent reigns were too short to fix confessional identities in Ireland. Even if there were signs of resistance to a Protestant reformation in the reign of Edward,[63] his reign was

---

[58] It could be argued against this terminology that Protestantism as well as the New English came to Ireland 'from outside'. I would, however, maintain that both the Protestant confession and the New English population became part of Irish society – which was of course heterogeneous and fluid – as soon as they settled in Ireland.

[59] Brendan Bradshaw, *The Irish constitutional revolution of the sixteenth century* (Cambridge: Cambridge University Press, 1979).

[60] The terminology is derived from W. Reinhard (ed.), *Power elites and state building* (Oxford: Clarendon Press, 1996), p. 79; see also Hiram Morgan, 'British policies before the British state', in Brendan Bradshaw and John Morrill (eds.), *The British problem, c.1534–1707: state-formation in the Atlantic archipelago* (London: Macmillan, 1996), p. 67.

[61] E.g., S. G. Ellis, 'The Kildare rebellion and the early Henrician reformation', *Historical Journal* 19 (1976), 808; Ciaran Brady, 'Court, castle and country: the framework of government in Tudor Ireland', in Brady and Gillespie (eds.), *Natives and newcomers*, p. 27.

[62] The most recent analysis of this process is Brady, *The chief governors*.

[63] See the letter by the Protestant Bishop Staples to Sir Edward Bellingham, 1548 in C. Maxwell (ed.), *Irish history from contemporary sources (1509–1610)* (London, 1923), pp.

too brief, especially in Ireland, where decrees arrived later, to have a lasting impact on society.[64] Similarly, Irish historiography now seems to have arrived at a consensus that Catholicism ('the counter-reformation') did not succeed in Ireland in Mary's reign.[65] People rejoiced in Kilkenny,[66] but they also, according to Eamon Duffy and Christopher Haigh, welcomed the return of the mass in England.[67] Mary's reign was also too short to determine the confessional development of Ireland. Moreover, the plantation projects, which later came to be associated with English Protestantism, were not yet confessionally determined; they were continued under Mary, not abandoned.[68]

Largely due to dynastic coincidences, the confessional and political future of Ireland remained open in 1558 and in this respect Ireland was not so much different from England and Wales.[69] It was, however, very different with regard to state-building and political penetration. Ireland was not under the political control of the English monarchs, but was divided into three political zones: Gaelic Ireland, the Anglo-Irish lord-ships and the 'English districts', i.e., the Pale and the towns.[70] This political fragmentation was to become decisive in Ireland's period of confessionalisation in the second half of the century and beyond.

152–3. On the other hand, Bishop Bale seems to have had a small Protestant following: S. G. Ellis, 'John Bale, bishop of Ossory, 1552–3', *Journal of the Butler Society* 2 (1984), 283–93.

[64] Due to a scarcity of sources, there is no monograph on the Edwardian reformation in Ireland: B. Bradshaw, 'The Edwardian reformation in Ireland, 1547–53', *Archivium Hibernicum* 34 (1977), 83–99.

[65] Above, note 55.

[66] The classic source for the enthusiasm over Mary's accession to the throne is P. Happé and J. N. King (eds.), *The vocacyon of Johan Bale* (Binghampton: Medieval and Renaissance Texts and Studies, 1990), p. 62.

[67] Eamon Duffy, *The stripping of the altars* (New Haven: Yale University Press, 1992), pp. 524–64; Haigh, *English reformations*, pp. 203–18.

[68] See the defense of plantation by the Catholic archbishop of Armagh, Dowdall: 'I call this a godly way of reformation to subdue or banish these people that be there always disposed to all naughtiness, as murder, stealth, robbery, and deceit, and do not obey God's or man's laws; and therefore, as it is written in the Civil Law quod Princeps debet purgare provinciam suam a malis hominibus, I do call it godly to plant good men in the stead of evil; and this was the occasion that moved the pope's holiness to give the king licence at the time of the first conquest to take their lands from them' (C. McNeill (ed.), 'Harris: Collectanea de rebus Hibernicis', *Analecta Hibernica* 6 (1934), p. 434).

[69] This is certainly one of the most important results of English revisionism for Irish history. See especially the review of Duffy, *Stripping of the altars* by Brian Jackson, *IHS* 24 (1994), p. 276.

[70] The term is from Ellis, *Age of the Tudors*, p. 31, see pp. 31–50. See also the differenti-ation from the English king's point of view into 'the King's Irish enemies', 'the King's English rebels' and 'the King's subjects' in State of Ireland, and plan for its reformation (1515): Maxwell (ed.), *Irish history*, pp. 79–85.

This first phase of political and legal reformation was followed by a phase of intensified state-building and increasing political resistance in an atmosphere of confessional uncertainty between 1558/60 and *c.* 1580. It was, in short, the preparatory phase of confessionalisation. This period also started with a political and legal reformation. After the accession of Elizabeth I in 1558 it quickly became clear that she would separate her dominions from the Catholic church. This became law in Ireland when in 1560 the Irish parliament adopted the English Acts of Supremacy and Uniformity.[71] At least theoretically, the Church of Ireland took control of the medieval church, its fabric and personnel. This political and legal reformation was to be followed up by a Protestant reformation. It was hoped by Elizabethan reformers that the Church of Ireland would gradually be transformed into a true Protestant church and that the people would be educated to the new faith. However, as Ford has stressed, Protestant reform strategies of all kinds (be they persuasive or coercive) lacked the means to be implemented[72] – and they lacked those means because the English state in Ireland was too weak effectively to assist Protestant confession-building. Therefore, rather than say that the English state did not succeed in enforcing the principle of *cuius regio, eius religio* in Ireland, we had better say that this mechanism was never really established because the English state in Ireland was incapable of doing so.

This had two important consequences: First, the all-embracing but not all-controlling Church of Ireland left a vacuum that was filled by traditional religion. This vacuum is most obvious in those areas which were not politically controlled by the Dublin government. But even where the queen's writ more or less ran, a similar situation prevailed: there was no active resistance to Protestantism, some conformity, little enthusiasm and a lot of clinging to 'the old ways'.[73] Catholic survivalism – also called crypto-Catholicism or church papistry – thrived

---

[71] H. A. Jefferies, 'The Irish parliament of 1560: The Anglican reforms authorised', *IHS* 26 (1988), 128–41.

[72] Ford, *Protestant reformation*, p. 27.

[73] E.g., the letter by Edmund Tanner, Catholic bishop of Cork, to Cardinal Moroni, 1571, in E. Hogan (ed.), *Ibernia Ignatiana seu Ibernorum Societas Jesu patrum monumenta* (Dublin, 1880), p. 16; see also the description of Ireland by Father David Wolfe, SJ, 1574, J. C. Begley (ed.), *The diocese of Limerick in the sixteenth and seventeenth centuries* (Dublin, 1927), pp. 507, 509; Lennon, *Sixteenth-century Ireland*, p. 312; Ciaran Brady, 'Conservative subversives: the community of the Pale and the Dublin administration, 1556–86', *Historical Studies* 15 (1985), 13. For the biography of Richard Creagh, an important figure of this preparatory phase, see Colm Lennon, *An Irish prisoner of conscience in the Tudor era: Archbishop Richard Creagh of Armagh, 1523–1586* (Dublin: Four Courts Press, 2000).

in a church that, while having to rely on the existing personnel, did not have the means to ensure this personnel's conformity with the new laws.[74]

Second, from the point of view of the government and the state church this period was one of 'missed opportunities', which afforded 'a crucial breathing space to the Catholic church in Ireland'.[75] The key mechanisms of confession-building and confessionalisation were not set in motion: the oath of supremacy and the act of uniformity were not and could not be systematically enforced;[76] schools and education were not brought under Protestant control; a Protestant university was not founded;[77] no use was made of the printing press;[78] medieval religious guilds were not, as Colm Lennon has shown, dissolved.[79] In short, Protestant confession-building and confessionalisation 'from above' did not take place.

However, this preparatory phase of confessionalisation saw important developments in the political sphere. The Desmond rebellions of 1569 and 1579 brought together two forms of noble resistance which would prove explosive in the future: resistance to English political interference and expansion in Ireland on the one hand, and the militant counter-reformation on the other.[80] Here I suggest retaining the term

---

[74] Ford, *Protestant reformation*, pp. 31–47.

[75] *Ibid.*, p. 222.

[76] See, e.g., R. G. Asch, 'Antipopery and ecclesiastical policy in early seventeenth century Ireland', *Archiv für Reformationsgeschichte* 83 (1992), 265; Bradshaw, 'Reformation in the cities', p. 465; Colm Kenny, 'The exclusion of Catholics from the legal profession in Ireland, 1537–1829', *IHS* 25 (1987), 338–9; Helga Robinson-Hammerstein, 'Erzbischof Adam Loftus und die elisabethanische Reformationspolitik in Irland', unpublished Ph.D. thesis, University of Marburg, 1976, pp. 46–50.

[77] Helga [Robinson-]Hammerstein, 'Aspects of the continental education of Irish students in the reign of Queen Elizabeth I', *Historical Studies* 8 (1971), 146; Robinson-Hammerstein, 'Erzbischof Adam Loftus', pp. 149–204.

[78] At the begining of her reign, Elizabeth I provided money to translate and print the *Book of Common Prayer*, but her bishops did not act and had to be warned in 1567 to either go ahead with the translation or return the money. Nevertheless, the *Book of Common Prayer* in Irish was printed only in 1608, while a catechism had appeared in 1571 and the New Testament had been published in 1603. Religious propaganda and controversy from both Catholic and Protestant authors started to appear in the early-seventeenth century. Brian Ó Cuív, 'The Irish language in the early-modern period', *NHI*, pp. 511–12; Declan Gaffney, 'The practice of religious controversy in Dublin, 1600–1641', in W. J. Sheils and Diana Wood (eds.), *The churches, Ireland and the Irish* (Oxford: Blackwell, 1989), pp. 145–58.

[79] Colm Lennon, 'The chantries in the Irish reformation: the case of St Anne's guild, Dublin 1550–1630', in R. V. Comerford, Martin Cullen, J. R. Hill and Colm Lennon (eds.), *Religion, conflict and coexistence in Ireland* (Dublin: Gill & Macmillan, 1990), pp. 8–25; Colm Lennon, 'The survival of confraternities in post-reformation Dublin', *Confraternities* 6 (1995), 5–12.

[80] Brady, *The chief governors*, pp. 189–208; Ciaran Brady, 'Faction and the origins of the Desmond rebellion of 1579', *IHS* 22 (1981), 289–312. Brady's analysis of the

'counter-reformation' because it conveys the aims and justification of this kind of opposition: political resistance combined with the idea of a 'religious war' against Protestantism.[81]

The second decisive political development was Old English resistance to the so-called cess.[82] The importance of this development cannot be overestimated. Due to the financial strain caused by the English military presence, the loyal Old English, who had originally been in favour of increased English involvement, developed a political grievance and began to resist English policies in Ireland. With the parliament of 1569 there begins a virtual 'string' of parliaments which mirrors the process of confessionalisation. Thus, the parliament of 1569 exhibits this prepara-tory phase. While the religious climate was still preconfessional, political opposition against the cess was already severe.[83]

The third phase from *c.* 1580 to 1603 marked the gradual transition to a confessionalised society. This phase began with the Baltinglass and Nugent rebellions of 1580–1 – two highly symbolic events, whose psy-chological consequences were much greater than their military and political significance. The government was shocked that the kind of fusion between political resistance and counter-reformation,[84] which they had previously associated only with the 'unruly' lordships not under government control, suddenly occurred so close to Dublin.[85] Their reaction was swift and harsh, but in its turn it shocked and antagonised the loyal Old English community of the Pale.[86] Moreover, the executions following the rebellion produced the first Catholic martyrs in Ireland, as

Desmond rebellions is oriented towards political aspects rather than the idea of a religious war which was especially prominent in the second Desmond rebellion. G. A. Hayes-McCoy, 'The completion of the Tudor conquest and the advance of the counter-reformation, 1571–1603', *NHI.*, pp. 104–5.

[81] Konrad Repgen, 'What is a "religious war"?', in E. I. Kouri and T. Scott (eds.), *Politics and society in reformation Europe* (London: Macmillan, 1987), pp. 311–28.

[82] Brady, 'Conservative subversives', pp. 11–32; Brady, *The chief governors*, pp. 209–244; Maxwell (ed.), *Irish history*, pp. 361–2, 389–90.

[83] Victor Treadwell, 'The Irish parliament of 1569–71', *Proceedings of the Royal Irish Academy*, section C, 65 (1966), 55–89.

[84] Helen Coburn-Walshe, 'The rebellion of William Nugent, 1581', in Comerford *et al.* (eds.), *Religion, conflict and coexistence*, pp. 34–5, 40; Hayes-McCoy, 'Tudor conquest' p. 107; Lennon, *Sixteenth-century Ireland*, p. 203.

[85] E.g., the letter by Sir Henry Wallop to Walsingham, 1581: 'the State is so far altered from former times, their hearts so much alienated from her (the Queen) and our nation, and so greatly affected to foreign nations and Papistry, as I fear she (the Queen) shall . . . lose even the Pale itself in very short time. This late discovered conspiracy and combination in the Pale, which stretcheth to all the best houses of English name, doth sufficiently prognosticate the same' (W. M. Brady (ed.), *State papers concerning the Irish church in the time of Queen Elizabeth* (London 1868), p. 56).

[86] Brady, 'Conservative subversives', pp. 27–8; Lennon, *Sixteenth-century Ireland*, p. 317.

some of the convicted declared on the scaffold that they died for their religion, not for treason.[87] This was followed in 1584 by Archbishop O'Hurley's martyrdom.[88] The fusion of religion and politics, of the religious and political grievances of the Old English community, was well on its way – and the process of confessionalisation along with it.

The parliament of 1585 can be seen as an event which mirrored the character of this phase of confessionalisation. Politico-confessional opposition became obvious in Sir John Perrot's parliament, whose legislative programme, which contained religious, political and economic measures, was rejected.[89] The gradual alienation of the Old English was in many respects a typical process of confessionalisation. Political opposition, which focused on the traditional rights and privileges of the Old English community, coalesced with religious opposition, understood as the defence of liberty of conscience. Catholicism, the 'old religion', was seen as an integral part of the traditions, rights and privileges to be guarded from an encroaching government.[90] As a consequence, important decisions for the future were taken. Sons of Old English families were sent to Catholic universities on the continent and a decisive 'generation shift' occurred: the children came back imbued with Tridentine Catholicism – and often as missionaries.[91]

In terms of aims and justification, the Nine Years War was a climax of the fusion between political and military resistance and the idea of a 'religious war' against Protestantism.[92] This was powerfully propagated by Hugh O'Neill in his twenty-two articles,[93] but he did not convince the

---

[87] See the account by the Protestant clergyman Thomas Jones, in Brady (ed.), *State papers*, p. 57; Coburn-Walshe, 'Rebellion of William Nugent', p. 40; Lennon, *Sixteenth-century Ireland*, p. 317.

[88] Lennon, *Sixteenth-century Ireland*, p. 205; see above, p. 1.

[89] Victor Treadwell, 'Sir John Perrot and the Irish parliament of 1585–6', *Proceedings of the Royal Irish Academy*, section C, 85 (1985), 259–308.

[90] *Ibid.*, 285–6; Brady, 'Conservative subversives', p. 29.

[91] Colm Lennon, 'The rise of recusancy among the Dublin Patricians, 1580–1613', in Sheils and Wood (eds.), *The churches, Ireland and the Irish*, p. 127; Colm Lennon, 'The counter-reformation in Ireland, 1542–1641', in Brady and Gillespie (eds.), *Natives and newcomers*, p. 83; Lennon, *Sixteenth-century Ireland*, p. 320.

[92] Ciaran Brady, 'The decline of the Irish kingdom', in Mark Greengrass (ed.), *Conquest and coalescence: the shaping of the state in early-modern Europe* (London: Edward Arnold, 1991), p. 107: ' the adoption of a religious justification for their resistance to English reform . . . formed the centrepiece of an ideological defence of the old ways which provided a far more powerful rallying point . . . than the material concerns of disappointed individuals or sectional interests . . . the disparate discontents of widely varied interests became fused in a "crusade" or holy war'. See also Hiram Morgan, 'Hugh O'Neill and the Nine Years War in Tudor Ireland', *Historical Journal* 36 (1993), 21–37.

[93] Hiram Morgan (ed.), 'Faith and fatherland or queen and country?' An unpublished exchange between O'Neill and the state at the height of the Nine Years' war', *Duiche Néill: Journal of the O Neill Country Historical Society* 9 (1994), 9–65.

Old English who preferred constitutional opposition.[94] Catholic confessionalisation in Ireland did thus not occur in the same form among all groups – but in this it was not different from Catholic confessionalisation in Europe in general.[95] For Ireland, I suggest differentiating between two movements of Catholic confessionalisation in this transitional period: the movement of Catholic reform, combined with constitutional opposition and upheld by the loyal Old English community, on the one hand, and the militant counter-reformation, upheld by Gaelic Irish and independent Old English nobles, on the other.

During this transitional phase Catholicism as well as Protestantism took their first steps towards confession-building – processes which would come to full fruition in the early seventeenth century. The religious vacuum left by the state church was increasingly filled by seminary priests and missionaries returning from the continent, who brought with them a well-defined confessional alternative in the form of Tridentine Catholicism.[96] In contrast to the traditional Catholicism which was prominent among the Old English up to this point, Tridentine Catholicism precluded conformity with the state church.[97] Towards the end of the sixteenth century, the most important order of reformed Catholicism, the Jesuits, successfully and permanently established themselves in Ireland, particularly in Dublin, where in 1597 Father Henry Fitzsimon celebrated the first high mass for forty years.[98] Meanwhile, the Church of Ireland's status as all-embracing state church was crumbling. Older conformist clergy died out or clergy even left their Church of Ireland benefices to live and work as Catholic priests; recusancy was massively

---

[94] E.g., the answer of David Barry, Viscount Buttevant, to Hugh O'Neill's campaign for support from the Old English: 'Her highness hath never restrained me for matter of religion . . . You shall further understand that I hold my lordships and lands immediately, under God, of Her Majesty . . . and none other, by very ancient tenure. Which service and tenure none may dispense withal, but the true possession of the Crown of England, being our sovereign lady, Queen Elizabeth' (*CSPI, 1599–1600*, pp. 493–4).

[95] Reinhard and Schilling (eds.), *Die katholische Konfessionalisierung*, especially the article by Reinhard, 'Was ist katholische Konfessionalisierung?', pp. 419–52; H. Molitor, 'Die untridentinische Reform: Anfänge katholischer Erneuerung in der Reichskirche', in W. Brandmüller, H. Immenkötter and E. Iserloh (eds.), *Ecclesia militans: Studien zur Konzilien- und Reformationsgeschichte, Festschrift Remigius Bäumer, vol. 1: Zur Konziliengeschichte* (Paderborn: Ferdinand Schöningh, 1988), pp. 399–431; M. R. Forster, *The counter-reformation in the villages: religion and reform in the Bishopric of Speyer, 1560–1720* (Ithaca: Cornell University Press, 1992).

[96] Lennon, *Sixteenth-century Ireland*, pp. 320–1.

[97] Alan Ford, 'The Protestant reformation in Ireland', in Brady and Gillespie (eds.), *Natives and newcomers*, pp. 57–8.

[98] Lennon, *Sixteenth-century Ireland*, pp. 303–304; Edmund Hogan, *Distinguished Irishmen of the sixteenth century* (London, 1894), pp. 208–9.

on the increase.[99] The state church had difficulty recruiting clergy in Ireland and increasingly resorted to 'importing' Protestant clergymen from England and Scotland. As a consequence, the Church of Ireland inaugurated a process of confession-building, which, however, embraced only the New English minority in Ireland.[100]

Ford has summed up the confessional situation most appropriately: 'As the religious divide between the two churches hardened, the middle ground crumbled.'[101] This was the phase which, through gradual confession-building on both sides, eliminated a conservative middle way within the state church. Clergy and people were forced to decide 'which side they were on'. Thus, the transition towards confession-building in Ireland was remarkably parallel to events in the Holy Roman Empire. There the 'pressure for confessionalization'[102] from the late 1570s onwards also led to a 'crumbling of the middle ground', particularly because Catholicism had been clearly defined by the Council of Trent and because the increasing antagonism between Lutheranism and Calvinism also forced people to decide between the two Protestant confessions.[103]

The pressure for confessionalisation in Ireland can be illustrated when we look at one of the key areas of confessionalisation: education, particularly university education. While attempts at establishing a university in Ireland had been made in the largely preconfessional and humanistic atmosphere of the 1560s and 1570s,[104] but proved unsuccessful for want of funding, the university which eventuated in 1592 was rapidly confessionalized. Trinity College, Dublin – while it aspired to be a college for the whole of Ireland – failed to recruit Catholics in significant numbers and quickly gained a reputation as a distinctly Protestant university.[105] As Helga Robinson-Hammerstein has remarked: 'The

---

[99] E.g., the report by Bishop Lyon of Cork in 1596: 'Also the priests of the country forsake their benefices to become massing priests . . . many have forsaken their benefices by the persuasion of those seminaries that come from beyond the seas' (*CSPI, 1596*, p. 15); Ford, *Protestant reformation*, pp. 36–7.

[100] This 'creation of a clearly Protestant church between 1590 and 1641' is analysed by Ford, *Protestant reformation*, p. 21.

[101] *Ibid.*, p. 40.

[102] The original German term by Wolfgang Reinhard is 'Zwang zur Konfessionalisierung', the translation is in Schilling, 'Confessionalization in the empire', p. 224.

[103] E.g., Schilling, 'Confessionalization in the empire', pp. 222–6; H. Schilling, 'the second reformation – problems and 'issues', in Schilling, *Emergence of early-modern society*, pp. 264–6.

[104] Above, note 77.

[105] Alan Ford, 'Who went to Trinity? The early students of Dublin University', in Helga Robinson-Hammerstein (ed.), *European universities in the age of reformation and counter-reformation* (Dublin: Four Courts Press, 1998), pp. 53–74, Elizabethanne Boran, 'Perceptions of the role of Trinity College, Dublin from 1592 to 1641', in Andrea Romano (ed.), *Università in Europa* (Messina: Rubbetino, 1995), pp. 257–66.

belated foundation of Trinity College, Dublin in 1592 was the most significant indication of the English government's inability to capture education and implant its Protestant order in the country.'[106] A parallel system of Catholic university education had already been established on the continent during this transitional phase of confessionalisation. The foundation in 1592 of Trinity College, Dublin and the Irish College in Salamanca – shortly to be followed by Douai in 1594 – symbolized the parallel processes at work.[107] The fourth phase from 1603 until 1632 was a period of confessionalisation 'inside' or 'within' Irish society in so far as confessionalisation between Protestantism and Catholicism, between the New English politicians and churchmen on the one hand and the Old English elite on the other hand, increased, while the London government often exercised a moderating influence from fear of rebellion.[108]

As a starting point for another phase in the history of Irish confessionalisation 1603 is chosen because it was the year that saw the end of the Nine Years War. The period that followed was – from the point of view of the government – characterised by a sense of new possibilities. In the early years of James I's reign, the Irish government believed that, as a consequence of the complete military conquest of Ireland, political and religious control could now be established effectively and completely. A programme of state-building and confessionalisation was launched. The extension of the common law over the whole island, the proclamation that all inhabitants were immediate subjects of the king,[109] the curbing of urban economic and political liberties[110] as well as the great regal visitations of 1615 and 1622[111] were all elements of this reform programme.

---

[106] [Robinson-]Hammerstein, 'Continental education', p. 140.

[107] *Ibid.*, pp. 144–8; Timothy Corcoran, 'Early Irish Jesuit educators', *Studies* 29 (1940), 545–8.

[108] Ford, *Protestant reformation*, pp. 51–7; Lotz-Heumann, *Die doppelte Konfessionalisierung*, pp. 159–65.

[109] Maxwell (ed.), *Irish history*, pp. 208–10; R. G. Asch, 'Kulturkonflikt und Recht: Irland, das *Common Law* und die *Ancient Constitution*', *Ius Commune: Zeitschrift für Europäische Rechtsgeschichte* 21 (1994), 194; H. S. Pawlisch, *Sir John Davies and the conquest of Ireland: a study in legal imperialism* (Cambridge: Cambridge University Press, 1985), p. 12.

[110] A. Sheehan, 'Irish towns in a period of change, 1558–1625', in Brady and Gillespie (eds.), *Natives and newcomers*, pp. 93–119; Anthony Sheehan, 'The recusancy revolt of 1603: a reinterpretation', *Archivium Hibernicum* 38 (1983), 3–13; Victor Treadwell, 'The establishment of the farm of the Irish customs 1603–13', *EHR* 93 (1978), 580–602.

[111] E.g., Trinity College, Dublin MS 1066; BL Add. MS 4756.

But this reform programme did not succeed, particularly with regard to the Church of Ireland's claim to a confessional monopoly. The process of confessionalisation now focused on the Old English community. They were still a very powerful social group in Irish society, controlling the towns and much of the land and wielding great political influence, not least in parliament.[112] Their religious allegiance was the issue at stake, for, as a politically loyal elite, their conformity would have been essential to any successful Protestant confessionalisation in Ireland.[113] However, Protestant efforts at confessionalisation 'from above' achieved effects that were the complete opposite of their intentions. Thus the process of state-sponsored Protestant confessionalisation in Ireland did not achieve religious and political integration as it did in many other European countries, but fundamental opposition – because it was inaugurated only after Catholic confessionalisation had made considerable inroads.

Again, the political and the religious aspects of this confrontation coalesced, particularly in the Old English towns. While Protestant confessionalisation 'from above' was combined with an attack on urban political and economic privileges, Catholic confessionalisation 'from below' also meant defending urban liberties against state encroachment.[114] For example, the recusancy revolt of 1603 in the Munster towns was sparked by a fusion of political, economic and religious grievances. It also attests to the fact that strong Catholic identities had already been formed during the preceding transitional phase.[115] Similarly, the firm resistance of Dublin's aldermen to the Mandates of 1605 was an expression of their strengthened Catholicism, but also confirmed the Dublin patriciate in their confessional stance.[116] Other events, such as the martyrdom of the Catholic bishop of Down and Connor, Cornelius O'Devany, in 1612, had similar effects.[117] Once again, the character of this phase of confessionalisation is mirrored in a parliament, that of

---

[112] The standard treatment is Aidan Clarke, *The Old English in Ireland 1625–42* (London: MacGibbon & Kee, 1966).

[113] N.P. Canny, 'Irish, Scottish and Welsh responses to centralisation, c. 1530–c. 1640', in Alexander Grant and K. J. Stringer (eds.), *Uniting the kingdom? The making of British history* (London: Routledge, 1995), p. 150.

[114] Bottigheimer and Lotz-Heumann, 'Irish reformation'.

[115] Sheehan, 'The recusancy revolt', pp. 3–13, esp. p. 10.

[116] Lennon, *The lords of Dublin*, pp. 178–82; John McCavitt, 'Lord Deputy Chichester and the English government's "mandates policy" in Ireland, 1605–7', *Recusant History* 20 (1991), 320–35.

[117] Lennon, *The lords of Dublin*, pp. 197–8; see also the report by Richard Conway, SJ, in P. F. Moran (ed.), *Spicilegium Ossoriense* (Dublin 1874), I, pp. 123–26.

1613–15. While 1585 had been characterised by the gradual merging of confessional and political opposition and the defence of traditional liberties against an increasingly encroaching government, by 1613 the process of confessionalisation had led to such fundamental politico-religious opposition on the part of the Old English that parliament could no longer function.[118]

In 1626, English foreign policy considerations brought about a new development in Irish history. In return for their financial support of the army, Charles I offered the 'graces', concessions most of which would have made life easier for the Catholic Old English by, for example, abolishing recusancy fines and enabling the Old English to inherit and practice as lawyers, despite their religion.[119] The graces could have prepared the way for an official toleration of Catholicism and a biconfessional settlement in the Irish kingdom. However, the failure of the graces was inherent in the fact that they did not grow out of – and thus did not find sufficient support in – Irish society as a whole, but were offered by the crown in reaction to developments in foreign policy.

In fact, Protestant reaction to the graces reveals how deeply Irish society was confessionalised at that time. Resistance was organized by the Protestant archbishop of Armagh, James Ussher, and found expression above all in sermons and during church services. Protestant arguments against the graces focused on the sinfulness of granting toleration to potentially disloyal Catholics and 'setting religion to sale'.[120] Religion and politics were thus closely intertwined in the conflict over the graces and this points to the nature of the process of confessionalisation: the two spheres converged in the eyes of contemporaries.

The years 1629 to 1632 furnish more evidence of the fact that Irish society was confessionalised along Protestant–Catholic lines. We have only to think of the 1629 Catholic riot in Dublin which occurred when the Protestant archbishop and mayor raided a Franciscan chapel.[121] Or of the Dublin government's order to destroy St Patrick's Purgatory in

[118] Aidan Clarke with R. D. Edwards, 'Pacification, plantation, and the Catholic question, 1603–23', *NHI.*, pp. 210–19; T. W. Moody, 'The Irish parliament under Elizabeth and James I: a general survey', *Proceedings of the Royal Irish Academy*, section C, 45 (1938–40), 57–64. For an Old English view of this parliament see B. Jackson (ed.), 'A document on the parliament of 1613 from St Isidor's College, Rome', *Analecta Hibernica* 33 (1986), 47–58. It is an interesting parallel that at about the same time – in 1608 and again in 1613 – the imperial diet was dissolved because of insoluble confessional antagonism.
[119] Clarke, *Old English*, pp. 28–59; Aidan Clarke, *The Graces, 1625–41* (Dublin 1968); Aidan Clarke, 'Selling royal favours, 1624–32', *NHI.*, pp. 233–42.
[120] See the 1626 statement by the Church of Ireland bishops, cited above, p. 5; and Clarke, *Graces*, pp. 12–13; Ford, *Protestant reformation*, pp. 208–10).
[121] *CSPI, 1625–1632*, p. 500; *Wadding Papers*, p. 330.

1632.[122] Or of the enforcement of recusancy fines by the Dublin government under the earl of Cork in the same year.[123] All in all, this period was characterised by mounting confessional tensions, although there was no war. The development in central Europe was very similar to this. Although the Peace of Augsburg of 1555 inaugurated a long period of calm in the empire, confessional tensions mounted severely in the late sixteenth and early seventeenth centuries.

Last but not least, this phase in the process of confessionalisation saw an unprecedented level of rival confession-building in Ireland. The Church of Ireland became a Protestant minority church with its personnel being increasingly 'imported' from England and Scotland. It was in this phase that the state church became a confessional church in the true sense of the word. In 1615 convocation agreed upon the markedly Calvinist 104 Articles. Thus, the Church of Ireland was put on a consciously broad – but nevertheless clearly defined – Protestant footing. The correlative of this was its strong anti-Catholicism.[124] Consequently, Protestant confessionalisation in Ireland shared important characteristics of the so-called 'second reformations' (Calvinist confessionalisations) in the territories of the Holy Roman Empire: first, its Calvinist doctrine; second, the late Protestant reformation in Ireland was a pure 'reformation from above' and was embraced only by an elite in state and church, the New English.[125]

After establishing a Tridentine mission at the end of the sixteenth century, Catholic confession-building also accelerated in the early seventeenth century. Major synods were held in 1614 and 1618 to ensure acceptance of the Tridentine decrees and to regulate Catholic confession-building along Tridentine lines.[126] It is certainly a sign of the parallel development towards confession-building in Catholicism and Protestantism that these major synods took place almost at the same time as the convocation of 1615. And by establishing a resident

---

[122] Shane Leslie (ed.), *Saint Patrick's purgatory: a record from history and literature* (London: Burns, Oates and Washbourne, 1932), pp. 70–80.

[123] Clarke, *Old English*, p. 67; Aidan Clarke, 'The government of Wentworth, 1632–40', *NHI.*, pp. 244–5.

[124] The standard treatment of the formation of the Church of Ireland as a consciously Protestant church is Ford, *Protestant reformation*, pp. 155–90.

[125] Described in more detail in Bottigheimer and Lotz-Heumann, 'Irish reformation' pp. 293–305.

[126] Daniel McCarthy (ed.), *Collections on Irish church history*, I (Dublin, 1861), pp. 116–46; P. F. Moran, *History of the Catholic archbishops of Dublin since the reformation* (Dublin, 1864), pp. 439–63, 427–30; Alison Forrestal, *Catholic synods in Ireland, 1600–1690* (Dublin: Four Courts Press, 1998).

hierarchy,[127] Catholicism developed, to vary the famous sentence by Patrick Corish, from a mission to a visible underground church.[128]

Very late in the day – from a European comparative perspective – both confessional churches now began to make more active use of the printing press. The government did not manage to monopolise confessional propaganda: Catholic books and pamphlets were printed on the continent and brought back to Ireland. As a consequence, the atmosphere of increasing and rivalling confessionalisation also found expression in religious controversy, particularly between the Dublin Jesuits and Church of Ireland theologians.[129] And, what is equally important, both confessions began to write their own versions of Irish history.[130]

The fifth phase between 1632 and 1649 can be called confessionalisation 'from outside' because it was mainly fuelled by influences and developments from outside Ireland, namely by the British and European contexts of Irish political and religious history. From 1632 to 1641 the new lord deputy, Thomas Wentworth, attempted to transform Ireland into an absolutist confessional state, which was to be a model for England.[131] His programme for Ireland consisted of strong elements of absolutist state-building on the one hand and an attempt to enforce confession-building within Protestantism on the other. Wentworth

---

[127] This process began with the appointment of David Rothe to the bishopric of Ossory in 1618.

[128] P. J. Corish, *The Irish Catholic experience* (Dublin: Gill & Macmillan, 1985), p. 96: 'Not a mission, but a church'; Corish, *Catholic community*, pp. 18–42; P. J. Corish, 'The reorganization of the Irish church, 1603–41', *Proceedings of the Irish Historical Committee* (1957), 9–14; Cregan, 'Episcopate'; Kearney, 'Ecclesiastical politics', pp. 202–12.

[129] Gaffney, 'Religious controversy', pp. 145–58.

[130] Brendan Bradshaw, 'Geoffrey Keating: apologist of Irish Ireland', in Brendan Bradshaw, Andrew Hadfield and Willy Maley (eds.), *Representing Ireland: literature and the origins of conflict, 1534–1660* (Cambridge: Cambridge University Press, 1993), pp. 166–90; Bernadette Cunningham, 'Seventeenth-century interpretations of the past: the case of Geoffrey Keating', *IHS* 25 (1986), 116–28; Bernadette Cunningham, 'Geoffrey Keating's *Eochair Sgiath An Aifrinn* and the Catholic reformation in Ireland', in Sheils and Wood (eds.), *The Churches, Ireland and the Irish*, pp. 133–43; Bernadette Cunningham, *The world of Geoffrey Keating* (Dublin: Four Courts Press, 2000); Bernadette Cunningham, 'The culture and ideology of Irish Franciscan historians at Louvain 1607–1650', *Historical Studies* 17 (1991), 11–30; Alan Ford, '"Standing one's ground": religion, polemic and Irish history since the reformation', in Ford, McGuire and Milne (eds.), *As by law established*, pp. 1–14; Alan Ford, 'James Ussher and the creation of an Irish Protestant identity', in Bradshaw and Roberts (eds.), *British consciousness and identity*, pp. 185–212; Ute Lotz-Heumann, 'The Protestant interpretation of history in Ireland: the case of James Ussher's *Discourse*', in Bruce Gordon (ed.), *Protestant history and identity in sixteenth-century Europe*, II (Aldershot: Ashgate, 1996), pp. 107–20; and below, ch. 5.

[131] The standard treatment of Wentworth's deputyship is H. F. Kearney, *Strafford in Ireland, 1633–41: a study in absolutism*, 2nd edn (Cambridge: Cambridge University Press, 1989); see also R. G. Asch, *Der Hof Karls I. von England: Politik, Provinz und*

believed that Catholic strength and the economic weakness of the Church of Ireland had produced a situation where conformity with the state church could not be successfully enforced. Moreover, and here Wentworth's confessional programme connects with his absolutist agenda, he realized that the Church of Ireland could not be effectively controlled by the state because of the strong New English lay influence on it. Therefore, Wentworth intended to transform the Church of Ireland into an institution which could be controlled by the state and thus enhance state power[132] and which would be a formidable opponent to Catholicism.[133] His programme of confessionalisation was to be realized in two steps.

The first step meant tolerating Catholicism in Ireland for the time being and meanwhile transforming the Church of Ireland. The state church was to be put on a sound financial footing and at the same time New English lay influence was to be restrained.[134] The Church of Ireland's theological and doctrinal basis was to be tightened and at the same time it was to be given greater capacity to control its personnel. Wentworth succeeded in forcing convocation in 1634 to replace the 104 Irish by the 39 English articles and to accept the English canons. He thus tried to enforce confession-building within Protestantism in Ireland 'from outside' – an attempt which convocation resisted vigorously, but unsuccessfully. Its clergy sought to maintain a broad and united Protestant front against

Patronage 1625–1640 (Cologne: Böhlau, 1993), pp. 206–87; R. G. Asch, 'Die englische Herrschaft in Irland und die Krise der Stuart-Monarchie im 17. Jahrhundert', *Historisches Jahrbuch* 110 (1990), 399; Clarke, 'Government of Wentworth', p. 243.

[132] 'Ireland was to be reformed in order to spread the Protestant gospel and to secure the English crown. The starting-point would be to raise and repair the clerical estate to make it capable of acting as an effective servant of the crown with which it was in a near hypostatic union.' J. McCafferty, 'John Bramhall and the Church of Ireland in the 1630s', in Ford, McGuire and Milne (eds.), *As by law established*, p. 101. However, I do not agree with McCafferty's analysis of Wentworth's political programme as an 'anglizising strategy' (p. 111). In my opinion, Wentworth's aims were clearly absolutist. As on the continent, he wanted to transform the Church of Ireland into a pillar of the state, controlling the state church was to be a 'key monopoly' in the process of absolutist state-building. As Wentworth remarked, church and crown 'mutually prosper and decrease together' (quoted in McCafferty, 'John Bramhall'), p. 100.

[133] 'In the view of Laud and Wentworth the Irish Protestant church was too weakened to undertake the work of evangelism. It was better not to attempt fruitless religious persecution until that church was recovered, properly endowed and resourced with an educated and effective clerical establishment backed by efficient ecclesiastical regiment. The reform programme of Laud and Wentworth was not primarily intended to bring the Irish church into conformity with England. It was to equip it for the deferred task of bringing the Irish nation to a saving knowledge of and obedience to the will of God.' John Morrill, 'A British patriarchy? Ecclesiastical imperialism under the early Stuarts', in Anthony Fletcher and Penny Roberts (eds.), *Religion, culture and society in early-modern Britain* (Cambridge: Cambridge University Press, 1994), p. 229.

[134] See the measures taken by Bramhall and Wentworth to regain church property: E. P. Shirley (ed.), *Papers relating to the Church of Ireland, 1631–39* (Dublin, 1874).

Catholicism on the basis of the 1615 articles.[135] Wentworth and Bramhall, on the contrary, used new and old instruments of confessionalisation (e.g., subscription and the High Commission of Ecclesiastical Causes) not, as Protestants had long demanded, against Catholicism, but to control – and exclude – Puritan- and Presbyterian-minded ministers in the Church of Ireland.[136]

The second step of Wentworth's programme targeted Catholicism. First, he wanted to render the Old English elite politically and economically powerless. On the one hand, he denied the graces to them and displaced them from the 1641 parliament.[137] On the other hand, he intended to destroy their economic power by initiating the plantation of Connacht.[138] Second, with the help of a 'streamlined' Church of Ireland Wentworth intended to suppress Catholicism and to enforce the *cuius regio, eius religio* principle in Ireland.[139] But his attempt at transforming politics and religion in Ireland ended when he was impeached in England and into the power vacuum he left behind came the rebellion of 1641.

During the Confederation of Kilkenny, Catholicism also experienced a process that can be characterised as 'confessionalisation from outside'. During his presence in Ireland as nuncio to the Confederation, Archbishop Rinuccini was an agent of confessionalisation within Catholicism because the aims of his mission in Ireland were derived from his continental background. Once again, this had political and religious aspects. On the one hand, Rinuccini advocated a militant counter-reformation, aiming at the establishment of Catholicism as the state religion in Ireland. This, however, caused the latent differences of opinion within the Confederation of Kilkenny to flare up. While the Old English sought an accommodation with the Protestant king, the Gaelic Irish refused to accept this accommodation – strongly backed by the nuncio's sentence of excommunication.[140] On the other hand, Rinuccini also brought his strict Tridentine convictions to bear on his Irish mission. Consequently, he

---

[135] On the 1634 convocation see TCD MS 1062; John McCafferty, '"God bless your free Church of Ireland": Wentworth, Laud, Bramhall and the Irish Convocation of 1634', in J. F. Merritt (ed.), *The political world of Thomas Wentworth, earl of Strafford, 1621–1641* (Cambridge: Cambridge University Press, 1996), pp. 187–208.

[136] Kearney, *Strafford in Ireland*, pp. 104, 116–17.

[137] *Ibid.*, pp. 61–3, 66–7; Clarke, *Old English*, pp. 86–7; Clarke, *Graces*, p. 30.

[138] Kearney, *Strafford in Ireland*, pp. 85–103; Clarke, *Old English*, pp. 90–110; B. Cunningham, 'From warlords to landlords: political and social change in Galway, 1540–1640', in Gerard Moran, Raymond Gillespie and William Nolan (eds.), *Galway: history and society* (Dublin: Geography Publications, 1996), pp. 121–4.

[139] Above, n. 133.

[140] 'Coming from a continental background, he had little sympathy with the arguments of Old English Catholics that they could hope for religious toleration from a Protestant monarch. Instead, he wanted all Catholics in Ireland to combine their resources to

criticised the Catholic church in Ireland which had adapted to its status as underground church by compromising Tridentine standards.[141] But Rinuccini's attempt at a Catholic confessionalisation from outside was cut short because he left Ireland shortly before the Cromwellian conquest.

Conclusion

Although Ireland did not experience a popular first reformation in the early sixteenth century, it entered a process of confessionalisation from about 1580. Ireland in the late sixteenth and early seventeenth centuries experienced a process of 'dual confessionalisation' within one territory. That is, Protestant confessionalisation 'from above', supported by the New English, confronted Catholic confessionalisation 'from below', lead by the country's traditional elites and after 1603 focusing on the Old English. In the history of parliament one can see the gradual fusion of religious and political grievances among the Old English and one can also see the increasingly fundamental nature of their opposition.

Catholicism filled the vacuum left by the preconfessional state church and developed from an exploratory mission into a full-fledged, if illegal and underground, Tridentine church. The Church of Ireland developed from an all-embracing state church into a minority, but legal, confessional church. Thus, Catholic and Protestant confession-building were parallel processes in Ireland as they were perhaps nowhere else in Europe, which created a situation of intense confessional rivalry. While Protestantism came to be associated with colonial state-building, Catholicism came to be associated with resistance to that state – be it constitutional or military.

Neither process of confessionalisation succeeded: the state-sponsored Protestant one failed because it could not achieve an integration of politics and religion in Ireland, the oppositional Catholic one failed because it could not break the legal status and theoretical confessional monopoly of the Church of Ireland.

---

achieve a political solution whereby Catholicism would be established as the exclusive religion in Ireland' (N.P. Canny, 'Early-modern Ireland, c. 1500–1700', in R. F. Foster (ed.), *The Oxford illustrated history of Ireland* (Oxford: Oxford University Press, 1991), p. 145; Tadhg Ó hAnnracháin, 'Vatican diplomacy and the mission of Rinuccini to Ireland', *Archivium Hibernicum* 47 (1993), 78–88; Tadhg Ó hAnnracháin, *Catholic reformation in Ireland: the mission of Rinuccini 1645–1649* (Oxford: Oxford University Press, 2002).

[141] E.g., A. M. Hutton (ed.), *The embassy in Ireland of Monsignor G.B. Rinuccini* (Dublin, 1873), p. 141; Aidan Clarke, 'Colonial identity in early seventeenth-century Ireland', *Historical Studies* 11 (1978), 70; P. J. Corish, 'Ormond, Rinuccini, and the Confederates, 1645–9', *NHI*, p. 317.

3   Protestant prelates or godly pastors? The dilemma of the early Stuart episcopate

John McCafferty

Two texts, one scriptural, one historical, have been applied to the Church of Ireland bishops of the early seventeenth century. The first is St Paul on the question of atonement, often appropriated to the episcopal office. 'And who', he says, 'is sufficient for these things?'[1] The second is taken from the Annals of the Four Masters for the year 1537: 'a heresy and new error [sprang up] in England, through pride, vain-glory, avarice and lust . . . so that the men of England went into opposition to the Pope and Rome . . . [and] they also appointed archbishops and bishops for themselves'.[2] Paul's depiction of the holy, austere and diligent bishop found above all in his letters to Timothy and Titus enjoyed definitive status in Jacobean England.[3] This image, relayed through biographies, consecration sermons and patristic studies, was the one placed before that first generation of settled Protestants attending the universities in the late 1550s and before their successors. The Four Masters, for their part, offered the first generation of committed recusants the historical proof that these same preaching pastors were mere novelties, sprung from venal and immoral impulses. Their own Roman church presented the people of Ireland with another episcopate which also claimed godliness and scriptural warrant. Vitally these other bishops proclaimed they were no set of innovators. So early modern Ireland saw a particular confrontation – a genuine clash of crosiers.

The fact that the Church of England and, by extension, the Church of Ireland, retained bishops has become an important component of what Diarmaid MacCulloch has dubbed 'the myth of the English

---

[1] 2 Cor 2.16.

[2] John O'Donovan (ed.), *Annála rioghachta Éireann: annals of the kingdom of Ireland by the Four Masters from the earliest period to the year 1616*, 3rd edn, 7 vols. (Dublin: De Búrca, 1990), VII *s.a.* 1537, pp. 1445–9.

[3] Kenneth Fincham, *Prelate as pastor: the episcopate of James I* (Oxford: Oxford University Press, 1990), ch. 1; Jessica Martin, *Walton's lives: conformist commemorations and the rise of biography* (Oxford: Oxford University Press, 2001), Chapter 3.

Reformation' or the myth of Anglicanism[4] This is, in essence, the belief that the settlements of 1559 and 1662 represent a judicious *via media* between Catholicism and Protestantism. Among the creators-in-exile of the Anglican identity was an Irish bishop, John Bramhall, whose tag, 'I make not the least doubt in the world but that the Church of England before the Reformation and the Church of England after the Reformation are as much the same church as a garden before it is weeded and after it is weeded is the same garden', has launched a thousand apologetic pamphlets.[5] Recent historians, especially Fincham and Collinson, while withering on the notion of a judicious *via media*, have been kind to James I and his English episcopate. The core of the argument is that James I, still famous for his aphorism on the matter, was a warm defender of *iure divino* episcopacy, but flexible enough, or rather canny enough, to bring Protestant opinion along with him and rescue his bishops 'from the hostility of the Elizabethan ruling class and the vociferous minority who were pressing ministerial parity'.[6] James' new model episcopacy put out fresh Pauline shoots from the decayed bulb of medieval prelacy. Here were teachers, preachers, pastors. Most of them were resident, they personally supervised visitations, they scrutinised ordinands, they balanced careful oversight of their jurisdiction and their clergy with the institutional realities of being officers of state, landowners and important country gentlemen.[7] Some were lazy, some incompetent and some corrupt, but on the whole the Jacobean bishops won 'respect . . . even popularity from lay society chiefly as a consequence of royal favour and the dominance of evangelical prelacy'.[8] The switch in Charles I's reign to a more disciplinarian, more narrowly conformist style of episcopal government, it has been argued, squandered the good will generated by his father and paved the way for a final collapse.

While the bishops appointed by James I and Charles I to the Irish church had to operate in a radically different environment the *bischopsideal* was the same. How did they cope? Did they try to be both prelate and pastor? If they did how did their labours affect their own flocks?

---

[4] Diarmaid MacCulloch, 'The myth of the English reformation', *Journal of British Studies* 30 (1985), 1–19; G. Bernard, 'The Church of England, c.1529–c.1642', *History* 75 (1990), 183–206. For a recent overview of the debate, see P. Lake and M. Questier, 'Introduction', in P. Lake and M. Questier (eds.), *Conformity and orthodoxy in the English church, c. 1560–1660* (Woodbridge: Boydell Press, 2000), pp. ix–xx.

[5] A. W. Haddan (ed.), *The works of the most reverend father in God, John Bramhall,* 5 vols. (Oxford: 1842–5), I, p. 113.

[6] Fincham, *Prelate as pastor,* p. 5. Kenneth Fincham and P. G. Lake 'The ecclesiastical policies of James I and Charles I', in Kenneth Fincham (ed.), *The early Stuart church* (London: Macmillan, 1993), pp. 23–50.

[7] Fincham, *Prelate as pastor,* pp. 295–304.   [8] *Ibid.,* p. 297.

How did they affect those other flocks or rather herds, herds of goats, not theirs? Between 1603 and 1641 there were seventy-three Church of Ireland bishops.[9] James inherited sixteen and he appointed thirty-four. Charles appointed twenty-three. They ranged from Miler McGrath, born about 1523, minimal conformist and pluralist on a Wolseyan scale, to John Atherton born at the other end of the century, in 1598, and hanged for sodomy in 1640.[10] They were English, Scottish, Welsh, Gaelic Irish and Old English and New English alike. One had been a Jesuit and another a Franciscan.[11] Some had no degrees, others the bare MA but others the DD. This was a motley crew and even with a box of index cards and a desk covered in comparative tables it is difficult to generalise about the Irish bishops from 1603 to 1641. Much of the real story is in the messy details of individual careers rather than in lists and tables. Even then most of the details are lost and witty and instructive vignettes are few and far between.

Two connected royal policies dominate the history of the Irish bishops in the first half of the seventeenth century. The first was the

---

[9] Apart from manuscript and printed contemporary sources, the biographical and chrono-logical information which follows for Irish bishops is drawn from: *NHI*, XI; Leslie Stephen and Sidney Lee, *Dictionary of national biography*, 66 vols. (London, 1885–1901); Henry Cotton, *Fasti ecclesiae Hibernicae*, 6 vols. (Dublin, 1848–78); J. B. Leslie, *Ardfert and Aghadoe clergy and parishes* (Dublin: Church of Ireland printing and publishing Co., 1940); *Armagh clergy and parishes* (Dundalk: W. Tempest, 1911); *Clogher clergy and parishes.* (Enniskillen: R. H. Ritchie, 1929); *Clergy of Connor* (Belfast: Ulster Historical Foundation, 1993); *Biographical succession lists of the clergy of the diocese of Down* (Enniskillen: Fermanagh Times, 1937); *Succession lists of the diocese of Dromore* (Belfast: Carswell, 1933); *Derry clergy and parishes* (Enniskillen: R. H. Ritchie, 1937); *Ferns clergy and parishes* (Dublin: Church of Ireland printing and publishing Co., 1936); *Ossory clergy and parishes* (Enniskillen: Fermanagh Times, 1933); *Raphoe clergy and parishes* (Enniskillen: R. H. Ritchie 1940). St J. D. Seymour, *The diocese of Emly* (Dublin: Church of Ireland printing and publishing Co., 1913); E. A. Cooke, *The diocesan history of Killaloe, Kilfenora, Clonfert & Kilmacduagh, 639–1886* (Dublin, 1886); W. M. Brady, *Clerical and parochial records of Cork, Cloyne and Ross*, 3 vols. (Dublin, 1863–4); Philip Dwyer, *The diocese of Killaloe* (Dublin 1878); J. Begley, *The diocese of Limerick in the 16th & 17th centuries* (Dublin, 1927); A. Cogan, *The ecclesiastical history of the diocese of Meath* (3 vols, Dublin, 1867–74); John Healy, *History of the diocese of Meath* 2 vols., (Dublin: APCK, 1908); W. H. Rennison, *Succession lists of the bishops, cathedral and parochial clergy of the dioceses of Waterford & Lismore* (Waterford: Crocker & Co., 1920); Walter Harris (ed.), *Whole works of Sir James Ware concerning Ireland*, 3 vols. (Dublin, 1739); John Leland, *Antiquarii de rebus Brittaninicis Collectanea*, 6 vols. (London, 1774), V, pp. 261–8 has a Latin verse autobiography by William Chappell.

[10] Francis Gough of Limerick was only thirty-two when appointed to that see in 1626, while Lewis Jones of Killaloe was a full seventy-two when consecrated in 1632. Most bishops were between forty and fifty-five years old on consecration. For William Laud's insistence that forty be the minimum allowed age: Laud to Wentworth, 14 October 1633, *WL*, 6, p. 322.

[11] John Todd of Down & Connor and Dromore (1607–12) and Miler McGrath of Cashel (1571–1622).

re-establishment of a full hierarchy. James inherited an incomplete bench from Elizabeth but he bequeathed a full complement of twenty-three to his son who, in turn, raised the number to twenty-five by 1641. Quite simply James made an end of protracted vacancies and gave the Armagh province its first full bench since the Reformation.[12] The Stuarts overcame the Tudor vacancies by 'Briticizing' the episcopate. This second policy meant that James, who began his reign with ten Irish-born bishops and six English-born, died leaving behind him twelve English, five Scots, one Welshman and only four of Irish birth. Of these four, only one, William Daniel, was of Gaelic stock. By the end of 1641 there were fourteen English, three Irish-born, five Scots and three Welsh. The three Irish-born were all Old English.[13] A predominantly British episcopate had implications beyond place of education, ties of origin or, indeed, outlook, because it was not equipped to preach to the mass of the Irish people.[14] Where James inherited over half a dozen bishops (including the archbishop of Armagh) who could speak Irish, they were almost invariably succeeded by anglophone Scots or English. Few newcomers appear to have learned the language.[15]

A very few of James' own appointees took the trouble to learn the language and some others encouraged clergy to do so.[16] In his son's reign the record of acquisition is even less impressive, being confined to William Bedell who was, in any case, a natural linguist.[17]

In Ireland, as in England and Wales, higher degrees became an episcopal hallmark. By the 1620s and 1630s plain MAs were giving way to degrees in divinity of which many were DDs. The vast majority of Stuart appointees had been at Oxford and Cambridge which come in at a level pegging of eighteen each. The failure of Trinity College, Dublin to

---

[12] There had been 306 years of vacancy under Elizabeth; 200 of those years were in the Armagh province alone.

[13] Anthony Martin (Meath 1625–50), James Ussher (Meath, 1621–5; Armagh 1625–56), Robert Ussher (Kildare 1635–42).

[14] There is an extensive literature on the language question. A useful survey can be found in Nicholas Williams, *I bprionta i leabhar: na Protastúin agus prós na Gaeilge, 1567–1724* (Dublin/Baile Átha Cliath: An Clóchomhar, 1986).

[15] Reference to Primate Henry Ussher's command of Irish is found in Lord Deputy and Council of Ireland to Privy Council of England, 30 September 1605, *CSPI, 1603–06*, p. 320, PRO SP 63/217/63.

[16] John Crosbie (Ardfert 1600–21), Nehemiah Donnellan (Tuam 1595–1609), Robert Draper (Kilmore 1604–12) did take the trouble, see Fenton to Cecil, 14 September 1603, *CSPI, 1603–6*, p. 86; PRO SP 63/215/92. Others such as John Rider (Killaloe, 1612–32) and George Downame (Derry, 1616–34) were anxious to encourage the study of Irish but probably did not learnt it themselves.

[17] Ussher wished to see Irish-speakers educated in Trinity College, Ussher to Laud, 6 May 1629, Bodl. MS Sancroft 18, p. 9.

provide a crack teaching ministry for the Church of Ireland was reflected on the bench. Only three of its undergraduates became bishops – James and Robert Ussher and John Richardson of Ardagh. These surviving bishops of Gaelic origin, if university educated, had attended the English universities which is in itself an interesting continuation of medieval patterns and a comment on attitudes to the recent Dublin foundation. Three provosts of Trinity did go on to be Irish bishops.[18]

English and Scottish historians have placed much emphasis on the growing participation of bishops in civil government under the early Stuarts.[19] James rescued them from Elizabethan rustication and brought them back to court and back into the Privy Council. Juxon's appointment as lord treasurer is often seen as the high-tide mark. Irish bishops, by contrast, in a smaller establishment had stayed at Dublin Castle and stayed at the board. Adam Loftus and Thomas Jones of Dublin both had spells as lords justices. Loftus was chancellor of Ireland for a total of twenty-seven years, Jones for fifteen and even James Ussher (albeit in commission) for eighteen months.[20] While James I vigorously defended the Irish church and its interests by inquiries, commissions and grants and Charles and Wentworth put reconstruction at the heart of their programme for the 1630s the part played by prelates at the higher level of government actually tapered off. John Bramhall never made it to the Privy Council and, although hotly tipped and backed by Laud, failed to become lord chancellor after the fall of Viscount Adam Loftus in June 1638.[21]

Anglican apologists have made much of the preservation of what was, according to them, best in the medieval church. The particular inheritance of the Irish church as by law established came in the form of a large number of dioceses. Perpetual and personal unions notwithstanding, the number of sees never fell below twenty-five between 1541 and 1641. The largely intact thirteenth-century territorial structure of the

---

[18] William Bedell, Robert Ussher and, controversially, William Chappell who held it with the diocese of Cork.

[19] A. Foster, 'The clerical estate revitalised', in Fincham (ed.), *Early Stuart church*, pp. 139 – 60; B. Quintrell, 'The church triumphant? The emergence of a spiritual lord treasurer, 1635–1636', in J. F. Merritt (ed.), *The political world of Thomas Wentworth, earl of Strafford, 1621–1641* (Cambridge: Cambridge University Press, 1996), pp. 81–108. For the Scottish perspective, see Maurice Lee, 'James VI and the revival of episcopacy in Scotland: 1596–1600', *Church History* 43 (1974), 49–64; A. R. MacDonald, *The Jacobean Kirk, 1567–1625: sovereignty, polity and liturgy* (Aldershot: Ashgate, 1998), chs. 6 and 7; A. I. Macinnes, *Charles I and the making of the covenanting movement, 1625–1641* (Edinburgh: John Donald, 1991), ch. 4.

[20] J. L. J. Hughes (ed.), *Patentee officers in Ireland, 1173–1826* (Dublin: Irish Manuscripts Commission, 1960).

[21] John McCafferty, 'John Bramhall and the reconstruction of the Church of Ireland 1633–1641', unpublished Ph.D. thesis, University of Cambridge (1996), pp. 12–13.

Church of Ireland accounted for seventy-three episcopal incumbents from the accession of James I to the Long Parliament. The figure for Wales and England in the same period is ninety-two. There is little point here in slogging through the endless pleas of Irish prelatical poverty or the grimy catalogue of despoiled bishoprics and the vacancies brought on by the impossibility of finding someone vain enough or desperate enough to take them on.[22] Yet out of the mire of detail it is possible to discern something of the particular impact that straitened episcopal circumstances had on the church as a whole. For example, the poverty of the archbishopric of Tuam led to an arrangement by which the incumbent was also dean of Christ-church cathedral. The need to maintain a full national hierarchy at any decent standard hobbled the cathedrals. Was there much point in having bishops if the effect was to suck cathedral revenues dry? Archbishop Laud certainly didn't think so. He may well have had a point.[23]

Not only was there no reduction in the number of bishoprics in the early seventeenth century, but the Church of Ireland, a church which had jogged on through Elizabeth's reign with a skeletal presence and minimal inquiry into the religious attitudes of many of its clergy, a church which then began to contemplate a national preaching ministry, ended up offsetting unions by the restoration of two bishoprics as autonomous units. William Bedell's passion for primitive episcopacy led him to shed Ardagh which became independent again in 1633 under his *protégé* John Richardson. John Bramhall's equal passion for catholicity led, with King Charles' enthusiastic endorsement, to a separate see of Cloyne for the first time since 1429. George Montgomery's 'triple mitre' of Clogher, Derry and Raphoe from 1605 to 1609, supported by nineteen 'painful' preachers, might seem to represent a blueprint for a more streamlined and missionary kind of episcopate except for the fact, as Alan Ford has shown, that his actions in office were based on legal and constitutional strategies and assumptions that would retain the full panoply of bishop-rics and not on any 'first concern . . . [for] . . . evangelization or a gentle missionary approach to winning over local clergy and people'.[24] The 1622

---

[22] For surveys of Irish eccesiastical poverty, see S. G. Ellis, 'Economic problems of the church: why the reformation failed in Ireland', *Journal of Ecclesiastical History*, 41 (1990), 239–65 and Alan Ford, *The Protestant reformation in Ireland, 1590–1641*, 2nd edn, (Dublin: Four Courts Press, 1997), ch. 4.

[23] Laud to Ussher, 28 January 1629, W. Scott and J. Bliss (eds.), *The works of the most reverend father in God, William Laud, D.D.*, 7 vols. (Oxford: John Henry Parker, 1847–60), VI, p. 258.

[24] McCafferty, 'John Bramhall and the reconstruction', pp. 49–50. Quoted in Ford, *Protestant reformation*, p. 135, see also pp. 132–40. Montgomery himself also intended the restoration of separate bishoprics when the plantation had been completed, E. P. Shirley (ed.), *Papers relating to the Church of Ireland, 1631–9* (London, 1874), p. 36. See

Commissioners proposed the kind of rationalisation that the Church of Ireland did not carry out until the nineteenth century. Their scheme involved perpetual unions of Ferns and Leighlin, Kildare and Ossory, Tuam and Killala, Elphin and Achonry, of Cork, Cloyne and Ross and of Killaloe and Kilfenora. This would have left four archbishoprics and sixteen bishoprics.[25] It is tempting to speculate as to whether such a strategy concerned with husbanding of financial resources might have had significant results. Unions in the Irish church had, in reality, been far from edifying. Miler McGrath's tenure of Cashel and Emly with Waterford and Lismore and later on Killala and Achonry was a byword for venality and long leases.[26] Furthermore, apart from a natural instinct for preservation of the order, too many unions might have looked like a managed retreat in the face of a revived Catholic episcopate. In 1605 Sir Arthur Chichester spelled out the problem of fight or flight when he proposed Lewis Jones for Dromore so as 'in that vast country [there will be] at least some show of a church'.[27] Alternatively, he suggested, Dromore could be extinguished. Dromore was not extinguished and Jones had to wait until he was seventy-two for a diocese. The see went, along with Down, to the ex-Jesuit John Todd. He promptly crippled both dioceses with indiscriminate leasing and later fled the country after a dodgy divorce in the very same week that the Catholic bishop of Down, Cornelius O'Devaney, was executed, which in turn prompted Primate Lombard to push for the re-establishment of a full resident Roman hierarchy.[28] The Irish bishops themselves favoured a reform of the ramshackle parochial system. George Montgomery's 1610 report envisaged the abolition of rectors and vicars for each parish and their amalgamation into one along with proper glebes. Permission to grant new lands without licence of mortmain was granted by the 1640 Act for endowing churches

---

also H. A. Jefferies, 'Bishop Montgomery's survey of the parishes of the Derry diocese', *Seanchas Ard Mhacha* 17 (1996–7), 46–76.

[25] BL Addit. MS., 4756 fol. 21r.

[26] Lawrence Marron (ed.), 'Documents from the State Papers concerning Miler McGrath', *Archivium Hibernicum,* 21 (1958), 75–189.

[27] Chichester to Devonshire, 17 February 1605, *CSPI*, 1603–6, p. 403, PRO SP63/218/16. This came in the wake of an offer of Kilfenora and Dromore to Adams of Limerick to be held *in commendam*, James VI & I to the Lord Deputy, *CSPI 1603–6*, p. 331. One of the many wild errors which may say something.

[28] For Todd's details, see Cotton, *Fasti*, I, 55, 108, III, 205, 238, 280, V, 5, 534; *CSPI, 1611–14*, pp. 171, 232, 241, 248. On Catholic hierarchy, see Cregan, 'Episcopate'; and Tadhg Ó hAnnracháin, *Catholic reformation in Ireland: the mission of Rinuccini 1645–1649* (Oxford: Oxford University Press, 2002), ch. 2.

with glebe lands, but the subsequent tumult of the parliament scuppered a bill for 'the real union and division of parishes and exchanges'.[29]

In short, the Church of Ireland failed entirely, from top to bottom, to reorganise its administrative units in the century following its legal inception. One consequence was this very large cohort of bishops. The English canons of 1571 and, indeed, the Council of Trent, acknowledged preaching to be the prime episcopal duty.[30] Well into the reign of Charles, 'preacher' crops up in almost every recommendation and every letter of appointment: 'grave preacher', 'constant preacher', 'learned preacher', 'painful preacher', 'diligent preacher', 'preacher at the court and in the university'.[31] Such were the early Stuart bishops. Between them the seventeen of the seventy-three bishops whose printed works are extant had well in excess of 150 books and pamphlets printed and of these ninety were sermons.[32] After the sermons came works of controversy – on kneeling at communion, on the Pope as Antichrist, on church history, on obedience to the crown and, repeatedly, on *iure divino* episcopacy and the high calling of bishops. Often preached before they were promoted these sermons were preached at Paul's Cross, to the king, to English and Irish parliaments, to the General Assembly in Scotland, to the lord deputy and Council and even to 1622 Commissioners. James, as is well known, preferred those he had heard himself and he appointed four of his chaplains in ordinary.[33] Of the remaining thirty-three it is likely that he had witnessed the majority preaching. Historians now insist that James took great care with his English

[29] 15 Charles I *c.* xi (Ire.), A bill 'for the real union and division of parishes' received its first, and only, reading in the Irish Commons on 26 October 1640, *Journals of the House of Commons of the Kingdom of Ireland, 1613–1800*, 19 vols. (Dublin 1796–1800), I, p. 161. A similar fate befell a bill for 'the uniting and dividing of parishes', recommitted on 20 February 1635 and subsequently vanished. A version was revived and passed as 14 & 15 Charles II. Sess. 4. c. x (Ire.).

[30] *A booke of certaine canons, concernyng some parte of the discipline of the Churche of England* (London, 1571), p. 3, Fincham, *Prelate as pastor*, p. 12, Patrick Collinson, *Religion of the Protestants* (Oxford: Clarendon Press, 1982), pp. 44–9.

[31] References are far too numerous to list since they occur, almost without exception in letters of recommendation and appointment. William Chappell even wrote a treatise on the subject which was published as *Methodus conciandi* (London, 1648).

[32] These figures are drawn from Tony Sweeney, *Ireland and the printed word: a short descriptive catalogue of early books, pamphlets, newsletters and broadsides relating to Ireland* (Dublin: De Búrca, 1997).

[33] George Downame (Derry 1616–34), Christopher Hampton (Derry 1611–13, Armagh 1613–25), John Lancaster (Waterford & Lismore 1608–19), James Wheeler (Ossory 1613–40). N. W. S. Cranfield, 'Chaplains in ordinary at the early Stuart court: the purple road', in Claire Cross (ed.), *Patronage and recruitment in the Tudor and early Stuart church* (York: University of York, Borthwick Institute, 1996), pp. 120–47. See also 'Calendar of sermons preached at court, 1558–1625', diskette enclosed in P. E.

appointments by selecting heads of houses and deans or archdeacons with the requisite administrative experience as well as ensuring representation of a wide range of theological opinion.[34] It is hard to avoid the impression that the Irish episcopate was, in this light, somewhat of a 'B' league. Out of the thirty-seven new men appointed between 1603 and 1625 there were two Trinity provosts. After them the next most senior academic was the Ramist, George Downham, former professor of logic at Cambridge. Deans and archdeacons often took Irish sees but their senior cathedral careers before appointment were quite short.[35] It is difficult, too, to discern signs of judicious balance, theological or otherwise. Imported clergy held out for the better dioceses. Irish bishoprics received, at best, intermittent royal attention. In 1611 the agent and inhabitants of Derry recommended John Tanner to succeed Brutus Babington. Chichester sprinkled a little light enthusiasm on their request and the deal was done.[36] It is hard to imagine the same for any English see. In 1633 when Bedell's conscience caused him to slough off Ardagh he simply named John Richardson as his successor and with very little pushing the deal was done.[37] It is not until Wentworth's viceroyalty that anything like a coordinated policy on higher appointments emerged and even then it was sometimes necessary to take the one candidate in the field because no-one else presented himself.[38]

So, necessity, the necessity of having 'a show of a church' created a good portion of the early Stuart episcopate. What policy there was gave Ireland a British episcopate. Scottish bishops were concentrated mainly in the north and the north west, the English and the few Old English scattered about elsewhere, with the odd surviving Gaelic Irish man thrown in. In the North of England and in Wales, Elizabeth and James favoured locals with local connections. The same was not true (and not true as policy) in Ireland. Many of these bishops were exiles and hoped

McCullough, *Sermons at court: politics and religion in Elizabethan and Jacobean preaching* (Cambridge: Cambridge University Press, 1998).

[34] Fincham, *Prelate as pastor*, pp. 22–34.

[35] The strict average under James is nine years, but closer to five when a small number of longstanding applicants are eliminated. At least thirteen and possibly fifteen of the bishops had no previous Irish career. Only three of Charles I's appointees had no Irish experience, and this includes John Maxwell of Ross's 'emergency' translation in 1641. The average wait was fourteen years, and in this case the figure is lowered by the presence of a handful of rapid promotions. Sources for these calculations are as cited in note 9 above.

[36] Chichester to Salisbury, 17 September 1611, *CSPI, 1611–14*, p. 103, PRO SP63/231/71.

[37] E. S. Shuckburgh (ed.), *Two Lives of William Bedell* (Cambridge: Cambridge University Press, 1902), p. 328.

[38] McCafferty, 'John Bramhall and the reconstruction', pp. 139–51.

to return home. A string of Irish bishops held on to their English and Scottish benefices. Andrew Knox of the Isles and Raphoe became the only bishop before 1641 to be provided to sees in two of the Stuart kingdoms simultaneously by holding the Isles and Raphoe together from 1610 to 1619. While Wentworth and Bramhall endeavoured to end transmarine holdings they still held out the carrot of plush retirement schemes in Britain.[39] There were huge variations in the level of experience these bishops had in the Irish church. James parachuted some men straight in. The shock of seeing a remote diocese for the first time could be considerable. Writing to Laud in August 1630 James Heygate was blunt: 'I have seen Kilfenora but would never go there again if it were not for duty.'[40] The majority of Jacobean bishops had come to Ireland as senior clergy so there was almost nobody who had been in the parishes. Charles I's appointees were, on the whole, slightly more experienced but not significantly so. There were, however, three fast-track appointees and there are indications that more were intended.[41] So these bishops of varying backgrounds and with widely varying Irish experiences in turn acted as magnets for clients, relations and other dependants. This is not to say that the bishops did not take care in their selections of clergy. No matter how punctilious they were it was still inevitable that the extreme diversity of episcopal appointments came to be reflected in diocesan personnel and promotions. The need to reward clients and oblige patrons *helped* to push aspirations to train up a native clergy further off into the background. Knox of Raphoe furnishes a partial example. He did encourage indigenous clergy even as he appointed Scottish ministers to serve the new planters. Two of his imported clergy, James Dundas and Archibald Adair, went on to Down and Connor and to Killala. They, not the O'Kellys, O'Downeys and McNelus' were the future.[42]

Arriving on the Irish bench by a score of different routes, the Irish bishops did not function well as a group. Perhaps no episcopate ever does, but it can be argued that the diversity of these Stuart bishops had an adverse effect on the Church of Ireland. This is not to say that they were without influence. Irish bishops were good attenders and made up

---

[39] Wentworth to Laud, 9 September 1633, Sheffield City Archives, Wentworth Woodhouse Muniments, Strafford Papers, letterbook 8, p. 17; Laud to Wentworth, 12 May 1635, *Works of . . . Laud*, VII, p. 131.

[40] Heygate to Laud, *CSPI, 1625–32*, p. 568, PRO SP63/251/1784.

[41] John Bramhall (Derry 1634–1660), Robert Dawson (Clonfert 1626–43), Henry Tilson (Elphin 1639–55).

[42] Ford, *Protestant reformation*, pp. 127–54. 'The churchmen through out the kingdom are mere idols and ciphers', John Davies to Cecil, 20 February 1604, *CSPI, 1603–14*, pp. 143–4, PRO SP63/216/4.

a substantial part of the House of Lords even when they were not all present.[43] Smaller groups of bishops might work together on a provincial basis. The bishops in the escheated counties acted to defend their plantation interests right throughout the 1610s, 1620s and 1630s, eventually securing for themselves a special statute in 1634.[44] In a gloomy report on a meeting (which he called a convocation) of July 1611 Andrew Knox had this to say about the four archbishops and three other bishops in attendance to discuss royal articles for church reform:

> The Archbishop of Armagh [Henry Ussher] somewhat old and unable . . . the Archbishop of Cashel [Miler McGrath] old and unable whose wife and children will not accompany him to church, the Archbishop of Dublin [Thomas Jones], Chancellor, old and burdened with the cares of state and the Archbishop of Tuam [William Daniel], well willed, but wants maintenance and help. The bishops of Waterford [John Lancaster] and Limerick [Bernard Adams] were also here but they have no credit. The Bishop of Meath [George Montgomery] is reserved to a special part and diocese of this realm.[45]

Waiting for the likes of Miler McGrath to die was all very well, but he lived until 1622. Charles even inherited one Elizabethan survivor, Roland Lynch, who had been a bishop since 1587. The Irish episcopate remained incoherent right throughout the early Stuart period. Even on the one issue which might be expected to have united them – recusancy – opinions varied. James Ussher presented his November 1626 declaration as 'a meeting of all the prelates who with one voice protested'. It was in reality signed by only twelve out of twenty-three bishops and only two of four archbishops.[46] Whatever political reasons some of the Irish bishops might have had for not signing, there can be no doubt but that the Church of Ireland and its bishops were tightly wedded to the official apocalypticism of the late Elizabethan and early Stuart church. The catch cry of many of these bishops was 'compel them in' or, at least, 'compel them to listen'. This was important not only in relations with the Catholic majority but also because established episcopacy needed to demonstrate vigorous promotion of the Gospel and active opposition to popery in order to maintain its own godly self-image.

---

[43] For example, in May 1613 there were twenty-seven lords temporal and twenty lords spiritual present: *CSPI, 1611–14*, p. 345.

[44] Petitions of Connacht bishops and clergy in Strafford Papers, letterbook 20, items 145, 167; *An act for the confirmation of leases made by the lord primate and other bishops in Ulster*, 10 Charles I, Sess 3, c. v (Ire.).

[45] Knox to George Abbott, 4 July 1611, *CSPI*, pp. 80–2, PRO SP63/231/56.

[46] Ussher to Abbott, 9 February 1627, *UW*, XV, p. 366. First printed without names of signatories as *A Protestation of the archbishops and bishops of Ireland* (London, 1641) and

Irish bishops were only too happy to fulfil these conditions. For them to declare that the pope was Antichrist was not simply a matter of repeating the quodlibets of Oxford, Cambridge, Glasgow and St Andrews – it was also an act of self-definition, of legitimation of their order in a country where they faced an opposing hierarchy. 'There is no diocese that does not have a bishop appointed by the Pope', mourned Andrew Knox.[47] But here was something worse than an alternative source of authority, here was a rival episcopate making the exact same, the identical, claims to jurisdiction – same dioceses, same titles, same ecclesiastical courts. Still worse, the Catholic episcopate was inspired by similar reforming impulses and exalted a similar primitive pastorate.[48] A very brief comparison of canons and decrees will illustrate the similarities in approach. Take catechesis as an example. The Catholic Armagh Synod of 1614 and Church of Ireland Canon 12 of 1634 both require clergy to offer systematic cathechesis every Sunday at services. Again, the Tuam synod of 1631 and Canon 11 of 1634 require almost identical religious knowledge for entry to sacraments.[49]

In these circumstances both sets of bishops were forced to confront the existence of the others by presenting their efforts as part of a struggle between good and evil or between truth and lies.[50] For their part, the Church of Ireland bishops did not shirk. Many of them were experienced controversialists – Ussher as a professor in Trinity, as author of *The religion anciently professed*, George Downham in his *Papa Antichristus*, George Synge against Dublin Jesuits and even John Bramhall against Yorkshire priests.[51] William Daniel's preface to his 1608 translation of the Book of Common Prayer is a gem of self-consolatory antipopery. The translation, he explained, was undertaken in order to undeceive the Irish and in itself was a cause for optimism: 'though Satan do now rage

with their names in Nicholas Bernard, *The life and death of the most reverend and learned father of our church, Dr James Usher* (London, 1656).
[47] Knox to George Abbott, 4 July 1611, *CSPI*, p. 81, PRO SP63/231/56.
[48] See A. D. Wright, 'The people of Catholic Europe and the people of Anglican England', *Historical Journal* 18, 3 (1975), 451–66 esp. 453–9 for one of the very few comparisons between Catholic and Church of England bishops. J. Bergin, 'The counter-reformation church and its bishops', *Past and Present* 165 (1999), 30–73 and Alison Forrestal, *Catholic synods in Ireland* (Dublin: Four Courts, 1998) offer excellent insights into the Catholic episcopate.
[49] *Constitutions and canons ecclesiastical* (Dublin, 1634); Forrestal, *Catholic synods*, pp. 55–74.
[50] Forrestal, *Catholic synods*, pp. 140–3 points to legislation intended to avoid giving scandal to Protestants.
[51] George Synge, *A rejoynder to the reply published by the Jesuits* (Dublin, 1632); Bramhall's disputation, 'The summe of a conference', Bodl. MS Rawlinson D320, fols. 33r–45v.

more among us than ever heretofore. His rage argues his desperate estate and the utter ruin of his kingdom.'[52]

Irish bishops were sorely in need of consolation. Many of their clergy had recusant wives and children. The wives of Bishop Roland Lynch and Bishop Miler McGrath did not attend church. One wonders if reports that Catholic wives refused to sleep with their excommunicate husbands affected Robert Draper of Kilmore whose widow was noted in 1622 as a convert to Catholicism. Some Irish prelates may have found recusancy in their very bedrooms or, rather, not in their bedrooms.[53]

Uniquely in the three kingdoms, antipopery was a matter of official doctrine enshrined in Irish Article 80 of 1615. Having explicitly said so, any compromise was unthinkable. In a letter berating Claud Hamilton of Abercorn for sheltering recusant priests, Downham of Derry stated bluntly: 'as your church is heretical and your Pope an Antichrist I think it my duty to oppose you'.[54] In 1622 James Ussher (then bishop of Meath) was taken severely to task by Primate Hampton for the heat of a sermon against recusancy which threatened the state's 'way of pacifi-cation'.[55] A similar clash between the government's politic drifts and rhetorical necessity, indeed, the religious necessity of denouncing popery as intrinsically Antichristian led to a very public clash in 1626–7.[56] The episcopal declaration and the ensuing dramatic preaching campaign strained relations between the spiritual lords and their earthly source of authority. On one side a church which validated its mission through the insistence that the pope was Antichrist, and on the other side kings who believed that the pope's status as Antichrist was based on the claim to depose princes. If that claim were to be dropped, then the pope might not be Antichrist after all.[57] At the same time, the Church of Ireland freely admitted and freely demanded the assistance of the secular arm to sustain and preserve itself and its claim to national jurisdiction. The distinctive authority of the bishops in that church was expressed in their power to excommunicate. But if episcopal sanctions were to have any teeth at all

---

[52] *Leabhar na nUrnaightheadh gComhchoidchiond* (Dublin, 1608), sig. A2.
[53] Knox to George Abbott, 4 July 1611, *CSPI, 1611–14*, p. 81, PRO SP63/231/56, Cotton, *Fasti*, V, p. 294, *UW*, I, appx. v, p. lviii.
[54] Quoted in Ford, *Protestant reformation*, p. 188.
[55] Hampton to Ussher, 17 October 1622, *UW*, XV, pp. 183–4.
[56] Bernard, *Life and death . . . Usher*, pp. 59–80; Alan Ford, 'James Ussher and the godly prince in early seventeenth-century Ireland', in Hiram Morgan (ed.), *Political ideology in Ireland, 1541–1641* (Dublin: Four Courts Press, 1999), pp. 203–28.
[57] Fincham and Lake, 'James I and Charles I', p. 28. On 4 August 1633 in his capacity as chaplain to the lord deputy, John Bramhall preached on the text *'tu es Petrus'* (Matt 16.18) holding 'the church of Rome to be only schismaticall and the Pope to be a patriarch', Dublin, Gilbert Library, MS 169, p. 211.

they needed to be further strengthened.[58] If the English bishops were disturbed occasionally by the crown's foreign policy in matters like the Spanish match, Irish bishops were apt to find that the crown's domestic policy undermined their position on a more regular basis.

James supported his bishops as key promoters of civility. Charles supported his bishops as adjuncts in the task of giving his Irish crown greater solidity. Up to 1634 the Church of Ireland had not only formally denounced the pope as Antichrist but the situation with regard to subscription was very fluid and there were no canons.[59] Dissenting accounts of James Ussher treat him in hagiographical tones as a man who would not force consciences and who himself had scruples about the church settlement.[60] The very model of a puritan primitive who like his English counterpart Arthur Lake of Bath and Wells was 'apter to reconcile differences then make them'.[61] It comes as no surprise then that many Irish bishops viewed the imposition of the Thirty Nine Articles and the English Canons in the Convocation of 1634 with alarm. The rejection of Antichrist, the rejection of the pope as Antichrist, picking up momentum through the 1630s, threatened to deprive the Church of Ireland of one of its chief rallying points. Writing to Samuel Ward just after the Convocation, Ussher pointedly lashed out at Robert Shelford's *Five Pious and Learned Discourses* which had identified the Grand Turk rather than the pope as Antichrist. Writing to Laud five months later he reiterated 'whatsoever others do imagine of the matter, I stand fully convinced that the Pope is Antichrist'.[62]

Uneasiness about the very tight subscription imposed by the 1634 canons did not mean that Church of Ireland bishops were prefiguring Ussher's *Reduction of Episcopacy*. Downham of Derry had been a famous defender of the order long before high-profile Scottish exiles like John Maxwell came on the Irish scene. Ussher himself revived confirmation which had been a symbol of the increasing confidence of bishops under James I. The primate's historical research gave his confreres Patrician pedigree.[63] He carried out his provincial visitation of 1629 in person and made pointed use of Armagh cathedral for the consecration of John

---

[58] James I to St John, 26 February 1620, *CSPI, 1625–32*, pp. 275–7.

[59] John McCafferty, 'Where reformations collide', in A. I. Macinnes and Jane Ohlmeyer (eds.), *The Stuart kingdoms in the seventeenth century: awkward neighbours* (Dublin: Four Courts Press, 2002), pp. 186–203.

[60] Ibid. pp. 200–1.

[61] Collinson, 'Episcopal', p. 89.

[62] Ussher to Ward, 15 September 1635, *UW*, XVI, p. 9; Ussher to Laud, 4 January 1636, Bodl. Sancroft 18, p. 16.

[63] Ussher to Laud, 4 January 1636, Bodl. MS Sancroft 18, p. 16: 'On St Stephen's day I confirmed.' For St Patrick and the Church of Ireland, see Alan Ford, 'James Ussher and

Richardson in 1633. He even pushed for the new style of patriarch for himself. He also had a short-lived obsession with trying to prove to Wentworth that archbishops were of equal rank with earls.[64] William Bedell, of course, was the last word in apostolic episcopacy – 'this good, evangelical and primitive bishop': Frugal in diet, plentiful in hospitality, generous to the poor, a reader of good books, an indefatigable preacher, a spotless administrator, an incorruptible judge, an exemplary visitor and a stern disciplinarian. Beyond the *Speculum Episcoporum* we can glimpse a quintessentially Jacobean figure. Here was a man who on his Venetian mission forged friendships with Sarpi and de Dominis and was influenced by Italian defenders of local episcopal privileges. Like Borromeo who defended the Ambrosian tradition, the more modest Bedell railed against the septennial suspension of his powers and famously and disastrously held his own synod. Yet this patristic scholar and grudging admirer of some Tridentine decrees was also a man who spied the Antichrist in the dedication of the Jesuit Caraffa's book.[65]

So Irish bishops were very far from being Presbyterian fellow travellers. They were committed to their order and brought both vitality and dedication to their office. Yet their location had its consequences. As in England qualified assent by puritans had been implicit in the revivification of the episcopacy and went on to shape it to some extent. To put it another way, if it is true that in the English case the price of puritan support for prelacy was antipopery and enthusiastic sermonizing, the price in Ireland was even higher – higher to the point of stretching episcopacy to near snapping. Irish bishops caught between the crown and their own godly impulses had little room for manoeuvre.

It is widely accepted that the Church of Ireland settled for an 'exclusivist' model of church and that bishops and clergy ended up by serving New English and Scottish congregations. Nonetheless it is important to remember that the bishops remained committed not only to the rhetoric of a national church but to its physical presence across the island. This was true even after the naive optimism of the post-conquest period gave way to the more hard-bitten predestinarian

---

the creation of an Irish Protestant identity', in Brendan Bradshaw and Peter Roberts (eds), *British consciousness and identity: the making of Britain 1533–1707* (Cambridge: Cambridge University Press, 1998), pp. 185–212; U. Lotz-Heumann, 'The Protestant interpretation of the history of Ireland: the case of James Ussher's *Discourse*', in Bruce Gordon (ed.), *Protestant history and identity in sixteenth-century Europe, ii: The later reformation* (Aldershot, 1996), pp 107–20; John McCafferty, 'St Patrick for the Church of Ireland: James Ussher's *Discourse*', *Bullán* 3 (1997–8), 87–101.

[64] H. Bourchier to Ussher, 4 December 1629, *UW*, XV, p. 454; Ussher to Laud, n.d. [? late 1633], *UW*, XV, p. 572.

[65] Shuckburgh, *Two lives*, p. 124, on Antichrist, p. 250, see also pp. 38, 110, 250, 311.

equations of the 1610s and 1620s. There are numerous indications that
bishops tried to reside or made preparations for doing so – though
provision of an armed guard for the bishop of Raphoe in 1612 and
the king of Elphin's financing of a small but 'strong' castle in 1635
speak volumes about the type of presence involved.[66] Hard evidence of
length of residence is hard to come by. We can say it was aspired to and
that a fair number of bishops spent a lot of money on attempting it.
Hand-in-hand with residence went sustained efforts to give substance to
a national network of cathedrals first as beacons of reformation and then
as anchors of Irish episcopacy. James and then Charles issued new
charters, instituted commissions of investigation, made new grants,
while many of their Irish bishops, from the late 1610s onwards, sought
to staunch the flow of revenue away from deans and chapters and then
endeavoured to recover them.

The claim to be a national church did not stop at the doors of the
episcopal palaces or the boundaries of cathedral closes. It was also manifest in the claim to exclusive jurisdiction. This, perhaps, turned out to be
the most noxious part of the medieval legacy. Bedell put his finger on the
matter: 'I do thus account that amongst all the impediments to the work of
God amongst us, there is not any greater than the abuse of ecclesiastical
jurisdiction.'[67] Given that the landed patrimony of the church had
been squandered or tied up, the temptation to push the system of tithe
and of ecclesiastical courts to produce maximum revenue was overwhelming. Complaints about fees and horror stories about tithes are
almost as shrill as the cries of episcopal poverty. A man went into court
for 3 pence worth of tithe-turf and it cost him £5 before he got off.[68]
Officials vexed the country with their 'too frequent' courts.[69] Bishops who
sat in their own courts, like Babington and Bedell, found their efforts to
prevent official profiteering vitiated by appeals, counter-suits and cheap
dispensations from the Court of Faculties.[70] Punch-ups and brawls
followed on the attempts of Protestant clergy to extract fees from recusants for christenings, burials and weddings. The countryside, it was often

[66] 'The king's direction in favour of the Bishop of Raphoe', 1 February 1612, *CSPI,
1611-14*, p. 315, PRO SP63/232/30; Wentworth to Laud, 14 July 1635, Strafford
Papers, letterbook 6, p. 209.
[67] Bedell to Laud, 10 August 1633, Shuckburgh, *Two lives*, p. 311.
[68] Shuckburgh, *Two lives*, p. 123.
[69] George O'Brien (ed.), *Advertisements for Ireland* (Dublin: Royal Society of Antiquaries of
Ireland, 1923), p. 54.
[70] Babington to Salisbury, 20 January 161, *CSPI*, 1611–14, pp. 3–5, PRO SP63/231/4;
Shuckburgh, *Two lives*, pp. 119–20.

alleged, was terrorised by those tough characters, 'kern, bailiffs-errant and the like' to whom ministers had farmed out their tithes.[71]

It is true that many bishops were not happy and they did make efforts and lobbied for the regulation of the tithe system for curbs on the taking of clandestines and for a mucking out of the courts. Diocesan government, however, designed as it was to run during vacancies was by its very nature more judicial and institutional than pastoral and personal. Thus by the middle of the seventeenth century formal interactions between Catholics and Protestants took place almost entirely in the context of a highly bureaucratised set of ecclesiastical tribunals. These courts, which even Ussher contemplated with a kind of embarrassed fatalism, were widely perceived as an extortion racket.[72] Bishops of the established church also had to contend with the fact there was often a rival set of courts functioning within their own dioceses which were better attended and more popular. These were no mute rivals either – Catholic officials had no hesitation in excommunicating members of their own flock who ventured to set foot in the Protestant courts.[73] Church of Ireland bishops then found themselves at the apex of a system of ecclesiastical justice which was threatened externally by competition and compromised internally by financial excesses and inappropriate uses. Nothing simpler, then, than, for the Four Masters, writing in the 1630s, to depict avarice as one of the original sins of the Church of Ireland. The drive by Charles I, Laud and in Ireland, Wentworth and Bramhall, to recover the fortunes of the Stuart church required the services of bishops who were not primarily preachers but rather lawyers, disciplinarians, conformists, hierarchs. Irish bishops might have shuddered at the cloaking of their 1615 Articles but they received good measures in return. Much of what was given they found far from unpalatable. Long, expensive and vexatious cases involving church lands were swiftly settled. A battery of statutes answered three decades of grievance and complaint and most bishops experienced a rapid and exhilarating increase in revenues. The court officials were purged and the system was streamlined.[74] Even the tense canonical settlement of 1634 gave them powers to discipline clergy

---

[71] O'Brien (ed.), *Advertisements*, p.16; Chichester to English Privy Council, *CSPI, 1615–25*, p. 32, 'Account of the state of the church in Ireland', *CSPI, 1625–32*, PRO SP63/248/1348.

[72] Ussher to Bedell, 23 February 1630, *UW*, XV, pp. 473–6.

[73] 'Notes', 12 April 1627, *CSPI, 1625–32*, p. 297, PRO SP63/245/883; 'State of the difference between seculars and regulars', Strafford Papers, letterbook 20, item 175; Bedell to Ussher, 15 February, *UW*, XV, p. 471.

[74] John McCafferty, 'John Bramhall and the Church of Ireland in the 1630s', in Alan Ford, James McGuire and Kenneth Milne (eds.), *As by law established: the Church of Ireland since the reformation* (Dublin: Lilliput Press, 1995), pp. 100–11.

and intervene in their dioceses well beyond those of their English colleagues. Naturally, there was a price to pay for the new prelacy. It took
flesh in the form of the 1636 High Commission which was dominated by
Bramhall and a clique of deans. This tribunal trained its sights on clerical
non-residence, irregularities and on non-conformists. It thought nothing
of bringing down Archibald Adair of Killala in 1640.[75] Scottish exiles
found themselves up against the new aggressive and confident Henry
Leslies and John Bramhalls rather than the irenical and flexible James
Usshers and Andrew Knoxs.

Ruthless recovery of revenues and unrelenting insistence on a narrowly conceived conformity left the Irish bishops without many friends.
The golden years of Irish Protestant prelacy ended in the black farce of
Atherton's execution for sodomy and in Protestant revolt, typified by the
physical assault on Raphoe's officials in open court by a local notable and
the lock-out of conformist clergy all across Down and Connor.[76] Catholic and Protestant MPs joined in tumultuous condemnation of continued use of Gaelic customary dues, excessive charges and naked
profiteering. Irish bishops had given their assent and support to a campaign for the recovery of rights and they never, not even the most godly
and primitive of their number, disassociated themselves from the
methods employed by Lord Deputy Wentworth and his *gauleiter* Bramhall.[77] Vilified as insatiable and ravening they also, bizarrely and ironically, found themselves smeared with accusations of popery. A
declaration of Convocation in June 1641 made a late vain bid to occupy
the high moral ground of antipopery.[78] The simple truth was that the
resumption campaign of the 1630s had cut the cords binding the Protestant bishops and gentry. By choosing, even with misgivings, to go
down the prelatical high road the bishops had torn up the 'social
contract' of Irish Protestantism.

[75] McCafferty, 'John Bramhall and the reconstruction', pp. 153–68.
[76] Aidan Clarke, 'A woeful sinner: John Atherton', in V. P. Carey and Ute Lotz-Heumann,
Taking sides? Colonial and confessional mentalités in early modern Ireland (Dublin: Four
Courts, 2003), pp. 138–49; Bramhall to Laud, 23 February 1638, Shirley (ed.), *Papers*,
pp. 53–5; H. Leslie to Wentworth, 18 October 1638, Strafford Papers, letterbook 20,
item 138.
[77] For a full account see Aidan Clarke, 'The breakdown of authority, 1640–41', *NHI*, III,
pp. 270–88. For a discussion of petitions against bishops, see John McCafferty, '"To
follow the late precedents of England": the first Irish impeachment proceedings in
1641', in D. S. Greer and N. M. Dawson (eds.), *Mysteries and solutions in Irish legal
history* (Dublin: Four Courts, 2000), pp. 51–72.
[78] *CSPI, 1647–60*, pp. 254–8, PRO SP63/274/44–49.

The majority of bishops appointed by James and Charles were qualified to be godly pastors. They were well-educated, accomplished preachers, enthusiastic about primitive episcopacy, hearty subscribers to a papal Antichrist. But the particular conditions of the Irish church mutated those godly strains. Poverty turned primitive pastors into busy litigants and constant supplicants. Politics polluted their relations with their godly prince which made them uneasy and suspicious and occasionally rebellious. The presence of rival bishops forced them to focus above all on the legal, institutional, indeed the titular, claims of their church. To survive at all, to justify their existence, these seventy-three bishops had little choice: to be Protestant prelate first and godly pastor after.

4 'In imitation of that holy patron of prelates the Blessed St Charles': episcopal activity in Ireland and the formation of a confessional identity, 1618–1653

Tadhg Ó hAnnracháin

I

In February 1630, David Rothe, the Catholic bishop of Ossory, justifying himself first by the example of Clement VIII, who had delegated Bellarmine to act as his conscience concerning the exercise of his authority, and second by the practice of Saint Charles Borromeo, who welcomed frank admonitions concerning any lapses in his behaviour, took it upon himself to direct a letter of criticism to his metropolitan superior, the archbishop of Dublin. The response of the archbishop, Thomas Fleming, was a barbed refutation of the charges contained in the letter but, while clearly seething with indignation, he accepted the legitimacy of Ossory's behaviour and 'in imitation of that holy patron of prelats saint Charles' he dignified his suffragan's admonitions with an extensive answer and thanked him for his 'brotherly freedom and frenly cenceritie'.[1] The sincerity of Fleming's own thanks in this regard is perhaps open to question but it is interesting that the parameters of their exchange were defined by a consciously Tridentine notion of episcopal practice.

That two seventeenth-century bishops should model their behaviour on Charles Borromeo in particular is, on the one hand, in no way surprising. The archbishop of Milan, canonised only twenty-six years after his death, quickly became *the* iconic saint-bishop of the Catholic reformation.[2] By the end of the sixteenth century, editions of the *Acta ecclesiae mediolanensis* were circulating widely in France and inspiring a host of examples, while Borromeo's instructions to confessors remained one of the staples of French pastoral literature throughout the early

---

[1] *Wadding papers*, pp. 479–81.
[2] Peter Burke, 'How to become a counter-reformation saint', in *The historical anthropology of early-modern Italy* (Cambridge: Cambridge University Press), pp. 50–5.

modern period.[3] On the other hand, there is a certain incongruity in the fact that the inflexible and intransigent archbishop of Milan, a hammer of Italian heresy who was prepared to push his investigation of unorthodoxy into the most sensitive areas of political jurisdiction,[4] should be accepted so readily as an exemplar by two bishops of an illegal church, who had already seen or were about to see several of their colleagues fall victim to the persecution of a Protestant state up to and including imprisonment and exclusion from their dioceses.

A certain amount of incongruity should, however, be expected of the first Irish counter-reformation hierarchy of the 1620s and 1630s, because to some extent the very existence of that body, to which no fewer than nineteen episcopal provisions were made between 1618 and 1630, was incongruous. A functioning Catholic episcopate in a kingdom where the state was Protestant was, as Patrick Corish pointed out long since, a European anomaly.[5] Even in contemporaneous Transylvania, where, despite the Calvinism of the seventeenth-century princes, Catholicism was at least one of four officially recognised confessions, it was not considered feasible to attempt the establishment of a hierarchy and the pastoral care of the Catholic population was administered within a fairly *ad hoc* system, in which the local lay elite and the regular orders of the church played the principal role.[6] Yet paradoxically these anomalous Irish bishops in some respects approximated more closely to the blueprint of a post-Tridentine hierarchy than any other episcopate in Europe.[7] Their role in the elaboration and refinement of confessional Catholic attitudes within Ireland was of undeniable importance during a period of roughly three and half decades from 1618 until 1653, by which time the impact of the Cromwellian conquest had effectively shattered the institutional structure of the Irish Catholic church. The objective of the present investigation is two-fold: first to contextualise the background in which the Irish counter-reformation church developed, and

---

[3] Marc Venard, 'La grande cassure (1520–1598)', in Jacques Le Goff and René Rémond (eds.), *Histoire de la France religieuse, Tome II: Du christianisme flamboyant à l'aube des Lumières* (Paris: Éditions du Seuil, 1988), p. 302.

[4] Christopher Cairns, *Domenico Bollani, Bishop of Brescia: devotion to church and state in the Republic of Venice in the sixteenth century* (Nieuwkoop: B. DeGraaf, 1976), pp. 202–4.

[5] Patrick Corish, *The Catholic community in the seventeenth and eighteenth centuries* (Dublin: Helicon, 1981), pp. 20–1.

[6] See Mihály Balázs, Ádám Fricsy, László Lukács and István Monok (eds.), *Erdélyi és hódoltsági jezsuita missziók 1/2 1617–1625* (Szeged: Scriptum KFT, 1990), esp. pp. 279, 292, 345, 355, 439.

[7] D. Cregan, 'The social and cultural background of a counter-reformation episcopate, 1618–60', in Art Cosgrove and Donal MacCartney (eds.), *Studies in Irish history* (Dublin: University College Dublin, 1979), pp. 85–117.

second to analyse aspects of the official attitudes of the Catholic clerical establishment towards rival confessional groupings and temporal authority.

II

The pointed contradiction of the background in which they were trained and that in which they functioned threw into sharp relief the difficult pastoral mission of the first resident post-Tridentine episcopate. Given their education and selection, it was hardly surprising that the Irish bishops proved keen exponents of the religious culture of Trent. But as an illegal body of pastors they encountered unique problems in their attempts to preside over a Tridentine-type movement of reform and discipline.[8]

With regard to the very reception of the decrees of the Council of Trent, for instance, there can be no doubt concerning the positive attitude of the Irish hierarchy. During the 1630s, every prelate who communicated to Rome concerning the *Decreta pro recto regimine ecclesiarum hiberniae* expressed their enthusiasm for the fullest possible implementation of Trent.[9] And, as has been noted by Alison Forrestal, the decrees of the council were a key point of reference for practically every Catholic synod convened within the island in the first half of the seventeenth-century.[10] Ironically, however, the regular holding of synods according to Tridentine legislation was never remotely possible during this period. While the Irish church was hardly unique in seventeenth-century Europe in failing to achieve the degree of synodal regularity recommended by Trent, the circumstances which prevented this within the island were not replicated in continental Catholic jurisdictions. In 1637, for instance, the bishop of Elphin, Boethius MacEgan, frankly informed Rome that he was unable to convene annual diocesan synods because it was simply too dangerous, and instead he resorted to the expedient of meeting annually with the priests of the seven individual deaneries into which he had divided his see.[11]

---

[8] P. Hoffman, *Church and community in the diocese of Lyons 1500–1789* (New Haven: Yale University Press, 1984), p. 6, contrasts the hierarchical episcopal model of Tridentine reform with less conservative models of missionary work.

[9] Michael Olden, 'Episcopal comments on the "Decreta pro recta regimine ecclesiarum hiberniae, 1635–6"', *Archivium Hibernicum* 27, (1964) 1–12.

[10] Alison Forrestal, *Catholic synods in Ireland, 1600–1690* (Dublin: Four Courts Press, 1998), p. 39.

[11] Tadhg Ó hAnnracháin, *Catholic reformation in Ireland: the mission of Rinuccini, 1645–49* (Oxford: Oxford University Press, 2002), p. 63.

If this represented a clear example of the difficulties created for the Catholic clergy as a whole by the Protestant nature of the jurisdiction in which they discharged their functions, it can be noted that the selective nature of the state's intolerance of Catholicism also operated as a more insidious challenge to the Tridentine project. The anti-Catholic legislation of the seventeenth-century Irish kingdom was far less draconian than its English counterpart. In effect, the relatively mild penalties against Catholic practice introduced by the parliament of 1560 represented the statutory basis of governmental policy down until the abolition of the separate status of the Irish legislature in the Cromwellian period. It is true that acts of state, deriving their authority from the royal prerogative, were a far more accepted aspect of early modern Irish governance than was the case in England,[12] and prerogative powers could be used as, for instance, during the interlude of the mandates, to supplement the deficiencies of the reformation legislation.[13] Nevertheless, even with this additional ace, the state's hand in the western island was notably weaker than across the Irish sea, as the Catholic population evidently appreciated.[14] This was demonstrated in 1613, when the fear of the introduction of additional anti-Catholic legislation was the major preoccupation of the recusant population concerning the parliamentary proceedings of that year.[15] Indeed, even in the wake of Wentworth's abusive government, it seems evident that the threat posed to the king's prerogative by the activities of the Long Parliament was actually a major factor in priming the keg of Catholic insurrection in 1641.[16]

From the perspective of the Catholic clergy, a major consequence of the limitations of Irish penal legislation related to the relative status of priests and bishops. In brief, a case could be made, and by the 1640s Ormond as lord lieutenant was convinced that the point was incontestable, that neither the saying or hearing of mass rendered an individual vulnerable to the penalties outlined in the Irish Act of Supremacy.[17] The exercise of an episcopal jurisdiction derived from Rome, on the other hand, clearly contravened not only articles of the reformation settlement

---

[12] W. N. Osborough, *Studies in Irish legal history* (Dublin: Four Courts Press, 1999), p. 83.

[13] John McCavitt, *Sir Arthur Chicester: Lord Deputy of Ireland 1605–16* (Belfast: Institute of Irish Studies, 1998), pp. 111–28.

[14] See below, ch. 8.

[15] P. F. Moran (ed.), *The Analecta of David Rothe, Bishop of Ossory* (Dublin, 1884), pp. 60–7.

[16] J. T. Gilbert (ed.), *History of the Irish confederation and the war in Ireland,* 7 vols. (Dublin, 1882–91), I, 16.

[17] Robert Armstrong, 'Ormond, the Confederate peace talks and Protestant royalism', in Micheál Ó Siochrú (ed.), *Kingdoms in crisis: Ireland in the 1640s* (Dublin: Four Courts Press, 2001), p. 135.

but could also be interpreted as violating the statutes of *praemunire*, which is why the repeal of these acts became incorporated into Confederate demands during the negotiations of the 1640s.[18] The practical effects of the state's different perception of the activity of Catholic bishops and priests, however, had already become visible during the previous decades. In a series of cases throughout the country, reforming Catholic bishops found themselves in difficulties with the state authorities. Convention of a synod, or the consecration of priests, certainly attracted unfavourable attention, but the bishops were at their most vulnerable in their attempts to discipline their own clergy, because this offered the disgruntled objects of their attention an easy opportunity for revenge. A succession of bishops fell victim to this procedure during the 1620s and 1630s.[19]

In a sense this was a logical response on the part of priests who resented the attempts of reforming bishops to force them to conform to new standards of behaviour and who threatened their livelihood in the event of non-compliance by depriving them of their parishes. Indeed, a close contemporary parallel with this situation can be noted in the Turkish Balkans. There, the intrusion of a band of Jesuit missionaries, hallmarked with the religious culture of Catholic reform, encountered enormous resistance from the indigenous Bosnian Franciscan friars who were quite prepared to denounce the newcomers to the Turkish authorities in the course of the elaboration of the feud. As in Ireland, a clash between a more traditional mode of clerical formation and a self-consciously remodelled style of ecclesiastical activity intertwined explosively with a competition for basic resources. The eventual outcome of this struggle was that the *Congregatio de Propaganda Fide* was more or less forced to modify its own programme for the Balkans and to accept the critical role of the Bosnian Franciscan province in the region.[20] As a result, a peculiar local pattern of regular dominance in church organisation consolidated itself in a manner far removed from the classical template of Trent.[21]

In Ireland, on the contrary, the newly created hierarchy managed to maintain the standard of reform, at least into the 1650s when it fell

---

[18] Tadhg Ó hAnnracháin, 'Rebels and Confederates: the stance of the Irish clergy in the 1640s', in J. R. Young (ed.), *Celtic dimensions of the British civil wars* (Edinburgh: John Donald, 1997), p. 105.

[19] Ó hAnnracháin, *Catholic reformation*, pp. 42–5.

[20] Antal Molnár, 'A Belgrádi kápolna-viszály (1612–1643). Kereskedelem es katolikus egyház a hódolt Magyarországon', *Századok* 134 (2000), 373–429.

[21] Antal Molnár, 'Pietro Massarecchi Antivari Érsek és Szendröi Apostoli Adminisztrátor Egyházlátogatási jelentése a hódolt dél-Magyarországról (1633)', *Fons* 2 (1995), 179.

victim to Cromwellian repression. One critical difference between the contemporaneous situations in Ireland and in the Balkans was that, in the former, the clash between more traditional forms of Catholicism and the new religious culture of Trent was not infected by the poisonous ethnic tensions which emerged between Bosnian and Ragusan merchants in Belgrade and elsewhere. This is not to deny that often considerable levels of ethnic tension between Gaelic and Old English clergy existed within the Irish church. But, contrary to the assumption which has sometimes prevailed, during the era of the first counter-reformation episcopate, there was no general pattern of confrontation on the ground where the division between reformed and traditional clergy corresponded with ethnic differences between Old English and Gaelic Irish. In predominantly Gaelic areas of the island, it generally devolved to continentally trained native Irish bishops to take on the dangerous task of disciplining what they saw as the excesses of their unreformed subordinates. Thus, with regard to the denunciation of bishops to the state, it can be noted that the bishop of Raphoe, John O'Cullenan, fell victim to the resentment of Maurice Ward; the archbishop of Armagh, Hugh O'Reilly, was imprisoned on the instigation of Donal Casey;[22] while the bishop of Down and Connor, Edward Dungan, was accused by Patrick Mulvaney.[23] The surnames in each of these cases strongly suggest that ethnic resentments did not substantially influence the situation. Similarly, the Old English (and Franciscan) archbishop of Dublin, Thomas Fleming, traced the origin of his chief disciplinary difficulties, not to unreformed Gaelic Irish clergy in his diocese, but to the example of the English priest, Paul Harris, and his confederates, Luke Rochford and Patrick Cahill.[24]

The fact that the episcopal leadership of the Tridentine movement of reform in Ireland was present in both the principal ethnic communities in the island was arguably a point of cardinal importance in defining the wider Catholic identity which emerged in the first half of the seventeenth century. That it resulted in the new religious culture establishing deeper roots throughout the country seems undeniable. This was of particular significance in Gaelic Ireland as the Old English wing of the hierarchy developed first and there was initial strong opposition on the part of some Old English prelates to the appointment of Gaelic Irish bishops, largely on the grounds that their doubtful loyalty might excite the wrath of the state against all Catholics. The struggle against the development

[22] Ó hAnnracháin, *Catholic reformation*, pp. 42–3.
[23] *CSPI, 1625–32*, pp. 295–6, 315, 330.
[24] Ó hAnnracháin, *Catholic reformation*, p. 43.

of a Gaelic episcopal branch, even in Ulster where the state's anxieties concerning the possibility of insurrection and/or invasion were most acute, however, was largely lost in the course of the 1620s. In that regard, the development of the new congregation of *Propaganda Fide* and the personality of its influential secretary, Francesco Ingoli, was probably of key importance.[25] A pivotal moment in this regard was the death of the absentee Archbishop of Armagh, Peter Lombard, in 1625. A native of Waterford, Lombard had been never able to fulfil the part of a resident pastor in his archdiocese, not least because he lacked the network of local connections to maintain himself there. In the course of the debate which was ignited concerning his successor, a variety of individuals of Gaelic stock successfully emphasised that sufficiency in the Irish tongue and a web of local support, precisely the points which had prevented Lombard from discharging his responsibilities on the ground, were critical ingredients in allowing a resident bishop to function in Ireland's anomalous conditions.[26] That such arguments weighed heavily with Ingoli appears particularly probable. As a result, over the next twenty years, until the arrival in Ireland in 1645 of the papal nuncio to the confederate Catholics of Ireland, GianBattista Rinuccini, the importance of an ability to preach in the dominant language of the population of a diocese and good local connections gradually emerged as centrally important elements in appointments to the Irish hierarchy.

Thus throughout the island, even in predominantly Gaelic areas, in the course of the 1620s and 1630s, a bishop-directed movement of ecclesiastical reorganisation began to take root. The limitations of what was achieved in this context have received considerable emphasis, in particular by Patrick Corish.[27] More recently, also, based principally on synodal evidence, even Corish's argument that what was constructed in Ireland by Rome prior to 1641 constituted an actual church rather than a mission has been contested. It has been argued that lack of adequate numbers of parish clergy undermined the attempt to provide a diocesan and parochial church and the fact that a bishop was not provided to each Irish diocese meant that the hierarchical structure was unable to provide a coherent system of ordination or confirmation.[28] While the provisional

---

[25] Concerning Ingoli see Josef Metzler, 'Francesco Ingoli, der erste Sekretär der Kongregation (1578–1649)', in Josef Metzler (ed.), *Sacrae Congregationis de Propaganda Fide memoria rerum 1622–1972* (Rome: Herder, 1972), pp. 197–243; István Gy. Tóth, 'A propaganda megalapítása és magyarország (1622)', *Történelmi Szemle* 42 (2000), 37–8.

[26] Ó hAnnracháin, *Catholic reformation* p. 61; *Wadding papers*, pp. 125–78; Hugh Kearney, 'Ecclesiastical politics and the counter-reformation in Ireland, 1618–48', *Journal of Ecclesiastical History* 11 (1960), 202–12.

[27] Corish, *Catholic community*, pp. 18–42.   [28] Forrestal, *Catholic synods*, p. 51.

nature of the clandestine ecclesiastical organisation of the period of the first Irish counter-reformation episcopate must always be borne in mind, there is a danger, however, of underestimating the genuine impact of Catholic reform in the localities. In terms of the numbers of parish clergy, for instance, the evidence suggests a consistent increase in the period leading up to 1641.[29] Furthermore, the pattern of dividing sees into deaneries and of using these as the units for supervision and instruction of priests was almost certainly not confined to those dioceses, namely Tuam, Elphin and Ossory, for which the evidence has survived. Such an organisational model probably operated to diffuse the education and example of continentally educated priests across a wider range.[30] In terms of ordination, it seems unlikely that the absence of a bishop from a 'widowed' see such as, for example, Derry or Leighlin during the 1620s and 1630s, posed much of a problem for any would-be ordinand. Setting aside the probability of previous ordination in an Irish continental college, and since 1623 Urban VIII had authorised the ordination of students in all the Irish continental seminaries on the sole title of a mission to Ireland,[31] the close proximity of resident bishops in neighbouring dioceses such as Raphoe or Kilmore in the case of Derry, and Ossory, Ferns and Kildare in the case of Leighlin would have ensured fairly easy access to a bishop. Irish dioceses were after all relatively small: the island contained far more sees than neighbouring England and it is arguable that there was no real pastoral need for a full complement of thirty-odd bishops, particularly in view of the economic difficulties of the church.

There is little evidence concerning the practice of Catholic confirmation in Caroline Ireland but it seems likely that bishops, particularly metropolitans, did not necessarily confine their activities to their own diocese. Indeed, Malachy O'Queely, the archbishop of Tuam, in boasting that he had confirmed 100,000 people, explicitly stated that he had performed this function both inside and outside his own diocese.[32] Again, it appears probable that the other metropolitans duplicated this behaviour. Certainly far more complaints were directed to Rome during the 1630s about metropolitans' interference in other dioceses than about their neglect.[33]

The case for a functioning Catholic church, rather than a mission, in Ireland prior to 1641 can therefore continue to be sustained.[34] Indeed, it

[29] Ó hAnnracháin, *Catholic reformation*, pp. 57–8.   [30] *Ibid.*, pp. 60, 63.
[31] T. J. Walsh, *The Irish continental college movement: the colleges at Bordeaux, Toulouse, and Lille* (Dublin and Cork: Golden Eagle, 1973), p. 14.
[32] Ó hAnnracháin, *Catholic reformation*, p. 60.
[33] Olden, 'Episcopal comments', p. 3.
[34] For much additional evidence see Ó hAnnracháin, *Catholic reformation*, pp. 39–68.

seems evident that it was principally the widespread and successfully directed activity of the clergy in the decades immediately prior to 1641 which underpinned the important position which the church hierarchy was able to assume in Irish politics during the 1640s. In Ireland, as in Scotland, but in sharp contrast to England, the clerical leadership was to emerge as a key political constituency in the course of the wars of the 1640s. It has been hypothesised that in both Ireland and Scotland the clergy operated to fill a vacuum in the power structures of local society which the gentry occupied to their exclusion in England.[35]

In a specifically Irish context, the clergy demonstrated an ability to both make and break governments. In 1642 the initial genesis of the confederate Catholic association rose directly from the Catholic synods of Kells and Kilkenny in March and May of that year.[36] Four years later, the synod of Waterford was the chief instrument in dismantling the first Ormond peace of 1646, and the clerical convocation then reconstructed a new Confederate executive with the papal nuncio as its president.[37]

Given the political role which devolved, and not always to their satisfaction, on the clerical leadership during this tumultuous decade, it was of no small importance that the Irish hierarchy had evolved as a genuinely national body representing both major traditions and all four provinces of the island. One result of that was that its politics was not exclusively dominated by the conciliatory demeanour towards the state of the kind that Lombard himself had espoused in the latter part of his life.[38] Within the Irish episcopate the political attitudes of the Old English bishops, William Tirry of Cork, David Rothe of Ossory and Thomas Dease of Meath, appointed during Lombard's dominance, tended to be more moderate towards state authority than most of their colleagues. This was to be demonstrated most pointedly at the provincial synod of Kells in 1642 when the largely Gaelic Irish leadership threatened Dease with excommunication because of his refusal to legitimise the war which they conceived to be then in progress in defence of the Catholic religion.[39]

This point assumed even more importance in 1648 when the Old English branch of the hierarchy was hopelessly split between opponents

---

[35] John Morrill, 'Historical introduction and overview: the un-English civil war', in Young, *Celtic dimensions*, p. 5.

[36] Donal Cregan, 'The Confederation of Kilkenny', in Brian Farrell (ed.), *The Irish parliamentary tradition* (Dublin, 1973), pp. 103–4.

[37] Micheál Ó Siochrú, *Confederate Ireland: a constitutional and political analysis* (Dublin: Four Courts Press, 1999), pp. 111–17.

[38] J. J. Silke, 'Primate Lombard and James I', *Irish Theological Quarterly* 22 (1955), 137–49.

[39] Stanislaus Kavanagh (ed.), *Commentarius Rinuccianus, de sedis apostolicae legatione ad foederatos Hiberniae Catholicos per annos 1645–9*, 6 vols. (Dublin: Irish Manuscripts Commission, 1932–49), I, pp. 317–18.

and partisans of the papal nuncio, while the Gaelic Irish bishops almost uniformly opted to support him. The fact that any national synod would inevitably have confirmed the nuncio's position impacted materially on the Supreme Council's conduct of the confederate civil war and greatly inflamed the nuncio and his supporters against them.[40]

Yet while the tensions which bubbled up in 1648 can not be ignored, and while they stress the urgency of appreciating how alternative loyalties and antipathies operated to undercut and restrict naked confessionalism in an Irish context, it would be a mistake to assume that these divisions within Irish Catholicism were constantly active in the preceding years. For most of the 1640s the clergy at least operated according to a general consensus. In seeking to analyse the wider confessional identity which, as individuals and as a collective body, they attempted to promote, two keys areas of investigation immediately present themselves, namely the proper relationship between clerical and temporal power, and the problem of the co-existence of different religious traditions within both the island and the archipelago of the Stuart multiple monarchy.

III

Despite their key political role in the foundation of the confederate Catholic association, in many ways the Irish bishops proved unwilling participants in confederate politics. The pastoral focus of many obviated an active political role. Moreover, from the beginning the clergy encouraged the formation of an executive which would pool clerical and temporal authority, and then accepted the dominant role of a secular leadership with remarkable equanimity.[41] Under Rinuccini, the clergy did become significantly more assertive but even the papal nuncio did not aspire to political leadership and only rather reluctantly embraced it. In 1646 after the rejection of the Ormond peace, the clergy moved immediately to reconstruct a Supreme Council with both lay and clerical membership, and the plan to re-establish confederate constitutional structures in 1647 by reconvening the general assembly clearly owed much to the initiative of the bishop of Ferns, Nicholas French.[42] In June 1647, the Irish clerical leadership resisted the nuncio's attempts to unite them in criticism of the Supreme Council's policies. And it seems clear that the divisions which emerged within the Irish church concerning the

---

[40] Ó hAnnracháin, *Catholic reformation*, pp. 217–19.
[41] Ó hAnnracháin, 'Stance of the clergy', pp. 101–5.
[42] Ó Siochrú, *Confederate Ireland*, pp. 124–5.

Inchiquin truce and Rinuccini's censure of that year stemmed from the belief that the nuncio's policy was invasive of the proper sphere of temporal authority.[43]

What the clergy did articulate strongly was both their legitimate property rights as members of the confederate Catholic association and their right to judge independently of matters which pertained to the spiritual sphere. On this latter point they could indeed become very irate, as in 1646 when they contemptuously dismissed the contention, which they compared to the apostasy of Henry VIII, that only within the context of the confederate general assembly did they enjoy the right to debate and question the association's policy.[44] The following year the declaration by the bishops at the second General Assembly of 1647 that they would be bound by no resolutions inimical to the interests of the church represented the culmination of this particular strand of clerical thinking.[45]

Throughout the 1640s, therefore, the Catholic clerical leadership in Ireland envisaged its proper role as a close cooperation with temporal authority, while protecting the just rights and demands of the church. Had the clergy been dealing with a simple Catholic government it seems probable that far less friction would have disturbed the relationship. The Catholic executive represented by the confederate Supreme Council was unique, however. From the conclusion of the first cessation with the royalist party in 1643, its chief preoccupation had become the negotiation of its own dissolution and the confederate Catholics' readmission as loyal subjects into the sphere of royal authority. This was the context which made clerical aspirations practically unattainable, for the king's lord lieutenant, the marquis of Ormond, was adamantly opposed to wide-ranging concessions to the Catholic church.[46]

Confederate clerical positions traced a clear lineage from those which had been formulated in the decades prior to 1641. In this regard some attention has previously been focused on Peter Lombard, traces of whose distinction between the subjective heresy of a monarch such as Elizabeth and the objective heresy of the Stuarts[47] resurfaced again in Confederate debates in 1645.[48] Rather more forthright than Lombard was the Jesuit William Malone, whose *A Reply to Mr James Ussher his*

[43] Tadhg Ó hAnnracháin, 'Lost in Rinuccini's shadow: the Irish clergy, 1645–9', in Ó Siochrú, *Kingdoms in crisis*, pp. 186–7.
[44] Kavanagh (ed.), *Commentarius Rinuccianus*, II, pp. 331–6.
[45] *Ibid.*, pp. 792–3.
[46] Armstrong, 'Ormond and the confederate peace talks', pp. 135–7.
[47] Silke, 'Primate Lombard and James I', p. 138; and see below, chapter 8, pp. 188, 198f.
[48] In this regard see the fifth query put to the congregation of clergy, 17 May 1645: Kavanagh (ed.), *Commentarius Rinuccianus*, I, p. 525.

Answere[49] is of interest not only for the opinions advanced but for the nature of Catholic clerical reaction to the text. Most controversy centred around Malone's dedicatory epistle to the king at the beginning of the book where, following the example of his adversary who had 'allreadie brought this controversie into the highest court',[50] he offered the debate between himself and Ussher 'unto the censure of that your most excellent wisdome'.[51] He continued to argue that even Protestants had come to accept that 'our Religion doth not any way diminish or weaken the force of our obliged duty to your sacred Crowne, no not though the Pope himselfe should attempt to withdraw us from the same',[52] and quoted Ussher's own conviction that 'neither the names of any schole-men . . . nor of the Pope himselfe . . . wilbe of any force to remove them [Irish Catholics] from the alleageance and duty which they owe unto their King and country'.[53] Having referred to the previous loyalty of the Catholic Irish in times of rebellion and attempted seduction by foreign powers he declared to Charles:

by God's divine assistance yow shall find it dayly more and more assured, that the free exercise of our Religion is our strongest tye and union to your Crowne: for the more united and familiar that we are with him by whom 'Kings do raigne, the more awfull also shall wee be found unto yow his Holie anointed: whose Regall Power, as we acknowledge it to be subiect unto none but unto God himselfe.[54]

These points aroused a good deal of anxiety among Catholic clergy on both sides of the Irish Sea. For many English clergy and apparently for the Irish Jesuits the chief cause of concern was that an official condemnation of Malone's epistle would reignite the controversy concerning Catholic loyalty, with potentially disastrous implications for the Stuarts' recusant subjects. In this regard, William Barlow, president-general of the English congregation of Benedictines, wrote urgently to the Irish Franciscan, Robert Chamberlin, in Louvain, urging the need to guard against such a condemnation.[55] In Barlow's estimation the epistle

---

[49] William Malone, *A Reply to Mr James Ussher his Answere wherein it is discovered how Answerlesse the said Mr Ussher returneth. The uniforme consent also of Antiquity is declared to stande for the Roman Religion: And the Answerer is convinced of vanity in challenging the Patronage of the Doctors of the Primative Church for his Protestancy* (Douai?, 1627).

[50] *Ibid.*, 'The epistle dedicatory', p. 2.

[51] *Ibid.*

[52] *Ibid.*, p. 3.

[53] *Ibid.*, p. 4.

[54] *Ibid.*

[55] See the extract from Barlow's original letter in Chamberlin's letter to Luke Wadding, 4 August 1628 (*Wadding papers*, pp. 265–6).

'displeaseth most, not because it contayneth expressele ene false doctrin as I will declare heerafter, but because it doeth not express the Catholique trueth inteerlie and completlie'.[56] Expanding on this topic, he argued:

The words of the proposition concerning the king of England's authoritie are these: 'Whose regal power, as we acknowledg it to be subject unto none but unto God himself from whom it is, soe ettc'; by which it may be thought that he would say how that regal power is immedeatelie from God, and therfor not subject to the pope in temporalities or spiritualities.[57]

Catholics could clearly not support such a position. But Barlow believed an alternative interpretation was possible:

And if we construe him favorabilie it may be understood thus: 'Whose regal power, as wee acknowledge it directlie subject *in temporalityes* [my emphasis] unto none but unto God himself from whom it is by the free consent of the people, soe ettc.' And this construction is most suitable to the text, for in the first proposition he speakes of our *obliged* duty to the crowne; and in the second of *allegeance* and duty which wee ow to the king; the which is to be understood of temporalities.[58]

Barlow's objective in writing to Chamberlin may well have been to enlist the Irish Franciscan's influence with Luke Wadding in Rome to prevent a condemnation of Malone's propositions. And indeed Chamberlin evidently promised to bring Barlow's arguments to Wadding's attention.[59] For his own part, Chamberlin was evidently not convinced that such a favourable interpretation of Malone's work was possible. He objected to the idea that the court of England represented the highest court for the decision of the controversy between Ussher and Malone. Malone's previously noted willingness to submit the right of the debate to the king's judgement was equally unacceptable:

To submit the equity and justice of his case, which is a case of faith, to the judgement of the king of England, who not only is a public heretic, but also a persecutor of Catholics and a sower of heresy, does not seem to be other than to agree with English heretics, who hold the king to be the judge of controversies of the faith in his dominions.[60]

The bluntness of this particular description of the king is noteworthy for its rarity value. In this regard, the context of the remarks, a letter between two continentally based exiles that was effectively immune from the

---

[56] *Ibid.*   [57] *Ibid.*   [58] *Ibid.*   [59] *Ibid.*

[60] 'Submittere aequitatem sive justitiam suae causae, quae est causae fidei, censurae regis Angliae, quin non solum est publicus haereticus, sed etiam Catholicorum persecutor et seminator heresis, non videtur esse aliud quam sentire cum hereticis Anglis, qui tenent regem esse judicem controversiarum fidei in suis dominiis' (*ibid.*, p. 266).

possibility of English interception, is probably significant and certainly gives some ground for suspicion that the privately held opinions of all Irish Catholic clergy were not necessarily as effusively positive towards their monarch as public utterances might suggest. Nevertheless it is also noteworthy that Wadding seems to have exerted himself to prevent the formulation of any condemnation of Malone's propositions. For this he received congratulations from the bishop of Ferns, John Roche, who welcomed his decision principally on political grounds.[61] Roche saw little reason to stir up trouble concerning a person as intellectually insignificant as Malone but the bishop also evidently believed that Malone was not necessarily erroneous, remarking indeed that his opinions were 'susceptible of good Catholicke sense'.[62]

The spectrum of clerical attitudes brought to bear on the Malone controversy does reveal a number of enduring features of Catholic thought *vis-à-vis* their heretical monarch. First, among both laity and clergy, individuals of Malone's stamp were to be found who were personally fervent and sincere in their loyalty and who were willing to push to the borders of contemporary Catholic thought to champion the compatibility of spiritual affiliation with Rome and temporal allegiance to the Stuarts. Second, even men of the stamp of Wadding or Roche, who in the hierarchy of their allegiances clearly placed Rome first, evidently had some sympathy with Malone's position. However, the guiding principle in their inclination to allow to go unchallenged propositions which offensively, at least in tone, delineated the limits of papal power and authority was evidently political. Third, a figure such as Chamberlin was clearly far less sympathetic to Malone, or to the king whom he so enthusiastically encomiumised, but tactical utility also dictated the parameters of his response.

The confederate period ultimately witnessed a strong official reformulation by the clergy of the idea of Catholic loyalty to the Stuarts. The confederate oath of association itself, the membership criterion of the organisation, was also an oath of allegiance to Charles,[63] although in 1645 delegated theologians of the congregation of clergy explained that this apparently absolute offering of allegiance was tacitly qualified by the impossibility of Catholics accepting any order from the king which was

---

[61] John Roche to Wadding, 20 October 1628: *Wadding papers*, p. 274.
[62] *Ibid.*
[63] There were several confederate oaths but the text relevant to the present discussion was that adopted by act of the General Assembly, 26 July 1644: for a copy of this oath see Walter Enos, *The second part of the survey of the articles of the late reiected peace wherein the invaliditie and nullitie of the said peace proved* (Kilkenny, 1646), pp. 104–5.

repugnant to natural or divine law.[64] The theologians subsequently drew extremely wide conclusions from this particular inference, most importantly, that the oath not only did not permit the confederates to accept the king's positions on the future of ecclesiastical property in Ireland, but actually required the association to retain possession of all churches and church livings which they had gained in the course of the rebellion and war in any treaty with their monarch.[65]

From 1645 this issue was to represent the Gordian knot of the confederate/royalist negotiations in Ireland and it was a problem anchored in vaster and potentially insoluble questions concerning the possibility of mutual toleration and coexistence between Catholics and Protestants in early modern Europe. Officially, none the less, the Irish clerical leadership never acknowledged the enormous problems inherent in any attempt to reconcile their basic demands with the king nor did they swerve from their professed loyalty to the person of Charles Stuart as their legitimate monarch. Conor O'Mahoney's *Disputatio Apologetica* received no public support from any major clerical figure for its exhortation that the Irish should deprive Charles of his kingship and select a new king of native stock.[66] Elsewhere I have suggested that one of the factors predisposing the Catholic clergy to ignore O'Mahony's arguments was their lack of tactical utility. In effect, fervent expressions of loyalty to their monarch did not prevent the clergy from utilising the confederate oath of association to insist on the attainment of concessions which the king both politically and morally was deeply reluctant to grant publicly.[67] Nevertheless, the at times apparently naïve insistence of the Catholic clergy that no essential conflict existed between allegiance to the Protestant Charles Stuart as a monarch and the profession of Catholicism,[68] cannot be dismissed as mere contrivance. Even the papal nuncio, Rinuccini, was under instructions not to attempt anything which would undermine Stuart sovereignty in Ireland, although his public declaration 'clapping his hand upon his breast' that 'serenissimo vestro Principi

---

[64] Kavanagh (ed.), *Commentarius Rinuccianus*, I, pp. 525–6.

[65] I have discussed this episode in 'Conflicting loyalties, conflicted rebels: political and religious allegiance among the Confederate Catholics of Ireland', *English Historical Review* 483 (2004), 851–72.

[66] Conor O'Mahony, *Disputatio Apologetica de Iure Regni Hiberniae pro Catholicis Hibernis adversus haereticos Anglos. Accessit eiusdem authoris ad eosdem Catholicos exhortatio* (Lisbon, 1645).

[67] Tadhg Ó hAnnracháin, 'Though hereticks and politicians should misinterpret their goode zeal: political ideology and Catholicism in early-modern Ireland', in Jane Ohlmeyer, *Political thought in seventeenth-century Ireland* (Cambridge: Cambridge University Press, 2000), pp. 166–7.

[68] I address this point in detail in 'Conflicting loyalties, conflicted rebels'.

meipsum devoveo'[69] ultimately earned him a sharp reproof from Rome.[70]

If the clergy refused to acknowledge any obstacle to their allegiance to their Protestant monarch, what of their attitude towards coexistence with Protestant cosubjects during the 1640s. The first official reaction of the church hierarchy, as opposed to the individual responses of friars and priests in the localities,[71] became evident at the metropolitan synod of Armagh in March 1642. The third proposition of that synod prescribed excommunication for any person who had invaded, intruded on or usurped the goods and property of any Irish person (*Ibernus*), whether Catholic or Protestant (*sive Catholici sive Protestantis*), in the province.[72] This explicit defence of the Protestant right to property is of extraordinary interest although it requires a closer examination of those who might have been comprehended under this terminology. In the first place, did the reference to Irishness exclude people of English or Scottish birth? The strong possibility exists that it did. In this regard, it can be noted that two months later the national synod of the Irish church decreed: 'that all and every such as from the beginning of this present warr have invaded the possessions of goods, as well moveable as unmoveable, spirituall, or temporall, of any Catholique whether Irish or English, or also of any Irish Protestant being not adversarie of this cause . . . shall be excommunicated'.[73]

The omission of any reference to English Protestants in this decree is certainly heightened by the pointed reference to English Catholics in the previous clause.[74] The Armagh decree concerning the protection of the property of *Iberni* may thus have had a significantly more limited impact than might appear at first glance. Nor, as the decree of the national synod helps to clarify, should the censures against invasion of the property of Protestants necessarily be taken as a protection for all non-Catholic proprietors. Those who were 'aversarie' to the cause were exempted in this regard. Throughout the 1640s, Catholics, both clerical

[69] *Historical Manuscripts Commission, 13th report, appendix 1: the manuscripts of his Grace the Duke of Portland* (London, 1891), p. 313.
[70] Ó hAnnracháin, 'Political ideology and Catholicism', p. 155.
[71] These have been analysed in detail by Nicholas Canny in a number of publications culminating in *Making Ireland British* (Oxford: Oxford University Press, 2002), pp. 513–24.
[72] Kavanagh (ed.), *Commentarius Rinuccianus*, I, p. 315.
[73] Gilbert, *Irish Confederation*, II, p. 39.
[74] It can be noted also that the Acts of the General Assembly offered to preserve and cherish the life, goods and estates of 'every Roman Catholick, as well English, Welsh, as Scotch who was of that profession before the troubles' if they settled in the kingdom: see *ibid.*, p. 79.

and lay, often opted for the convenient term 'puritan' as a shorthand to distinguish their Protestant foes. Indeed in 1642, the first General Assembly of the Confederate Catholics chose to emphasise this distinction on 29 October when it ordained: 'It is this day ordered, that every person or persons whatsoever talking or discoursing, in writing or otherwise, of the enemies, shall not call them by the name or names of English or Protestants, but shall call them by the names of Puritanical or malignant party.'[75]

What constituted the difference between Protestants and Puritans was evidently partly a matter of political interpretation in the early years of the rebellion. But by the middle years of the decade, Walter Enos, perhaps the most influential theological voice among the Confederate clergy, declared that the Confederate Catholics were prepared to guarantee security to the Protestant subjects of the king, adding:

By Protestants we understand such as professe the Protestant doctrine established in England and comprized in the 39 articles and not any new Parliamentarie Protestants, who, as they have demolished the ecclesiastical hierarchy maintained in the said articles, soe have they (as much as in them lay) monarchicall government: such a brood of vipers which devoureth both church and state, both king and prelate, may not be licensed to cohabit with the Confederate Catholics. *Qui enim dicit illlis ave, communiscat operibus eorum malignis.*[76]

In a similar spirit to the order of 1642, for Enos the 39 Articles were probably important as a touchstone of royalist loyalty. Fundamental to the confederate position during the 1640s was the argument that they were not rebels but loyal subjects, defending the king's prerogative power, which in the past had protected Catholics by dispensing from the penal laws. Catholics, of course, were also acutely aware that Charles' foes in the British struggle were markedly hotter in their anti-Catholicism than the king's own party. Yet Enos' reference to ecclesiastical hierarchy was not without significance. For many Catholics within the Stuart dominions were in a sense in agreement with Godly critics of the church establishment concerning its popishness. To them it was evident that the episcopal structure of the church by law established brought it closer to Rome. This was not to accept that it could be considered a true church: even John Lynch in the 1660s merely confined himself to a description of the king's church as 'administered by bishops similar to Catholics',[77] and deduced that in terms of a truce 'of two evils

---

[75] *Ibid.*, p. 84.   [76] Enos, *Second part of the survey*, pp. 29–30.
[77] 'More Catholicorum ab episcopis administraretur': John Lynch, *Supplementum Alithinolgiae* (St Malo, 1667), p. 97.

the lesser is to be preferred. It was less of a sin, if a sin at all to pact with those of whose sect fewer points differed from the Catholic faith, than with those who completely turned away from all conformity with Catholics.'[78] From a Catholic perspective, the structure of the established church acted as a bulwark for the maintenance of necessary hierarchical order in both the religious and political spheres. Enos' comment on the subversive tendency of Puritanism was echoed and reinforced in the post-confederate period by Lynch who argued that Puritanism execrated ecclesiastical hierarchy and that its objective was 'to reduce provinces and kingdoms to the form of anarchy or democracy'.[79]

Moreover the survival of the Protestant hierarchy might ultimately ease the way to the restoration of its Catholic counterpart. The confederates indeed had already given proof of this during the 1640s when they simply assigned the property and revenues of dignitaries within the established church to their Catholic equivalents.[80] Sir Kenelm Digby made a similar point with great force in Rome in 1646, arguing that it was in the interest of the Church of Rome to preserve the Elizabethan church settlement because while it remained in existence the prospect for a swift restoration of Catholic structures at some future date remained infinitely more practicable.[81] And there is evidence that some Catholic clerics in the preconfederate period were prepared to assist their Protestant counterparts in the recovery of alienated revenues in the hope that their own successors would eventually reap the benefit of this process.

If Protestants could be distinguished from Puritans, then what did Catholic assurance of their security entail? The example of the earl of Thomond would appear to indicate a willingness to allow Protestants of secure Irish origin quiet enjoyment of their estates. In the vast majority of cases this did not apparently extend to the permitting of public religious ceremonies by ministers of the established church. In Limerick up until 1646, it appears that the economic importance of local Protestant artisans had inclined the city to allow them to continue to hold religious services in a former Augustinian friary. The papal nuncio, Rinuccini, was evidently appalled at this situation and, realising that Limerick was unique in confederate quarters in this respect, successfully pressurised the city to put an end to the practice in 1646. He himself

---

[78] 'Duorum malorum minus eligendum est. levius delictum (si delictum fuit) cum his pacisci, ut quorum sectae pauciora capita a fide Catholica discrepant, quam cum illis, qui omnem cum Catholicis conformitatem penitus aversantur' (*ibid.*, p. 140).

[79] 'Ut provincias et regna ad Ararchiae vel Democraciae formam redigat' (*ibid.*, p. 96).

[80] Ó hAnnracháin, 'Lost in Rinuccini's shadow', p. 178.	[81] *Ibid.*

reconsecrated the church for Catholic worship in an overt display of religious triumphalism.[82] The attitudes of the nuncio, consistent with his Italian formation, were evidently towards the harder end of the Irish clerical spectrum. Unlike a figure such as Enos, the nuncio showed little appreciation of the nuances within Protestant opinion and little inclination to differentiate between more and less acceptable types of heresy. Indeed, as I have suggested elsewhere, even after his return from Ireland the nuncio continued to confuse the different strands of British Protestantism in his published work.[83] During the negotiations for a renewed truce with Ormond in 1647, the nuncio was to the fore in attempting to ensure that no Protestant ministers could return to any area which had previously been regained for the Catholic religion and in this regard his anxieties seem to have been more acute than any of the Irish bishops on the Supreme Council.[84] Later in the year the nuncio clashed sharply with the bishops of Clonfert and Ferns who were prepared to sign a mandate from the Supreme Council offering positions within the confederate forces to defecting Protestant royalists. One of the conditions of this offer was that such Protestant acquisitions would be permitted the exercise of their religion, although the bishop of Ferns insisted that this would not involve the use of churches. The sharp exchange which this provoked between Ferns and the nuncio can be taken as an indication that, at least in certain conditions, some members of the Irish hierarchy were more prepared than the Italian nuncio to consider a little leeway in the practice of Protestant worship in confederate controlled territory.[85]

One of the sharpest indications of a discrepancy between Irish and Italian clerical opinion occurred in 1648 concerning the Inchiquin truce. The nuncio's basic position in this regard was that the truce was unnecessary because units of O'Neill's Ulster army would be capable of defending the province from Inchiquin's forces. It was probably none other than William Malone, then acting as the superior of the Jesuits, who took it upon himself to inform the nuncio that Ulster men were not wanted in Munster. In what was evidently a heated exchange the nuncio responded that ultimately it was better to have Catholics than heretics in the province only to be shocked by a crude rejoinder that this was not always true.[86]

This exchange occurred at a particularly volatile moment in confederate politics when the issue of the Ulster army had become a lightning rod

[82] Kavanagh (ed.), *Commentarius Rinuccianus*, II, pp. 272–3.
[83] Ó hAnnracháin, *Catholic reformation*, p. 90.
[84] Kavanagh (ed.), *Commentarius Rinuccianus*, II, p. 526.
[85] *Ibid.*, pp. 695–9.   [86] Ó hAnnracháin, *Catholic Reformation*, p. 196.

for a series of accumulated grievances. Consequently, traditional ethnic antipathies received a fresh airing in a variety of contexts. On 10 September 1648, for instance, a veritable roll call of scions of the major Pale families, Viscount Dillon, the barons of Trimleston and Slane, Robert Talbot, Sir Luke FitzGerald, Gerard Wall, Richard Barnewall, Walter Dungan and Thomas Preston among them, signed a letter to Michael Jones in Dublin urging him to desist from any contact with Owen Roe O'Neill, whose objective, they asserted, was the complete ruin of the 'British nation'.[87] No Englishman with a sincere heart they judged could join such a figure against them, whose desire to preserve English government had never weakened.[88] As the principal author of the *Commentarius Rinuccinianus*, Richard O'Ferrall, later pointed out, the use of the Protestantly loaded term 'British' in this context was highly significant, reflecting a conscious attempt to rearticulate the primary line of division on the island in national/ethnic rather than confessional terms.[89] For his part, Owen Roe O'Neill unsuccessfully attempted to sway Donough McCarthy, Viscount Muskerry, by appealing to their common Gaelic identity. In this context it was not surprising that the ranks of the clergy came to reflect wider societal divisions.

Rinuccini, for his part, consistently adhered to a strictly confessional definition of party and interest. It can be noted that the Monck truce of 1649 contrived to alienate him somewhat from Owen Roe O'Neill.[90] Two years previously, he had also clashed with the Ulster general over the issue of Athlone. Essentially, Rinuccini had been willing to see the fortress of Athlone pass into the hands of a former royalist, Viscount Dillon of Costello and Galen, after that nobleman's public conversion to Catholicism. The nuncio, who had personally presided over the viscount's reception into the Catholic faith,[91] was deeply irritated by O'Neill's (subsequently justified) suspicions about Costello's future loyalty.

If the nuncio was more absolutist in his convictions concerning the primacy of confessional allegiance, and less willing to differentiate between varieties of Protestant opinion and political stance, it seems clear, nevertheless, that his opinions merely represented a harder band on the spectrum of Irish clerical opinion, rather than a fundamentally different perspective. Rinuccini may have been the force which moved against public Protestant worship in Limerick but it appears as if the Irish

[87] 'Nationem Britannicam': Kavanagh (ed.), *Commentarius Rinuccianus*, III, p. 504.
[88] *Ibid.*
[89] *Ibid.*, p. 505.
[90] Ó hAnnracháin, *Catholic reformation*, p. 208.
[91] Kavanagh (ed.), *Commentarius Rinuccianus*, II, pp. 467–8.

bishops had already pre-empted the nuncio's position in other confederate controlled cities. In this regard, it is of interest that the year prior to the bishop of Ferns's clash with the nuncio concerning the right of Protestant soldiers to exercise their religion, the same bishop ordered that

the body of Francis Talbot, who died an obstinate heretic be buried . . . with only one candle at his grave at nine of the clock by night without a bell in the church or street, without priest, cross, book or prayer. Any person exceeding this manner of burial to incur church censures. No wax taper nor candle nor torch to be used.[92]

Ferns' willingness to countenance the exercise of Protestant rites was therefore curtailed by very definite limits. In his clash with Rinuccini he had defended his position with reference to continental jurisdictions where contact with Protestants was forbidden only in cases concerning illicit communication concerning divine matters, or where danger of perversion existed, or where scandal might be created.[93] Nevertheless, the straitness of the limits prescribed by these conditions was very considerable and certainly acted to make the idea of public Protestant worship inadmissible under normal circumstances.

Overall, a certain similarity can be detected between Catholic clerical attitudes towards Protestantism and those of certain Protestant observers concerning the Church of Rome, a point which the brief interlude of Catholic dominance in the 1640s allows to be glimpsed. Just as Walter Enos or John Lynch could agree that Protestantism was not as heinous a heresy as Puritanism, so Griffith Williams could argue the case that Puritans were worse than papists, that Catholics might wish 'to squat in the temple' but that Puritans aspired 'to overturn it completely'.[94] When they enjoyed positions of dominance, the prelates of both confessions clearly distinguished between the public and private exercise of religion by ecclesiastical rivals. Both clerical establishments claimed the power of keys and the weighty responsibility which this entailed meant that neither confession had much freedom for manoeuvre in terms of the endorsement of toleration and mutual coexistence.

[92] *Historical Manuscripts Commission thirteenth report, appendix 1: the manuscripts of his Grace the Duke of Portland* (London, 1891), p. 403.
[93] Ferns to Rinuccini, 6 September 1647: Kavanagh (ed.), *Commentarius Rinuccianus*, II, p. 696.
[94] This phrase is Robert Amstrong's; see his 'Protestant churchmen and the confederate wars', in Ciaran Brady and Jane Ohlmeyer (eds.), *Making good: British interventions in early-modern Ireland* (Cambridge: Cambridge University Press, 2005). I am deeply indebted to Dr Armstrong for allowing me to read this article prior to its publication.

Naturally, it would be foolish to consider that either entirely moulded the confessional attitudes of those they considered their flocks. In the course of the peace negotiations during the 1640s the evidence suggests that Ormond tended to look more often to the judges than the bishops concerning what was permissible to offer the confederates,[95] while, for their part, the confederates ultimately broke with the majority party of the clergy and the papal nuncio in accepting the second Ormond peace of 1649. Equally, however, it would be excessively reductive to deny the influence of developed ecclesiastical hierarchies in helping to define the intellectual space in which sectarian identities became established. Seventeenth-century Ireland was not merely a flatly confessional landscape but the articulation of two distinct and antagonistic ecclesiastical institutions allowed for a formidable intellectual superstructure of intolerance to sprout from the existing cultural and political divisions.

[95] *Ibid.*

5   A haven of popery: English Catholic migration to Ireland in the age of plantations

David Edwards

On 22 February 1594 the Privy Council issued instructions to the mayor of Chester requiring him to detain and examine all strangers arriving in the city who were then passing either to or from Ireland.[1] Unlike its previous instructions, the Council insisted that this time the mayor should not confine his inquiries exclusively to people of Irish birth. *Every* traveller was to be stopped, English, Irish or foreign, for it was concerned by the activities of religious, not ethnic, interlopers moving between the two kingdoms. Within barely six weeks stop-and-search tactics had produced the desired result: the arrest and detention of three fugitive English Catholics *en route* to Ireland, in the shape of two boys, aged eleven and twelve, and a disfigured middle-aged man with 'an artificiall lefte eye'.[2] The man, Edward Cowper, was a servant of Mrs Agnes Mordaunt, a convicted recusant[3] from Oakley in Bedfordshire and a relative through marriage of Lord Mordaunt, a senior Catholic nobleman. The Mordaunt connection seemed significant. For several years the heir-apparent to the Mordaunt title, Henry Mordaunt, had been defying the Elizabethan government over religion; punishment had not tamed him. In the period prior to the Chester arrests he had become a close associate of Sir Thomas

A previous version of this paper was presented to a meeting of the Royal Society of Antiquaries of Ireland in May 2002. I wish to thank Con Manning and the members of the Society for a stimulating discussion of some key points. My thanks also to Clodagh Tait, Kenneth Nicholls, Brian Donovan, Alan Ford, Julian Walton and Helen Davis for helping me locate additional evidence. Initial research was aided by a HEA/PRTLI grant to the Department of History, University College, Cork.

[1] Chester City Record Office, ML/1/56.

[2] *Ibid.*, ML/5/218–19.

[3] Tried and convicted in 1588, Agnes was still an active recusant in 1601: A. G. Petti (ed.), *Recusancy documents from the Ellesmere MSS* (London: CRS, 1968), p. 140; H. Bowler and T. J. McCann (eds.), *Recusants in the Exchequer pipe rolls, 1581–92* (London: CRS, 1986), p. 123.

Tresham, the principal English recusant then imprisoned in the Fleet in London.[4] The mayor was authorised to question the detainees.

Subsequent inquiries revealed that they were known to an imprisoned Jesuit, Thomas Pound; also, that they were headed for Ireland because they had kin, friends and other connections there. Cowper's brother had a house in Dublin, while it seems a 'Mr Cole', another Dublin resident, was waiting to receive them.[5] Moreover, there were other Irish links that the Chester authorities were unable to discover. It is recorded in the published recusant rolls that Mary Warnford, the mother of one of the boys in Cowper's care, was incarcerated in London with a well-to-do Irishwoman from the Co. Meath area, and a prominent member of the London Irish community, Anne Plunkett;[6] likewise Mrs Mordaunt. She was related to the English soldier and martial law commissioner, Captain Nicholas Mordaunt, a figure of some celebrity – even notoriety – in Ireland. During the recent Armada crisis he had served the crown west of the Shannon, chiefly in Co. Clare.[7] Finally, there was Pound the Jesuit. Evidently the idea to smuggle the boys into Ireland had been his, because, as he was reported to have said, he was confident he could 'place' them there, through contacts of his own.[8]

The three made a strange party, each speaking with a different regional accent. Cowper, the adult guardian, came from Bedford. In contrast, one of the boys hailed from Enmeth, near Wisbech in Cambridgeshire, while the other came from a village near Winchester in Hampshire. Given their diverse origins it seemed that only their common Catholicism had brought them together, though they may also have been linked to Sir Thomas Tresham and his circle.[9] Whatever the case, the scheme to spirit the boys away was clearly quite sophisticated, involving a far-flung network of friends and contacts that stretched across southern England

[4] A. Morey, *The Catholic subjects of Elizabeth I* (London: George Allen & Unwin, 1978), p.163; H. Bowler (ed.), *Recusant Roll 2 (1593–4)* (London: CRS, 1965), pp.116, 118; G. E. C., *Complete Peerage*, sub 'Mordaunt'; Chester City RO, ML/1/74, ML/5/222, 224, 226–7, 228–31.

[5] Chester City RO, ML/5/220–1.

[6] H. Bowler (ed.), *Recusant Rolls 3 & 4 (1594–6)* (London: CRS, 1970), p.184. For the London Irish at this time see David Edwards, 'The Irish of London, c. 1400–1610: a preliminary survey' (forthcoming).

[7] *Irish Fiants*, Eliz. I, nos. 4053, 5223. The likelihood of his being known to the travellers is increased by the fact that the boys claimed they were going to serve with Sir Richard Bingham, his superior officer, in Connacht (Chester City RO, ML/5/218–19).

[8] Chester City RO, ML/1/60–2. A relative of the earl of Southampton, Pound was an associate of Edmund Campion, who, of course, had many connections in Ireland. For his career see M.D.R. Leys, *Catholics in England, 1559–1829: a social history* (London: Longman, 1961), pp. 28–32.

[9] Like Agnes Mordaunt's kinsman, Lord Mordaunt, Mary Warnford was a fellow inmate of Tresham's in the Fleet (n. 7 above).

and parts of eastern (and perhaps western) Ireland: so much so, indeed, that it is possible to characterise it, as one historian has done, as 'a highly organised transit'.[10] Its sophistication is further underlined by the fact that Ireland was not to be the boys' final destination. Rather, having interrogated all three and got the younger lad to blab, the mayor of Chester and his agents were able to report that the ultimate destination of the intercepted party was continental Europe, where the boys were probably destined for a seminary education, and the priesthood.

On 29 April the mayor signed a warrant for their release from Chester jail. His signature did not bring freedom. The Privy Council ordered that the eleven-year-old be transferred to the custody of Lord North, the Protestant governor of Cambridgeshire, and the twelve-year-old be given to the lord mayor of London, who promptly had him sent to join his mother in prison in the Fleet.[11] Thereafter they disappear, replaced in the records by another, much larger, group of 'Popishe' English children who were detained and questioned in Chester in June 1594, having been arrested in Dublin trying to use a very similar escape network.[12]

Though apparently trivial, this curious little drama is actually of some importance. The plight of the three travellers is reflective of the wider experience of the Catholic community of England at the close of the sixteenth century when, because of Queen Elizabeth's war with Spain, government suspicion of Catholics as potential 'traitors within' was at its peak.[13] Plainly, too, the story of 'the Chester Three' (and those who followed them) shows Ireland in an interesting light. It is usually assumed that the main destination of recusant English emigrants was Catholic Europe, and, after 1634, Maryland in North America. Ireland barely figures in such studies. Yet, as the foregoing story indicates, it was clearly part of a wider international Catholic network which closely involved Ireland. The information gleaned from this case suggests that the number of English Catholics in Ireland was quite high. Other sources confirm this impression. In 1592, for instance, the Antwerp-based English Catholic writer and publisher Richard Verstegen informed a friend that 'sondry English Catholiques are gon over into Ireland',[14] an observation confirmed by the Protestant archbishop of Cashel writing at almost exactly the same time.[15] It seems that for much of the period

---

[10] K. R. Wark, *Elizabethan recusancy in Cheshire* (Manchester: Chetham Society, 3rd series, 19, 1971), p. 112.
[11] Chester City RO, ML/1/65–6, 69–70, ML/5/232–4, 242–3.
[12] A third party of youths was caught in 1595: Wark, *Elizabethan recusancy*, pp. 112–13.
[13] *Calender of state papers, domestic, 1591–4*, p. 389.
[14] A. G. Petti (ed), *The letters and despatches of Richard Verstegen* (London: CRS, 1959), p. 87.
[15] *CSPI, 1588–92*, p. 494.

before 1641 considerable numbers of English Catholics travelled to Ireland, some like 'the Chester Three' seeking a temporary refuge, others in pursuit of career opportunities, and others still a new land in which to settle permanently.

This chapter is intended to explore this mysterious community for the first time. How many English Catholics were there in Ireland during the late 1500s or early 1600s? Did their numbers rise or fall before 1641? Were they only to be found clustered along the eastern seaboard, close to England, around Dublin and the Pale? Or, as hinted at by the case of 'the Chester Three', were they settled more widely? What was their background? Did they exist on the margins of English Ireland, like so many of their coreligionists in England and Wales increasingly forced underground into hiding, or were they part of the colonial establishment, protected by the cloak of their Englishness, able to live without fear of persecution by the English authorities? How did they get on with the native population? Were they very much 'new colonials', holding themselves aloof from the Irish? Or did a shared religion enable some form of social and political fusion between English and Irish Catholics to occur as the Protestant grip on power tightened in the early seventeenth century?

Religion and emigration

Viewed from the larger perspectives of continental and Atlantic history, the existence of an English Catholic community in early modern Ireland is not unusual. The pressures of religious conflict in post-reformation Europe often led to persecuted minorities seeking refuge abroad. In the mid-1550s Geneva had filled with the English Protestant refugees known as the 'Marian exiles', as well as many Huguenots from France,[16] and from the 1560s Protestant immigrants from the Netherlands had settled in south-eastern England in large numbers, fleeing the 'Spanish Fury' in their homeland.[17] During the 1620s there was a huge Protestant exodus westwards out of Bohemia, Moravia and Austria into neighbouring

---

[16] C. H. Garret, *The Marian exiles* (Cambridge: Cambridge University Press, 1938). The exiles also appeared in Italy: K. Bartlett, 'The English exile community in Italy and the political opposition to Mary I', *Albion* 3 (1981), 223–41. For the French Huguenots, see esp. R. M. Kingdon, *Geneva and the coming of the wars of religion in France, 1555–63* (Geneva: Droz, 1956).

[17] Joan Thirsk, *Economic policy and projects: the development of a consumer society in early modern England* (Oxford: Clarendon Press, 1988), pp. 43–4, 46–7; D. M. Palliser, *The age of Elizabeth, 1547–1603* (London: Longman, 1983), pp. 258–9, 260–1; V. Morant, 'The settlement of Protestant refugees in Maidstone during the sixteenth century', *Economic History Review*, 2nd series, 6 (1951). There were also many French Hugue-

Saxony and farther afield, and eastwards into Hungary, in order to escape the Emperor Ferdinand's drive for Catholic uniformity.[18] Across the ocean, the European colonisation of the Americas during this period could not have occurred without the active involvement of religious immigrants. Huguenots played a leading role in the French settlement of Canada in the 1540s, and of Florida and Brazil in the 1550s and 1560s.[19] The English colonisation of North America of the early seventeenth century went hand-in-hand with religiously motivated emigration: on the Protestant side, the colonies founded by the Pilgrim Fathers and the various Puritan sectaries; while the colony of Maryland was established after 1634 as a refuge for Catholics from all parts of the British Isles.[20]

However, in the narrower context of British and Irish historiography the simple observation that English Catholics existed in some numbers in Ireland is significant in itself. It challenges an established assumption that English settlement in early modern Ireland was Protestant settlement, and that Protestantism was 'the religion of the New English'.[21] To date, the main published histories of English colonial settlement in Ireland have concentrated chiefly on the great state-sponsored colonies, the plantations of Munster (1584) and Ulster (1610).[22] Both occurred

nots in England, especially in London: Andrew Pettegree, *Foreign Protestant communities in sixteenth-century London* (Oxford: Clarendon, 1986).

[18] Hajo Holborn, *A history of modern Germany: the reformation* (Princeton: Princeton University Press, 1982), pp. 281–3, 290–3, 319–20.

[19] Frank Lestringant, *Le Huguenot et la sauvage* (Paris: Aux Amateurs des Livres, 1990); Frank Lestringant, 'Geneva and America in the Renaissance: the dream of the Huguenot refuge, 1555–1600', *Sixteenth Century Journal* 26/2 (1995), 285–95. The idea of a programmatic pursuit of Huguenot havens in the New World has recently been challenged: J. McGrath, 'Polemic and history in French Brazil, 1555–1560', *Sixteenth Century Journal* 27/2 (1996), 385–97.

[20] There is currently an interesting debate on the extent to which religion was the prime motivator for migration to New England, or just one factor in several. See, e.g., V. DeJohn Anderson, 'Migrants and motives: religion and the settlement of New England, 1630–1640', *New England Quarterly* 58 (1985), 339–83; T. H. Breen and S. Foster, 'Moving to the New World: the character of early Massachusetts immigration', *William and Mary Quarterly*, 3rd series, 30 (1973), 189–222; David Cressy, *Coming over: migration and communication between England and New England in the seventeenth century* (Cambridge 1987), ch. 3; N. M. Crouse, 'Causes of the great migration, 1630–1640', *New England Quarterly* 5 (1932), 3–36.

[21] B. Fitzpatrick, *Seventeenth-century Ireland: the War of religions* (Dublin: Gill & Macmillan, 1988), p. 3. See also Aidan Clarke, *The Old English in Ireland, 1625–42* (London: MacGibbon & Kee, 1966), p. 18; Margaret MacCurtain, *Tudor and Stuart Ireland* (Dublin: Gill & Macmillan, 1972), p. 66.

[22] Philip Robinson, *The plantation of Ulster* (Dublin: Gill & Macmillan, 1984); Michael MacCarthy-Morrogh, *The Munster plantation: English migration to southern Ireland, 1583–1641* (Oxford: Clarendon Press, 1986); T. W. Moody, *The Londonderry plantation*

under a Protestant monarch, Elizabeth I and James VI & I respectively. For reasons of state, both of these rulers approved the creation and enlargement of a New English and *Protestant* planter class in the country, in order to displace and diminish the troublesome native Catholic elite who had conspired with England's continental Catholic enemies. Given the acknowledged importance of these two state projects, it has become an unquestioned 'fact' of Irish history, articulated with the certainty of a mathematical equation, that from the middle of the sixteenth century onwards English settlement = plantations = Protestantism. Yet there were other forms of colonial settlement apart from the great plantations, and other plantations besides Munster and Ulster. Moreover, as yet, little detailed study has been done of religious attitudes in any of the colonies (plantations or otherwise) introduced after 1550. The under-lying assumption that *Hibernia Anglicana* was one and the same thing as 'the Protestant Ascendancy' is almost entirely untested.

The presence of English Catholics in early modern Ireland has been further obscured by the tendency of political historians to lump them in with the native Anglo-Irish, or 'Old English'. In his brief biographical list of the members of the Irish parliament of 1634, Hugh Kearney identified the Co. Limerick MP, Richard Stevenson, as a 'prominent Anglo-Irish landowner'.[23] In fact Stevenson was an English Catholic colonist whose family had settled in Limerick during the previous fifty years.[24] Such misidentifications are commonplace in the secondary literature. In one of the best, and most influential, interpretations of politics and religion in early modern Ireland, Aidan Clarke's *The Old English in Ireland*, the author admitted to deliberately downplaying the ethnic origins of some of the characters in his study in order to recapture the seventeenth-century perspective in which religion, not ethnicity, determined political identity.[25] His point (as always) was well made, but it did mean that his analysis necessarily defined 'New English' as exclusively Protestant. Figures such as Colonel Walter Bagenal of Dunleckny, Co. Carlow, the Catholic commander of 1641, whose ancestors had first arrived in Ireland from Staffordshire in the 1540s and played an important part in

---

(Belfast 1939); N. P. Canny, *Making Ireland British, 1580–1650* (Oxford: Oxford University Press, 2001).

[23] H. F. Kearney, *Strafford in Ireland, 1633–41: a study in absolutism* (Manchester: Manchester University Press, 1959), p. 241.

[24] MacCarthy-Morrogh, *Munster plantation*, p. 133.

[25] Thus the Irish-born and bred twelfth earl of Ormond, James Butler, is treated as one of the 'New English' because of his Protestantism, and the English-based fifth earl of Clanricarde, Ulick Burke, as 'Old English' because of his Catholicism: Clarke, *Old English*, p. 16.

the Tudor conquest of Ireland, are left rootless by this approach.[26] Although the most famous representatives of the line, Sir Nicholas and Sir Henry Bagenal,[27] seem to have been Protestants, this was not necessarily the case with other family members. Take Sir Samuel Bagenal, who brought a levy of troops from Staffordshire and the surrounding area to Ireland in 1598. He was a Catholic, as were most of his men.[28] He is hardly likely to have agreed that the purpose of the Tudor conquest in which he participated was to bring about what scholars have since dubbed a 'Protestant conquest'.[29] For him, as for other Catholic Bagenals, the purpose of the mid-Tudor and Elizabethan wars was to complete an *English* conquest. Their religious differences with the state only became fully apparent after March 1603 and the accession of James VI of Scotland to the English and Irish thrones. Their subsequent alienation from the state, as exemplified by the actions of Colonel Walter Bagenal in the 1640s, is important because of the journey they had travelled in just a couple of generations, from English conquerors to Catholic rebels. To put it another way, a sense of Englishness did not obscure the attachment of some of the Bagenals to Catholicism; it is historians who have done that.

Developments in the writing of English history since the 1970s highlight the need for recognising the existence of an English Catholic community in early modern Ireland. It is now accepted that large parts of England remained linked to Rome long after the Elizabethan religious settlement of 1559.[30] Even by 1580 it is far from clear that Protestantism

[26] For the strength of Catholicism in Staffordshire, see A. G. Petti (ed.), *Roman Catholicism in Elizabethan and Jacobean Staffordshire*, Staffordshire Record Society, 4th series, 9, 1979).

[27] The religious and political identity of these Bagenals is indicated in J. G. Crawford, *Anglicising the government of Ireland: the Irish Privy Council and the expansion of Tudor rule, 1556–1578* (Dublin 1993), pp.443–4; Canny, *Making Ireland British*, pp. 79–82; H. Morgan, *Tyrone's rebellion: the outbreak of the Nine Years War in Tudor* Ireland (Dublin: Gill & Macmillan, 1993).

[28] John McGurk, *The Elizabethan conquest of Ireland: the 1590s crisis* (Manchester: Manchester University Press, 1997), pp. 70, 153, 208. The Catholicism of Sir Samuel's troops probably explains why William Turner, the recusant-baiting spy, tried to obtain a command under him in Ireland: Francis Edwards, 'The 1st earl of Salisbury's pursuit of Hugh Owen', *Recusant History* 26/1 (2002), 5.

[29] Clarke, *Old English*, p. 9.

[30] John Bossy, *The English Catholic community, 1570–1850* (London: Darton, Longman & Todd, 1976); Christopher Haigh, *Reformation and resistance in Tudor Lancashire* (Cambridge: Cambridge University Press, 1975); Morey, *Catholic subjects*; Alexandra Walsham, *Church papists: Catholicism, conformity and confessional polemic in early modern England* (Woodbridge: Boydell, 1999); J. C. H. Aveling, *The handle and the axe: the Catholic recusants in England from reformation to emancipation* (London: Blond & Briggs, 1976); J. C. H. Aveling, *Northern Catholics* (London: Chapman, 1966); M. J. Havran, *The Catholics in Caroline England* (London: Oxford University Press, 1962); Leys,

was the religion of choice of the majority of the English population; while it had made rapid progress in all areas, the number of genuine converts was not as great as the Protestant authorities hoped. Many people were 'church papists', who publicly conformed, but remained privately Catholic.[31] The number of Catholics dropped dramatically in the 1590s and early 1600s, ministered to by fewer and fewer clergy, but conditions improved somewhat in the 1630s. According to one estimate, as many as 60,000 English Catholics were 'regular clientele' of missionary priests in 1640; how many more were irregular clients is not known, but the number was probably considerable.[32] Despite decades of Protestant policing, certain regions of the country remained not only stubbornly traditionalist or 'survivalist' in religious matters, but increasingly 'recusant' in disposition also, actively rejecting Protestant doctrine while accepting new, post-Tridentine, Catholic ideas and practices. According to government records, the strongest areas of 'popish recusancy' were Lancashire and Cheshire (close to Ireland), with numbers relatively high in Derbyshire, Staffordshire, along the Anglo-Welsh border, in Hampshire and Sussex, and also in the north. However, given the problem of 'outward conformity' there is reason to suspect that the number of Catholics in the south and south-east, where Protestantism was dominant, was higher than official documents indicated. As Haigh has observed, more than half of the seminary-trained priests despatched to England in 1580 went to work in London and throughout the Thames Valley, in the belt of counties from Middlesex through Bedfordshire to Oxfordshire. Plainly, the priests would not have based themselves in these parts unless there was a sizeable Catholic community requiring their ministry.[33]

The fact that two of 'the Chester Three' had London and Bedfordshire connections is therefore not so surprising . Nor is the fact that they were headed for Ireland, or knew a number of English settlers there. During the reign of Henry VIII the English royal government had embarked on a policy of military and political reintervention in the country. Steadily, more and more Englishmen received administrative

---

Catholics in England; W. R. Trimble, *The Catholic laity in Elizabethan England* (Cambridge, MA: Harvard University Press, 1964); Arnold Pritchard, *Catholic loyalism in Elizabethan England* (London: Scolar Press, 1979); Eamon Duffy, *The stripping of the altars* (New Haven: Yale University Press, 1992); M. B. Rowlands (ed.), *English Catholics of parish and town, 1558–1778* (London: CRS, 1999), 17.

[31] Walsham, *Church papists*; Christopher Haigh, 'The continuity of Catholicism in the English reformation', in Haigh (ed.), *The English reformation revised* (Cambridge: Cambridge University Press, 1987), pp. 176–208.

[32] Bossy, *English Catholic community*, p. 101; K. J. Lindley, 'The Lay Catholics of England in the reign of Charles I', *JEH* 22 (1972).

[33] Haigh, 'The continuity', pp. 196–7.

appointments in central and local government, and the size of the royal army was enormously increased.[34]

Whereas early in King Henry's reign the English army had numbered just 200 men, after 1534 it rarely dropped below 1,600, and was often as high as 2,500 or more. In a major conflict, such as the Nine Years War (1594–1603), the total royal force ballooned to 17,500.[35] Without these troops, transported to Dublin through the ports of Chester, Liverpool, Holyhead and Bristol, English colonial settlement would not have been possible in early modern Ireland. The first official plantation, Laois/ Offaly (1549–50), occurred while the military establishment stood at 2,500; significantly, many of the original planters were soldiers, rewarded for their part in suppressing the local Gaelic rulers.[36] The plantation's survival paved the way for further military and colonial expansion. Even before the next state-sponsored plantation scheme, in Munster (1584), English soldiers, officials and colonial adventurers had established themselves as landholders around the country. Their posses- sions dotted the map from Stillorgan, Co. Dublin (acquired by the Wolverstones, a Suffolk family) and St Wulfstan's, Co. Kildare (the Alens of Norfolk), south to Tintern, Co. Wexford (the Colcloughs of Staffordshire), and west as far as Ballinasloe, Co. Galway (the Brabazons of Warwickshire).[37] Where the soldiers and adventurers went, New English tenants sometimes followed, in the form of kindred, friends and clients. Precise figures cannot be given, but it is clear that midway through the reign of Elizabeth I thousands of New English men and women were working and living in Ireland, from the Leinster–Ulster border to the southernmost parts of Munster, and many points in between.

Little wonder, then, that 'the Chester Three' had so many Irish connections. Prior to the 1570s the new settlers who arrived in Ireland had as likely been Catholics as Protestants, for the simple reason that many of them would have been born at a time when England was still predominantly a Catholic country. Take the Laois/Offaly plantation.

[34] S. G. Ellis, *Ireland in the age of the Tudors, 1447–1603* (London: Longman, 1998), pp. 146, 157, 225. See also R. Loeber, *The geography and practice of English colonisation in Ireland, 1534–1609* (Athlone: Group for the Study of Irish Historical Settlement, 1991).

[35] Ellis, *Ireland in the age of the Tudors*, pp. 178–9; Colm Lennon, *Sixteenth-century Ireland: the incomplete conquest* (Dublin: Gill & Macmillan, 1994), pp. 171, 181. This was despite regular attempts to cut troop numbers: e.g., Ciaran Brady, *The chief governors: the rise and fall of reform government in Tudor Ireland, 1536–1588* (Cambridge: Cambridge University Press, 1994), pp. 85, 103, 119–20, 129, 135–6, 145.

[36] Lennon, *Sixteenth-century Ireland*, 171; Loeber, *Geography*, pp. 16–17.

[37] Loeber, *Geography*, pp. 12–16, 34–5, 43.

Contradicting the orthodox assumption that it was somehow 'inextricably bound up with the Elizabethan [Protestant] church settlement',[38] one authority on the English colony there has noted 'the original settlers were of mixed religion'.[39] Thus prominent soldier-planter families such as the Cosbys, Barringtons and Pigotts were seemingly Protestants, at least before 1600, while others like the Hovendons, Davells and Harpoles were Catholics.[40] Evidence concerning central government personnel reveals a similar pattern. The East Anglian legalist Sir John Alen, despite taking a prominent part in the dissolution of the monasteries and being reappointed lord chancellor of Ireland by the Protestant king, Edward VI, in 1548, did *not* oversee the growth of a Protestant lineage after settling in Co. Kildare. Rather, his successors became strongly identified with Catholic recusancy in the Pale.[41] Similarly, Henry Draycott from Derbyshire, who was appointed to the Irish Privy Council by Elizabeth I in 1566, and served as a commissioner for ecclesiastical causes before his death in 1572. Though sometimes identified by historians as 'a loyal Protestant', the evidence for his religious sympathies is equivocal at best. All that can be said with certainty is that following his passing his family became closely involved with the Catholic families of Co. Meath, and was soon to the fore among the recusant gentry there.[42] And as the behaviour of Sir William Stanley in Flanders in 1587 revealed, some of the highest-ranking English commanders from Queen Elizabeth's Irish army (and the captains and lieutenants who followed them) were privately committed to the Catholic religion, some even to the point of committing treason.[43]

Given all this, scholars should perhaps adopt a new chronology for the relationship between English colonisation and religious change in early

---

[38] MacCurtain, *Tudor and Stuart Ireland*, p. 166.

[39] Ivan Cosby, 'The English settlers in Queen's county, 1570–1603', in P. G. Lane and William Nolan (eds.), *Laois: history & society* (Dublin: Geography Publications, 1999), p. 291. Rolf Loeber is less cautious, claiming 'most of the settlers were Roman Catholic': Loeber, *Geography*, p. 27.

[40] Cosby, 'English settlers', pp. 283–9.

[41] Crawford, *Anglicising the government*, p. 442. For Thomas Allen of Dublin, his grandnephew, see Lennon, *Lords of Dublin*, p. 225.

[42] S. Barnewall, 'Henry Draycott and the Draycotts of Mornington, Co. Meath', *Ríocht Na Midhe* 6 (1977), 68–77, esp. 70, 75–6. For a different view, see Helen Coburn-Walshe, 'Responses to the Protestant reformation in sixteenth century Meath', *ibid.* 8/1 (1987), 100–1.

[43] A. J. Loomie, *The Spanish Elizabethans: the English exiles at the court of Philip II* (London: Burns & Oates, 1963), ch. 5. Of the officers of Stanley's Catholic regiment, the greater part was English or Welsh; the rank and file mainly Irish: Grainne Henry, *The Irish military community in Spanish Flanders, 1586–1621* (Dublin: Irish Academic Press, 1992), pp. 54–5, 149–50.

modern Ireland. For new settlers who arrived during the period *c.* 1540–
70 it is safer to assume they were Catholic than Protestant. Thereafter,
from 1570 until the early 1590s the number of Protestants arriving in
Ireland probably expanded rapidly, but it is still not safe to assume that
they outnumbered the Catholic arrivals. Only from the 1590s onwards is
it certain that Protestantism passed Catholicism out as the religion of the
newcomers. Even then, and for reasons that will be discussed below,
English Catholics continued to appear in significant numbers throughout
the early seventeenth century.

Reasons for migration

Ireland had much to recommend it as a possible place of refuge for
English Catholics. It was nearer than the European mainland, and safer
to sail to, but it was also a place where many people of English descent
were already settled and where the English language was widely spoken.
Best of all, it was the one country in the British Isles where Catholicism
remained the dominant religion. The Protestant reformation gained only
the smallest of toeholds in sixteenth-century Ireland – the government's
efforts to impose doctrinal uniformity on the parochial clergy only began
in earnest in the 1590s, by which time the Catholic counter-reformation
was already well under way, with seminary-trained clergy appearing in
increasing numbers.[44] Up till then the old pre-Tridentine order prevailed in most Irish parishes. Probably to an even greater extent than
in England and Wales, this 'Catholic survivalism' proved fertile ground
for the new version of Catholicism that began gradually taking root in
the country after the closure of the Council of Trent in 1563. In addition,
far more than in England, the right to appoint clergy to parish livings was
controlled largely by the local lords and gentry, who displayed little
interest in Protestant doctrine.[45]

The main reason, however, why English Catholics settled in Ireland
was political. Although the early modern period is generally seen as the
time of 'the Penal Laws', when Catholicism was suppressed by statute, it
is not generally recognised that the anti-Catholic measures adopted by
the Dublin government were mild in comparison to those that were
taken up in England. For more than a century after 1560 the principal
law against Catholicism in Ireland was the statute 2° Elizabeth cap. 1.

---

[44] A. Ford, *The Protestant reformation in Ireland, 1590–1641*, 2nd edn. (Dublin: Four
Courts Press, 1997); Helga Hammerstein, 'Aspects of the continental education of
Irish students in the reign of Elizabeth I', *Historical Studies* 8 (1971), 137–53.
[45] Lennon, *Sixteenth-century Ireland*, ch. 11.

This authorised the imposition of the oath of supremacy (acknowledging the queen as head of the church instead of the pope) on all office-holders, with a mandatory fine and period of imprisonment as the penalty for those who failed to attend Protestant divine service on Sundays.[46] True, early in the 1600s Irish Catholics discovered that this statute, once enforced, was capable of inflicting considerable discomfort on local communities and their leaders.[47] However, this should not detract from the fact that under Elizabeth I, and also under her early Stewart successors, the anti-Catholic statute bearing her name was only intermittently enforced.[48]

This contrasts markedly with England. From early in Queen Elizabeth's reign much harsher anti-Catholic measures were introduced. In 1563 a law was passed which at once made the lot of the English Catholic population markedly worse than that of its Irish equivalent: those who (in conscience) refused a second time to take the supremacy oath were to be charged with treason and face the death penalty.[49] Eight years later, directly as a result of the 1563 Act, no Catholic MPs were elected to the Westminster parliament (in Ireland, Catholic MPs continued being returned down to 1641). Three statutes were passed further eroding the Catholic position: the Treasons Act, which made it treasonable to describe the queen as a heretic or schismatic; an act which made it treason to convert or 'reconcile' anyone to Rome, or to receive Catholic absolution; and an act to outlaw Catholic exiles who had crossed to the continent.[50] Conditions worsened further following the parliament of 1593, when acts were passed excluding Catholics from all offices and professions, and forcing them even out of the guilds. This parliament was remarkable for going beyond the regulation of public religious life, reaching into family and domestic affairs. Thus it was enacted that recusant housewives were to have their dowries forfeited, and a man who married a recusant heiress was to lose two-thirds of his moveable goods and possessions. Perhaps worst of all, the 1593 parliament agreed to a new law whereby the children of recusant Catholics were to be forcefully taken from their parents to be reared as Protestants by others.[51]

---

[46] *Statutes at large, Ireland*, 15 vols. (Dublin, 1786), I, pp. 279–81.

[47] John McCavitt, 'Lord Deputy Chichester and the "Mandates" policy in Ireland, 1605–7', *Recusant History* 20/3 (1991).

[48] However, it is important to remember that anti-Catholic policy was sometimes pursued rigorously under Elizabeth, and not always in wartime; see David Edwards, *The Ormond lordship in County Kilkenny, 1515–1642: the rise and fall of Butler feudal power* (Dublin. Four Courts, 2003), pp. 225–8, 239–42, 246–7.

[49] Morey, *Catholic subjects*, pp. 46–7.   [50] *Ibid.*, p. 60.   [51] *Ibid.*, pp. 70–1.

Hence, then, the 1594 fugitives at Chester, bound for the would-be haven of Catholic Ireland, and the many other migrants who both preceded and succeeded them. As Richard Verstegen noted, in Ireland English Catholics 'are at more quiet than yf they were in England'.[52] Contemporary documents confirm that the Catholic settlers moved to Ireland because they felt they had been driven out of England. Take the Lancashire-born priest and future martyr, John Almond (b. 1567). As a teenager, if not a little earlier, he had had to go Ireland to receive a Catholic education.[53] Similarly, Ralph Corby, who was destined to be hanged, drawn and quartered at Tyburn in September 1644 for serving as a Jesuit missionary in England. He was born in Dublin in March 1598 'of English parents, natives of the bishopric of Durham'. As 'zealous converts' to Catholicism, in the 1590s they had gone over into Ireland 'for the freer exercise of their religion' and to escape persecution – and the threat of family separation – at home.[54]

Nor did English conditions improve in the early 1600s. Following the discovery of the gunpowder plot, anti-Catholic laws were intensified. Repeatedly, Protestant MPs demanded action against 'popery', and Catholics were fined and imprisoned. Even in the 1630s, after the marriage of Charles I to the French Catholic Princess Henrietta Maria, and despite the assertions of some historians, conditions for Catholicism remained prohibitive.[55] In 1633–4 recusants living in many parts of England, from London to Oxford to Chester, lived in constant fear of arrest and punishment. As with 'the Chester Three' forty years earlier, a clandestine transit network existed that smuggled recusants out of England 'speedely into Ireland' (sic), and also overseas to Europe.[56] Fear of punishment also explains the appearance of Henry Norton of Westham, Sussex, at Freshford in Co. Kilkenny, where he died and was buried in May 1627. Having been convicted of recusancy many times over at the Sussex assizes, he was dangerously exposed to the rigours of English anti-Catholic legislation. Documents about him compiled ten years after his death imply that 'disappearance' into Ireland may have been his only

---

[52] Petti (ed.), *Letters and despatches*, 87.
[53] George Anstruther, *The seminary priests*, 4 vols. (Durham: Ushaw College, 1968–77), I, p. 6.
[54] Corby and his parents returned to northern England only in 1603, following the death of Elizabeth I: R. Challoner, *Memoirs of missionary priests*, ed. J. H. Pollen (London, 1924), pp. 461–2; G. F. Nuttall, 'The English martyrs, 1535–1680: a statistical review', *Journal of Ecclestical History* 22/3 (1971), 191, n.3.
[55] Conditions may have relaxed at court, but in the country difficulties remained: e.g., Leys, *Catholics in England*, pp. 78–85; Havran, *Catholics*, pp. 27–8, 39–60, 91–4, 99, 134–5.
[56] Bibliotheque Royale De Belgique, Brussels, MS 3824, ff. 19 r–v, 24 r–v.

way to frustrate the efforts of the authorities to seize what remained of his estate.[57]

Escape to Ireland offered the opportunity to live as Catholics with a far lower risk of detection than in England. Indeed, if evidence from Co. Tipperary is anything to go by, in the early seventeenth century Ireland became increasingly important to Catholics in England as a place where the full practice of Catholicism remained readily available despite government opposition. The religious celebrations associated with the public display of the fragment of the True Cross kept at Holy Cross Abbey, *including* 'the procession of the Cross' across the county border to Kilkenny city, were attended by a number of pilgrims from England, who purchased as many medals, images and bottles of holy water from the nearby shrine of Monahincha as they could carry back to England. On being asked by an Irish monk in 1623 why they purchased 'so many pious objects', one of them, 'a venerable old man', explained that a cult of the Irish Holy Cross had recently emerged in England, and that the miracles attributed to it had enabled 'many [English] Catholics . . . [to] openly practice the Catholic faith'.[58]

Even in Dublin it was possible for an Englishman to live almost undisturbed as a Catholic, presumably because his Englishness protected him from suspicion by Protestant authorities hopelessly overstretched by the task of having to control so many Irish Catholics. One of the best private collections of Catholic devotional literature to have survived from early modern times in Ireland belonged to an Englishman, 'F.S.', 'an old Popish gentleman'. For the final years of his life, *c*.1590–1608, and despite all the religious turmoil then taking place in the state capital, he was able to read and transcribe a wide range of European and English Catholic treatises, and to write spiritual meditations of his own such as 'Of the Sacraments of the body and blode of Christe' (1592) and 'Of Contynency and Sole Lyfe' (1605).[59] The knowledge that such a fulfilling religious life was possible in Ireland helped in no small way to boost the number of potential immigrants from England. As John Pym, the great Protestant parliamentarian, put it in November 1640, to Englishmen early Stewart Ireland seemed to be a land of 'popery without restraint'.[60]

---

[57] East Sussex Record Office, Lewes, MS SAU 1321.

[58] Malachy Hartry, *Triumphalia chronologica monasterii Sanctae Crucis in Hibernia*, ed. D. J. Murphy (Dublin: Sealy, Bryers & Walker, 1891), pp. 159–61.

[59] BL, Harleian MS 1714.

[60] Michael Perceval-Maxwell, *The outbreak of the Irish rebellion of 1641* (Dublin: Gill & Macmillan, 1994), p. 110.

Of course, English Catholic settlers were economic migrants too. The Elizabethan wars were hugely destructive in Ireland. In Munster the Desmond rebellion of 1579–83 led to a virtual depopulation of the province, with tens of thousands of natives killed.[61] Similar mortality crises accompanied the Nine Years War, and early in the 1600s large parts of each province, but especially of Ulster and Connacht, were severely underpopulated. North America was not the only new colonial destination where Englishmen were summoned by the promise of open space. In Ireland economic opportunities abounded for immigrants.[62]

Another reason for migration to Ireland was the certainty of being welcomed by a native host community. It is not usually recognised that, at least among the upper strata of society, transinsular marital links existed between English Catholic families and their Irish counterparts. Several of the leading Anglo-Irish noble lineages were well connected in England, as they had been since medieval times. The Butlers of Ormond, the Fitzgeralds of Kildare, the Flemings of Slane, the St Lawrences of Howth, as well as branches of the Dillons, Fitzharrises and others, had property interests in England during the sixteenth and seventeenth centuries,[63] and it was not unusual for them to consolidate these interests through marriage. Gradually, religion seems to have become an additional factor behind such unions, particularly in the early 1600s. Shortly after the discovery of the gunpowder plot, marriage with the Butlers of Kilcash (heirs-presumptive to the earldom of Ormond) brought Elizabeth Pointz of Acton in Gloucestershire, her servants and companions, to Tipperary where they earned a reputation for Catholic piety[64] Also in the Butler territories, but a little lower down the social scale, scions of the Audleys of Norfolk and the Knatchbulls (or Nashpoles) of Kent settled in Kilkenny and Tipperary following marriages with the Butlers of Callan.[65]

---

[61] See David Edwards, 'War's grim audit: the demographic impact of the conflict in Munster, 1579–83', in David Edwards, Padraig Lenihan and Clodagh Tait (eds.), *Age of atrocity: violent death and political change in early modern Ireland* (forthcoming).

[62] MacCarthy-Morrogh, *Munster plantation*, 203–8; N. P. Canny, 'Migration and opportunity', *Irish Economic & Social History* 12 (1985), 7–32.

[63] E.g., B. C. Donovan and David Edwards, *British sources for Irish history, 1485–1641* (Dublin: Irish Manuscripts Commission, 1997), pp. 7, 41, 69, 86, 122, 169, 203; PRO, PCC Wills, 7 Milles (Lord St Lawrence of Howth), 52 Drury (Burke of Limerick), 86 Nevill (Fitzharris of New Ross), 27 Maynwaring (Eustace of Kildare), 29 Wood (Fitzsimons of Louth), 14 Ketchyn (Leonard of Kilkenny and Waterford).

[64] B. M. Mansfield, 'A mid-seventeenth century Butler dedication', *Butler Society Journal* 2/4 (1985), 401–2.

[65] *The Visitations of Oxfordshire, 1566, 1574 and 1634*, ed. W. H. Turner (London: Harleian Society, 1871), 278; St Kieran's College, Kilkenny, Carrigan MSS, vol. 21 (un-paginated); PRO, PCC Wills, 170 Grey.

Government awareness

Until late in the reign of Elizabeth I the Protestant authorities in London and Dublin paid little attention to the religious allegiance of New English settlers in Ireland. The government's intelligence-gathering apparatus, such as it was, was chiefly concerned with accumulating military and political information to counter the threat of native insurrection or foreign interference. As the majority of English Catholic settlers were loyal subjects, and like their Protestant countrymen expected to benefit from government expansion, they did not register as a problem group that needed to be watched. A rare exception was in 1570–1, when a few stragglers from the English northern rebellion of 1569 sought temporary refuge in Munster with the Irish Catholic forces led by James Fitzmaurice Fitzgerald.[66] Ten years later, again in Munster, the government was greatly concerned by the appearance of the English Catholic clergyman Dr Nicholas Sander in the ranks of the Desmond rebels, but less because of his English origins, and more because he was a papal representative who had arrived from Rome.[67]

It was the coming of war with Spain in 1585 that finally persuaded the government to begin monitoring English Catholics in Ireland. One of the first to fall under suspicion was the auditor general, Thomas Jenison, a native of Durham who despite more than thirty years' service in Ireland was unable to silence his critics because of the open recusancy of his eldest son, William, who lived in Co. Kildare. In 1587 Jenison had to disinherit William and bequeath his burgeoning estate in England to his second son, John, in order to prevent it being seized in accordance with English anti-Catholic inheritance laws.[68] The defection of Sir William Stanley (January 1587) seemed to confirm what some Protestant servitors in Ireland had long been insisting, namely that Catholic officers could not be trusted with important posts and would have to be systematically rooted out of the royal administration. During the Armada crisis of 1588 the crown authorities learned that disaffected English papists had been using Ireland as a safe haven for several years, with leading recusants such as Sir John Arundel receiving covert shelter in parts of the country before going to Europe to offer their services to the crown's

---

[66] Ellis, *Ireland*, 297; W. Palmer, *The problem of Ireland in Tudor foreign policy, 1485–1603* (Woodbridge: Boydell, 1994), pp. 94–7.

[67] Palmer, *Problem of Ireland*, p. 111; Ellis, *Ireland*, 312–14; Lennon, *Sixteenth-century Ireland*, pp. 223–4.

[68] David Edwards, 'Thomas Jenison (*c.* 1525–87)', *Oxford Dictionary of National Biography*.

enemies.[69] As more information was gathered the government briefly feared that English Catholic exiles on the continent might gather around Stanley and Lord Westmorland, Lord Paget or Henry De La Pole, and try to invade Ireland, where Stanley's connections with the Irish and his knowledge of the terrain could prove dangerous.[70]

Yet at this date even the most paranoid commentators did not view English Catholics living in Ireland as a security risk. For the most part this optimistic analysis was correct. When Ireland emerged as the main theatre of the Anglo-Spanish war in 1594, only a handful of English Catholic settlers joined the rebels. Most famously, the Hovendons, a planter family from Laois, accompanied the main rebel leader, Hugh O'Neill, earl of Tyrone, into battle.[71] O'Neill had been fostered with the Hovendons during his youth; and his later decision to represent his insurrection as a religious crusade, issuing a proclamation to the Catholic loyalist gentry of the Pale and midlands, may have owed something to their influence.[72] Another English Catholic to join the rebellion included an unnamed man executed by martial law at Ballymartin, Co. Kilkenny, in 1597.[73] O'Neill had cause to be disappointed by such a poor showing. In the Catholic regions of England, particularly in Lancashire, Cheshire and the north-west, recusants became increasingly restive throughout the 1590s,[74] and according to spies' reports late in 1596 O'Neill had made contact with them.[75] Not only did they fail to respond positively to his overtures: so too did their Catholic countrymen in Ireland. Evidently, though many English Catholics wanted rid of Elizabeth Tudor few were prepared to join an Irish rebellion in order to expedite her removal. Like their fellow papists the Anglo-Irish, or 'Old English', they remained tied to the monarchy and were quite prepared to wait for better days under a different sovereign.

In the event, of course, the new king was not inclined to authorise any major new anti-Catholic measures, and was content merely for Jesuits and known troublemakers such as the English Catholic printer, Henry Owen (or 'Oven'), to be hunted down and arrested as and when they

---

[69] Donovan and Edwards, *British sources*, p. 262.

[70] *Ibid.*, 262–3. These fears soon subsided as a constant trickle of desertions gradually diminished Stanley's regiment: Henry, *Irish military community*, pp. 55–6, 93–4.

[71] Morgan, *Tyrone's Rebellion*, pp. 96–7, 106; Canny, *Making Ireland British*, p. 98.

[72] Hiram Morgan, '"Faith and Fatherland" in sixteenth-century Ireland', *History Ireland* 3/2 (1995), 16–20.

[73] The document, a list of executed persons, notes 'one of them was an Englishman': PRO, SP 63/198/60.

[74] McGurk, *Elizabethan conquest*, pp. 117–19, 151.   [75] E.g., PRO, SP 63/197/6.

appeared in Ireland.[76] However, the summoning of the English parliament in 1604, followed in 1605 by the gunpowder treason, led immediately to a toughening of policy. In Dublin Castle the new lord deputy, Sir Arthur Chichester, sought to enforce a proclamation banishing all Catholic clergy from the country; local Protestant informers were encouraged to spy on leading recusant families, so that discovery of English Catholics became less accidental, more systematic. For instance, an extraordinarily detailed list compiled about 1610 for Co, Kilkenny, 'A note of the priests, commissaries, friars and Jesuits, . . . their relievers and maintainers', drew explicit attention to the presence of English recusants in the shire. At Castle Eve, near Callan, on the lands of the Anglo-Irish Sweetman family, there resided an English gentleman tenant called 'Mr Brooksbury', who 'keepeth an English priest'. The priest, we are told, held mass 'every Sunday', attracting a large rural congregation that included the tenants from a neighbouring estate. The activities of this English priest clearly aroused the interest of the informer, who attempted without success to discover his name and identity.[77] Not that the informer's inquiries were entirely fruitless. Further on in the list he records the name of another English recusant who had recently settled in the Kilkenny countryside around Callan, 'Mr Nashpole' (Knatchbull), who was a tenant on the Ormond manor of Pottlerath. Knatchbull too kept an English priest, whose name the informer was likewise unable to discover.[78] Not all lists were as detailed, or as comprehensive, as the Kilkenny list, but others referred to English Catholics, especially in the south-east. A list of priests resident in Waterford city mentions two persons who, to judge by their names, were English newcomers to the port, the priest William Readen, and his protector, Thomas Howe;[79] a similar list for Co. Wexford names another English cleric, William Hampton, who lived near Moyglass, while John Peerce, who resided at Carne, was possibly English.[80]

Chichester's pursuit of the policy of 'mandates' uncovered other English Catholic elements in the country, particularly in the Pale. Between November 1605 and April 1607, of the thirty-three Catholic gentry resident in Cos. Dublin, Meath, Kildare and Louth to receive orders ('mandates') requiring them to attend Protestant religious service and to repair the Protestant parish churches on their lands, at least nine were

[76] Owen was captured in 1603 'as he was flying with his press and letters, so it is said, into Ireland': H. R. Plomer, 'Ireland and secret printing', *Irish Book Lover* 1/3 (October 1909), 27.
[77] TCD, MS 567, fol. [11v et seq].   [78] *Ibid.*
[79] *Ibid.*, fol. 37v.   [80] *Ibid*, fol. 42r.

New English.[81] The best known of this group is Francis Marshall and his father-in-law Philip Bassett.[82] Brought to trial in Castle Chamber in late 1605 they were fined and banished, given just thirty days to get out of Ireland.[83] Bassett seems to have complied, disappearing from Irish records, but not Marshall. By July 1619 he was living in Co. Kilkenny, a tenant of the Catholic eleventh earl of Ormond, Walter Butler 'of the beads and rosary'.[84] Evasion was not an option for some of the other victims of 'mandates'. As well as being fined and incarcerated for a time in Dublin Castle in 1606–7, Christopher Worrall had his career as a government official in Drogheda terminated.[85]

English Catholics in Munster were also exposed by 'mandates'. In June 1607 Thomas Prater and John Sherwood were jailed 'for obstinate recusancy', after which arrangements were made for their banishment from Cork into England.[86] And again, as in the Pale, the government identified Catholics among its administrative personnel. One such was the second justice of the province, Robert Marshall – a kinsman of the aforementioned Francis Marshall? – whose servant was caught smuggling Catholic religious items into Munster from France in February 1607. Marshall had already relinquished his post as justice, being described as a 'late' official of the king in Munster,[87] an understandable response to the aggressive anti-Catholicism of the lord president of Munster, Sir Henry Brouncker.

Finally, in 1612, as the government began to realise the extent of English Catholic settlement in Ireland, new measures were proposed. Before the parliament of 1613 met, officials decided what bills should be brought forward for enactment. One was a bill 'that English recusants flying to Ireland shall be subject to the laws made against recusants in England'. A marginal comment by an anonymous government official underlined the problem: 'Ireland swarms with English recusants, for the laws [of Ireland] have no power to deal with them.'[88] Significantly,

---

[81] These were Francis Marshall, Philip Bassett, Thomas Orpy, Bartholomew Elcock, John Elliott, Robert Chillam and Christopher Worrall: NAI, Catalogue of Fiants, James I, pp. 714–15, 738. Another, William Turner, may also have been English. Two more, John Gooding and James Jans, both Dublin merchants, are recorded in HMC, *Egmont MSS*, I, 31.

[82] Lennon, *Lords of Dublin*, pp. 178, 180.

[83] *CSPI, 1603–6*, 348, 353; TCD, MS 852, fols. 89r–90r; HMC, *Egmont MSS*, I, 30–1.

[84] NLI, D. 3633.

[85] HMC, *Egmont MSS*, I, 32.

[86] HMC, *Salisbury MSS*, XIX, 1607, pp. 160–2.

[87] West Devon Record Office, Plymouth, Miscellaneous Borough Papers, MS W359/38–40, 43.

[88] *CSPI, 1611–14*, p. 290.

although the clashes in this parliament between the crown and the Catholic MPs are usually seen as a serious setback for Irish Catholics, English Catholics had cause to be pleased with the outcome. Because of all the controversy, the government had to abandon much of its legislative programme – including, crucially, the English recusants bill. Henceforth, immigrants could continue to avoid English anti-Catholic laws by moving to Ireland. The country remained, comparatively, a haven of popery for many years to come.

Geographical spread after 1603

A steady stream of English Catholics continued to settle in Ireland before 1641. Indeed, their numbers grew appreciably during the 1620s and 1630s, when economic migrants – arriving to escape the agricultural depression in England – swelled the ranks of more purely religious refugees.[89] Whereas before 1603 settlement was mainly in the east, the midlands and the south-east, after that date Catholic immigrants spread themselves much more widely, appearing in each province and almost every county.

Leinster, and particularly the east and south-east, remained the main destination. Thanks to its proximity to Chester and the main recusant enclaves in England and Wales, Dublin and the shires of the Pale continued to draw large numbers of Catholic settlers. The 1641 Depositions identify a number of English 'papists' who had arrived in the greater Dublin area in the course of the previous thirty years, such as the Frend family at Newcastle, and the Parkers and Woodfields at Templeogue.[90] Likewise in Co. Kildare, where recently arrived English Catholics included the Ordes at Castlemartin, the Lekes at Rathbride and the Brittans at the Lyons.[91] Also in Leinster, but moving west, by 1616 the Hedwich family had emerged at Mullingar, Co. Westmeath.[92] The most interesting developments occurred in south and south-east Leinster. In Co. Wexford after 1610, English colonisation

---

[89] Some of these newcomers are recorded in the series of 'Licenses to pass beyond the Seas' (PRO, E157), a valuable source for economic history, but frustratingly silent about religion. For an introduction to the series, see A. M. Breen, 'To pass beyond the seas', *Irish Roots* 48 (Autumn 2003), 24–5.

[90] The Frends were associates of another New English family, the Bretts; the Parkers and Woodfields were tenants of the Anglo-Irish lineage, the Talbots (TCD, MS 809, fols. 264r, 278). The Frends had appeared by 1607: J. Ohlmeyer and E. Ó Ciardha (eds.), *The Irish Statute Staple Books, 1596–1687* (Dublin 1998), p. 227.

[91] TCD, MS 813, fols. 8r, 10v.

[92] HMC, *Egmont MSS*, I, 47.

was spearheaded as much by English Catholics as by Protestants. By this time the Mastersons of Ferns (who hailed originally from Cheshire) had ceased to conform to the established church and turned to Catholicism. If only for the time being they avoided conflict with the authorities when the head of the family, Sir Richard Masterson, 'discovered' crown title to the north of the county, thereby facilitating the introduction of a new plantation. While much of the plantation territory was subsequently granted to English Protestant officials and servitors, Masterson also benefited, and his expanded estate formed a Catholic enclave at its heart.[93] A few years later, in 1625, the English Catholic cause in Wexford was greatly boosted by the conversion to Catholicism of a leading colonist, the courtier and official Sir George Calvert, Lord Baltimore, who had previously acquired the Cloghamon estate along the border with Wicklow. Subsequently, as the idea of founding a Catholic colony in North America began to obsess him, Baltimore recruited tenants in England to farm his Wexford holdings. Estate documents of 1638 show that the majority of these tenants were Catholics, recruited from Bedfordshire, Lincolnshire and elsewhere.[94] English Catholics appeared elsewhere in the plantation: in 1641 the estate of the Protestant planter Sir Walsingham Cooke had at least two English Catholics as tenants, the yeomen John Chandler and Hugh Clarke.[95] Elsewhere in the county the manor of Enniscorthy, securely in Protestant hands before 1599, subsequently turned Catholic as a result of the prolonged absenteeism of its landlords, the Wallops, and in 1640 it returned an English recusant, Ralph Waddington, to the Irish parliament.[96]

There was also a growing English Catholic presence in Cos. Carlow and Kilkenny, one of the few regions of the country where, for a time, Catholic newcomers may actually have outpaced Protestant arrivals in the early seventeenth century. The fact that Protestant settlement levels were comparatively low no doubt helped to attract Catholics to the area – all the more so as the smallness of the Protestant community undermined the repeated efforts of the government to create a new local elite in its own image, and the dominating influence over local affairs enjoyed by the Butlers of Ormond and their Catholic supporters survived

---

[93] W. F. Butler, *Confiscation in Irish History* (London, 1917), pp. 60–75.

[94] Articles of agreement, 17 August 1638 (Sheffield City Library, MS WWM Add, Brown parcel 4, Loose Deeds/6); Schedule of indentures, 28 August 1638 (ibid., Loose Deeds/7).

[95] TCD, MS 818, fols. 9, 73.

[96] Waddington had lands in Queen's County (Laois): Clarke, *Old English*, pp. 260–1. My thanks to Brian Donovan for helping me untangle the circumstances behind this election.

(bruised, but essentially intact).[97] The weakness of the state was perhaps most visible in Co. Carlow, where rather than appoint a Butler as county governor the crown looked instead to the principal New English land-owner in the area, Walter Bagenal of Dunleckny. Of course, Bagenal was no Protestant, and was closely associated with senior Butler figures from Kilkenny such as Richard Butler, third Viscount Mountgarret, Edmund Butler of Baleen (future fourth Viscount Mountgarret) and Pierce Butler of Barrowmount.[98] Hence the arrival in Co. Carlow of English Catholic immigrants such as the Cookes and the Eversons,[99] while in Kilkenny the likes of the Pointzes, Knatchbulls, Audleys and Marshalls were joined by the Baskervilles, Smyths, Greenes, Bests and Crispes by the 1630s.[100] Subsequently, Protestant settlement levels increased markedly following the acquisition of the Gaelic territory of Idough in north-east Co. Kilkenny by the senior crown administrator, Christopher Wandesford, but even here Catholics appeared among the new arrivals. On the eve of the 1641 rebellion, it was reported that 'gentlemen papists' living near Idough, using 'evill counsels and practices', had introduced 'their priests' into the area. Able to say mass openly, these succeeded in converting some of the Wandesfords' English tenants.[101]

The most striking evidence about English Catholic settlement in early seventeenth-century Ireland pertains to Munster. When the Munster Plantation was first introduced in 1584 the government went to consid-erable lengths to ensure that English Protestants settled the new colony. Accordingly, it was their Protestant credentials as well as their high connections that secured plantation grants for the likes of the provost marshal George Thornton (Dunnaman, Co. Limerick), the poet Edmund Spenser (Kilcolman, Co. Cork), the soldier Robert Cullum (Ardagh,

---

[97] *Ibid.*, 291, 295.

[98] Perceval-Maxwell, *Outbreak of the Irish rebellion*, pp. 257, 259.

[99] A rare surviving fragment of the Co. Carlow Civil Survey mentions William Cooke as occupying land at Ullard in the barony of Forth circa 1640, but misidentifies him as an 'Irish Papist' (NLI, MS 2560, fol. 51). He was probably the son of the settler James Cooke, indicted as a Carlow recusant juror in 1612 (HMC, *Egmont MSS*, I, 40). For the Eversons, see ibid., 44–5.

[100] John Baskerville's arrival at Skeirke and William Smyth's at Dammagh was due to the patronage of Walter Butler, eleventh earl of Ormond: NLI, MS 2510, fol. 41r; Patricia Coughlan, '"The model of its sad afflictions": Henry Burkhead's *Tragedy of Cola's Furie*' in Micheál Ó Siochrú (ed.), *Kingdoms in crisis: Ireland in the 1640s* (Dublin: Four Courts Press, 2001), p. 194. The Greenes, alternatively, seem to have settled in Kilkenny city through their cousins the Audleys, who were married to the Butlers of Callan (PRO, PCC Wills, 170 Grey), while the Bests and the Crispes, who settled at Parksgrove and Lismaine, were brought in by their Knatchbull kin and the Mountgarret Butlers (*Funeral entries of Ireland* (appendix to *Irish Memorials of the Dead, VII:* Dublin 1907), pp. 41, 197).

[101] 'The case concerning the territory of Idough', n.d. [1641]: NLI, Prior Wandesford MSS.

Co. Limerick), and the anti-recusant agent Hugh Cuffe (Kilmore, Co. Cork). Equally, Catholics who had applied for plantation grants in 1584 had had their applications denied.[102] However, as Michael MacCarthy-Morrogh has shown, Catholicism replaced Protestantism as the religion of several of the planters in the years after 1603, when the colony was re-established after being destroyed by Irish rebels.[103] In some cases, previously Protestant seigniories passed into Catholic hands through marriage. This was the fate of Hugh Cuffe's estate, which passed to the Yorkshire knight Sir Francis Slingsby, who married one of Cuffe's daughters, Elizabeth, a coheiress. Although Sir Francis was outwardly Protestant – at least until 1633 – after the conversion of his eldest son to Catholicism, his family was not. First his wife and then all his children became recusants.[104] Other plantation estates in Munster changed religion because of the conversion of the original family. Thus two of Edmund Spenser's sons, Silvanus and Peregrine, were Catholics by the 1630s;[105] so too Thomas Fleetwood's son, Sir Richard Fleetwood, who left Staffordshire for Cork in 1626 to escape punishment as a recusant.[106] On the eve of the 1641 rebellion at least eight of the original thirty-five (Protestant) plantation seigniories were possessed by English Catholic families: the Thorntons, Stevensons and Cullums in Limerick, the Slingsbys, Spensers and Fleetwoods in Cork, and the Brownes and Springs in Kerry.[107] As documents concerning the Slingsbys suggest, Catholic recruitment did not stop at the manor house door, since priests would also have had access to servants and tenants. Lady Slingsby maintained an English priest, 'one Alexander', to provide such services;[108] most of the others would probably have kept Irish priests.

In the rest of Munster, outside the plantation, English Catholics were also present in considerable numbers, part of the 'swarm' of recusants so frequently complained of by Protestant officials after 1603. As elsewhere, the patronage of Anglo-Irish lords facilitated settlement. In the 1630s, Viscount Roche of Fermoy had a small group of English Catholics as tenants on his lands in north Co. Cork, headed by one 'Mr Henly'.[109]

---

[102] MacCarthy-Morrogh, *Munster plantation*, pp. 191–2.   [103] *Ibid.*, 195–6.
[104] Anstruther, *Seminary priests*, II, 297–8; Bibliotheque Royale De Belgique, Brussels, MS 3824, fols. 1–4.
[105] Silvanus Spenser's Catholicism is well known; Peregrine's is indicated in Bodl., Carte MS 67, fol. 29v.
[106] MacCarthy-Morrogh, *Munster plantation*, 195.
[107] Not four families, as MacCarthy-Morrogh claims (*ibid.*).
[108] NAI, M 2448, fols. 128–9.
[109] R. S., *A collection of some of the murthers and massacres committed on the Irish in Ireland Since the 23rd of October 1641, with some observations and falsifications on a late printed abstract of murthers said to be committed by the Irish* (London, 1662), p. 24.

The port towns proved to be particularly popular destinations, because of the economic opportunities they offered and the number of priests they usually contained. Quite simply, compared to England and Wales, where there were fewer and fewer priests, the main towns of Munster seemed to be full of Catholic clergy. In 1636, detained by Protestant officials at Dover, Robert and Barbara Cluett admitted that three years earlier they had been married 'by a masse priest' at Youghal, Co. Cork, where they continued to live because of the ready availability of all the Catholic sacraments, properly ministered by trained clergy.[110]

English Catholic immigrants were thinnest on the ground in Connacht and Ulster, but they were not entirely absent. The fact that there were not more in Connacht, especially in Co. Galway, is a little surprising, given the assumed influence over local affairs of the Catholic earls of Clanricarde – all the more so as the fourth earl, Richard Burke, had attempted a 'planting of the English' on his lands during the 1620s. In fact, none of the English tenants who were subsequently attracted to Galway were Catholics, and in 1641 the fifth earl, Ulicke, described the newcomers on his estates as all 'English Protestants'.[111] Perhaps the fact that the Clanricardes were usually absentees, and that their grip on the provincial government of Connacht was not all that it could have been – the fourth earl had resigned the lord presidency in 1615 – served to discourage prospective Catholic settlers from venturing so far west. As it was, however, a few English Catholics did establish themselves in the province after 1603.[112] One such was an unnamed 'Englishman' living 'without the Westgate of Galway' in 1618, when a friar (possibly also English) was discovered being taken to his house for safekeeping.[113] Another was Anthony Brabazon of Ballinasloe, who was assumed a Protestant by crown representatives because he was 'an English man's sonn', but revealed himself an energetic Catholic leader in 1641.[114]

Remarkably, even the Ulster Plantation (1610), which did so much to establish Protestantism in Ireland, contained a Catholic element. Apart from sizeable communities of Scottish Catholics under the Hamiltons at

---

[110] Breen, 'To pass beyond', 24.

[111] Bernadette Cunningham, 'From warlords to landlords: political and social change in Galway, 1540–1640', in G. Moran, R. Gillespie and W. Nolan (eds.), *Galway: history and society* (Dublin: Geography Publications, 1996), pp. 111, 114.

[112] For the earls' partial displacement by central officials, see McCavitt, *Sir Arthur Chichester*, pp. 105–8.

[113] *Ibid.*, 54. The friar's name was 'Richard Carrene alias John Woodlock'.

[114] TCD, MS 817, fol. 40.

Strabane, Co. Tyrone,[115] and the Gordons in Co. Cavan,[116] there were a handful of English Catholics to be found on plantation land. By far the most visible group of English recusants, remembered years later as all 'Roman Catholiques', seems to have been settled in Co. Cavan under the sponsorship of 'Mr De La Pole, an English Gentleman' who acquired an estate in the county sometime before 1641.[117] Co. Monaghan also had an English Catholic group, mainly in Monaghan town, but also at Eniskeane, Glaslough and Clones.[118]

Integration

Since many of the English Catholics first came to Ireland as soldiers or settlers, they might be expected to have had a strained relationship with the native population. Certainly, the antics of Sir Thomas Masterson in north Co. Wexford in April 1580, slaughtering sixty of the Kavanaghs who were under government protection, ensured he was perceived as an unprincipled aggressor, and unwelcome newcomer, by many Leinster Irish.[119] The same could be said of Francis Cosby and Robert Harpole, respectively the founders of the Cosbys of Stradbally and Harpoles of Shrule in Queen's County, who were hated by the Irish of the midlands, having been involved in the massacre of Mullaghmast and other frontier atrocities in Elizabethan times.[120] Other examples could be cited. Sir George Thornton, the founder of the Thorntons of Dunnaman, Co. Limerick, Henry Davells, the first of the Davells of Carlow, and several of the Bowens of Ballyadams, Queen's County:[121] all of these played a prominent part in the bloody transformation of Irish society between 1556 and 1603, their Catholicism seemingly no hindrance to their violent subjugation and dispossession of the Catholic Irish. Moreover, there is little evidence to suggest that the descendants of these men, despite being born and raised in Ireland, were in any way troubled by

---

[115] Michael Perceval-Maxwell, *Scottish migration to Ulster in the reign of James I* (Belfast: Ulster Historical Foundation, 1999), pp. 272.

[116] R. S., *Collection*, p. 4.   [117] *Ibid.*

[118] D. M. Schlegl, 'An index to the rebels of 1641 in the County Monaghan Depositions', *Clogher Record* 15/2 (1995), 69–89.

[119] B. C. Donovan, 'Tudor rule in Gaelic Leinster and the rise of Feagh McHugh O'Byrne', in C. O'Brien (ed.), *Feagh McHugh O'Byrne: the Wicklow firebrand* (Rathdrum: Rathdrum Historical Society, 1998), pp. 135–7.

[120] Vincent Carey, 'John Derricke's *Image of Irelande*, Sir Henry Sidney, and the massacre at Mullaghmast, 1578', *IHS* 31/123 (1999), 319–22.

[121] I will deal in greater detail with these in a book on martial law in Ireland, 1556–1641 (currently in preparation). For the general background see David Edwards, 'Ideology and experience: Spenser's *View* and martial law in Ireland', in Hiram Morgan (ed.), *Political ideology in Ireland, 1541–1641* (Dublin: Four Courts Press, 1999), pp. 127–57;

their forebears' actions. Rather, their predecessors' brutal exploits were if anything a source of familial pride, evidence of the martial valour that had conquered the country and earned their descendants privileged places in the new colonial order. Indeed, for some, involvement in further acts of dispossession during the early seventeenth century was a matter of maintaining family tradition. Thus, the plantation of north Wexford was largely the result of the actions of Sir Richard Masterson, son and heir of Sir Thomas. As provosts marshal of Leinster before 1623, Richard and John Bowen made the plantations of Wexford, Longford, and Ely O'Carroll possible by executing without trial opponents of the various schemes, by power of martial law.[122] Less dramatically, but equally revealing of the grasping colonial mentality of many of the New English Catholics, in the late 1630s Thomas Davells instigated proceedings to dispossess members of the O'Lawlor lineage, one of the banished 'seven septs of Laois', of such lands as they continued to occupy in Queen's County.[123]

Yet even those descended from the most notorious founding figures found it possible to integrate into Irish society. Despite a long history of violence towards native groups, 'borderers' such as the Mastersons had had of necessity to enter into contact with Irish lineages during the Elizabethan period, in order the better to establish their position as the new local rulers. Several married native women. Sir Thomas Masterson had married Katherine Clere, a native of Kilkenny, probably before 1564, after which he was joined in his military exploits by a gang of Gaelic and Anglo-Irish natives from the Kilkenny/Tipperary area comprised of Cleres, O'Brennans, Waddings, Clintons, O'Meaghers, Graces, O'Lonegans, Wales and Purcells.[124] In Munster, some of the original planters also married natives – for instance, Sir George Thornton, Oliver Stevenson and also Sir Nicholas Browne, the latter marrying a daughter of O'Sullivan Beare, as he put it, 'for my better strength and to maintain my own'.[125] The Wolverstones of Stillorgan, for many years responsible for policing part of the troublesome Dublin/Wicklow border, had (like

---

David Edwards, 'Beyond reform: martial law and the Tudor reconquest of Ireland', *History Ireland* 5/2 (1997), 16–21.

[122] Bodl. Carte MS 62, fol. 247. For state violence and the new plantations, see David Edwards, 'Legacy of defeat: the reduction of Gaelic Ireland after Kinsale', in Hiram Morgan (ed.), *The battle of Kinsale* (Dublin: Wordwell Publishers, 2004).

[123] Bodl., Carte MS 176, fol. 41r.

[124] St Kieran's College, Kilkenny: Carrigan MSS, vol. 21, unpaginated abstract of Katherine Clere's funeral entry, 1596; *Irish Fiants*, Eliz. I, nos. 618, 1305. In 1571, having settled permanently at Ferns, he recruited a new gang, chiefly of Wexfordmen, but the Cleres remained with him (*ibid.*, no. 1692).

[125] MacCarthy-Morrogh, *Munster plantation*, pp. 85–6, 133.

Sir Thomas Masterson) recruited most of their soldiers from the local
Gaelic population, and they intermarried with the O'Byrnes and the
Kavanaghs.[126]

Marriage with natives was equally widespread among those who
settled in less volatile regions. Within the Pale English Catholics often
married into the ranks of the medieval colonists, the Anglo-Irish. Take
Alderman James Jans. He was born in Dublin of an English father, from
Kent, and an Anglo-Irish mother, from Tobbersool. Married three
times, only his third and final wife was an Englishwoman, from a
Catholic family from the north of England. His two previous spouses
were, like his mother, Anglo-Irish gentlewomen from the Pale.[127] Before
his death in 1572, Henry Draycott, the founder of the Draycotts of
Mornington, Co. Meath, had arranged the marriage of his eldest son
and heir, John (aged 14), to a daughter of the influential knight, Sir
Christopher Barnewall of Turvey.[128] Thereafter the Draycotts quickly
established themselves as one of the leading families not just of Meath,
but of the Pale, and subsequent marriages saw them tie the knot with the
Plunketts, Lords Louth and the Dowdalls of Dundalk.[129] Plainly, being
Catholic made intermarriage with the Irish easier. Evidence concerning
the New English as a whole in sixteenth- and early seventeenth-century
Ireland suggests that their marriage patterns divided chiefly along religious rather than ethnic lines, with a relatively high number of English
Catholics intermarrying with the Anglo-Irish and Gaelic Irish, unlike
English Protestants, who, because native Protestants were so few, were
more inclined to marry mainly among themselves or in England.[130]

Marriage, of course, was the threshold to further integration. Testa-
mentary records of the period suggest that the extended family and
affinity networks of the New English Catholics were also ethnically
mixed. In particular, compared to New English Protestants, English
Catholic settlers were much more likely to have Anglo-Irish and Gaelic
people act as parties to the family trusts and deeds of conveyance.[131]
Two examples will have to suffice: in 1561 three of the four witnesses to

---

[126] E.g., *Irish Fiants*, Eliz. I, no. 1162; *CSPI, 1625–32*, 425; TCD, MS 809, fol. 286; Bodl.,
Carte MS 61, fol. 166r.
[127] Lennon, *Lords of Dublin*, p. 258.
[128] M. C. Griffith (ed.), *Calendar of inquisitions, Co. Dublin* (Dublin: Irish Manuscripts
Commission, 1991), pp. 212–15.
[129] *Funeral entries of Ireland*, pp. 109, 120.
[130] For an introduction to this subject, see Donald Jackson, *Intermarriage in Ireland, 1550–
1650* (Montreal: Cultural and Educational Productions, 1970).
[131] I am grateful to Julian Walton for allowing me to consult his copy of R. E. F. Garret's
catalogue of abstracts of Irish wills and administrations in the Prerogative Court of
Canterbury.

the last will and testament of the East Anglian Sir John Alen of St Wulfstan's, Co. Kildare, were Anglo-Irish (named Dillon, Bath and Ussher);[132] while in 1640 the Oxfordshire-born William Clarke, owning property in the Pale, named twenty-one people in his will, of whom five were Anglo-Irish (called Fleming and Hadsor) and one was Gaelic Irish (MacMahon).[133] The extent to which the New English Catholics 'went native' is difficult to determine. In a few isolated cases, hibernicisation occurred to a significant degree, especially in frontier areas, where settlers needed to learn the Gaelic language in order to carry out day-to-day business. Many of those who were born in Ireland of Irish mothers knew Gaelic, while others probably picked up a smattering of key words. The 1641 Depositions record instances of English Catholics intermingled with the Gaelic-speaking masses, indicating that communication was not a serious problem. For the most part, however, the English Catholics retained their cultural distinctiveness. They rarely adopted Gaelic-style sobriquets such as 'Mac', 'Oge' and 'Roe', in contrast to the Anglo-Irish, among whom such nicknames were commonplace. In truth, they probably had not been out of England long enough before 1641 – just one or two, sometimes three, generations – to experience any major dilution of their English culture. It is inappropriate, therefore, for historians to simply lump them in with the Anglo-Irish because they were Catholic.

The political fate of the New English Catholics is one of the most important things about them. For all their having played their part in the English recolonisation of Ireland, early in the seventeenth century, as Catholics, they began to suffer much the same treatment as the native population. As power was increasingly Protestantised, they were cut adrift. Like their Gaelic and Anglo-Irish coreligionists, they fell under suspicion because of their sheltering of priests, which (particularly in the years 1604–32) the state viewed as almost as serious as treason.[134] They were unable to evade the dreaded oath of supremacy, so that advancement in the crown service, both in central and local government, was closed to them;[135] worse, some even suffered dispossession because of

---

[132] PRO, PCC 28 Loftus.

[133] *Ibid.*, PCC 11 Fairfax. For another example, see Carrigan's abstract of the 1635 will of Vincent Knatchbull, making five bequests, two of which were to Gaelic natives of Kilkenny named Maddan and Ryan (St Kieran's College, Kilkenny: Carrigan MSS, vol. 83, unpaginated).

[134] In addition to the examples given above, see Bodl.,Carte MS 61, fol. 360, and Carte Ms 62, fols. 440–3, for the February 1618 examination of Marcus Draycott over his involvement with certain priests.

[135] E.g., following the replacement of Sir George Thornton as provost marshal of the province in 1604, and the resignation of Richard Marshall as justice, the personnel of the Munster presidency was all Protestant.

the oath, which prevented them in conscience from suing for livery of
their inheritance following the death of the head of the family.[136] Jury
service also became a cause of anxiety, because of the fines, imprison-
ments and forfeitures of property that would ensue if they refused to
'present', or try, their co-religionists in the county courts.[137] Like other
Catholics they felt let down by the collapse of 'the Graces' in 1628–9,
and angry over Lord Deputy Wentworth's false promise of better times
made before the parliament of 1634.[138] Some became involved in
unrest: for example, in Co. Dublin and Co. Kilkenny several English
Catholics refused to pay Wentworth's subsidy in 1636;[139] more omin-
ously, in north Wexford English and Gaelic Catholics joined together in
attacks on Protestant settlers in November 1637.[140] As students of
politics know only too well, nothing unites like a common enemy.
Whatever their level of integration with Irish neighbours, by autumn
1641 the New English Catholics were as one with Anglo-Irish and Gaelic
'papists' in fearing the worst as 'the Puritan faction' grew in strength after
Wentworth's downfall. Unless something was done to reverse the trend
Ireland might become as uncomfortable for Catholicism as England.

1641

The Ulster rebellion of October 1641 caused the Protestant government
to address anew the problem of English Catholics moving freely about
the country. It was suspected that the Ulster revolt was but a curtain-
raiser for a general papist uprising all across the British Isles. Responding
to the news from Ulster, and convinced that evil was afoot, on 1 November the House of Commons at Westminster issued an order recalling
home 'all Papists of quality yt have estates in England and have repaired
to Ireland', on pain of confiscation of their estates.[141] Such was the level of
panic and confusion in official circles that it is difficult to discern which
came first – the notion of English Catholic collusion with the Ulster
rebels, or the supposedly corroborative evidence that individual English
Catholics were indeed behaving suspiciously. The Northamptonshire

---

[136] E.g., Richard Stevenson, son of the Munster planter Oliver, who was dispossessed of
Dunmoylin, Co. Limerick, in April 1615. To regain it, he had to purchase it back from
the crown grantee: Griffith (ed.), *Calendar of inquisitions*, p. 412.
[137] Aidan Clarke and R. D. Edwards, 'Pacification, plantation and the Catholic Question,
1603–23', *NHI*, III, pp. 187–232.
[138] Clarke, *Old English*, pp. 75–152; Aidan Clarke, *The Graces, 1625–41* (Dublin: Dublin
Historical Association, 1968).
[139] NAI, Ferguson MSS, vol. 12: Equity Exchequer Orders, 1618–38, 285, 301, 305.
[140] BL, Harleian MS 430, fol. 406.   [141] Bodl., Carte MS 68, fol. 345v.

Catholic Luke Marriott was a case in point. On 23 October, 'being lieutenant of a company of souldiers . . . licensed to goe for Spaine', he was aboard a ship in Dublin harbour waiting for permission to sail with his men when news broke of the rebellion and the arrest of Lord Maguire. According to an eyewitness, immediately on hearing the news Marriott and several of the company 'were for joining the rebels'.[142] It was further alleged that Marriott said he hoped 'to doe any hurt to the Protestants' that he could, that he boasted how 'he would make them [the Protestants] smoke', and that it would be 'a good deede to cutt their throats'.[143]

Until the latter part of November, such evidence as the government considered about the possibility of English Catholic collusion with the Irish rebels was all of a like sort – isolated reports of individual Englishmen bringing suspicion on themselves through dangerous talk and bravado. For their part, with rumours flying of government-sanctioned atrocities against Catholics in the south during October and November, the English Catholics were forced to choose between loyalty to their country of origin or their religion. From late November on it seems the majority chose religion. It is well known that by Christmas 1641 and throughout the early months of 1642 the Protestant government began to collect and assemble detailed reports of the losses incurred by Protestant settlers around the country as a result of the rebellion – the 1641 Depositions. What is not so well known is that for most counties outside Ulster the names of English Catholics appear in the lists of rebels. This may seem odd, given that some Irish historians have argued that 1641 was essentially an ethnic conflict between English and Irish, colonisers and colonised.[144] Moreover, the oddity of there being English Catholic rebels in Ireland seems all the stranger when it is noted that, in a few places, the Irish rebels attacked English Catholic as well as English Protestant settlers.[145] It is important, however, to distinguish between what were only exceptional cases and the general trend in Ireland, which was towards a purely religious war.[146] In most areas inhabited by English Catholics the Irish did *not* attack them, a fact that did not go unnoticed by their less fortunate Protestant neighbours.

[142] TCD, MS 809, fol. 129r.
[143] These alleged quotations were put to him during his examination (*ibid.*, fol. 131r).
[144] B. I. Bradshaw, 'The invention of the Irish: was the Ulster Rising really a bolt from the blue?', *Times Literary Supplement* (14 October. 1994), 8–10.
[145] TCD, MS 814, fol. 264r.
[146] N. P. Canny, 'Religion, politics and the Irish Rising of 1641', *Religion and Rebellion: Historical Studies XX* (UCD Press, Dublin 1997), pp. 40–68.

The Depositions record how in many parts of southern Ireland English Protestant colonists were robbed, even killed, by armed groups including English Catholic colonists. In Co. Dublin, for instance, Protestants living at Terenure and Coolock were attacked by groups of rebels that included English Catholics such as Edward Parker, John Woodfield and John Hayward,[147] while on the Dublin/Wicklow border, the yeoman John Woodfen served in the O'Toole forces that attacked a Protestant settler near Rathfarnham.[148] There was a similar pattern in Queen's County. On different occasions over Christmas 1641 and early 1642 English Protestants were beset by rebel forces commanded by the colonists William Cosby and Francis Barrington, and an English tenant farmer living on the outskirts of Maryborough was robbed by Thomas Davells of Ballykide and his Gaelic accomplices.[149] A little later, when Ballyleman Castle, the government stronghold, was besieged, the besiegers included Sir John Bowen of Ballyadams and other New English Catholics such as Thomas Smyth of Water Castle, Richard Glascock and several of the Hetheringtons.[150] In Co. Roscommon, Anthony Brabazon of Ballinasloe was to the fore among those who laid siege to Athlone Castle. Some of the most violent confrontations between New English elements occurred in Co. Limerick, where Catholic forces commanded by the planters Oliver Stevenson and William Collum besieged Castle Matrix for six months from January to August 1642, and hanged a number of its English Protestant defenders when the siege was over.[151] English Catholics were said to have killed English Protestants in other parts of the country. The murder of ten Protestants at Graiguenamanagh, Co. Kilkenny, on the night of 2–3 May 1642 was associated (not necessarily accurately) with Colonel Walter Bagenal of Dunleckny,[152] while William Harpole of Shrule was reputedly present at the hanging of English Protestant prisoners in Co. Carlow.[153] It is impossible to know for certain how many English Catholics participated in the revolt; geographically, the depositions are too patchy to supply a reliable estimate. All that can safely be said is that Englishmen comprised a significant minority of named rebels, somewhere between 5 per cent and 8 per cent, depending upon region.[154] In addition, there is no doubt that in the upper strata of society, among the gentry, lists of officers of the Catholic

---

[147] TCD, MS 809, fols. 278, 280.   [148] *Ibid.*, fol. 294.
[149] *Ibid.*, MS 815, fols. 13r, 21v, 60v.   [150] *Ibid.*, fols. 62v–64v.
[151] TCD, MS 822, fols. 190r–191v.   [152] Edwards, *Ormond Lordship*, pp. 323–4.
[153] Bodl., Carte MS 67, fols. 18v–19r.
[154] E.g., of 388 known rebels in Co. Monaghan, approximately 20 were English Catholics (*c.* 5.25 per cent), while in Co. Kilkenny there were 11 English rebels named out of a total of 162 (*c.* 7 per cent): Schlegel, 'An index'; TCD, MS 812, fols. 165–85.

rebel forces read like a who's who of English Catholics in Ireland: in Dublin and Wicklow the Wolverstones were prominent commanders, in Carlow the Bagenals were to the fore, in Limerick it was the Stevensons, in Cork the Slingsbys, in Wexford the Colcloughs, and so on. From top to bottom the Irish Catholic rebellion of 1641 was partly English. So too was the Catholic Confederation that succeeded it. Catholic New Englishmen were present at every level of the Confederate movement. In the General Assembly convened in Kilkenny after October 1642 one of their number, James Tuchet, third earl of Castlehaven, sat in the Lords, while at least eight English Catholics (Robert Harpole, John Allen, Walter Bagenal, Henry Slingsby, Anthony Colclough, George Green, Francis Wolverstone and William Young) sat in the Commons.[155]

Conclusion

If the foregoing study reveals anything about life as it was lived in early modern Ireland, it is surely that religion and ethnicity were unequal partners in the forging of group identities in the country. For the best part of a century, from 1540 to 1640, English Catholics coming to Ireland seem to have felt they had less to fear from, and more in common with, Irish Catholics, than English Protestants. Politics were primarily about religion, not race; nationalism, while certainly a contributory factor in events, was increasingly confessional in form, not ethnic. The existence of so many New English Catholics in Kilkenny after 1642, active at the very heart of the Confederate Irish government, indicates how the early modern concept of *patria* was far less ethnically derived than its modern successor. Scholars may emphasise 'faith and fatherland' as the emerging political ideology of the time, but clearly 'faith' came first, and it did so by a considerable distance. So dominant was it, indeed, that it was able to close the potentially enormous distance separating colonisers from the very natives they colonised, and make them natural allies as coreligionists. It is difficult to think of a parallel situation anywhere else in the history of British or European colonial societies.

---

[155] Micheál Ó Siochrú, *Confederate Ireland, 1642–1649* (Dublin: Irish Academic Press, 1999), pp. 256–8.

6 The Irish historical renaissance and the shaping of Protestant history

Alan Ford

The later sixteenth and early seventeenth centuries were marked by an outpouring of historical work about Ireland. From Holinshed's *Chronicles of England, Scotland and Ireland* in 1577, to the publication of the lifetime's labours of Colgan and the Irish Franciscan hagiographers from 1645, the writing of history was at the forefront of Irish scholarship. Indeed, such was the scale of intellectual endeavour that this period can justly be designated the Irish historical renaissance, the beginning of the investigation of Ireland's past using recognisably modern scholarly methods.

The intellectual currents which nourished this dramatic growth can easily be outlined. An essential foundation was provided by the medieval method of annalistic compilation, together with the antiquarian instinct for unearthing manuscripts and artefacts, both of which helped to establish essential facts and chronologies without which history could not have been written. The methodological breakthrough in identifying and analysing original sources was provided by Renaissance humanism, with its determination to return *ad fontes*.[1] More specific to Irish scholarship were the professional historians, poets, brehons and scribes who sought to maintain the vitality of the Gaelic historical tradition with its rich inheritance of genealogies, annals and saints' lives, and the distinctive form of Anglo-Irish colonial historiography created by that master of racial stereotyping, the twelfth-century Welsh historian, Giraldus Cambrensis.[2] And, finally, there were two crucial driving forces common

---

[1] Antonia Gransden, *Historical writing in England: c.1307 to the early sixteenth century* (London: Routledge, 1982); Graham Parry, *Trophies of time: English antiquarians of the seventeenth century* (Oxford: Oxford University, 1995); D. R. Woolf, *The idea of history in early Stuart England* (Toronto: University of Toronto Press, 1990); F. S. Fussner, *The historical revolution: English historical writing and thought, 1580–1640* (London: Routledge, 1962); F. J. Levy, *Tudor historical thought* (San Marino: Huntingdon Library, 1967).

[2] For a summary of the traditional Irish sources available to a seventeenth-century Irish historian, see Bernadette Cunningham, *The world of Geoffrey Keating* (Dublin: Four

across all European nations: the growing sense of patriotic pride which
led scholars to try and defend and glorify their native land and its past;
and the polemical historiography of the reformation and the counter-
reformation, inspired by each side's determination to establish its own
exclusive historical legitimacy.[3] Identifying the mutual dependence, and
independence, of these various factors is made more difficult in the case
of Ireland by the lack of any clear chronology of the key intellectual
movements, since the reformation and counter-reformation, arguably,
took place at virtually the same time.[4] Rather than engaging upon the
difficult task of sorting out the complex horizontal interrelationships
between movements which are, in any case, of limited explanatory value
in the Irish context, it is easier and more useful to construct a vertical or
linear account of Irish historiography by concentrating on a particular
strand, in this case confessional history.[5] The late sixteenth and early
seventeenth centuries saw the emergence of two competing religious
traditions, whose power and persistence – right down to the twentieth
century – are evident in the way they appropriated and reduced even the
most apparently recondite of subjects to a matter of sectarian pride,
where scholarly conclusions were shaped by confessional allegiance,
opponents being dismissed as lying heretics, coreligionists *ipso facto*
trusted as sound.[6] Tracing the origins and early development of these
competing traditions has the potential to clarify a complex nexus of
issues in early modern Irish history relating to religion, community and
identity. On the Catholic side, two leading early modern historians,
Richard Stanihurst and Geoffrey Keating, have been identified as instru-
mental in the creation of a colligatory sense of national feeling; the work
of Irish martyrologists from the late sixteenth-century has been highlighted as creating a narrative of shared suffering which decisively influenced the self-image of Irish Catholics; and the efflorescence in Irish

---

Courts, 2000), ch. 4, and Nollaig Ó Muraíle, *The celebrated antiquary Dubhaltach Mac Fhirbhisigh (c.1600–1671)* (Maynooth: An Sagart, 1996), ch. 11; Michael Richter, *Giraldus Cambrensis* (Aberystwyth: National Library of Wales, 1976); Robert Bartlett, *Gerald of Wales* (Oxford: Clarendon Press, 1982).

[3] For a helpful general discussion of the intellectual elements involved in the creation of modern historiography see D. R. Kelley, 'Johann Sleidan and the origins of history as a profession', *Journal of Modern History* 52 (1980), 573–4.

[4] See Introduction, pp. 5f.

[5] I have sketched the development of confesional history in ' "Standing one's ground": religion, polemic and Irish history since the reformation', in Alan Ford, James McGuire and Kenneth Milne (eds.), *As by law established; the Church of Ireland since the reformation* (Dublin: Lilliput, 1995), pp. 1–14.

[6] Canice Mooney, 'Father John Colgan O.F.M., his work and times and literary milieu', in Terence O'Donnell (ed.), *Father John Colgan O.F.M., 1592–1658* (Dublin: Assisi Press, 1959), pp. 35–7.

hagiography in the early seventeenth century was used to define the uninterrupted heritage of Irish Catholicism dating back to the second century AD, enabling Ireland to be seen as 'a distinct religious and cultural entity, united by allegiance to "national" patrons'.[7] The purpose of this investigation, however, is to examine the other side of the coin – to identify when a distinctively Protestant historiography emerged, where its intellectual roots lay and how it contributed to the creation of Irish Protestant religious and national identities.

I

The origins of Irish Protestant historiography lie, paradoxically, in the intertwined works of two notable Catholics, Stanihurst, and his 'fast & sure friend' Edmund Campion.[8] Stanihurst was the son of a prominent Anglo-Irish family. He studied at Oxford and the Inns of Court in London, acquiring in the process a sound training in the humanities.[9] In 1570 he returned to Ireland and was joined there by his fellow Oxford scholar, Edmund Campion, whose doubts about the Elizabethan settlement eventually led him to abandon a promising academic career to join the Jesuit order.[10] Campion stayed with the Stanihursts until mid-1571, when the threat of arrest forced him to flee Ireland. But before he left he had compiled the first complete English history of Ireland, relying upon his hosts' library, his own historical and geographical knowledge, manuscripts provided by local gentry, official records and, where written sources broke down, oral history.[11]

---

[7] Thomas O'Connor, 'Towards the invention of the Irish Catholic *Natio*: Thomas Messingham's *Florilegium* (1624)', *Irish Theological Quarterly* 64 (1999), 174; Cunningham, *Geoffrey Keating*; P. J. Corish, 'The Irish martyrs and Irish history', *Archivium Hibernicum* 47 (1993), 89–93; Clodagh Tait, 'Adored for saints: Catholic martyrdom in Ireland c.1560–1655', *Journal of Early Modern History* 5 (2001), 128–59; Alan Ford, 'Martyrdom, history and memory in early modern Ireland', in Ian McBride (ed.), *History and memory in modern Ireland* (Cambridge: Cambridge University Press 2001), pp. 43–66; Bernadette Cunningham and Raymond Gillespie, '"The most adaptable of saints": the cult of St Patrick in the seventeenth century', *Archivium Hibernicum* 49 (1995), 82–104.

[8] Barnaby Rich, *A new description of Ireland: wherein is described the disposition of the Irish whereunto they are inclined, etc.* (London: 1610), p. 2.

[9] Colm Lennon, 'Richard Stanihurst (1547–1618) and Old English identity', *IHS* 21 (1979), 121–43; Colm Lennon, *Richard Stanihurst the Dubliner 1547–1618* (Dublin: Irish Academic Press, 1981).

[10] T. M. McCoog (ed.), *The reckoned expense: Edmund Campion and the early English Jesuits* (Woodbridge: Boydell, 1996).

[11] A. F. Vossen (ed.), *Two bokes of the histories of Ireland compiled by Edmunde Campion* (Assen: van Gorcum, 1963), pp. 13–78.

The result, *Two bokes of the histories of Ireland*, was not published until 1633, but it lurked behind the three sections on Ireland which appeared in 1577 as part of Raphael Holinshed's famous *Chronicles of England, Scotland and Ireland*.[12] Holinshed himself related how, whilst searching for an authoritative, indeed any, account of Ireland to add to his collections on England and Scotland, he was given a copy of Campion's manuscript, which he set about adapting to produce *The historie of Irelande* from earliest times to 1509. Holinshed then had another piece of good fortune, coming across Richard Stanihurst, who had come to England again, this time to look after the further education of the son of the earl of Kildare. Stanihurst provided two further pieces for the *Chronicles*: a continuation of *The historie* covering the reign of Henry VIII, and a *Description of Irelande*, loosely based upon Campion.[13]

The Irish section of the *Chronicles* laid one of the foundations for the study of Irish history in the early modern period. It represented the application to Irish history of the humanist ideals and tools which had become commonplace in the hands of other European historians.[14] Two obvious tests can be posed for the application of these skills to Irish sources in this and other works of early modern history: first, how did they handle the first inhabitants of Ireland – those wonderful but frustrating early Irish origin myths; and second, what did they make of the conversion of Ireland and the role of St Patrick. The plethora of invasions and mythical stories and characters, most notably brought together in the various versions of the *Leabhar Gabhála*, and popularised by Giraldus Cambrensis, were immensely attractive to Irish historians: they filled in the yawning gap before written records began; and they provided the modern Irish with a noble ancestry that gave them, like other European nations, respectable biblical roots. St Patrick was of even greater symbolic importance as the heroic founding father of Christian Ireland, whose life and achievements were elaborated and expanded by Muirchú, Tirechán and countless other later hagiographers and biographers. Both provided a classic challenge for humanist historians, of distinguishing myth from fact, original from later sources.

---

[12] Raphaell Holinshed, *The chronicles of England, Scotland and Ireland. The history of Ireland from the first inhabitation thereof, unto the year 1509. Collected by Raphaell Holinshed, and continued till the year 1547 by Richard Stanyhurst* (London, 1577); Levy, *Tudor historical thought*, pp. 182–6.

[13] Holinshed (ed.), *History of Ireland*, dedication by Holinshed to Sir Henry Sidney.

[14] Peter Burke, *The Renaissance sense of the past* (London: Arnold, 1970), p. 1; Campion's use of official records broke important new ground: Colm Lennon, 'Edmund Campion's *Histories of Ireland* and reform in Tudor Ireland', in McCoog (ed.), *The reckoned expense*, p. 69.

The three Irish pieces in the *Chronicles* were, of course, far from perfect in their response to these challenges – this was, after all, the *beginning* of modern Irish historical scholarship. Campion had no Irish, and was therefore unable to use Gaelic sources.[15] But he did display a shrewd critical sense in trying to sort through the pre-history of Ireland. He dismissed the account of the first inhabitants of Ireland popularised by Giraldus as a 'fable not only false but also impossible'.[16] But Campion also included much that modern historians would categorise as mythological, as in his peopling of Ireland with giants, and his belief that Gurguntius, King of Britain, had included Ireland in his dominions.[17] Stanihurst is even more credulous, on occasion restoring some of the fabulous elements that the more rigorous Campion omitted or rejected.[18]

The *Chronicles*, though, were more than just the first printed renaissance history of Ireland. They also contained another ideological subtext, being a notable example of what might be termed, at the risk of anachronism, the English imperialist approach to Irish history.[19] The founding father of this school was Giraldus Cambrensis, who wrote two works on Ireland, the *Topographia*, a *National Enquirer* style description of Irish geography, people and wonders, and the *Expugnatio*, which provided a shrewd and valuable account of the Anglo-Norman invasion of Ireland. Not surprisingly, his work proved popular, both in England – where extracts were included in some of the earliest printed books – and in Ireland where it was translated into English and circulated in manuscript copies.[20] Giraldus viewed the Irish as an interesting, almost quaint, race, but one which was fatally flawed by its backwardness: 'All their habits are the habits of barbarians.'[21]

---

[15] See his ambiguous dismissal of the 'Iryshe chronicles' as 'freight of lewde examples, idle tales, and genealogies', 'yet concernyng the state of that wilde people, specially before the Conquest, I am perswaded that with choise and judgement I might have sucked thence some better store of matter, and gladly wold have sought them, had I fownd an interpretour, or understode their toungue': Vossen (ed.) *Two bokes*, p. [6].

[16] *Ibid.*, p. [26].

[17] *Ibid.*, p. [34].

[18] *Ibid.*, p. 67.

[19] John Gillingham, 'Images of Ireland, 1170–1600: the origins of English imperialism', *History Today* 27 (1987), 16–22; John Gillingham, 'The beginnings of English imperialism', *Journal of Historical Sociology* 5 (1992), 392–409.

[20] Campion when writing his history at the Stanihursts obtained two different copies from neighbouring Anglo-Irish families: Vossen (ed.), *Two bokes*, p. 75; Ralph Higden in his monumental *Polychronicon*, used Giraldus' *Topographia*: Gransden, *Historical writing in England*, p. 48.

[21] Gerald of Wales, *The history and topography of Ireland*, (ed.), J. J. O'Meara (Harmondsworth: Penguin, 1982), pp. 102–3.

This sense of superiority is Giraldus' most notable and notorious contribution to Irish history. The confidence and vigour of his judgements more than offset his limited acquaintance with Ireland, and ensured that his views became the received wisdom of the subsequent colonial tradition, shaping the attitudes not only of the descendants of the Anglo-Normans, the Anglo-Irish, but also the outlook of those later invaders, the new-English settlers of the early modern era. For Giraldus not only confirmed their cultural superiority, he also, by justifying the Norman invasion of the twelfth century, proleptically sanctioned the completion of the conquest 400 years later. Thus in the *Expugnatio* he provided a series of reasons supporting the English claim to Ireland: he cites Gurguntius, and adds the story that King Arthur had ruled Ireland (both from Geoffrey of Monmouth); he points out that Ireland was originally peopled from Bayonne, part of the English province of Gascony; that the Irish kings had voluntarily submitted to Henry II; and, finally, he adduces that controversial papal endorsement of English rule in Ireland, *Laudabiliter.*[22] And when in 1569 the Act of Attainder of Shane O'Neill was drawn up, it was to Giraldus that the drafters, like Campion and Stanihurst after them, turned to provide an historical underpinning for English rule.[23]

The Irish histories of Campion, Stanihurst and Holinshed's *Chronicles*, then, relied heavily upon Giraldus and shared two essential ideological assumptions: the rightfulness of the English claim to rule Ireland; and the superiority of English to Irish civilisation.[24] They do not, though, demonstrate any strong denominational or sectarian religious commitment. Campion and Stanihurst can almost certainly be described broadly as Catholics when they wrote their histories. But their precise religious position at that stage in their lifelong journey from conformity to the counter-reformation is impossible to identify.[25] The histories can

---

[22] Giraldus Cambrensis, *Expugnatio Hibernica*, (ed.), A. B. Scott and F. X. Martin (Dublin: Royal Irish Academy, 1978), p. 149.

[23] Richard Bolton (ed.), *The statutes of Ireland* (Dublin, 1621), pp. 315ff.

[24] There was, of course, a marked difference in emphasis between Giraldus, a visitor to Ireland, and Stanihurst, proud to term himself an Irishman. The latter specifically aimed large parts of his description against the Gerald-like slanders of 'Alan Cope', an English author whose jaundiced view of Ireland was summed up in his verdict that the only venemous beasts there were its people. In a work published in 1584, *De rebus in Hibernia gestis*, Stanihurst published a further description of Ireland, together with an account of the Norman invasion, which was again heavily dependent upon Giraldus, but at the same time omitted some of the Welshman's more negative comments: Richard Stanihurst, *De rebus in Hibernia gestis libri quattuor. Richard Stanihurst accessit his libris Hibernicarum rerum appendix ex Silvestro Giraldo Cambrensi pervetusto scriptore collecta cum eiusdem Stanihursti adnotationibus* (Antwerp, 1584).

[25] Vossen (ed.), *Two bokes*, pp. 4–11; Lennon, *Stanihurst the Dubliner*, pp. 125–6.

best be described as religiously dispassionate. Campion was happy to stress Ireland's medieval allegiance to the papacy, but his references to the reformation, like those of Stanihurst, were terse and neutral.[26] This may of course have been a product of self-censorship (and the history of Holinshed's publication would amply justify such caution); what we are left with, for whatever reason, is two classic examples of the application of humanist methodology to Irish history.[27]

II

The contrast between 'humanist innocence and evangelical commitment' becomes abundantly apparent when first and second editions of the *Chronicles* are compared.[28] By the time a new edition appeared in 1587 Campion had been executed as a Catholic martyr and Stanihurst was a counter-reformation exile, so the task of revising the sections on Ireland fell to a very different author. John Hooker was a native of Exeter and notable historian of Devon. Educated at Oxford and on mainland Europe, his early intellectual ambitions were stymied by marriage: being 'dryven to take a wyffe, and then all his desyres and zeale to learnynge and knowledge therewith abated'.[29] But he more than made up for this in later life. Through his connection with the local Carew family, he came to Ireland in 1568, where he served as an MP, and began to develop his antiquarian skills by studying Irish history. On his return to England after the death of Sir Peter Carew in 1575 he was an obvious choice to help edit the new edition of the *Chronicles*. Leaving Holinshed's and Stanihurst's histories of Ireland untouched, he added two new sections: the first was a rather good translation of Giraldus' *Expugnatio*, the second a continuation of Stanihurst's history from the end of Henry VIII's reign to 1586. In both of these, Hooker's strong commitment to the reformation and his New-English perspective are apparent. This, for the first time, is Irish history seen through Protestant eyes.

In the dedication to his fellow Devonian, Sir Walter Raleigh, Hooker touched upon two linked, and strongly Protestant, themes to which he regularly returned. The first was the way in which God, through his providential judgements in history reinforced the biblical requirement,

---

[26] Vossen (ed.), *Two bokes*, pp. [42]–[46], [72], [133]–[135].
[27] C. S. Clegg, *Press censorship in Elizabethan England* (Cambridge: Cambridge University Press, 1997), ch. 7; Annabel Patterson, *Reading Holinshed's Chronicles* (Chicago: University of Chicago Press, 1995).
[28] The quotation is from Kelley, 'Sleidan', 581.
[29] Quoted in May McKisack, *Medieval history in the Tudor age* (Oxford: Clarendon Press, 1971), p. 128.

so firmly expounded by Luther and his English followers, that subjects must obey their monarch as a divinely appointed ruler. English history, Hooker insisted, taught important lessons about morality and behaviour.

I would to God I might or were able to saie the like, or the halfe like, of Ireland, a countrie, the more barren of good things, the more replenished with actions of bloud, murther, and lothsome outrages; which to anie good reader are greevous and irkesome to be read and considered, much more for anie man to pen and set downe in writing, and to reduce into an historie.[30]

This, he goes on, explains both the lack of any histories of Ireland, and his own initial reluctance to undertake one. And, indeed, when he began to write, he 'found no matter of an history worthy to be recorded: but rather a tragedy of cruelties to be abhorred, and no historie of good things to be followed'.[31]

Closer examination, however, uncovered a providential pattern in recent Irish events, which revealed the 'great and wonderous workes of God, both of his severe judgement against traitors, rebels, and disobedient; and of his mercie and loving kindnesse upon the obedient and dutifull'.[32] There were, of course, examples in English history of the foolishness of rebellion against divinely appointed kings (Hooker had experienced the 1549 Prayer Book rebellion in Devon), but 'none to be compared to this tragicall discourse of Ireland, and the most unnaturall wars of the Desmonds against hir sacred majestie. Whose disobedience the Lord hath . . . so severlie punished and revenged, as the like hath not in our age been seen nor knowne.'[33]

But Hooker's explanation for the Desmond risings went much further than God's just punishment of traitors. He also introduced into Irish history a second distinctively Protestant idea by placing such events into a new overarching framework – the apocalyptic struggle between Christ and Antichrist. The idea that the apocalyptic books of the Bible could be read as containing hidden clues as to the operation of the forces of good and evil, Christ and Antichrist in the present and the immediate future, was one which became closely associated with Protestant reformers. Luther and Melanchthon on the continent, and John Bale and John Foxe in England, saw their task as working out how the biblical prophecies were being worked out in history. The challenge was made all the more urgent by the parallel conviction that history was rapidly drawing

[30] Raphaell Holinshed, *The first and second volumes of chronicles, comprising 1 The description and historie of England, 2 The description and historie of Ireland, 3 The description and historie of Scotland*, 2nd edn (London, 1587), II, Dedication to Sir Walter Raleigh, sig. Aii verso.
[31] Ib.   [32] Ib.   [33] Ib.

to a close, as the end of the world drew nigh.[34] Hooker set about placing
the events of his history in this framework. Thus Giraldus' positive view
of the papacy was replaced by a negative, Protestant one.[35] The fourth
Lateran Council of 1215 was a step in the advancement of 'the Romish
antichrist'.[36] Thomas á Becket, treated as a holy martyr by Giraldus and
by the post-reformation Catholic writers, was cast in an entirely different
light by Hooker, who omitted the section in *Expugnatio* which dealt with
his martyrdom, and referred readers instead to that classic text of the
Protestant apocalyptic, Foxe's Book of Martyrs.[37] And finally, the Desmond rising was seen as the most recent manifestation of the ongoing
struggle between the forces of Christ and Antichrist.[38] Rebellion in
Ireland was therefore transformed from a political into a religious act,
with Catholics now portrayed as pawns of Antichrist in his nefarious
plan to defeat the forces of light.

Not only did Hooker identify Irish Catholics as Antichristian, he also
casually discarded the distinction, carefully maintained by Stanihurst,
between the loyal Anglo-Irish and the rebellious native Irish. Stanihurst
had gone to great lengths to emphasise the continuing faithfulness to
king and country of his patrons, the Fitzgeralds, even though this involved him in contortions when explaining the revolt of Silken Thomas.
Hooker had little time or sympathy for such tergiversations, fusing
Anglo-Irish and native Irish together in their Catholicism and rebelli-
ousness by dismissing the Geraldines as having been a noble family
whilst they remained true to the English monarchy: 'but when they
leaving English government, liked the loose life of that viperous nation,
then they brought in coine and liverie, and a number of manie other Irish
and divelish impositions, which . . . in the end will be the overthrow of all

[34] R. A. Bauckham, *Tudor apocalypse* (Appleford: Courtenay, 1978); Paul Christianson, *Reformers and Babylon* (Toronto: University of Toronto Press, 1978); K. R. Firth, *The apocalyptic tradition in reformation Britain 1530–1645* (Oxford: Oxford University Press, 1979).

[35] Another near-contemporary Protestant translator of the *Expugnatio*, Richard Robinson, challenged the pope's right to grant Ireland to Henry II: Hiram Morgan, 'Giraldus Cambransis and the Tudor conquest of Ireland', in Hiram Morgan (ed.), *Political ideology in Ireland, 1541–1641* (Dublin: Four Courts, 1999), p. 28.

[36] Holinshed, *Chronicles* (1587), II, *The conquest of Ireland*, p. 48.

[37] *Ibid.*, p. 16; Hooker also left out two of Thomas á Becket's prophecies: J. S. Brewer, J. F. Dimock and G. F. Warner (eds.), *Giraldi Cambrensis opera*, 4 vols. (London, 1861), V, p. lxxix; for an Irish Catholic view of Beckett, see Stephen White, *Apologia pro Hibernia adversus Cambri calumnias* (Dublin, 1849), p. 114; Hooker was here following the pattern set early in the English reformation of identifying Becket as a traitor rather than a saint: R. E. Scully, 'The unmaking of a saint: Thomas Becket and the English reformation', *Catholic Historical Review* 86 (2000), 579–602.

[38] Holinshed, *Chronicles* (1587), II, *The conquest of Ireland*, p. 183; I intend to examine the development of early modern Irish Protestant apocalyptic in more detail elsewhere.

their houses and families'.[39] In sum, Hooker's translation of the *Expugnatio* provided those engaged in the early modern conquest of the country with a standard source which reinforced their sense of superiority over the native inhabitants, Irish and Anglo-Irish alike.[40] He thus helped transform Giraldus from an Anglo-Irish into a New-English historian and the *Expugnatio* from a medieval Catholic to an early modern Protestant, even apocalyptic, text.[41]

Similar undercurrents can be traced beneath the most famous example of early modern English writing about Ireland – Edmund Spenser's *View of the present state of Ireland*. Part polemic, part learned discourse, the 'clinical ruthlessness' of the *View's* prescriptions for Ireland have created serious problems of scholarly interpretation; was this a humanist reform programme, a Machiavellian master-plan or a violent cry of despair? For our purposes, it is sufficient that Spenser demonstrates a serious and subtle interest in the Irish past: 'Above all, the *View* is a history.'[42] And, in his treatment of the history, it seems at first that Spenser shared both Hooker's apocalyptic framework and Giraldus', Campion's and Stanihurst's negative evaluation of all things Irish. Indeed, Spenser at times seemed to argue for the simple extirpation of native culture and its replacement by 'English civility'.[43]

But there are nuances. Eudoxus not unexpectedly dismisses the reliability of the accounts which the native Irish sources gave of the early history of Ireland:

howe can theare be anie truthe in them at all since the auncient nations which firste inhabited Ireland were alltogither destitute of lettres muche more of learninge by which they might leave the veritie of thinges written, And those bardes comynge alsoe soe manie hundred yeris after, could not knowe what was done in former ages owr deliuer certentye of anie thinge but what they fayned out of their owne heades.[44]

---

[39] Holinshed, *Chronicles* (1587), II, *The conquest of Ireland*, p. 42.
[40] Andrew Hadfield, 'Briton and Scythian: Tudor representations of Irish origins', *IHS* 28 (1993), 390–408; Andrew Hadfield, *Edmund Spenser's Irish experience: wilde fruit and savage soyl* (Oxford: Clarendon Press, 1997), pp. 94–5.
[41] This transformation was not to everyone's taste: Barnaby Rich lumped Stanihurst, Campion and Giraldus together as 'Papists' and 'lying authorities': see below, n. 59.
[42] G. E. McLean, 'Spenser's territorial history: book V of the *Faerie Queene* and *A view of the present state of Ireland*', unpublished Ph.D. thesis, University of Arizona (1986), p. 66.
[43] Edmund Spenser, 'A view of the present state of Ireland', Gonville and Caius College Library MS 188/221, p. 145 (transcribed by Andrew Zurcher at http://www.english.cam.ac.uk/ceres/haphazard/vewe/veweindex.html); Rudolf Gottfried (ed.), *The works of Edmund Spenser, a variorum edition, the prose works*, 11 vols. (Baltimore, 1932–49), p. ix.
[44] Spenser, 'A view', Gonville and Caius MS 188/221, p. 49; Gottfried (ed.), *Prose works*, p. 87.

His conversation partner, Irenius, accepts that ancient tradition is slippery and unreliable, but goes on rather surprisingly:

yett for the auncientnesse of the written cronickles of the Irishe geive me leave to saye some thinge not to iustifye them but to shewe that some of them might saye truthe. For where ye saye that the Irishe haue allwaies beene withowte lettres ye are therin muche deceyved. For it is certeine that Ireland hathe hadd the use of lettres very aunciently and longe before England.[45]

Again, Eudoxus acts as *provocateur*, seeking to problematise the whole question of the sources for the earliest history of Ireland:

yea doe verie bouldly Irenius adventure vppon the history of soe auncient tymes and leane to confidently vnto those Irishe cronicles which are most fabulous and forged in that oute of them ye dare take in hand to laie open the originall of a nation soe antique, as that noe monyment remayneth of her begyninge and inhabitinge, here speciallie havinge bene allwaies withowt lettres but only bare tradicion of tymes & remembrances of bardes which vse to forge and falsefie every thinge as they liste to please or displease anie man . . .[46]

Such a full-frontal assault on the native historical tradition fits, of course, with Spenser's disdain for things Irish. But Irenius' reply is, again, more thoughtful:

Trulie I must confesse I doe soe, but yet not so absolutelie as yee suppose. But I doe herein relye upon those bardes or Irishe cronicles, though the Irishe themselves, through their ignorance in matters of learninge and deepe judgement, doe most constantly beleve and avouch them. But unto them besides I adde my owne readinge; and out of them both togeather, with comparison of tymes, likenes of manners and customes, affinitie of words and names, properties of natures and uses, resemblances of rights and ceremonies, monuments of churches and tombes, and many other like circumstances I doe gather a likelyhood of truth; not certenly affirminge any thinge, but by conferringe of tymes, language, monuments, and such like, I doe hunt out a probabilitie of thinges, which I leave unto your judgement to beleve or refuse . . .[47]

Irenius outlines a hierarchy of authorities, which is, it is true, founded, in best humanist style, upon classical authors, from Caesar to Pliny.[48] But he again refuses to dismiss the native Irish scholars:

---

[45] Ib.

[46] Spenser, 'A view', Gonville and Caius MS 188/221, p. 48; Gottfried (ed.), *Prose works*, p. 84.

[47] Spenser, 'A view', Gonville and Caius MS 188/221, p. 48; Gottfried (ed.), Prose works, pp. 84–5.

[48] Spenser, 'A view', Gonville and Caius MS 188/221, pp. 48–9; Gottfried (ed.), *Prose works*, p. 86.

Besides, the bardes and Irish croniclers themselves, though through desier of pleasinge perhappes to much, and ignorance of arte and pure learninge, they have clouded the truth of those tymes; yet there appeareth amongest them some reliques of the true antiquitie, though disguised, which a well eyed man may happilie discover and finde out.[49]

Spenser uses these principles to deconstruct the Spanish origin of the Irish, arguing that the lack of confirmatory evidence makes it impossible to prove. Rather, he sees this as a story akin to the inventions of Geoffrey of Monmouth, which traced the origins of the English back to Brutus: 'the Irish doe heerein no otherwise, then our vaine English-men doe in the tale of Brutus'.[50] This was a promising application of humanist historical criticism to the origin myths of Ireland. But progress here was offset by Spenser's reluctance to apply his hermeneutic principles across the board. Having ditched the tale of Spanish origins so beloved of later Irish Catholic historians, he then opted for an alternative myth – that of the Scythian origin of the Irish. This not only had more respectable classical roots, it also, of course, justified Spenser's dismissive attitude towards native culture – the barbarian Scythians gave birth to the uncivil-ised Irish.[51] His unwillingness to use his historical methodology impar-tially is also evident in Spenser's embracing of those seductive legends of Geoffrey of Monmouth concerning King Arthur and Gurgunitus, both, it would seem, for the same reason – they strengthened the English claim to sovereignty over Ireland.[52] In short, Spenser's attitude towards Irish culture was more ambivalent than has been supposed. He lived long enough in Ireland to become acquainted with its language and history; he knew and used Irish words, had Irish poetry translated so that he could assess its literary merit, and was clearly familiar with the *Leabhar Gabhala* and other traditional accounts of Irish origins.[53]

---

[49] Spenser, 'A view', Gonville and Caius MS 188/221, p. 49; Gottfried (ed.), *Prose works*, p. 86.

[50] Gottfried (ed.), *Prose works*, p. 82.

[51] Though clearly viewed as barbarians, the early modern view of the Scythians was not wholly dismissive, since they could also be seen as noble savages: J. W. Johnson, 'The Scythian: his rise and fall', *Journal of the History of Ideas* 20 (1959), 250–7; and see below, n. 74.

[52] Spenser, 'A view', Gonville and Caius MS 188/221, p. 57; Gottfried (ed.), *Prose works*, p. 95; Hadfield, *Spenser's Irish experience*, pp. 98–100; Willy Maley, 'The British prob-lem in three tracts on Ireland by Spenser, Bacon and Milton', in B. I. Bradshaw and Peter Roberts (ed.), *British consciousness and identity* (Cambridge: Cambridge University Press, 1998), pp. 164–5; J. H. Anderson, 'The antiquities of fairyland and Ireland', *Journal of English and Germanic Philology* 86 (1987), 199–214.

[53] Clare Carroll, *Circe's cup: cultural transformations in early modern writing about Ireland* (Cork: Cork University Press, 2001), pp. 61–8.

But if he was at least ambivalent towards Gaelic culture, he was straightforwardly dismissive of Irish religion. He did not even give it the traditional Protestant concession of having declined from original purity. Rather, he saw Christianity as fatally flawed from its first arrival in Ireland.

> The generall faulte commeth not of anie late abuse either in the people or their preistes whoe can teache noe better then they knowe nor shewe noe more light then they have sene but in the first institution & plantinge of religion in all that realme which was (as I reade) in the time of Pope *Celestine* whoe (as it is written) ded firste sende over thither *Palladius* whoe theare deceassing he afterwardes sent over *St Patrick* beinge by nation a Britton whoe converted the people beinge then infidells from paganisme and christned them, in which popes time & longe before it is certeine that religion was generallie corrupted with their popishe trumperie.[54]

The Protestant apocalyptic underpinnings of this judgement are evident in Spenser's conclusion, inspired by Revelation 17: 'Therfore what other coulde they learne then soche trashe as was taught them and drincke of that cupp of fornication with which the purple harlott hadd then made all nations druncken?'[55]

This negative identification of Gaelic learning and religion with savagery and popery had obvious implications not only for the writing of history but also for the public sphere. In the view of that perennial polemicist, Barnaby Rich, all Catholic historians, even those from the medieval period, were *ipso facto* misleading: he therefore lumped Stanihurst, Campion and Giraldus together as 'Papists' and 'lying authorities'.[56] In terms of official policies, this dismissive attitude had the radical implication that progress in Ireland could best be achieved by eradicating the native culture. There had long been enactments in Ireland seeking to preserve the purity of the Anglo-Irish and English against Gaelic infection, ranging from the medieval Statutes of Kilkenny to the sixteenth-century Act for English order habit and language. But where these had been defensive (and usually ineffective), later proposals, such as those by Lord Chancellor Gerard that the Irish statutes requiring those of English race to refrain from Irish speech, customs, 'spottes and blemishes' be collected into one statute and made 'more sharpe and severe', took on an added importance as English power in Ireland

---

[54] Spenser, 'A view', Gonville and Caius MS 188/221, pp. 104–5; Gottfried (ed.), *Prose works*, p. 137.

[55] Spenser, 'A view', Gonville and Caius MS 188/221, p. 105; Gottfried (ed.), *Prose works*, p. 137.

[56] Rich, *New description*, p. 3.

grew, and enforcement became possible.[57] As Protestant bishops and officials in Ireland pressed for the suppression of the traditional Irish cultured classes and the rigorous enforcement of conformity to an anglicised established religion, the subversive role of native poets and chroniclers became almost an obsession. 'There is nothing that hath more led the Irish into error, then lying historiographers', 'idle poets . . . bardes and Irish rythmers', according to Barnaby Rich.[58] Parr Lane, a retired English soldier and Munster official, in his rambling poem *The holy ile* of c. 1620, influenced by Spenser's *View*, queried whether Ireland was a sacred isle or rather an 'Ile of swyne', and went on to list the twelve plagues of Ireland, chief amongst which were the bards, rhymers and harpists, whom he collectively dismissed as 'vermin'.[59]

This view of the Gaelic cultural tradition as hostile to the English presence in Ireland, indeed as inherently traitorous and fomenting rebellion, together with the deconstruction of noble Spanish origins, suggested strongly that Protestant history of Ireland was primarily concerned with an English or an anglicising sense of identity – with St George's triumph over St Patrick, as it were – and had very little interest in the riches or power of Ireland's Gaelic heritage.[60] David Rothe, the bishop of Ossory, complained in the early seventeenth century at the way in which the new English invaders, from the lord deputies to the common soldiers, had sought in the recent wars to destroy treasured Irish historical manuscripts, as if they were trying to wipe the historical record clean.[61] Such wanton destruction fuelled the other half of the Irish historical renaissance, the efflorescence of Roman Catholic scholarship both in Ireland and in mainland Europe, which, realising 'that extinction was hovering over the story of Ireland's national past, and that the prejudices of English historians were like to write her epitaph', set out on the Herculean tasks of rescuing the records of this threatened civilisation and disproving English slanders about Irish barbarity.[62]

---

[57] 'Lord Chancellor Gerard's notes of his report on Ireland', *Analecta Hibernica* 2 (1931), 184.

[58] Rich, *New description*, p. 3, sig. A3r.

[59] Alan Ford (ed.), 'Parr Lane, "Newes from the holy ile"', *Proceedings of the Royal Irish Academy*, section C, 99 (1999), 123 line 31, 127 line 233; cf. Joseph Leerssen, *Mere Irish and Fior Gael: studies in the idea of nationality, its development and literary expression prior to the nineteenth century*, 2nd edn (Cork: Cork University Press, 1996), p. 49.

[60] On the cult of St George in Ireland, see R. A. McCabe, *Spenser's monstrous regiment: Elizabethan Ireland and the poetics of difference* (Oxford: Oxford University Press, 2002), 101–20.

[61] P. F. Moran (ed.), *The analecta of David Rothe* (Dublin, 1884), p. 343.

[62] J. F. Kenney, *The sources for the early history of Ireland, ecclesiastical: an introduction and guide* (New York: Columbia University Press, 1929), p. 37; for examples of recent

III

But not all colonists were wedded to the idea of a *Kulturkampf*. The first parliament of James I repealed the anti-Irish legislation in a new spirit of inclusiveness, seeking an 'utter oblivion and extinguishment of all former differences' and 'a perfect agreement . . . betwixt all his Majesties subjectes in this realme'.[63] A Protestant could embrace the Irish language and the Gaelic tradition and write the history of Ireland without dismissing its culture as backward or somehow inferior to England. It was possible to use in a creative way the scepticism which Spenser had hinted at in his discussion of the early sources of Irish history to try to cut through the mists and distinguish myth from fact without leaving Ireland as a product of barbaric Scythians. And finally and most importantly, it was also possible for Catholic and Protestant to cooperate in this process of identifying, rescuing and interpreting the remnants of Ireland's past, united in a shared commitment to its true glories.

Here another Welshman led the way. Meredith Hanmer's background did not obviously equip him to be a culturally or religiously sensitive Irish historian. Having published anti-Catholic polemic directed at Campion, and served in the Church of England, he emigrated, possibly under a cloud, and came to Ireland in the early 1590s, where he eventually settled in Dublin as a prebendary of Christ Church.[64] He did, though, have some claim to be an historian, having edited that essential early Christian sourcebook, Eusebius' *Ecclesiastical history*.[65] And by March 1594 he had decided to apply his skills to Ireland, writing to Burghley to announce his intention to 'collect the antiquities of this land and to registre them unto the posteritie'.[66] Though he died of the plague in 1604, the results of Hanmer's labours have survived in two forms: his historical notes in the Irish state papers; and his treatise on Irish history,

---

scholarship on Catholic historiography, see: Cunningham, *Geoffrey Keating;* O'Connor, 'Thomas Messingham's *Florilegium* (1624)'; Breandán Ó Buachalla, *Aisling ghéar: na Stíobhartaigh agus an t-aos léinn* (Dublin: An Clóchomhar, 1996); Ó Muraíle, *Dubhaltach Mac Fhirbhisigh.*

[63] Bolton (ed.), *Statutes of Ireland*, p. 428.

[64] Meredith Hanmer, *The great brag and challenge of M. Campion a Jesuit* (London, 1581); Meredith Hanmer, *The Jesuit's banner. Displaying their original and success: their vow and oath: their hypocricy and superstition: their doctrine and positions* (London, 1581); Peter Holmes, *Resistance and compromise: the political thought of Elizabethan Catholics* (Cambridge: Cambridge University Press, 1982), p. 56; the only actual evidence concerning Hanmer's character concerns his abuse of church property and his possible perjury: NDNB, sv Hanmer.

[65] Meredith Hanmer, *The ancient ecclesiastical histories . . . written by Eusebius, Socrates and Evagrius* (London, 1577).

[66] SP 63/173/93 (*CSPI, 1592–6*, p. 229).

preserved in manuscript by Archbishop Ussher, which was edited by Daniel Molyneux, Ulster king of arms, and published in 1633 by James Ware as part of a distinguished trio of Irish histories.[67]

In his own words, Hanmer was an 'antiquarie and collector of antiquities' writing for 'the Christian reader'. He was capable of distinguishing among myth, fable and history, but was respectful of the material he found in his sources, and wanted to bring the antiquaries' legends and stories to the attention of his audience so that they could judge for themselves. The *Chronicle of Ireland* began by surveying the stories about the origins of the Irish people. Here he was following in the footsteps of Giraldus, Campion and Stanihurst – indeed, Hanmer pointedly referred to 'Richard Stanyhurst, the great philosopher and antiquary of Ireland'.[68] He retails the familiar stories about the peopling of Ireland by the descendants of Noah, but Hanmer is made of sterner stuff than Campion or Stanyhurst. He refuses, he says, to put these fables and lies at the start of his history 'as all Irish antiquaries doe', because 'I would not abuse the reader, being purposed beginning and ending to deliver the truth'.[69] Similarly, when retailing from the fabulous stories about Patrick from the saints' lives, he repeatedly questions their authority with asides such as '(say the Irish antiquaries)', and distances himself from them – 'I will now neither confirme nor refute, but acquainte the reader with such antiquities as I finde.'[70] Similarly he places contradictory accounts side-by-side in order to expose their manifest contradictions – 'see (gentle reader) how these reports hang together'.[71] In true humanist fashion he seeks out the source of some of these untruths, tracing some of them back beyond Giraldus to Higden's Polychronicon, and others to 'that silly writer', Hector Boece, the notable but highly inventive renaissance Scottish historian.[72]

Hanmer himself, like Spenser, opts for the Scythian origin of the Irish, engaging in some typically dubious early modern philological fantasies to demonstrate the derivation of Scottish from Scythian.[73] But he refuses to discard the Scythians as mere barbarians – rather he sees them as a blessed race, descended from Noah's son Japheth.[74] Hanmer takes a

---

[67] SP 63/214 (*CSPI, 1601–3*, pp. 661ff.); James Ware (ed.), *The historie of Ireland, collected by M. Hanmer. . . E. Campion. . . and E. Spenser* (Dublin, 1633); *UW*, XV, p. 378.

[68] Ware (ed.), *Historie*, 'The chronicle of Ireland', p. 6.

[69] *Ibid.*, p. 3; which, of course, does raise the question of what comes in between.

[70] *Ibid.*, pp. 44, 13, 20, 23.

[71] *Ibid.*, p. 15.

[72] *Ibid.*, 6.

[73] Ib, 6f.; etymology was one of the favourite means of tackling insoluble problems in ancient history in the early modern period: see Parry, *Trophies of time*, pp. 30, 58.

[74] *Ibid.*, p. 7.

similarly positive attitude towards the Irish language. Far from being dismissive, he had actually made the effort to learn Irish.[75] He can confidently reject the idea that Gathelus shaped the native language: 'I finde no Greek in the Irish tongue.'[76] Instead he correctly identified Irish as cognate with Welsh, using his knowledge of his native language to demonstrate the common roots.[77]

The fact that Hanmer respected his Irish sources, and did not get as far as the reformation (his work was cut short by his death) nor deal with earlier religious issues in a contentious manner, means that, for the most part, his account of Irish history is religiously neutral.[78] Nevertheless, this is still recognisably Protestant history, as when he comments on such 'superstitious' practices as the veneration of the Brigid's bell: 'Where-unto, to deceive the simple people, they attribute great vertue and holinesse, the which together with other toyes, they carried about, not onely in Ireland, but also in England.'[79] Similarly in relation to St Patrick's purgatory, Hanmer sets out to debunk the pious Catholic belief that it dated back to Patrick himself and offered a way into the under-world. It was, he argued a hangover from pagan times, a holy cave where the wind entering in 'whisteleth and crieth like dolefull ghosts; the silly, ignorant and simple people being deceived through perswasion of covet-ous priests that some soules and spirits doe penance there for their sinnes, call it Purgatorie'.[80] A contemporary agenda can also be ob-served in his claim that eleventh-century Irish kings 'had negative voyce in the nomination of bishops' throughout their realm, and in the exag-gerated assertion that the archbishops of Canterbury traditionally had jurisdiction over Irish bishops.[81] And, finally, he added a significant and clearly Protestant dimension to Irish historiography in his treatment of St Patrick, where, almost in an aside, he implicitly distanced himself from Spenser's dismissal of early Irish Christianity as papist, by hinting that it was in fact more like bible-based Protestantism: 'The onely

---

[75] SP 63/214, fol. 122r.
[76] Ware (ed.), *Historie*, 'The chronicle of Ireland', p. 7.
[77] *Ibid.*, pp. 8–12; Camden had made the same point, William Camden, *Britannia* (London, 1610), p. 64; Camden, like Hanmer, calls Welsh 'British': Parry, *Trophies of time*, p. 29; I would like to thank Jenny Lloyd-Mills for her assistance with matters relating to the Welsh language.
[78] On the unfinished nature of Hanmer's history, see Ware (ed.), *Historie*, Preface to the subsequent histories.
[79] *Ibid.*, p. 45.
[80] *Ibid.*, p 86. The Patrick associated with Lough Derg was, according to Hanmer, an abbot who lived around 850: cf. Keating, *History of Ireland*, I, pp. 46–98, IV, pp. 193–4.
[81] Ib, pp. 95, 97; cf. Keating's correction, *History of Ireland*, III, pp. 300–1.

doctrine Patricke read and expounded unto the people, was the foure evangelists, conferred with the Old Testament.'[82]

Hanmer's private papers reveal an eclectic range of interests, from traditional Irish war cries to genealogical lists, and show that he was collecting a range of antiquarian material from both cultures.[83] He was thus more sympathetic to the native tradition, less interested in the apocalyptic, and much less polemical and hostile than Spenser or Giraldus. Though he was later criticised by the foremost Catholic historian, Geoffrey Keating, rather incongruously, as 'an Englishman, who never either saw or understood the history [seanchus] of Ireland', and placed in the company of Giraldus, Campion, Stanyhurst, Spenser and other anti-Irish authors, this is unjust. The Welsh Hanmer points to a very different approach to Irish history from that taken by anglicising historians, one which seeks to transcend, or at least ignore and set to one side, religious and cultural boundaries in order to uncover the full riches of Ireland's past.

This ability was notably exemplified by one of the foremost English scholars of his day, William Camden, in his magnum opus first published in 1586, *Britannia*.[84] Initially Camden's treatment of Ireland was brief, but in subsequent editions it grew considerably, until by 1607 it included a description of the island and its geography, customs and inhabitants collected out of classical and contemporary authors, accounts of the O'Neills and the Nine Years War and the texts of two Irish chronicles.[85] Camden was primarily interested in the early history of Ireland. Like Hanmer he demonstrated a politic ability to recount without entirely rejecting the mythological elements from the *Leabhair Gabhála* and other early sources. 'My purpose is not either to averre these reports for true, nor yet to refute them: in such things as these let antiquity bee pardonable, and enjoy a prerogative.'[86]

It is true that, following Stanyhurst and Campion, from whom he borrowed, and Giraldus, whom he (rather badly) edited, Camden exhibited a dismissive and negative attitude towards native Irish

[82] *Ibid.*, p. 43.
[83] Public Record Office, Kew, SP 63/214 (*CSPI, 1601–3*, pp. 661–87); *CSPI 1600–1601*, pp. 115, 446.
[84] William Camden, *Britannia sive florentissimorum regnorum, Angliae, Scotiae, Hiberniae, et insularum adiacentium ex intima antiquitate chorographica descriptio* (London, 1586); R. B. Gottfried, 'The early development of the section on Ireland in Camden's Britannia', *ELH* 10 (1943), 17–30.
[85] Camden, *Britannia* (London, 1610), II, 55–201.
[86] *Ibid.* (hereafter references are to the 1610 edition), p. 64; see the similar strategy in his treatment of Geoffrey of Monmouth's tales of Britain's Trojan origins: Parry, *Trophies of time*, p. 28.

culture.[87] Thus he laments that Roman rule had never been extended across the Irish sea, since if it had been, Ireland might then have been 'reduced from barbarism to civility', and he identifies Ireland as being 'now for the most part . . . rude, half-barbarous, and altogether voide of any polite and exquisite literature'.[88] But he offsets this with his twin recognition that all the other races in Britain also began as savages, and that Ireland had indeed had a golden age in the seventh and eighth centuries as a *sanctorum patria*, sending out missionaries across Europe. Only after the disaster of the Viking invasions did Ireland relapse again into barbarism.[89] Ireland's savagery was a product of circumstance and providence, not the innate character of its people.

Camden's picture of the conversion of Ireland to Christianity represented a serious attempt to grapple with the confused sources, noting the difficulties over the relative roles of Palladius and Patrick, but insisting that it was the latter, sent by Pope Celestine, who converted the vast majority of the Irish people.[90] Though Protestant, Camden was not interested in using his history to provide ammunition for religious polemic. He recounted the miracles of St Patrick, and gave a neutral account of St Patrick's purgatory, ascribing to the *pie creduli* – the devoutly credulous – the idea that 'Patrick the Irishmens apostle, or else some abbat of the same name, obtained by most earnest praier at the hands of God, that the punishments and torments which the godlesse are to suffer after this life, might here bee presented to the eye: that so hee might more easily root out the sinnes which stuck so fast to his countrimen the Irish. . .'[91] He was a humanist scholar, a product of that late northern renaissance which transcended national and religious boundaries.[92] Thus he included in his section on Ireland both an account of Irish manners by a Jesuit schoolteacher in Limerick and material provided by a Protestant Irish scholar, James Ussher.[93]

---

[87] William Camden, *Anglica, Hibernica, Normannica, Cambrica, a veteribus scripta* (Frankfurt, 1602) contains editions of both the *Topographia* and the *Expugnatio*.

[88] Camden, *Britannia*, pp. 66, 68.

[89] *Ibid.*, p. 68. An explanation which found favour with later Catholic historians – see Alan Ford, 'James Ussher and the creation of an Irish Protestant identity', in Bradshaw and Roberts (eds.), *British consciousness and identity*, pp. 202–3.

[90] Camden, *Britannia*, p. 67.

[91] *Ibid.*, p. 115.

[92] Parry, *Trophies of time*, p. 26; Fussner, *Historical revolution*, ch. 3; Levy, *Tudor historical thought*, pp. 148–59.

[93] Camden, *Britannia*, pp. 93–4, 140; this assumes that the I. Good referred to by Camden in *Britannia*, p. 140, is in fact William Good: cf. Anthony a Wood, *Athenae Oxonienses*, 3rd edn, 4 vols. (London, 1813–20), I, 516–17; Edmund Hogan, *Distinguished Irishmen of the sixteenth century* (London, 1894), p. 10; *UW*, XV, 5–16; Gottfried, 'Early development', pp. 128–30.

As a result, later Irish writers, more attuned to history as a denominational bludgeon, were unsure where to place Camden. The Jesuit,
Henry Fitzsimon, labelled him a 'sectarist' historian, but acknowledged
him to be 'the learnedest of that kinde among the whole crue'.[94] Another
Catholic scholar, Stephen White, referred to the heretical Camden as 'an
enemy of the Irish and an admirer of Giraldus'.[95] But Keating, while
lumping him amongst the hostile foreign historians, generally quoted
him with respect, referring to him on one occasion as 'learned Camden',
whilst another Catholic, Robert Rochfort, praised him as 'the renowned
English antiquary', and David Rothe, bishop of Ossory, in his account of
the sufferings of Irish Catholics and the glories of Irish history, welcomed
Camden's account of St Patrick's miracles and even suggested that he
might be a closet Catholic.[96] Such praise so disconcerted one contemporary Protestant historian that he was reduced to writing to Camden to
seek reassurance about his religious orthodoxy.[97]

IV

This more positive evaluation of ancient Irish culture and Christianity
offered Protestant historians a significant choice: they could follow Spenser in opting for St George and dismissing Patrician Christianity as
Antichristian and popish, or they could take up Hanmer's hint that
St Patrick's religion had been pure and uncorrupted. A decisive step in
adopting rather than rejecting St Patrick was taken by John Rider, another
émigré English cleric with scholarly pretensions. As dean of St Patrick's,
1598–1608 (he later served as bishop of Killaloe 1613–32), Rider busied
himself with that recently discovered Irish pastime, religious controversy,
engaging in a public dispute with Henry Fitzsimon.[98] For the most part

---

[94] Henry Fitzsimon, *A Catholike confutation of M. John Riders clayme of antiquitie and a
caulming comfort against his caveat. In which is demonstrated, by assurances, even of
Protestants, that al antiquitie, for al pointes of religion in controversie, is repugnant to
Protestancie* (Rouen, 1608), sig. A3v–A4r.
[95] Matthew Kelly (ed.), Stephen White, *Apologia pro Hibernia adversus Cambri calumnias*
(ed.), Matthew Kelly (Dublin, 1849), pp. 28, 47.
[96] Keating, *History of Ireland*, I, pp. 46–7.; Jocelin, *The life of the glorious bishop S. Patricke
apostle and primate of Ireland. Togeather with the lives of the holy virgin S. Bridgit and of the
glorious abbot Saint Columbe patrons of Ireland* Robert Rochfort (ed.) (St Omer, 1625),
sig. A3r; Rothe, *Analecta*, pp. 89–90.
[97] William Camden, *Gulielmi Camdeni, et illustrium virorum ad Camdenum epistolae*
(London, 1691), pp. 236–9, 245–8, 257; *UW*, XV, 134–40.
[98] Declan Gaffney, 'The practice of religious controversy in Dublin, 1600–1641', W. J.
Sheils and Diana Wood (eds.), *The churches, Ireland and the Irish*, Studies in Church
History (Oxford, 1989), pp. 150–1; Edmund Hogan, *Distinguished Irishmen of the
sixteenth century* (London, 1894), pp. 196–310; Pádraig Ó Riain, 'The "Catalogus

the issues discussed were those typical early modern theological sticking-points, but there was one new dimension to the debate. Rider, according to Fitzsimon (we lack Rider's side of the exchange on this crucial point) claimed that there was 'a conformitie betwixt the first Christianitie planted among us, and their Puritan [=Protestant] profession'. Fitzsimon, in response, set out to prove that Ireland's primitive Christianity thoroughly conformed to 'our profession'.[99]

Though brief and second-hand, Rider's claim marked an important shift in Irish Protestant perceptions of their past, enabling them not only to adopt Patrick as their progenitor, but also to fit his mission in Ireland into their apocalyptic periodisation of Christian history. Early modern Protestants saw the early Christian church as relatively pure, but declining in the high middle ages with the rise of Antichrist in the papacy, until it was finally rescued at the reformation by Martin Luther and the other reformers. The greatest of the early Irish Protestant historians, James Ussher, applied this framework both to the whole of Christendom and then to Irish history. Though Ussher served for much of his career as Bishop of Meath (1621–5) and Archbishop of Armagh (1635–56), and played a significant political role in Irish and English ecclesiastical and secular politics, his first love was scholarship. He devoted as much of his time as he could (and, some complained, more than he should) to the pursuit of books and manuscripts in the libraries of Ireland and England, and even, and through his agents, further afield. The result was that he built up an extraordinary knowledge of the primary sources relating not just to Irish history, but to a whole range of areas of scholarly research, from the bible, to patristics, to early church history and chronology. His first book, *Gravissimae quaestionis. . . historica explicatio* combined apocalyptic and church history on a grand scale: *An historical investigation of that most important question – the continual succession and condition of the Christian church . . . from the time of the apostles to the present.* It tackled the problem of how the pure gospel truth of the early Christian church had been preserved through the increasing decay of the middle ages until it burst forth again in the Protestant reformation. The framework which Ussher used was based upon that seminal text in chapter 20 of the book of Revelation which told how Satan had been bound for a 1000 years in the bottomless pit.[100] During this period the power of Satan, and the inroads of Antichrist, had been restrained; it was not until the eleventh

   praecipuorum sanctorum Hiberniae"', in A. P. Smyth (ed.), *Seanchas: studies in early and medieval Irish archaeology, history and literature in honour of Francis J. Byrne* (Dublin, 2000), pp. 399ff.
[99] Fitzsimon, *Catholike confutation*, sig. A3v.   [100] Revelation 20.1–3.

century and beyond that the papacy had been taken over by that man of iniquity and the power of Rome ruthlessly extended. Ussher gave a detailed analysis of church history in which he showed how the truths of the early church had been preserved in the high and later middle ages by those heretical groups who had opposed Rome, such as the Waldensians.

In the early 1620s Ussher was challenged by a religiously (and, indeed, apocalyptically) minded friend, the Irish judge, Christopher Sibthorp, to apply this general European framework to Irish history. He did so in his *A discourse of the religion anciently professed by the Irish and Brittish*, which sought to prove that the religious practices and beliefs of the first Irish Christians under Patrick were very different from Spenser's 'trashe' and 'popish trumpery'. Rather, Patrick had introduced the gospel truth, and it was not till the eleventh century that this began to be corrupted by the introduction of Roman jurisdiction in to Ireland. As Ussher put it to Sibthorp:

I doe not deny but that in this countrey, as well as in others, corruptions did creep in by little and little, before the Divell was let loose to secure that seduction which prevailed so generally in these last times: but as farre as I can collect by such records of the former ages as have come into my hands . . . the religion professed by the ancient bishops, priests, monks, and other Christians in this land, was for substance the very same with that which now by publike authoritie is maintayned therein, agaynst the forraine doctrin brought in thither in later times by the Bishop of Rome's followers.[101]

Ussher's was a highly polished academic performance, but one which was nevertheless slanted. He was fully aware of the tension between propaganda and truth, and in fact openly admitted that he was scouring the primary sources in order to make his case, leaving the discovery of contrary evidence to his Catholic opponents.[102] The end result of Ussher's Protestant rewriting of Irish history was the confirmation of St Patrick as a suitable ancestor for the Church of Ireland. The early Irish church was pure and uncorrupted; only later, with the increase in papal power in Ireland, did it degenerate. Irish church history followed the broad pattern of European reformation history.[103]

---

[101] James Ussher, *A discourse of the religion anciently professed by the Irish and Brittish*, 2nd edn (London, 1631), sig. A2v–A3r.

[102] *Ibid.*, Afterword, 'To the reader', unpaginated (there are two 1631 printings of the discourse, one of which excludes the Afterword, the other, part of Ussher's 1631 *Workes*, includes it).

[103] Ford, 'Ussher and Irish Protestant identity', pp. 200–2; John McCafferty, 'St Patrick for the Church of Ireland: James Ussher's *Discourse*', *Bullán* 3 (1998), 87–102; Ute Lotz-Heumann, 'The Protestant interpretation of history in Ireland: the case of James

The scale of Ussher's achievement is evident in the power of this origin myth over the Protestant imagination in subsequent centuries. He had, almost single-handedly, rescued the early Irish church and, by implication, its traditions, from the hostility of those anglicising Protestants who despised it as corrupt, Gaelic and barbaric. But he had done so by appropriating it to an apocalyptic and anti-Catholic world-view which seemed to have little to offer in terms of common ground with his Catholic co-workers in the Irish historical renaissance. And, indeed, his work can be identified as the cornerstone of a distinctive tradition of Protestant Irish history which had a firm polemical undertone of hostility towards what it perceived as Antichristian Catholicism. The anti-Catholic tenor of Ussher's scholarship in the 1620s was only confirmed by his massive 1624 work of historical theology, *An answer to a challenge made by a Jesuite in Ireland*, which sought to show that beliefs and practices of the early church had been largely free from later Roman 'innovations and corruptions', and by his drafting of the 1626 statement by the Irish bishops that the Church of Rome was both erroneous and apostatical.[104]

V

Yet, though it was clearly propagandist, the *Discourse* was, for Ussher and for Irish Protestants, a tentative first step towards a more objective Irish history, since it provided them with a reason to identify proudly with the Irish, and, more importantly, the Gaelic Irish past. It helped to resolve the residual tension, dating back to Stanyhurst and Ussher's Anglo-Irish forebears, between their English or Norman origins and Irish culture. It thus cleared the way for the much more serious, and largely unpolemical and uncontroversial, works of the 1630s which explored that newly claimed Irish tradition.

This can most easily be seen in the work of Ussher, where in the latter half of his life the meticulous scholarship remained the same, but the apocalyptic and polemical edge largely disappeared. Instead he concentrated upon the endless task of sorting out texts and editions to establish the basic sources for Irish and British history, drawing up chronologies and succession lists to bring order to the early years of Christianity in these islands, mining Irish, English and Latin sources alike, and setting

Ussher's *Discourse*', in Bruce Gordon (ed.), *Protestant history and identity in sixteenth century Europe: the later reformation*, 2 vols. (Aldershot: Ashgate, 1996), II, pp. 107–21.
[104] James Ussher, *An answer to a challenge made by a Jesuite in Ireland: wherein the judgement of antiquity in the points questioned is truly delivered...* (Dublin, 1624); Richard Parr, *The life of the most reverend father in God, James Usher* (London, 1686), p. 28.

his conclusions down in as neutral and objective a fashion as possible. In 1632 he produced *Veterum epistolarvm hibernicarvm sylloge*, a collection of previously unpublished letters concerning the early Irish church, and in 1639 this was followed by his *magnum opus*, his history of the origins of Christianity in the British Isles, *Britannicarum ecclesiarvm antiquitates*.[105] His choice of subject matter – the arrival and spread of Christianity – enabled him to avoid the controversies concerning Noah's descendants and their role in peopling Ireland; Ussher was trying to establish the facts of the early Christianisation of these islands.[106] He did, however, devote the final chapter of the work to a detailed discussion of St Patrick. To the eyes of a modern scholar used to the minimalist approach to Patrician sources in the aftermath of Binchy's 1962 article, Ussher's attempts to accommodate the contradictions and inventions of such disparate texts as the Irish annals, the saints' lives, Tírechán and Jocelin appear strained and unconvincing.[107] In the context of contemporary early modern scholarship, however, his researches were based upon the fullest range of Patrician sources, both printed and manuscript, and offered the most comprehensive and thorough scholarly discussion yet of Patrick's career.

One reason why Ussher was different from those new English writers who followed Giraldus in viewing Ireland as a barbaric country was that he had a positive attitude towards Ireland's heritage, seeking to defend it from its detractors. He was, in short, Irish and proud of it. Ireland in *Britannicarum ecclesiarvm antiquitates* was 'Hibernia nostra'.[108] Irish was not a remnant of a barbaric past, but a language which was 'both elegant and rich'.[109] He was personally responsible for the preservation of numerous important early Irish manuscripts, most notably the Book of Kells. In the introduction to the *Sylloge*, Ussher quoted with obvious pleasure Camden's account of how Ireland had attracted Saxon scholars on account of its fame as a centre of learning.[110] And even in the *Discourse*, having cited a text which suggested that the kingdom of Ireland was older than that of England, he remarked: 'and this have I

---

[105] James Ussher, *Veterum epistolarvm hibernicarvm sylloge; quae partim ab Hibernis, partim ad Hibernos, partim de Hibernis vel rebus hibernicis sunt conscriptae* (Dublin, 1632); James Ussher, *Britannicarum ecclesiarvm antiquitates: quibus inserta est pestifera adversus Dei gratiam a Pelagio Britanno in ecclesiam inducta hareseos historia* (Dublin, 1639). I intend to deal with these works in much greater detail in my forthcoming book *James Ussher: theology, history and identity*.

[106] Though he did comment sarcastically on the stories about Gathelus and Scota the daughter of Pharaoh and queried the accuracy of Geoffrey of Monmouth: *UW*, VI, pp. 35, 105–6.

[107] D. A. Binchy, 'Patrick and his biographers: ancient and modern', *Studia Hibernica* 2 (1962), 7–173.

[108] *UW*, VI, 103.   [109] *Ibid.*, XVI, 25.   [110] *Ibid.*, IV, 393.

here inserted the more willingly, because it maketh something for the honour of my country, to which, I confess, I am very much devoted'.[111]

It was here, in the fusion of scholarly inquiry and national pride, that Protestants and Catholics, despite their deep theological differences, found common ground. One of the more surprising features of the 1620s and 1630s was the cooperation of scholars across the religious divide in their investigations into the early history of the church in Ireland. Ussher had a lengthy and detailed correspondence with Rothe (though Rothe did feel constrained to adopt a *nom de plume*), in which they exchanged information, references and transcripts of manuscripts.[112] Ussher also cooperated closely with Luke Wadding, the great Franciscan historian, providing him with material from his researches, whilst Wadding reciprocated by searching the Vatican archives for Ussher.[113] As a result, Thomas Strange, the intermediary between Ussher and Wadding, talked of his friendship with Ussher; and Ussher acknowledged Rothe's assistance in his *Britannicarum ecclesiarvm antiquitates*, and praised another prominent Catholic historian, the Jesuit Stephen White, as 'an expert in the antiquities not only of his own nation Ireland but also of other peoples'.[114]

Catholic and Protestant scholars were also bound together by their common distaste for one of the *bêtes noirs* of early modern Irish history, the Scottish writer and 'saint stealer', Thomas Dempster.[115] Dempster, inspired, like Ussher, White and Rothe, by pride in his own nation, had claimed for Scotland all those persons who were described in the early Christian sources as *Scoti*. This seemingly obvious step unfortunately ignored the fact that the term *Scoti* had referred primarily to the Irish. The resultant mass exodus of Irish saints to Scotland outraged Irish historians, and not only led to considerable controversy, but, in a fortunate by-product, fostered much serious historical research – as one later Irish historian put it, Dempster was 'the greatest boon that was ever conferred upon Irish literature'.[116]

[111] *Ibid.*, IV, 370.
[112] William O'Sullivan (ed.), 'Correspondence of David Rothe and James Ussher, 1619–23', *Collectanea Hibernica* 36–7 (1994–5), 7–49; Ussher had contact with a wide range of Catholic scholars: Aubrey Gwynn, 'Archbishop Ussher and Fr Brendan O'Connor', in Franciscan Fathers (ed.), *Father Luke Wadding* (Dublin: Clonmore & Reynolds, 1957), pp. 263–83; Brendan Jennings, *Michael O Cleirigh, chief of the four masters, and his associates* (Dublin: Talbot Press, 1936), p. 55; Joseph Leerssen, 'Archbishop Ussher and Gaelic culture', *Studia Hibernica* 22–3 (1982–3), 52–3.
[113] *Wadding papers*, pp. 266–7, 280, 349, 551.
[114] *Ibid.*, p. 551; *UW*, VI, 269, 274, 284, 286–7, 377; V, 458.
[115] *Ibid.*, VI, 285.
[116] William Reeves, 'Colgan's works', *Ulster Journal of Archaeology* 1 (1853), 295.

The shift of focus in the 1630s from confrontation and controversy to cooperation and compilation was also evident in the work of the other great Protestant scholar, James Ware. Born in 1594 and educated at Trinity College, Dublin, Ware combined a busy career as a government official with serious historical research. His library, in particular his collection of manuscripts, was only surpassed in early modern Ireland by that of his mentor and friend, James Ussher.[117] In 1626 he published his first work, an account of the archbishops of Cashel and Tuam, expanded by 1665 to cover all the Irish dioceses.[118] In 1633 he edited three earlier Irish histories, those of Campion, Spenser and Hanmer.[119] This was followed in 1639 by a bibliographical and biographical account of Irish authors.[120] And in 1654 and 1656 he published two more works, a treatment of Irish antiquities and an edition of the principal writings of St Patrick.[121]

The purpose of Ware's work on the Irish episcopate was – as his eighteenth-century editor, Walter Harris, put it – 'only to make a catalogue of the names and preferments of all the bishops'.[122] Its tone was neutral, avoiding controversial issues and exploiting Ware's extensive primary researches to reconstruct the lives of the archbishops and bishops in brief factual form. Similarly, his collection of writers was primarily bibliographical, referring to their religion where relevant, but refraining from making judgements. Unlike Ussher, Ware showed little interest in apocalyptic periodisation or causation in history. Thus the reason he gave for the decline of the island of saints and scholars was not the growth of Roman antichristian influence, but the more prosaic explanation of increasing unrest caused by civil war and Viking

[117] On Ussher's library, see T. C. Barnard, 'The purchase of Archbishop Ussher's library in 1657', *Long Room* 4 (1971), 9–14; H. J. Lawlor, *Primate Ussher's library before 1641* (Dublin, 1900); Elizabethanne Boren, 'The libraries of Luke Challoner and James Ussher, 1595–1608', in H. H. W. Hammerstein Robinson (ed.), *European universities in the age of the reformation* (Dublin: Four Courts, 1998), pp. 75–115; William O'Sullivan, 'A finding list of Sir James Ware's manuscripts', *Proceedings of the Royal Irish Academy*, section C, 97 (1997), 2–99; James Ware, *Librorum manuscriptorum in bibliotheca Jacobi Waraei equitis aur. catalogus* (Dublin, 1648).
[118] James Ware, *De praesulibus hiberniae commentarius a prima gentis hibernicae ad fidem Christianam conversione, ad nostra usque tempora* (Dublin, 1665).
[119] Ware (ed.), *The historie of Ireland*.
[120] James Ware, *De scriptoribus Hiberniae. Libri duo. Prior continet scriptores, in Hibernia natos. Posterior, scriptores alios, qui in Hibernia munera aliqua obierunt* (Dublin, 1639).
[121] James Ware, *De Hibernia et antiquitatibus eius disquisitiones* (London, 1654); James Ware (ed.), *S. Patricio, qui Hibernos as fidem Christi convertit, adscripta opuscula. Quorum aliqua nunc primum, ex antiquis MSS. codicibus, in lucem emissa sunt, reliqua, recognita; omnia, notis ad rem historicam & antiquariam spectantibus, illustrata* (London, 1656).
[122] James Ware, *The whole works of Sir James Ware concerning Ireland*, 3 vols. (Dublin, 1739), I, sig a2v.

invasion.[123] Indeed, the relative neutrality of Ware can best be seen when contrasted with the much more overt antipopery of his later editor, Walter Harris, whose additions to Ware's original texts have sometimes been mistaken for Ware's own writings.[124]

However bland and factual the content, though, the very choice of material had important subtexts. The English model for his work on the Irish episcopal bench, Francis Godwin's *Catalogue of the Bishops of England*, had an overt historical purpose, seeking to establish the early, even apostolic, credentials of the Church of England.[125] And, of course, Ware, by tracing the episcopal succession from the earliest Celtic prelates through the reformation to their modern Protestant rather than Catholic counterparts, presumed the rightful inheritance of the Protestant episcopal line and disowned the post-reformation Catholic episcopate, a highly sensitive and controversial issue in a period obsessed with ecclesiological legitimacy.[126] This was still identifiably *Protestant*, indeed, even polemical, history.

But it was also *Irish* history, and Irish history written by a proud Irishman. Ware, like his friend and master Ussher, saw himself as writing the history of his own country – he too used the phrase *Hibernia*

---

[123] Ware, *De scriptoribus*, sig A4r–v – echoing the explanation of Camden and Irish Catholic writers: see above, n. 92.

[124] See Harris's Preface to *The writers of Ireland* (Dublin 1746); and the much more sectarian additions (largely based on Ussher) he made to the entry on St Patrick: Ware, *Whole works*, I, 24–34.

[125] Francis Godwin, *A catalogue of the bishops of England, since the first planting of Christian religion in this island: together with a briefe history of their lives and memorable actions, so neere as can be gathered out of antiquity* (London, 1601); cf. Ware, *The historie of Ireland*, Preface, where he refers to Godwin.

[126] On the importance of episcopal succession in this period, see generally, Anthony Milton, *Catholic and reformed: the Roman and Protestant churches in English Protestant thought, 1600–1640* (Cambridge: Cambridge University Press, 1994); for later Irish arguments on the subject, see W. M. Brady, *The Irish reformation, or, The alleged conversion of the Irish bishops at the accession of Queen Elizabeth, and the assumed descent of the present established hierarchy in Ireland from the ancient Irish church, disproved*, 5th edn (London, 1867); W. M. Brady, *The episcopal succession in England, Scotland and Ireland A.D. 1400–1875*, 3 vols. (Rome, 1876–7); R. D. Edwards, 'The Irish bishops and the Anglican schism', *Irish Ecclesiastical Record*, 5th series, 45 (1935), 39–60; H. J. Lawlor, *The reformation and the Irish episcopate*, 2nd edn (London, 1932); A. T. Lee, *The Irish episcopal succession: the recent statements of Mr Froude and Dr Brady, respecting the Irish bishops in the reign of Elizabeth, examined* (Dublin, 1867); P. F. Moran, *The episcopal succession in Ireland during the reign of Elizabeth* (Dublin, 1866); E. A. Stopford, *The unity of the Anglican church and the succession of Irish bishops* (Dublin, 1867); the polemical subtext of the enterprise is explicit in Ware's English model, Francis Godwin's *The succession of the bishops of England since the first planting of Christian religion in this island*, 1st edn (London, 1601), where he appends to the list of bishops an account of the first settling of religion in Britain.

nostra.[127] Again like Ussher, he was anxious to distinguish between Ireland and Britain so that the former was not subsumed under the latter.[128] Nor did he follow Spenser in accepting those British sources that told of Arthur's invasion of Ireland: the fact that there was no *Irish* confirmation was sufficient for Ware to cast doubt on the story.[129] He was also critical of Giraldus' 'inventions' in his *Topographia*, expressing astonishment that they could still be repeated by contemporary scholars who were 'otherwise serious and learned'.[130] And, crucially, Ware shared Ussher's academic interest in the native Irish tradition. Though his knowledge of Irish was limited – he could 'make a shift to read and understand it . . . but was utterly ignorant in speaking it', he was an avid collector of Irish manuscripts, and employed Irish scholars 'to interpret and translate the language for him' – one of whom, in a neat fusion of the two historical traditions, was 'the last of the traditional antiquaries', Dubhaltach MacFirbisigh.[131]

Most revealing is Ware's editing of Spenser. This, the first printed edition of the *View* contains interesting variations on the manuscript versions which have come down to us. Repeatedly, he tones down Spenser's more hostile comments about Irish barbarism. In the opening page of the *View*, in changes that are repeated throughout the edition, 'that salvage nacion' becomes simply 'that nation'; and 'they are so barbarous still, and so unlearned' is altered to 'they are so unlearned still'.[132] Ware dropped entirely a long section which dismissed early Irish Christianity as 'generally corrupted with theire popish trumpery' and explained why the Irish have been left 'to wallowe in such deadly darknes' in apocalyptic terms.[133]

But Ware's emendations were also linked to a broader political and cultural vision. Superficially, his decision to publish Campion, Spenser's *View* and Hanmer in the same volume merely gathered together three different but pioneering Irish historians. But, by the contrast between the age when they were written and the time of their publication, Ware

---

[127] James Ware, *De scriptoribus Hiberniae* (Dublinii, 1639), sig. A3v.
[128] Hadfield and Maley, eds., Spenser, *A View*, pp. 52, 165.
[129] Ib.
[130] Ware, *De Hibernia et antiquitatibus eius*, p. 119; Harris (ed.), *Whole works*, I, 190.
[131] On Ware's knowledge of Irish, see Ware (ed.), *S. Patricio*, p. 144 and Harris (ed.), *Writers of Ireland*, p. 156; W. S. O'Sullivan, 'The Book of Domhnall O Duibhdabhoireann, provenance and codicology', *Celtica* 23 (1999), 277; for an important reassessment of his relationship to MacFirbisigh, see Ó Muraile, *Dubhaltach Mac Fhirbhisigh*, pp. 248–56.
[132] Hadfield and Maley (eds.), Spenser, *A View*, pp. 171–2.
[133] The passage quoted above, n. 55 is thus left out in 1633; Hadfield and Maley (eds.), Spenser, *A View*, pp. 173–4.

was seeking to make a point – that Irish historiography had progressed, that the nation had largely overcome the bitter divisions and hatreds chronicled, and even fostered, by the three writers. The *View*, with its savage remedy for Irish ills, could, Ware conceded, have 'bin tempered with more moderation'.[134] But he excused it as a product of violent times, which were to be contrasted with what had happened since the accession of King James. Ware was a firm royalist and a loyal servant of Lord Deputy Wentworth, and saw the peace of the 1630s as evidence that the various races and religions in Ireland could live together under an English monarch. Hence his use of the phrase of the Roman poet Claudian to refer to the way which the divisions of the Roman Empire had been overcome by his hero Stilicho – 'now we are united as one people':

And surely wee may conceive, that if hee had lived to see these times, and the good effects which the last 30 years peace have produced in this land . . . he would have omitted those passages which may seeme to lay either any particular aspersion upon some families, or generall upon the nation. For now we may truly say, *iam cuncti gens una sumus*. . .[135]

VI

As historians and politicians have repeatedly discovered, the Ireland where a shared national identity and a common historical awareness transcend religious and racial difference has an irritating tendency to be more ideal than real.[136] Ware's Platonic vision of mutual trust and harmony was soon shattered by the 1641 rising which amply confirmed the depth of sectarian division in Irish society.

There is a tension here between, on the one hand, the dream of a shared common history, based on disinterested historical research, part of the great European Erasmian tradition where religious difference and national divisions are overcome, or at least ignored or finessed, in the pursuit of academic truth, and, on the other hand, the inescapable underlying realities of religious division and sectarian polemic. It is undoubtedly possible, indeed, it is largely accurate, to portray the first half-century or so of Protestant Irish historical scholarship as representing significant progress from the latter to the former, as part of a wider

---

[134] Hadfield and Maley (eds.), Spenser, *A View*, p. 6.
[135] Ware (ed.), *The historie of Ireland*, Preface to Spenser, *View*; the quotation comes from Claudian, *De consulatu Stilichonis*, Bk. 3, 159; Michael Hendry (ed.), *Claudii Claudiani carmina Latina*, URL: http://www.curculio.org/claudian.
[136] Cf. Ian McBride, '"When Ulster joined Ireland": anti-popery, Presbyterianism radicalism and Irish republicanism in the 1790s', *Past & Present* 157 (1997), 63–93.

Irish historical renaissance that transformed the academic study of Irish history. One can compare the early works of English-born and instinct-ively 'imperialist' writers like Hooker and Spenser, which followed Giraldus in their negative evaluation of Ireland and the Irish, and es-poused an apocalyptic interpretation of the history of Ireland, with those of Irish-born Ussher and Ware, who, by the 1630s, were compiling scholarly works based on an impressive range of primary research in Gaelic as well as Latin sources, and drawing on the efforts of their fellow Catholic scholars to defend the reputation of their native land. One can compare the exclusivist and anti-Irish mentality of the Statute of Kilkenny with the Jacobean 'Act of repeale of diverse statutes concerning the natives of this kingdome of Ireland', which, recognising that the 'continuall hostilitie' between the English and their 'Irish enemies' was now over, sought to consign 'former differences' to 'utter oblivion' so that all in Ireland could live 'under one lawe as duetifull subjects of our sovereign lord and monarch'.[137]

One can also compare the English colonists of the later sixteenth century, holding on to their lands by martial law in the face of resistance and risings, with the willingness of their later successors, amidst the peace of the early seventeenth century, to put down roots and even to 'fabricate an Irish historical ancestry'.[138] Indeed the work of Ussher and Ware in the 1630s, in rescuing the records of early Ireland, and their 'discovery of a national culture practically at the very point of its expiry' was not fabrication, but rather primary research, and offered, it has been argued, an important example of the 'scholarly suspension of social and religious enmity'.[139]

But the reality is more complex than a neat journey from sectarian polemic to 'objective' or 'neutral' history, from a divided to a united nation, from racial hostility to cultural unity, since the tension between these poles often existed within the works of the same writer. As has been seen, even Spenser demonstrated a much more nuanced interest in Gaelic sources than his reputation for hostility to all things Irish might suggest; Ussher's researches into his native land may well have ended in praise for the scholarship of a Jesuit countryman, yet they still started from a strongly anti-papal apocalyptic framework. Similarly, Ware may indeed have had an inspiring vision of Ireland as one nation, but that

[137] Richard Bolton (ed.), *The statutes of Ireland* (Dublin, 1621), pp. 427–8.
[138] N. P. Canny, *The upstart earl: a study of the social and mental world of Richard Boyle, first Earl of Cork, 1566–1643* (Cambridge: Cambridge University Press, 1982), p. 128; Bianca Ross, *Britannia et Hibernia: nationale und kulturelle Identitäten im Irland des 17. Jahrhunderts* (Heidelberg: Winter, 1998), p. 189.
[139] Leerssen, 'Ussher and Gaelic culture', p. 58.

could not hide the fact that his *De praesulibus* was, bizarrely, a highly polemical recitation of boring and largely indisputable facts. And, for all their distancing of themselves from Giraldus, and their employment of Irish scholars, Ware and Ussher were still members of an essentially anglicising church and government, which *may* have come to recognise the importance of Irish as an historical language, but still saw the spread of English and the imposition of 'civility' as going hand-in-hand with political and social progress.

The resultant ambiguity was both powerful and lasting. It enabled Protestants on the one hand to identify with their native land and join with their Catholic fellow-countrymen in celebrating a shared history, thereby opening the way for them to transcend their colonial past and inherited racial prejudices. National pride could thus grow into some form of national feeling – it is no coincidence that the latter part of the eighteenth century, when the Anglo-Irish pressed for legislative independence, was also a period when historical scholarship was to the forefront of Protestant intellectual endeavour.[140] On the other hand, there remained a strong polemical undertone which readily surfaced in times of crisis when Catholic or Gaelic national feeling threatened the power of the elite in Ireland.[141] The Protestant historical renaissance of the early modern period thus gave rise to an ambiguous historical tradition which could encompass both the visceral polemic of Richard Cox in the aftermath of the battle of the Boyne, and the studied neutrality of Thomas Leland in the middle of the eighteenth century, which at its sectarian worst could tear a nation apart, but at its humanist best could greatly enhance the knowledge of Ireland's past.[142]

---

[140] Clare O'Halloran, *Golden ages and barbarous nations: antiquarian debate and cultural politics in Ireland, c.1750–1800* (Cork: Cork University Press, 2004).

[141] Hill, 'Popery and Protestantism', pp. 96–129; Clare O'Halloran, '"The island of saints and scholars": Views of the early church and sectarian politics in late eighteenth-century Ireland', *Eighteenth-century Ireland* 5 (1990), 7–20; Joseph Liechty, 'Testing the depth of Catholic/Protestant conflict: the case of Thomas Leland's "History of Ireland", 1773', *Archivium Hibernicum* 42 (1987), 13–28.

[142] Richard Cox, *Hibernia Anglicana: or, the history of Ireland from the conquest thereof by the English to this present time with an introductory discourse touching the ancient state of that kingdom* (London, 1689); Thomas Leland, *The history of Ireland from the invasion of Henry II*, 3 vols. (London, 1773); Liechty, 'Testing the depth', pp. 13–28.

7 Religion, culture and the bardic elite in early modern Ireland

Marc Caball

In her innovative study of religion and sectarian controversy in Ireland during the period 1400–1690, Samantha Meigs argues that the Gaelic *literati* played a pivotal role in the transmission and dissemination of a traditional Gaelic religious sensibility which effectively predetermined the failure of the Protestant reformation in Gaelic Ireland. While other European countries obviously had their scholarly elites, she suggests that none of these matched the influence which the Gaelic *literati* brought to bear on communal devotional experience in Ireland. Discerning a broad professional alliance, Meigs maintains that teachers, scribes, historians, jurists, physicians and high poets combined to form a particularly influential 'bardic' order to which she applies the collective term *aos dána*. This diverse group was, she claims, characterised by a shared corporate identity which was shaped by a common intellectual formation and frequently distinguished by reason of kinship ties. Significantly, because their training was influenced by an amalgam of Christian monastic and Gaelic cultural influences, Meigs portrays agents of this so-called bardic order as integrating both Gaelic and Latin learning while simultaneously mediating between written and oral cultures. Accordingly, although the *aos dána* occupied an elite social niche, its members also functioned as the purveyors of popular culture. Apparently the 'linchpin of Irish society', it seems that when Meigs' proposed combined bardic order moved to reject the Protestant reformation and consciously aligned itself with the counter-reformation church, its members collectively sealed the fate of Protestant evangelical ambitions in Ireland and imparted an enduring and distinctively Gaelic bardic ethos to Irish religion in the early modern period and beyond. Crucially, she proposes that counter-reformation Catholicism in Ireland was projected contemporaneously by means of Gaelic religious practices that are to be traced to the medieval period.[1]

---

[1] Samantha A. Meigs, *The reformations in Ireland: tradition and confessionalism, 1400–1690* (Basingstoke: Macmillan, 1997), pp. 2–3. Cf. Mícheál Mac Craith, 'The Gaelic reaction to the reformation', in S. G. Ellis and Sarah Barber (eds.), *Conquest and union fashioning a British state, 1485–1725* (London: Longman, 1995), pp. 139–61.

Given that the bardic order had by the late medieval period developed and successfully propagated a form of religious expression inextricably intertwined with Gaelic culture in both its elite and popular manifestations, the seamless intellectual fabric which constituted Gaelic religious and cultural identity easily withstood the challenges subsequently posed by Protestant reformers.[2] Indeed, Meigs asserts that as a result of the unparalleled symbiosis of religion and culture characteristic of late medieval Ireland, ideological phenomena common in other parts of Europe such as heresy and anti-clericalism were effectively alien to Gaelic modes of thought.[3] The continuity of this peculiarly bardic religious mindset is supposedly evident in Irish devotional ritual and practice down to the twentieth century. While offering no evidence in this regard, it seems that Meigs sees enduring quasi-bardic devotionalism negotiating profound social and linguistic change in the intervening centuries in much the same way as it apparently circumvented early modern Protestant reform.[4]

This chapter seeks to interrogate Samantha Meigs' ambitious interpretative model of a bardic Gaelic religio-cultural sensibility essentially predetermining the relatively limited impact of the reformation in Gaelic Ireland. More particularly, it proposes to examine the early modern religious attitudes of the professional literary caste commonly termed bardic poets in English. In contradistinction to Meigs' somewhat loose classification under the heading of 'bardic order' of a range of Gaelic learned professions which enjoyed quite varied contemporary status and influence, it is actually more appropriate to describe the poets as the bardic elite. While Meigs has reconstructed the religious outlook of the 'bardic' professions in rather broad terms, she has, for the purpose of supporting evidence necessarily relied largely on the evidence of bardic poets in her depiction of the late medieval Gaelic religious mindset which is the effective basis for her framework of confessional continuity and devotional conservatism. Although the Gaelic medieval and early modern legal and medical traditions have bequeathed a large corpus of manuscript material to posterity, its immediate relevance to the reconstruction of devotional *mentalités* is circumscribed by the specific technical remit of the literature. Because of these inevitable historiographical constraints, Meigs has for the most part drawn on the testimony of bardic poetry to support her argument. Although she employs the term 'bardic' to characterise her definition of the outlook of a supposed collective entity, its usage in this chapter applies exclusively to the work and attitudes of the classical poets.[5]

---

[2] Meigs, *Reformations*, p. 40.   [3] *Ibid.*, pp. 141–2.   [4] *Ibid.*, pp. 143–4.
[5] J. E. Caerwyn Williams, 'The court poet in medieval Ireland', *Proceedings of the British Academy* 57 (1971), 85–135.

With particular reference to the question of Gaelic awareness of the
reformation, it is argued here that the devotional *oeuvre* of sixteenth-
century bardic poets illustrates their commitment to a communal mode
of Christian piety which remained aloof for the most part from contemporary controversies generated by the Protestant reform movement or
Tridentine Catholicism. Utilising the religious poetry of Aonghus Fionn
Ó Dálaigh and drawing from a collection of bardic poems celebrating
St Patrick's Purgatory on Lough Derg, it is demonstrated that bardic
devotional lore and beliefs remained impervious to the broader European
confessional debate at a time of intense ecclesiastical and doctrinal
conflict.[6] This evidence reveals a picture of bardic Christian piety heavily
coloured by apocryphal influences filtered through a distinctly Gaelic
process of inculturation. As might be expected of the devotional culture
of a lay elite, bardic poets display no particular interest in abstract
theological debate concentrating instead on the more immediately ritu-
alistic and redemptive aspects of religion.[7] Therefore, while endorsing
Samantha Meigs' emphasis on the medieval incorporation of a Christian
devotional ethos within the bardic mindset, it must also be acknowledged that such an ethos coexisted with a decidedly profane poetic
ideology of political and dynastic validation. The vibrancy of lay devotional poetry in Irish possibly derived from the extrusion of traditional
Irish learning from the monasteries in the twelfth century and the consequent development of a vernacular devotional culture within a lay
environment. Given that in the immediate post-Norman conquest
period, control of the church was for the most part the preserve of the
English monarchy and the continental monastic orders, Gaelic lords
may well have turned to bardic poets to articulate a demotic religious
expression in much the same way as they required them to articulate an
ideology of lordship.[8] However, it should be remembered that expressions of Christian devotion in the bardic *oeuvre* were to a large extent
subsidiary to the corporate duties of the poets. The bardic elite primarily
functioned as political brokers and mediators. They drew from a
metaphorical armoury of thematic convention and pseudo-historical

[6] The broader scenario of religious practice and sectarian controversy in early modern
Ireland is discussed in Alan Ford, *The Protestant reformation in Ireland 1590–1641*, 2nd
edn (Dublin: Four Courts Press, 1997); Raymond Gillespie, *Devoted people belief and
religion in early modern Ireland* (Manchester: Manchester University Press, 1997).

[7] See also Raymond Gillespie, *The sacred in the secular religious change in Catholic Ireland,
1500–1700* (Colchester, VT: St Michael's College, 1993), pp. 6, 9; Gillespie, *Devoted
people*, pp. 8–10.

[8] Katharine Simms, *From kings to warlords: the changing political structure of Gaelic Ireland in
the later middle ages*, 2nd edn (Woodbridge: Boydell, 2000), p. 16.

precedent to impart communal ideological endorsement to aspiring and ascendant lords in Gaelic Ireland.[9] While it is certainly not plausible to go so far as to apply to a bardic context Jean Delumeau's controversial argument for superficial European Christianisation prior to the sixteenth-century reformations, nonetheless the syncretic fusion of Christianity and bardic traditions of considerable antiquity cannot have been effected without some degree of intellectual tension.[10]

In taking account of both conventional bardic piety and the ambiguity inherent in bardic modes of validation with regard to medieval Christian notions of social explication, it is proposed that the poets' awareness of religious controversy in the sixteenth century was primarily determined by considerations of a socio-cultural nature.[11] The integrity of Gaelic culture and identity constituted a central element in the bardic outlook and the threat posed to Gaelic society by aggrandising crown expansion in late sixteenth and early seventeenth-century Ireland was a matter of more immediate concern to classical bardic poets than questions of overt denominational commitment. The overwhelming political and cultural focus of early modern bardic debate is immediately evident from con-temporary poetry. It is further argued that while bardic poets reacted to the Protestant reformation with apparent lack of interest, the increas-ingly anglocentric emphasis of the established church scarcely served to secure the approbation of culturally conscious bardic poets. Nonetheless, occasional Protestant evangelical attempts to engage with the Gaelic Irish through the medium of their own culture and language in the sixteenth and early seventeenth centuries were not entirely unsuccess-ful.[12] This fact also cautions against Meigs' portrayal of reflexive Gaelic antagonism to religious innovation. While discounting the deterministic notion of an atavistic bardic loyalty to medieval Catholicism, it is

---

[9] The bardic validatory function is discussed in Marc Caball, 'Aspects of sixteenth-century elite Gaelic mentalities: a case-study', *Études Celtiques* 32 (1996), 203–16.

[10] Jean Delumeau, *Catholicism between Luther and Voltaire: a new view of the counter-refor-mation* (London: Burns and Oates, 1977), pp. 160–1. For Christian influence on native scholarship in early medieval Ireland see Donnchadh Ó Corráin, 'Irish vernacular laws and the Old Testament', in Próinséas Ní Chatháin and Michael Richter (eds.), *Irland und die Christenheit Bibelstudien und Mission* (Stuttgart: Klett-Cotta, 1987), pp. 284–307.

[11] In an analogous interpretative vein, Brendan Bradshaw has argued that the success of the counter-reformation in late sixteenth-century Ireland hinges on its incorporation as a central element in communal identities in contrast to the apparently alien character of the reformation church. Brendan Bradshaw, 'The English reformation and identity formation in Wales and Ireland', in Brendan Bradshaw and Peter Roberts (eds.), *British consciousness and identity: the making of Britain, 1533–1707* (Cambridge: Cambridge University Press, 1998), pp. 54, 70–2, 99.

[12] See, e.g., the evangelical activity of Sir William Herbert in his Kerry seigniory in the late 1580s: *CSPI, 1586–88*, p. 539; *CSPI, 1588–92*, pp. 133–4, 191–2.

arguable that the ultimate failure of the reformation in Gaelic Ireland was in large part due to the entrenched antipathy of the established church to indigenous culture which was in turn counterpointed by a systematic campaign on the part of Tridentine Catholicism from the later sixteenth century onwards to invoke Gaelic culture as a complementary social ancillary to Roman Catholicism. Unlike their Protestant antagonists, the clerical agents of the Gaelic counter-reformation were wholly conversant with native culture and in a number of cases boasted descent from hereditary learned families. Yet they were not bardic poets in the classical sense. In fact, the bardic corporate apparatus had been in protracted decline from at least the middle of Elizabeth's reign and the departure of the northern earls to the continent in 1607 effectively signalled the demise of the Gaelic polity to which the poets were bound by a Gordian knot. The early years of James VI and I's reign accelerated the cumulative transfer of bardic ideological primacy to a new cadre of counter-reformation clerics and lay gentlemen poets who articulated a potent and enduring amalgam of ethnically inclusive Irish nationality and Catholic allegiance. It was this radicalised generation of Irish intellectuals, who, combining the bardic ideological and cultural inheritance with a counter-reformation dynamic, formulated a potent inflection of religion, culture and nationality. In effect, the reception of the two reformations among the Gaelic elite had been determined by considerations of Gaelic cultural integrity and autonomy rather than by polemical issues of theology or denominational allegiance.[13]

The important collection of religious verse attributed to the elusive late sixteenth-century Munster poet Aonghus Fionn Ó Dálaigh (fl.1596) provides a relatively comprehensive body of material from which it is possible to reconstruct aspects of the bardic devotional mindset.[14] Of the fifty-five poems assembled in Lambert McKenna's edition of Ó Dálaigh's attributed *oeuvre*, fifty-one are religious in subject. Notwithstanding the large number of compositions extant, the thematic range of the poems is surprisingly limited. Seventeen of Ó Dálaigh's poems are addressed to the Virgin Mary, who is assigned a decisive role as an intercessor between Christ and sinners, especially on the day of judgement.[15]

---

[13] Marc Caball, 'Faith, culture and sovereignty: Irish nationality and its development, 1558–1625', in Bradshaw and Roberts (eds.), *British consciousness*, pp. 112–39.

[14] Lambert McKenna (ed.), *Dánta do chum Aonghus Fionn Ó Dálaigh* (Dublin: Maunsel, 1919). The problematic identity of Ó Dálaigh is discussed in Cuthbert McGrath, 'Ó Dálaigh Fionn cct.', *Éigse* 5 (1945–7), 185–95.

[15] For an historical overview of Marian devotion in Ireland see Peter O'Dwyer, *Mary: a history of devotion in Ireland* (Dublin: Four Courts Press, 1988). Mirroring contemporary bardic devotion to the Virgin, the fifteenth and sixteenth centuries in Ireland witnessed

Many of these pieces reveal bardic influences in their portrayal of the Virgin in a guise easily interchangeable with that of a Gaelic lord's wife. Perhaps reflecting the importance of familial links in Gaelic society, the poet hails Mary as a kinswoman (*bean ghaoil*) and in the manner of a trusted relative she can be relied on to make his case before God to avert divine wrath ('Saoradh ríoghain nimhe naoi/mise ar do dhíoghail a Dhé').[16] On the day of reckoning, she will plead in heaven for her kin and Ó Dálaigh prays for her personal intercession at that critical juncture ('Labhair damh ris an tí as triúr/a shiúr ler ghabh Rí na ríogh').[17] All human hope is best placed in the Virgin given that she has dedicated herself to the redemption of sin ('Muire . . . do bhí ar tí ceannaigh ar gcuil/níor luigh gur cheannaigh sí sin').[18]

Hailed as a 'salmon of knowledge' in the mythological Gaelic mode, Mary is nevertheless depicted in conventional bardic eulogistic terms in the poem entitled 'I mbréig ní mholaim Muire' ('In deceit I praise not Mary'). No amount of praise easily suffices to render appropriate homage to Mary and because of his affection for her person, the author vows to undertake his best effort in her honour.[19] There follows a distinctly sensual and nuanced account of the Virgin's physical traits more readily applicable to the persona of a Gaelic *chatelaine*. The attractiveness of her eyes, face and body are highlighted while it is remarked that her countenance never avoided human engagement and her glance is distinguished by an aura of love ('Is néal seirce na silleadh'). In a direct approach to the 'mother of the high-king's heir' ('A mháthair oighre an Aird-Ríogh'), Ó Dálaigh admits that a satisfactory description of her glories is beyond his abilities, and moreover, her corporeal embodiment merely serves as a physical representation of a nature incapable of sin.[20] Throughout these poems, the Virgin is presented in imagery indicative of natural abundance. The trope of fertility was commonly invoked by poets to sanction a lord's rule and the deployment of such imagery in a Marian context likewise seeks to underline her status as a legitimate and efficacious intercessor. Mary is a 'tree full of heavy fruit', a 'wave bearing wealth to the shore', a 'ripe berry of noblest wine', 'golden fruit for the cure of our sins' or 'the golden apple tree of

---

an increase in the production of representations of the madonna and child: John Bradley, 'The Ballyhale madonna and its iconography', in Etienne Rynne (ed.), *Figures from the past: studies on figurative art in Christian Ireland* (Dublin: Royal Society of Antiquaries of Ireland, 1987), p. 265.

[16] McKenna (ed.), *Dánta*, poem II, stanza 7.
[17] *Ibid.*, poem XIV, stanza 6.   [18] *Ibid.*, poem XIV, stanza 2.
[19] *Ibid.*, poem II, stanza 4; poem X, stanzas 1–2.   [20] *Ibid.*, poem X, stanzas 3–8.

the three fruits' while 'the juice of her wine-fruit is the Lord'.[21]
Evidently, Ó Dálaigh is primarily concerned to depict the Virgin in terms
immediately recognisable in a Gaelic context, while her role as the
sinner's advocate on the day of judgement is invested with a decisive
significance. A deliberate degree of local contextualisation is emphasised
by Mary's inclusion in the company of Irish saints like Patrick, Colm
Cille and Brigid who is described as 'bright Mary of the *Gaoidhil*'.[22]

The Gaelic literary tradition was historically enriched from the early
medieval period onwards by contact with broader European cultural
developments and bardic devotional poetry proves no exception in this
regard. Indeed, the work of poets like Aonghus Fionn Ó Dálaigh is
remarkable for the facility with which local themes are combined with
foreign influences to produce a remarkably coherent composite canon.
Aonghus Fionn's blending of traditions is perhaps most readily evident
in his use of the apologue device to illustrate a given point or to adduce
apparently exemplary testimony in favour of an argument or conclusion.
The use of apologues is a standard feature of the bardic repertoire and in
this instance Ó Dálaigh unselfconsciously applies the format to demonstrate Mary's miraculous powers. Significantly, the poet draws from a
common medieval European store of Marian lore to make his case. For
instance, in the poem entitled 'Iomdha sgéal maith ar Mhuire' ('Many
the fine tale of Mary'), the story of a pious young hermit in the desert is
recounted. Having renounced worldly pleasures in favour of a life of
contemplation and spiritual reflection, the youth is visited by the devil in
the form of an attractive young woman and predictably enough is rapidly
deflected from his more worthy previous course of action. Following the
pair's decision to marry, however, the Virgin intercedes and appears at
the former hermit's door in the guise of an ordinary woman. She
prompts the young man to show her how to make the sign of 'the
creator's cross' (*Cros an Dúilimh*) and what to say by way of verbal
accompaniment. On Mary's enactment of these rites, the young woman
or demon promptly disappears and the youth is saved from sin ('an
spiorad uaidh do imthigh').[23] Describing this tale as an adaptation of a
theme found in the *Vitae Patrum*, Robin Flower noted that it was often

[21] *Ibid.*, poem XI, stanza 6; poem XII, stanza 3; poem XIV, stanza 7; poem XXVI, stanza
1. For the golden apple as a sign of salvation see F. C. Tubach, *Index exemplorum: a
handbook of medieval religious tales* (Helsinki: Suomalainen Tiedeakatemia, 1969), p. 30.
[22] *Dánta*, poem XXX, stanzas 10–11.
[23] *Ibid.*, poem XLVIII. For the provenance of this exemplum see L. P. Ó Caithnia, *Apalóga
na bhfilí 1200–1650* (Dublin: An Clóchomhar, 1984), p. 160; T. F. Crane (ed.), *The
exempla of Jacques de Vitry* (London, 1890), no. CCXLVI, pp. 103–7, 236–7.

introduced to medieval collections of exempla.[24] In the poem entitled 'Ceanglaim mo chumann le Muire' ('I bind my affection to Mary'), Ó Dálaigh remarks that he knows of a story, unsurpassed by anything scripture has to offer, documenting the Virgin's power. This tale concerned the fate of a famous knight who having lost his wealth neglected his religious obligations and fell victim to the blandishments of the devil. Encountering an imposing horseman astride a black steed, the knight naively agrees to hand over his wife to his new acquaintance in exchange for a year's wealth. At year's end, the knight sets off unenthusiastically to deliver his wife to the rider to fulfil his side of the pact. On the way, they call at a church where she begins to pray to Mary's statue ('Dealbh Muire na híomháigh ann') and in response to the unfortunate wife's entreaty, Mary takes her place and foils the devil's attempt to corrupt this hapless woman.[25] Of course, the theme of a pact with the devil was common in medieval and early modern lore and this particular version is paralleled by a story recounted in Jacobus de Voragine's (c.1230–98) popular *Golden Legend,* a collection of saints' lives and short works on Christian festivals completed by 1265.[26] Such examples of cultural interchange remind historians of the inaccuracy of portraying the bardic religious experience in exclusively hermetic terms and highlight the extent to which bardic poets accessed a common European culture.

In conjunction with the presentation of Mary as the supreme heavenly intercessor, the notion of a vengeful Christ demanding expiation of his travails on earth is a thematic commonplace in the poems attributed to Aonghus Fionn. He places particular emphasis on Christ's suffering on the cross. Lambert McKenna, in his edition of the Ó Dálaigh corpus, remarked on what he termed 'a very strange and theologically incorrect view of the Passion' manifested in the poems. In such cases, Christ is presented as demanding the condign punishment of humankind because of the intense pain he suffered at the crucifixion. On Doomsday, Christ will invoke against mankind the wounds he incurred on the cross and the pain caused by the nails and thorns. In such fearful circumstances, Mary must plead the case of her children ('Mar as fheirrde inn t'aon-fhuil/ maoluigh rinn fheirge an aláidh'). She wields sufficient influence to assuage Christ's fury and her request will avert divine wrath ('Ceird

[24] Robin Flower, *Catalogue of Irish manuscripts in the British Library,* reprint, 2 vols. (Dublin: Dublin Institute for Advanced Studies, 1992), II, 153.
[25] *Dánta,* poem XLIX.
[26] Ó Caithnia, *Apalóga,* pp. 161–2. John Bossy, *Christianity in the west 1400–1700* (Oxford: Oxford University Press, 1985), p. 9; Peter Burke, *Popular culture in early modern Europe,* 2nd edn (London: Wildwood House, 1988), p. 171.

ríoghna cách do chaomhna').[27] The image of the vengeful Christ is given a peculiarly Gaelic resonance when the indigenous juridical concept of *éiric* or 'retribution price' is deployed to describe Christ's demand for satisfaction on the day of judgement. Of course, the poet himself cannot hope to satisfy the *éiric* demanded in this case and the Virgin's beneficial intervention on his behalf must be sought ('Díol t'fhola ní héidir liom/ t'éiric re tobhach is trom').[28] In a poem addressed to the holy cross, the poet promises a ransom of bardic praise to the cross for its intercession with God on his behalf ('Gabh ar gceannaigh-ne a chroch naomh . . . do bhéar ceannach duit im dhán'). This reference is further indicative of the cultural amalgam which infused bardic devotional mores. In fact, the Gaelic technical term *ceannuigheacht* denoted the payment made to secure protection and assistance from the party to whom it was made.[29]

Ó Dálaigh's seemingly obsessive fear of perdition must be set against a vibrant Gaelic devotional ambience which encouraged the production and reception of grotesquely lurid apocryphal texts such as the Harrowing of Hell.[30] In a version of this text which has recensions preserved in manuscripts dating to 1437 and 1575, Christ's descent, the torments of hell and the escape from captivity are accompanied by gory descriptions of Christ's wounds, the violence of his onset and the unspeakable horror of hell. The account of Christ's wounds in this text is rendered in minute detail: 'He arose, with the blood of His yellow-curled, sharp-eyed head in twisting, oblique-red encrustations and in spurred clots from the spiny crown . . . His snowy-white, long-fingered, slender hands oozing noble blood, bitter and crimson, and His slim, pierced-soft, bright-soled feet casting heavy bleeding to the green-sided earth.'[31] Christ's descent into the diabolical inferno, his sojourn there and his ascent with the tormented captive souls are described in vivid and startling detail: 'there were numerous spits there, roasting (people)

---

[27] *Dánta*, p. ix; poem VII, stanzas 1, 6. On the centrality of the passion in late medieval and early modern English worship, see Eamon Duffy, *The stripping of the altars* (New Haven: Yale University Press, 1992), pp. 234–56.

[28] *Dánta*, poem VIII, stanza 6.

[29] *Ibid.*, poem XXVII, stanzas 1, 2. Kenneth Nicholls, *Gaelic and gaelicised Ireland in the middle ages* (Dublin: Gill and Macmillan, 1972), p. 41.

[30] Máire Herbert and Martin McNamara, *Irish biblical apocrypha* (Edinburgh: T&T Clark, 1989). Martin McNamara suggests that from 1100 onwards the apocrypha of the Old and New Testaments attracted the interest of Gaelic poets and writers more frequently than the Bible itself because they were available in the vernacular and because they appealed more to the Irish imagination. McNamara, 'The bible in Irish spirituality', in Michael Maher (ed.), *Irish spirituality* (Dublin: Veritas, 1981), p. 45.

[31] Texts and translation in William Gillies (ed.), 'An early modern Irish "Harrowing of Hell"', *Celtica* 13 (1980), 47. Martin McNamara, *The apocrypha in the Irish church* (Dublin: Dublin Institute for Advanced Studies, 1975), p. 71.

alive, and dark-swirling, circular cauldrons bone-chopping, and black, green-toothed demons swiftly-executing, and the fugitive shouts of feeble (souls) being coerced in no uncertain manner'.[32] In keeping with the bardic habit of often gaelicising material of foreign origin, the administrative structure of hell is given a uniquely Irish character. The vile inferno so dramatically portrayed in this tract is presided over by two chief stewards ('airdfhedhmannaigh aigmhéle fhuairIfrinn') under whom serve seven *airchinnigh* ('atáit seacht n-oirchinnigh a n-Ifrionn'). The use of the peculiarly Gaelic quasi-ecclesiastical office of *airchinneach* or hereditary tenant of church lands in a diabolical context seems bizarre.[33] The author of the text may simply have wanted to give his description of hell a spurious aura of terminological authenticity and accordingly he invoked a pseudo-clerical office immediately intelligible to a Gaelic audience. William Gillies in his edition of the two earliest recensions of this text has remarked on stylistic similarities between them and the early modern Gaelic romantic prose tradition which is often heroic and martial in tone.[34] This mixture of the devotional and profane surely reflects an ongoing Gaelic tendency to incorporate late medieval Catholic religious expression within a recognisably indigenous framework and with a resulting blurring of boundaries between profane and sacred forms of cultural consumption. For instance, such a coalescence of religious and lay interests is evident in the book list of the minor Gaelic lord, Tadhg Ó Duinn (fl.1475) which records a diverse manuscript collection of apocryphal, hagiographical, romantic and mythological material assembled cheek by jowl.[35] A similar intermix of apocryphal and profane material is evident in a medieval Latin manuscript miscellany which belonged to Conor O'Brien (d.1581), earl of Thomond, in the sixteenth century and which in the early fifteenth century had been in the possession of the Dominicans of Limerick city.[36]

The emphatic sociological dimension of Gaelic religious expression is especially evident in a collection of sixteenth-century bardic poems

---

[32] Gillies, 'Harrowing', p. 48.

[33] *Ibid.*, p. 42. For *airchinnigh*, see Nicholls, *Gaelic and gaelicised Ireland*, p. 111; E. P. Shirley (ed.), *Papers relating to the Church of Ireland 1631–1639* (London, 1874), pp. 27–8; H. A. Jefferies, 'George Montgomery, first Protestant bishop of Derry, Raphoe and Clogher (1605–10)', in H. A. Jefferies and Ciarán Devlin (eds.), *History of the diocese of Derry from earliest times* (Dublin: Four Courts Press, 2000), pp. 151–2.

[34] Gillies, 'Harrowing', pp. 37–8.

[35] Cuthbert McGrath, 'Notes on Í Dhuinn family', *Collectanea Hibernica* 2 (1959), 16; K. W. Nicholls (ed.), *The O Doyne (Ó Duinn) manuscript* (Dublin: Irish Manuscripts Commission, 1983), pp. 116–17.

[36] D. J. G. Lewis (ed.), 'A short Latin *Gospel of Nicodemus* written in Ireland', *Peritia* 5 (1986), 263.

which take St Patrick's Purgatory as their thematic focus. Possibly part of a larger site of pagan worship in pre-Christian times and in turn the location of an anchoritic presence, Lough Derg's reputation as a place of pilgrimage spread through later medieval Europe thanks to such texts as the *Tractatus de Purgatorio Sancti Patricii* (c. 1184) and Gerald of Wales' *Topography of Ireland* (c. 1186). The cave or entrance to the otherworld traditionally associated with St Patrick was probably given a new lease of life by the arrival in the twelfth century of the Augustinian Canons and by their subsequent institution of a pilgrimage under the patronage of St Patrick.[37] These bardic poems present the Lough Derg penitential ritual as a Gaelic social phenomenon. The importance of the peniten- tial pilgrimage in Gaelic culture is exemplified by the case of Aonghus Mac Niocaill, who having strangled his son in 1543 appealed to the dean of Armagh, Edmund MacCawell, for absolution. As a condition of absolution, the dean obliged Mac Niocaill to embark on an arduous pilgrimage to a range of celebrated Irish shrines. Travelling for what must have been the best part of a year, he journeyed to sites as far apart as the Skelligs and Mt Brandon, Glendalough, Downpatrick, Croagh Patrick and of course Lough Derg. On his return the contrite pilgrim provided documentary proof of his sojourn at each holy place visited to secure his absolution.[38] In a related expiatory vein, the Lough Derg poems highlight the value of the pilgrimage in appeasing God's wrath against the sinful and in much the same way as Aonghus Fionn Ó Dálaigh sought the beneficial intervention of the Virgin, these authors make their case to St Patrick. Like Ó Dálaigh's work, this collection of poems illustrates the devotional *mentalité* of a lay elite and as such they are very much reflective of a general Gaelic mindset. The poems' illus- tration of the importance of Lough Derg in the socio-geographical context of Ireland underlines the centrality of communal cultural expression and identity in Gaelic devotional practice.[39]

[37] Yolande de Pontfarcy, 'The historical background to the pilgrimage to Lough Derg', in Michael Haren and Yolande de Pontfarcy (eds.), *The medieval pilgrimage to St Patrick's Purgatory Lough Derg and the European tradition* (Enniskillen: Clogher Historical Society, 1988), pp. 7–34.

[38] Aubrey Gwynn, *The medieval province of Armagh 1470–1545* (Dundalk: Tempest, 1946), pp. 268–9.

[39] For previous discussion of these poems see Tadhg Ó Dúshláine, 'Lough Derg in native Irish poetry', *Clogher Record* 13/1 (1988), 76–84; Próinséas Ní Chatháin, 'The later pilgrimage–Irish poetry on Loch Derg', in Haren and de Pontfarcy (eds.), *The medieval pilgrimage*, pp. 202–11. The texts of the poems are conveniently collected together in Shane Leslie, *Saint Patrick's Purgatory: a record from history and literature* (London: Burns Oates and Washbourne, 1932), pp. 163–80.

Tadhg Dall Ó hUiginn's (d.1591) poem beginning 'Teach leagha leaba Phádraig' ('Patrick's Bed is a healer's abode') emphasises Patrick's support for the 'men of Ireland' ('Do bhí Pádraig Phuirt Manaidh . . . ag síorchabhair fhear nÉireann') and he is hailed as the 'adored prophet of the Irish'. Significantly, the poet's employment of the ethnically inclusive term *Éireannach* ('Irish person') no doubt mirrors both the historic Anglo-Norman involvement in the development of the Lough Derg pilgrimage and the late sixteenth-century process of ethnic coalescence between the historic Irish communities in reaction to Tudor aggrandisement.[40] Unfortunately, death had deprived the Irish of their country's healer ('Liaigh cabhartha') and they now resembled a ship's crew without direction or a flock without a shepherd. Nonetheless, Ireland's patron has left behind him a place where his people may seek spiritual solace and healing, namely the 'cave of Patrick the primate'. The afflicted are required to enter Patrick's cave and having been healed, they must bathe their wounds in a nearby pool. The potency of these waters was such that no matter how grievous the wound, it could not remain beyond the reach of their efficacious cure.[41] In a poem extant in a fragmentary state, Tadhg Dall triumphantly describes the Purgatory as 'the bright Rome of the western world', while remarking that St Patrick, in this instance styled 'Archbishop of Ireland' ('ardesbuc Innsi hEalga'), spent a period in the cave struggling with demons.[42] Although Ó hUiginn's testimony in these poems is of intrinsic relevance to the history of Lough Derg, more generally and more importantly, the poems evidence an acute consciousness of ethnic and territorial integrity interwoven within the fabric of a conventional bardic devotional exercise.

Tuileagna Ó Maolchonaire's poem 'Loch Dearg aonRóimh na hÉireann' ('Lough Derg the one Rome [i.e. chief sanctuary] of Ireland') manifests a similar reflexive interchange between sacred and profane discursive modes and a correspondingly implicit juxtaposition of communal identity with devotional experience.[43] The poet recounts how

---

[40] De Pontfarcy, 'The historical background to the pilgrimage to Lough Derg', in Haren and de Pontfarcy (eds.), *The medieval pilgrimage*, pp. 32–4. In 1561 the Anglo-Norman Pierce Butler of Cahir requested An Cosnamhach Mac Flannchadha to transcribe Gaelic prose and poetic material relating to St Patrick's Purgatory. Flower, *Catalogue*, II, p. 477.

[41] Leslie, *Purgatory*, pp. 163–4.

[42] *Ibid.*, p. 165.

[43] I have followed Tadhg Ó Dúshláine's identification of the author of this poem with Tuileagna Ó Maolchonaire (fl. 1584–1603). Regarding the poet's extant biographical details see T. F. O'Rahilly, 'Irish poets, historians, and judges in English documents, 1538–1615', *Proceedings of the Royal Irish Academy* 36, C 6 (1922), 88–9. Cf. Ó Dúshláine, 'Lough Derg', pp. 80–1.

Patrick chose Lough Derg as a place of penance and he maintains that any person desiring to cleanse himself of sin is well advised to journey there. Ó Maolchonaire admits that he has come to this venerable lake in order to have his soul cured and he places himself at the mercy of St Patrick, the 'judge of Ireland' ('a bhreitheamh na Banbha a Phádraig') and 'patron of Ireland' ('a éarlaimh Éireann').[44] In particular, the poet implores Patrick or 'Ireland's patron' to intervene on his behalf to save him from God's wrath. He remarks that Lough Derg offers a path which leads directly to God and he must win the favour of the Almighty, for this sacred place favoured by kings promises salvation to one and all.[45] In 'Slán uaim ag oileán Phádraig' ('Farewell to Patrick's Isle'), Fearghal Óg Mac an Bhaird also frames his praise of the spiritual benefits of the site within the larger geographical context of Ireland, describing the Lough Derg experience as the 'chief pilgrimage of Ireland' ('ceann oilithre na hÉireann').[46] Significantly, Fearghal Óg Ó hUiginn claims that God had introduced Patrick and the Christian faith to Ireland with the specific purpose of cleansing ancestral transgression.[47] Patrick's ability to intercede with God on behalf of sinners is further highlighted in Aonghus Ó hUiginn's 'Mo chean théid i dteaghdhais Phádraig' ('Blessed is he who visits Patrick's house'). In this case, the poet in addition to seeking the aid of Patrick to effect his salvation also requests the intercession of other Irish saints such as Colm Cille, Brendan, Brigid, Mo Laise, Caillín, Tighearnach, Ciarán and others.[48] Generally, the Lough Derg poems' portrayal of Patrick as mediator corresponds to Aonghus Fionn Ó Dálaigh's desire to enlist the Virgin as a powerful spiritual advocate to represent his case before God and to secure the remission of earthly transgressions. In their emphasis on the evocation of place and atmosphere, the Lough Derg poems no doubt mirror the traditional Gaelic interest in *dinnsheanchas* or topographical lore. However, the specific awareness of the pan-Hibernian social and geographical context against which the penitential experience is located in these poems is not simply an incidental antiquarian detail, rather it is an indication of the extent to which medieval Christianity had been seamlessly inculturated within Gaelic modes of representation and identity.

The composition of bardic poetry was primarily politically focused and the extant corpus of devotional poetry is professionally marginal in

---

[44] Leslie, *Purgatory*, p. 169, stanzas 12–3.   [45] *Ibid.*, p. 170, stanzas 27–8.
[46] *Ibid.*, pp. 172–3, stanza 6.   [47] *Ibid.*, p. 179, stanza 4.
[48] *Ibid.*, pp. 174–5, stanzas 6–11. Cf. Ní Chatháin, 'The later pilgrimage', in Haren and de Pontfarcy (eds.), *The medieval pilgrimage*, p. 206; Henry Jones, *Saint Patrick's Purgatory containing the description, originall, progresse, and demolition of that superstitious place* (London, 1647), pp. 7–8.

terms of the central dominant emphasis on seigneurial validation. The
political repertoire of the poets remained firmly rooted in the indigenous
historical and poetic tradition and it is arguable that this dominant
bardic political strand coexists somewhat ambiguously with the Christian piety of the poets' religious work. Katharine Simms has identified a
late-medieval strain of church hostility to bardic poets which is probably
to be traced to the Gregorian reform movement and the consequent
separation of ecclesiastical and profane scholarship.[49] The antipathy of
some churchmen to the poets may also be attributed to the bardic mode
of dynastic endorsement which remained essentially non-religious in
character. Interestingly, it seems that Gaelic divines were represented
in clerical opposition to the poets and accordingly an attitude of aversion
does not appear to have been exclusive to clergy of Anglo-Norman
background. For instance, under Primate John Colton a provincial
synod of Armagh held in the 1380s enacted legislation against poets as
well as harpers, mimers, jugglers, drummers and kerns. Tellingly, these
measures were described as a renewal of statues passed previously
by Archbishop Dáibhidh Ó hOireachtaigh (d. 1346) and Archbishop
Richard FitzRalph (d. 1360).[50]

Earlier evidence of bardic and clerical dissension is contained in a
poem attributed to Giolla Brighde Mac Con Midhe (d.*c.* 1272). In this
piece beginning 'A theachtaire tig ón Róimh' ('Messenger who comes
from Rome'), the author vehemently criticises a supposed ban by the
church on the composition of praise poetry. Addressing an unnamed
clerical opponent of the poets, he demands documentary evidence from
Rome in support of a prohibition.[51] Denying that such a decision had in
fact been taken in Rome, he argues that poetry is a gift from God
('Donum Dei gach dán binn') and he demands rhetorically why St
Patrick had not suppressed the cultivation of poetry on his arrival in
Ireland if this were indeed the policy of the church.[52] Ironically, Mac
Con Midhe's defence of the bardic art and its function in Gaelic society

---

[49] Katharine Simms, 'The brehons of later medieval Ireland', in Daire Hogan and W. N.
Osborough (eds.), *Brehons, serjeants and attorneys: studies in the history of the Irish legal
profession* (Dublin: Irish Academic Press, 1990), pp. 54, 74; Katharine Simms, 'An
eaglais agus filí na scol', *Léachtaí Cholm Cille* 24 (1994), 21–36; Katharine Simms,
'Frontiers in the Irish church – regional and cultural', in T. B. Barry, Robin Frame
and Katharine Simms (eds.), *Colony and frontier in medieval Ireland: essays presented to
J. F. Lydon* (London: Hambledon Press, 1995), pp. 192–3.
[50] D. A. Chart (ed.), *The register of John Swayne Archbishop of Armagh and primate of Ireland
1418–1439* (Belfast: Stationery Office, 1935), pp. 8, 11.
[51] N. J. A. Williams (ed.), *The poems of Giolla Brighde Mac Con Midhe* (Dublin: Irish Texts
Society, 1980), no. XVIII, pp. 204–13.
[52] *Ibid.*, pp. 204–6, stanzas 7, 10.

can hardly have served to placate his clerical antagonists. Proclaiming that praise of men also glorified the power of the Almighty, he claims that bardic eulogy conferred lasting fame on patrons and their wealth. If poetry were suppressed, it would result in the loss of illustrious pedigrees and knowledge of heroic achievements. The composition of poetry underpins the genealogical and martial status of the nobility and if eulogy were abandoned it would entail the disappearance of critical social distinctions separating the elite from their inferiors ('gach saoirfhear ann budh aitheach').[53]

A poem composed for Diarmaid O'Brien (d. 1364) of Thomond also contains sentiments similar to those expressed by Mac Con Midhe. Of uncertain authorship, the piece beginning 'Damhaidh dúind cóir, a chléirche' ('Grant us justice, cleric') likewise denies that anti-poet measures were to be attributed to Rome. In fact, native divines had taken it on themselves to dislodge the poets of Ireland ('sgola Éireand d'athchar as') and to usurp the rewards which formerly accrued to the bardic profession ('Ar gcuidne ag cléirchibh Éireand').[54] This author also echoes Mac Con Midhe's argument that the neglect of eulogy would result in a detrimental dislocation of social hierarchies.[55] It is no coincidence that he develops the theme of clerical opposition to aristocratic expenditure on bardic compositions which was fleetingly raised by Mac Con Midhe.[56] Addressing O'Brien, the author specifically states that churchmen were seeking to divest poets of a professional income for their own ends.[57] These references hint at clerical jealousy of the material rewards accruing to poets and it seems that churchmen sought to redirect this wealth to ecclesiastical coffers. Clerical–bardic tension probably peaked in the fourteenth century.[58] The dramatic success of the Franciscan Observantine reform movement in Gaelic areas in the fifteenth century and the work of the Franciscan bardic poet Pilib Bocht Ó hUiginn (d. 1487) herald a new era in relations between the church and the bardic elite in Gaelic Ireland.[59]

---

[53] *Ibid.*, p. 212, stanza 33.
[54] Brian Ó Cuív (ed.), 'An appeal on behalf of the profession of poetry', *Éigse* 14 (1971–2), 93–2, stanzas 1, 6.
[55] *Ibid.*, pp. 95–6, stanzas 17–20.
[56] Williams, *Giolla Brighde*, p. 206, stanza 9.
[57] Ó Cuív, 'An appeal', p. 93, stanzas 6–7.
[58] For other examples of clerical–bardic hostility at this period see Simms, 'An eaglais'; T. F. O'Rahilly (ed.), *Measgra dánta*, 2 vols. (Cork: Cork University Press, 1927), I, no. 13, pp. 21–2.
[59] Lambert McKenna (ed.), *Philip Bocht Ó hUiginn* (Dublin: Talbot Press, 1931), pp. ix–xiv. Cf. Alan J. Fletcher, *Drama, performance and polity in pre-Cromwellian Ireland* (Cork: Cork University Press, 2000), pp. 33–4.

Nonetheless, evidence from the sixteenth century reveals a continued, if admittedly opaque, clerical–bardic opposition which suggests that the poets were not ideologically subordinate advocates of Christianity. Poets incorporated their religious beliefs within the compositional domain of devotional poetry but their central poetic function and ancillary bardic activities demonstrate that their primary commitment was to a socio-political tradition which privileged the primacy of Gaelic high culture. For instance, the testimony of two Gaelic contractual documents, dating to 1539 and 1580 respectively, provides evidence for a bardic regulatory role in the enforcement of the conditions agreed. In each case, it was stipulated that contravention of the given provisions would be punished by both bardic satire and ecclesiastical excommunication.[60] This material suggests no diminution of bardic status *vis-à-vis* the church. Significantly, the Franciscan cleric Eoghan Ó Dubhthaigh (d. 1590) severely criticised some bardic poets for an overriding professional focus and their failure to venerate the Virgin in their work.[61] Mindful of the ambiguity of the church's attitude to the poets, Aonghus Ó Dálaigh in a poem he composed for Felim O'Toole (fl. 1591) advocated his appointment as the latter's personal poet or *ollamh* in spite of clerical prohibition ('Gabhuimsi tar crois cléire/leatsa, a Fhéilim, d'éinchéile').[62] These references and the extensive corpus of bardic validatory poetry illustrate the extent to which poets operated within a dominant social and cultural framework which had subsumed medieval Christianity within the canon. Critically, the bardic elite continued to articulate an ideological rationale which predicated the primacy of Gaelic cultural sovereignty and this fact generated a latent tension in the interaction of the poets with the church.

In the remainder of this essay, it is argued that the small number of sixteenth-century bardic compositions which may be said to reflect contemporary religious dissension clearly illustrate the degree to which poets interpreted sectarian controversy in socio-cultural as opposed to strictly theological terms. In effect, bardic awareness of the reformation was influenced more by considerations of cultural integrity and autonomy than by notions of abstract allegiance to a particular denominational

---

[60] Maura Carney (ed.), 'Select documents III. Agreement between Ó Domhnaill and Tadhg Ó Conchobhair concerning Sligo castle (23 June 1539)', *IHS* 3 (1942–3), 282–96; K. W. Nicholls (ed.), 'The Lisgoole agreement of 1580', *Clogher Record* 7 (1969), 27–33.

[61] Cuthbert Mhág Craith (ed.), *Dán na mbráthar mionúr*, 2 vols. (Dublin: Dublin Institute for Advanced Studies, 1967–80), I, no. 27, pp. 139–40.

[62] Éamonn Ó Tuathail (ed.), 'A poem for Felim O'Toole', *Éigse* 3 (1941–2), 261, lines 17–18.

alignment. Bardic devotional lore constituted an integral if subsidiary element within a larger cultural mosaic which fused Gaelic and Christian traditions. The Gaelic cultural idiom was a contextual prerequisite to the formulation and expression of bardic piety. In fact, the poets mediated questions of faith within a larger explicative schema underpinned by an awareness of the Gaelic cultural autonomy which assured their intellectual and corporate prestige. Bardic depiction of religious turbulence within an interpretative framework characterised by cultural tension deriving from crown consolidation is discernible from a relatively early date in the sixteenth century. In the anonymous poem entitled 'Fúbún fúibh, a shluagh Gaoidheal' ('Shameful your stance, men of the *Gaoidhil*'), probably composed around 1542–3, the poet berates several leading Irish families for their acquiescence in English claims to dominion in Ireland.[63] In what is unquestionably a deliberately political poem in terms of its denigration of emollient Irish attitudes in the face of crown policy, the inclusion of an uncomplimentary reference to apparent Gaelic acceptance of Henrician church reform ('Fúbún séana Mheic Mhuire') is an important early indication of the extent to which politics and religion became enmeshed in the Gaelic assessment of conquest.[64]

An anonymous poem beginning 'Mairg rug ar an aimsirsi' ('Unfortunate the person overtaken by present times'), possibly composed in Munster during the years 1575–9, is blunt in its presentation of social and ecclesiastical chaos as constituent elements of a larger process of upheaval. Lamenting the troubled state of the country, the poet remarks that neither castle, monastery nor the sanctuary of the *literati* offers a haven from which to escape widespread danger ('Ní díon múr ná mainistir/ná tearmonn aosa dána').[65] Now the pope goes unregarded ('nach fiú pinginn an pápa') and both the country and church are degraded, while there is no place for the woodkern to seek protection since the clergy have already fled the sites which traditionally offered sanctuary ('cáit a ngeabha an ceithearnach, ag teitheadh ó 'tá an cléireach?').[66] The friars, notwithstanding the affection in which they had previously been held, were now obliged to discard their habits for fear of arrest ('folchuid siad a n-aibhidi/d'eagla go ngeabhthaoi orra'). On the other hand, the poet observes that some clergymen have little claim to respect given their indifference to honour and truth and their love of falsehood

---

[63] Brian Ó Cuív (ed.), 'A sixteenth-century political poem', *Éigse* 15 (1973–4), 261–76.
[64] *Ibid.*, p. 273, stanza 9.
[65] R. A. Breatnach (ed.), 'Anarchy in west Munster', *Éigse* 23 (1989), 58, stanza 4.
[66] *Ibid.*, p. 58, stanzas 4–5.

and bribes.[67] Bardic poets have likewise been humiliated and they should swap places with the nobility to avoid being plundered. Indeed, many of the so-called nobility are themselves culpable in this regard. Those who are hostile to poets merit the enmity of God.[68] Interestingly, the author presents the fate of the poets, friars and kern as interlinked examples of the general disregard for previously accepted norms of civility. Indeed, it is the collapse of the church's charitable role in the provision of sanctuary which is highlighted and the friars are depicted in terms suggestive of their participation in a communal network.

A similar depiction of religious expression integrated within the general context of Gaelic cultural and social experience is evident in the poem beginning 'Bráthair don bhás an doidhbhreas!' ('Poverty is a companion to death!'). Its author, Maoilín Óg Mac Bruaideadha, having apparently fallen victim to penury, composed this piece possibly sometime between 1576 and 1579 in an effort to regain the favour of a disaffected patron, Conor O'Brien, the third earl of Thomond.[69] The poet presents his case in a heavily ironic tone which reveals continued Gaelic adherence to customs which were opposed by the crown authorities. Divided into three distinct discursive episodes, the poet discusses the inevitable misfortune of the poor man in the first section, in the second and most interesting section he threatens to blackmail Thomond for his maintenance of various practices unacceptable to the English, while in the third section he anticipates his eventual rapprochement with O'Brien. In the second section, Mac Bruaideadha declares his intention to avenge his alleged desertion by Thomond with a public exposition of his continued exaction of a variety of forbidden Gaelic levies and dues, his support of elements openly defiant of the crown, his veneration of statues and patronage of holy wells ('Adéar go n-adhrann d'íomháigh . . . adéar go dtéid fá thobar'), and not least his connoisseurship of Gaelic poetry ('s go n-éistfeadh dán is duanlaoidh').[70] Once more, devotional practice is presented within the definitive context of a unified Gaelic cultural experience in which the rituals of worship form part of a comprehensive semiology of communal representation.

---

[67] *Ibid.*, p. 59, stanzas 6–7. For the pastoral role of the Franciscans in Gaelic Ireland see P. J. Corish, *The Catholic community in the seventeenth and eighteenth centuries* (Dublin: Helicon, 1981), p. 22; C. N. Ó Clabaigh, *The Franciscans in Ireland, 1400–1534: from reform to reformation* (Dublin: Four Courts Press, 2002).

[68] Breatnach, 'Anarchy', pp. 59–60, stanzas 8–15.

[69] O'Rahilly, *Measgra*, I, no. 26, pp. 41–4; notes pp. 79–81.

[70] *Ibid.*, pp. 42–3, lines 37–76. Regarding the continued popularity of traditional pilgrimages in Thomond in the late sixteenth century see Bernadette Cunningham (ed.), 'A view of religious affiliation and practice in Thomond, 1591', *Archivium Hibernicum* 48 (1994), 17.

Two poems which initially appear to suggest a Tridentine reaction to the Protestant reformation, on closer analysis reveal their authors' fairly conventional appreciation of the supreme spiritual efficacy of the mass expressed against the backdrop of a specifically Gaelic environment. Given the central importance of the mass to the Christian liturgy of pre-reformation Europe, it is no surprise to find that both Fearghal Óg Mac an Bhaird and Domhnall Mac Bruaideadha reflect common devotional wisdom in this regard.[71] It is, no doubt, an indication of the superficial influence of the reformation in the Gaelic heartlands in the sixteenth century that one of the most comprehensive of sixteenth-century bardic commentaries on contemporary religious controversy should have derived from its author's experience of developments in Scotland. Mac an Bhaird's piece beginning 'Dursan mh'eachtra go hAlbuin' ('Grievous my visit to Scotland') most likely dates from around the year 1581 when it is documented that the author received a payment for poems he composed for James VI.[72] The poet expresses bitter regret that pursuit of his bardic vocation and desire for material enrichment had encouraged him to journey to Scotland where the absence of the mass now imperilled his eternal salvation ('Do thréigeas ord is aifrionn . . . do ghrádh na séad saogholta'). Lamenting the rejection of belief in transubstantiation in Scotland, he affirmed his personal allegiance to received dogma ('Adhruim don reacht do-rinne').[73] By way of apocalyptic warning to Scotland, Mac an Bhaird recounts an exemplum in which a Jew who had deliberately defiled the blessed sacrament was drowned along with fellow unbelievers by a massive deluge of blood pouring from the violated host.[74] He remarks that Scotland is not the only country to have rejected the doctrine of transubstantiation and he once again bemoans his seduction by worldly interests. The sole possible resolution of his spiritual predicament is to return to his native land ('siar dom dhúthchos go ndeacham') and he prays that he will not die in Scotland ('Iarruim gan mh'éag i nAlbain').[75] While the poem's composition was obviously inspired by firsthand exposure to the ecclesiastical regimen engendered by the Scottish reformation, it is significant that the poet does not seek to categorise theological conflict in standard oppositional

---

[71] John Bossy, 'The mass as a social institution 1200–1700', *Past & Present* 100 (1983), 30; Duffy, *Stripping of the altars*, ch. 3.

[72] John Bannerman, 'The Scots language and the kin-based society', in D. S. Thomson (ed.), *Gaelic and Scots in harmony* (Glasgow: University of Glasgow, 1988), p.10.

[73] Lambert McKenna (ed.), *Aithdioghluim dána: a miscellany of Irish bardic poetry*, 2 vols. (Dublin: Irish Texts Society, 1939–40), I, pp. 204–5, no. 53, stanzas 1–8.

[74] *Ibid.*, pp. 205–6, stanzas 9–17; Ó Caithnia, *Apalóga*, pp. 192–3.

[75] *Ibid.*, p. 206, stanzas 21–2.

sectarian terms. In fact, the poet is content to report the actuality of the confessional situation in Scotland and he certainly does not attempt to locate his discussion within the contemporary context of polemical sectarian debate. Indeed, with the exception of references which reflect events in Scotland and the poet's stated desire to return to Ireland to benefit from the celebration of the mass there, the poem is essentially a traditional bardic exercise in piety.

Domhnall Mac Bruaideadha, who was active in Munster in the later sixteenth century, in the poem beginning 'Raghad d'éisteacht aifrinn Dé' ('I shall set off to hear God's mass') likewise seems at first glance to have been influenced by a Tridentine consciousness, although on more detailed examination it is arguable that the work is also a product of conventional bardic devotional composition. The poet opens on a some-what confrontational note when, declaring his intention to hear mass, he demands rhetorically if anyone can deny that Jesus is present at the sacrifice as both man and God ('Tig na Dhia agus na Dhuine ann, cia do'n uile nách admhann').[76] Although unwell, he vows to set out to hear mass which he depicts as the spiritual balm of mankind ('biadh gach nduine an t-aifrionn') and again in a tone which hints at a background of religious controversy, he declares that a person cannot claim to be Christian unless he believes that Christ is made present as man in the host ('Ní Críostaidhe nách creid sin'). Aside from these two topical allusions, the remainder of the poem is an unremarkable eulogy on the mass and the emphasis on the body of Christ corresponds to Eamon Duffy's description of this potent image as 'the focus of all hopes and aspirations of late-medieval religion'.[77] As in the case of Fearghal Óg Mac an Bhaird's Scottish poem, Mac Bruaidheadha seems to reflect the influence of contemporary religious controversy. His response is simi-larly abstract in political terms in so far as he does not adopt a sectarian polemical stance predicated on a Protestant/Tridentine Catholic oppos-itional basis. The mass is presented as the supremely beneficial act of Christian worship which guarantees the salvation of the community of the faithful. In effect, the sacrifice of mass represented a communal act of worship which promised the redemption of the world.[78] Mac Bruaideadha's sentiments highlight how central the communal dimension

---

[76] Cuallacht Cholm Cille, *Mil na mBeach* (Dublin: Gill and Sons, 1911), p. 35, lines 3–4.
[77] *Ibid.*, p. 36, lines 12, 17. Duffy, *Stripping of the altars*, p. 91.
[78] Duffy, *Stripping of the altars*, pp. 92–3. Flann Mac Cairbre in a manuscript marginal note written in 1554 interprets the reformation as essentially an unwelcome disruption of communal liturgical practice and not in terms of theological innovation or change: Charles Plummer (ed.), *Irish litanies* (London: Henry Bradshaw Society, 1925), pp. xi–ii, note 3.

was to bardic awareness of faith and how the expression of religious sentiment was symbiotically linked to representations of Gaelic cultural and social identity.

The material examined in the preceding paragraphs demonstrates that bardic poets articulated a collective Christian piety which bore a distinctive Gaelic imprint but which nonetheless would have been recognisable throughout contemporary western Europe. While expressed within the sociological format of the Gaelic cultural idiom, bardic emphasis on the passion, the sacrifice of the mass and Marian devotion is replicated by lay and clerical elites throughout Europe. What distinguishes bardic Christianity, however, is the fact that the poets combined a conventional late-medieval religious sensibility with a political ideology and validatory role which is profane in character. The supremacy of the bardic elite was intimately linked to the sovereignty of Gaelic culture and society. In so far as the poets' devotional outlook was conceptualised and formulated within a Gaelic cultural framework, bardic assessment of religious change was invariably undertaken within a referential schema embracing interconnected facets of a unified cultural experience and identity. The bardic combination of Christian and local traditional influences is not without parallel in early modern Europe. Carlo Ginzburg, for instance, has demonstrated how popular cultural consciousness in sixteenth-century Friuli reflects a rich medley of Christianity, folk cosmology and sorcery.[79] It would no doubt be anachronistic to attempt to reconcile or compartmentalise the apparent contradiction between the Christianity and political ideology of the poets. The poets surely made no such distinction between the sacred and the profane and consequently must have perceived both strands as exemplifying an integral Gaelic cultural identity. What is unusual in comparative terms in the case of the poets, however, is the extent to which their professional ideology overshadowed expressions of the Christian ethos which seems marginal to their primary ideological focus. On the other hand, this apparent dichotomy may simply reflect the vagaries of manuscript transmission which tended to favour the preservation of seigneurial compositions.

Samantha Meigs' theory that the Protestant reformation was doomed to failure because of an allegedly ingrained or reflexive bardic allegiance to Catholicism is belied by the evidence. In fact, bardic poets were for the most part reticent and possibly strategically detached in their response to the rival claims of the sixteenth-century reform movements. The attitude of the poets was no doubt also influenced by the vulnerable

---

[79] Carlo Ginzburg, *The night battles: witchcraft and agrarian cults in the sixteenth and seventeenth centuries* (Baltimore: Johns Hopkins University Press, 1983).

position of clerics and church tenants from bardic families who continued to remain *in situ* under the new ecclesiastical dispensation.[80] Given the inevitable degree of continuity in personnel between the old and new churches, it is possible that some poets remained publicly uncommitted with regard to confessional controversy to avoid compromising the prospects of clerical kinsmen *vis-à-vis* the established church.[81] Samantha Meigs, however, is correct to stress the extent to which bardic religious expression was integrated within the Gaelic cultural experience. In fact, considerations of cultural identity and sovereignty were dominant factors in the decidedly restrained bardic reaction to the Protestant reformation. There is no significant evidence extant to suggest that the poets were conscious of a transcendent loyalty to Tridentine Catholicism. Notwithstanding the fact that the poets articulate the faith of a lay elite, it is interesting that their devotional outlook seems little touched by an acquiescence in clerical oversight or intervention. In this regard, Meigs' claim that early modern Gaelic Ireland is exceptional in its lack of anti-clerical sentiment is far from accurate. The biting pseudo-elegy composed on the death of Tadhg O'Meara, last prior of Tyone priory near Nenagh which was dissolved in 1551, and the portrayal of the priest's ludicrous attempts to administer the last rites in *Pairlement Chloinne Tomáis* (*c.* 1608–11) attest to the existence of a current of early modern Gaelic anti-clericalism.[82]

---

[80] An apparently three-fold pattern of original recruitment to the bardic profession from the minor nobility, pre-Norman learned professions and church tenants is proposed by Katharine Simms, 'The brehons of later medieval Ireland', p. 60.

[81] The subject of recruitment from bardic families for ecclesiastical posts in the fifteenth and sixteenth centuries remains obscure. A sample examination of Canon Leslie's succession lists for clerics bearing the bardic surnames Mac an Bhaird and Ó hUiginn during these two centuries provides clear evidence of bardic occupation of church benefices. For Ó hUiginn clerics see Representative Church Body Library (Braemor Park, Dublin) MS 61/2/5 (Elphin), p. 16; MS 61/2/14/1 (Meath), p. 48; MS 61/2/15 (Tuam), pp. 148, 208, 291, 294; for Mac an Bhaird clerics see J. B. Leslie, *Clogher clergy and parishes* (Enniskillen: Fermanagh Times, 1929), pp. 99, 115, 126; J. B. Leslie, *Derry clergy and parishes* (Enniskillen: Fermanagh Times, 1937), pp. 301–2; RCB Library MS 61/2/5 (Elphin), p. 170; MS 61/2/8 (Kilfenora, Clonfert and Kilmacduagh), p. 516; MS 61/2/15 (Tuam), p. 101. Cf. Cuthbert McGrath, 'Í Eódhosa', *Clogher Record* 2/1 (1957), 9–10; Proinsias Mac Cana, 'The rise of the later schools of *filidheacht*', *Ériu* 25 (1974), 126–46; Henry A. Jefferies (ed.), 'Bishop George Montgomery's survey of the parishes of Derry diocese: a complete text from *c.* 1609', *Seanchas Ard Mhacha* 17/1 (1996–7), 71; Marc Caball, 'Politics and religion in the poetry of Fearghal Óg Mac an Bhaird and Eoghan Ruadh Mac an Bhaird', in Pádraig Ó Riain (ed.), *Beatha Aodha Ruaidh: the life of Red Hugh O'Donnell, historical and literary contexts* (London: Irish Texts Society, 2002), 95–7.

[82] Book of O'Conor Don, fo. 27b ('Marbhna abadh an Aonaigh'); Aubrey Gwynn and R. Neville Hadcock, *Medieval religious houses: Ireland* (Dublin: Irish Academic Press, 1988), pp. 214–15; N. J. A. Williams (ed.), *Pairlement Chloinne Tomáis* (Dublin: Dublin

While the course of the reformation in Ireland was beset by organisational and financial obstacles, the indifference of the bardic elite to the
new religion must be attributed largely to the intruded character of the
church by law established and its consequently largely unsympathetic
attitude to the culture of the indigenous majority. In spite of official
recognition of the evangelical implications of the linguistic realities of
Ireland as early as 1550, it was not until 1571 that the first Anglican
catechism in Irish was published.[83] Significantly, a bardic devotional
poem by Pilib Bocht Ó hUiginn (d. 1487) seems to have been chosen
as the printer's trial piece in advance of undertaking the more exacting
task of printing Seaán Ó Cearnaigh's primer. Possibly a native of Leyney
in Sligo, he was educated at Cambridge from where he graduated with a
BA degree in 1564/5. It was quite likely Ó Cearnaigh who chose
Ó hUiginn's poem as a trial piece and this choice may explain why in
the linguistic preface to his catechism he defers to the expertise of the
bardic poets in matters of Irish usage.[84] The product of a Gaelic milieu,
Ó Cearnaigh recognised the importance of engagement by reformers
with the *literati* and his comments in the catechism suggest that he
envisaged close contact between agents of the reformed faith and bardic
poets. The ongoing hostility of the crown authorities to the bardic elite,
who were perceived as advocates of opposition to crown hegemony, and
the cumulative anglocentric focus of the established church, ensured

Institute for Advanced Studies, 1981), pp. 37–8; Marc Caball, 'Pairlement Chloinne Tomáis I: a re-assessment', *Éigse* 27 (1993), 47–57. For later seventeenth-century expressions of Gaelic anti-clericalism see Seosamh Ó Dufaigh (ed.), 'Comhairle Comissarius na Cléire', *Studia Hibernica* 10 (1970), 70–83; Seosamh Ó Dufaigh and B. E. Rainey (eds.), *Comhairle Mhic Clamha ó Achadh na Muilleann* (Lille: Presses Universitaires de Lille, 1981).

[83] *The statutes at large, passed in the parliaments held in Ireland*, 20 vols. (Dublin, 1786–1801), I, p. 290; Richard Mant, *History of the church of Ireland* (London, 1840), pp. 261–2; E. P. Shirley (ed.), *Original letters and papers in illustration of the history of the church in Ireland, during the reigns of Edward VI, Mary and Elizabeth* (London, 1851), p. 40; F. R. Bolton, *The Caroline tradition of the church of Ireland* (London: SPCK, 1958), p. 3; Brendan Bradshaw, 'The Edwardian reformation in Ireland, 1547–53', *Archivium Hibernicum* 34 (1976–77), 90.

[84] Brian Ó Cuív (ed.), *Aibidil Gaoidheilge & caiticiosma* (Dublin: Dublin Institute for Advanced Studies, 1994), p. 67. John Carswell (d. 1572) in his translation of the *Book of Common Order* to classical Irish Gaelic, published in Edinburgh in 1567 for distribution in Gaelic Scotland and Ireland, readily recognised the scholarly authority of the poets. While lamenting their preoccupation with the historical traditions of the *Gaoidhil* and other profane concerns, he nonetheless envisaged bardic acceptance of the reformed church ('Gach seancha gan seanchus saobh, gach fear dáno nár aomh brég, cumand eadrad agas iad, a leabhráin bhig, bíadh go h-ég'). R. L. Thomson (ed.), *Foirm na n-urrnuidheadh* (Edinburgh: Scottish Gaelic Texts Society, 1970), pp. 8–13; D. E. Meek and James Kirk, 'John Carswell, superintendent of Argyll: a reassessment', *Records of the Scottish Church History Society* 19 (1975), 1–22.

that Ó Cearnaigh's vision of mutual interaction was short-lived.[85] Writing in 1605, Sir John Harington perceptively attributed the unsatisfactory progress of the reformed church to its deeply antipathetic attitude to indigenous religious sensibilities:

> By these and such kind of mild conferences many may be won, and not as our men have used them, by violent hewing down their crosses, burning and defacing their images, railing in the pulpit on all their saints and ceremonies, feasting on ash Wednesdays and good Fridays, going to plough on their Christmas days, and promising that all their ancestors are damned that did but pray to our Lady, with such like, as it is no marvel if such labourers have in 44 years made so slender an harvest.[86]

As late as the 1590s two bardic poets, Domhnall Óg Ó hUiginn and Maoilín Óg Mac Bruaideadha, assisted in the collaborative translation of the New Testament to Irish under way within the precincts of the newly founded Trinity College in Dublin.[87] In terms of establishing a bardic alignment with the Anglican church, their intervention was too little, too late. If bardic poets themselves remained largely aloof from sixteenth-century sectarian controversy, remaining faithful to an essentially traditional Christianity, an emergent cohort of gentlemen and clerical Gaelic poets actively embraced counter-reformation Catholicism. As the bardic caste declined in tandem with aristocratic Gaelic society, the new *literati* quickly developed what proved a powerful and enduring ideological nexus enshrining Gaelic culture and Roman Catholicism in contradistinction to the apparently unsympathetic intrusion of Protestantism to Ireland as the religious ancillary of the crown's programme of administrative consolidation.[88] When, at the end of the seventeenth century,

---

[85] Aidan Clarke, 'Varieties of uniformity: the first century of the church of Ireland', in W. J. Sheils and Diana Wood (eds.), *The churches, Ireland and the Irish* (Oxford: Blackwell, 1989), pp. 117–9; Colm Lennon, 'The shaping of a lay community in the church of Ireland, 1558–1640', in Raymond Gillespie and W. G. Neely (eds.), *The laity and the church of Ireland, 1000–2000: all sorts and conditions* (Dublin: Four Courts Press, 2002), p. 50.

[86] W. D. Macray (ed.), *A short view of the state of Ireland, written in 1605 by Sir John Harington, Knt.* (Oxford, 1879), p. 19. Cf. Gilbert Burnet, *The life of William Bedell, D.D. lord Bishop of Killmore in Ireland* (London, 1692), pp. 114–21; Peter Heylyn, *Cyprianus Anglicus* (Dublin, 1719), p. 130.

[87] Uilliam Ó Domhnuill (trans.), *Tiomna nuadh ar dtighearna agus ar slanaightheora Iosa Criosd* (Dublin, 1602); Nicholas Williams, *I bprionta i leabhar na protastúin agus prós na Gaeilge 1567–1724* (Dublin: An Clóchomhar, 1986), pp. 29–31.

[88] A somewhat similar paradigm developed in sixteenth-century Burgundy where the clerical and legal elites increasingly viewed loyalty to the Roman church as an essential component of French identity and in contradistinction Protestantism was seen as foreign or non-French. Mack P. Holt, 'Burgundians into Frenchmen: Catholic identity in

William King, then bishop of Derry, contrasted the success of the Protestant reformation in Wales and Gaelic Scotland with the situation in Gaelic Ireland, he readily admitted that the church had made a fundamental and costly error in its failure to engage with the Irish language, and by extension Gaelic culture.[89] Given the traditional emphasis on cultural sovereignty in the Gaelic world view, this was indeed to prove a decisive misjudgement on the part of the Protestant reformers. The reformation proved abortive in Gaelic Ireland not because the bardic elite determined so, but because counter-reformation Catholicism deftly and strategically appropriated a highly influential cultural patrimony neglected by the established church to its own cost.

sixteenth-century Burgundy', in Michael Wolfe (ed.), *Changing identities in early modern France* (Durham: Duke University Press, 1997), p. 361.

[89] William King, *A discourse concerning the inventions of men in the worship of God* (Dublin, 1694), pp. 91–2; cf. Phil Kilroy, *Protestant dissent and controversy in Ireland 1660–1714* (Cork: Cork University Press, 1994), p. 176. See also John Richardson, *A short history of the attempts that have been made to convert the popish natives of Ireland, to the established religion: with a proposal for their conversion* (London, 1712), pp. 10–12. Regarding the success of the reformation in Gaelic Scotland in a cultural environment remarkably similar to that of Ireland see Jane Dawson, 'Calvinism and the Gaidhealtachd in Scotland', in Andrew Pettegree, Alastair Duke and Gillian Lewis (eds.), *Calvinism in Europe, 1540–1620* (Cambridge: Cambridge University Press, 1994), pp. 231–53.

The political and religious thought of
Florence Conry and Hugh McCaughwell

Mícheál MacCraith

One of the striking features of Irish life in the first years of the seven-teenth century was the speed with which both the Gaelic *literati* and the Catholic hierarchy accepted James I as the legitimate monarch of Ireland.[1] Before granting recognition to James, however, the Catholic authorities had one major difficulty to overcome. After all, the pecu-liarities of the Irish scene with a Protestant monarch ruling over a Catholic people, was a complete contradiction of the solution proposed in Augsburg in 1555, *cuius regio eius religio*. If James was the *de facto* monarch, what were the obligations of his Catholic subjects *vis-à-vis* what was a heretical monarch according to the Catholic church?

The question was further complicated by James' own background. His mother, Mary Queen of Scots, was a Catholic. His wife, Anne of Denmark, had converted to Catholicism shortly before her husband's proclamation as king of England. There were even rumours, both at home and abroad, that James himself was about to become a Catholic, rumours that he did little to dispel, even if they had no basis in fact. English recusants were under the impression that James' accession to the throne of England would herald a new era of tolerance for Catholics. It is difficult to know exactly what promises James made during the nego-tiations prior to his succession and Antonia Fraser has drawn attention to his superb diplomatic skills in raising religious hopes without actually satisfying them.[2] His private correspondence with Cecil contains a more probable reflection of his real views: 'I will never allow in my conscience that the blood of any man shall be shed for diversity of opinions in religion, but I should be sorry that Catholics should so multiply as they

---

[1] Breandán Ó Buachalla, 'James our true king: the ideology of Irish royalism in the seventeenth century', in D.G. Boyce *et al.* (eds.), *Political thought in Ireland in the seventeenth century* (London: Routledge, 1993), pp. 1–35.
[2] Antonia Fraser, *The gunpowder plot: terror and faith in 1605* (London: Weidenfeld & Nicolson, 1997), p. 46.

might be able to practise their old principles upon us.'[3] On 24 March 1603, the very day Queen Elizabeth died, James wrote to the earl of Northumberland:

As for the Catholics, I will neither persecute any that will be quiet and give but outward obedience to the law, neither will I spare to advance any of them that will by good service worthily deserve it. And if this course will not serve to win every particular honest man, my privy dealings with any of them can avail but little.[4]

The consensus among contemporary historians is that any promises made by James were merely verbal, and in fact envisaged little more than a tolerated minority status for Catholics, similar to that enjoyed by French Huguenots. With the discovery of the gunpowder plot in 1605 and the subsequent framing of the oath of allegiance in 1606, Catholic hopes were finally crushed. Though both Catholics and Protestants believed it was justifiable to kill an evil or tyrannical monarch, James felt that this doctrine threatened both himself personally and also the principle of the divine right of kings. The discovery of the gunpowder plot only strengthened the king's convictions. James, however, wished to distinguish between Roman Catholics who were loyal subjects and those who were fanatics. The easiest way to overcome this problem lay in devising an oath of allegiance that strongly refuted any doctrine that held regicide to be pleasing to God. English Roman Catholics had no difficulty with the first part of the oath that asserted James to be the legitimate monarch of the kingdom. Other aspects of the oath, however, contained a number of disquieting features. Because of the issues involved and their impact on Catholic subjects of the crown, the oath bears quoting in full:

I A.B. doe trewly and sincerely acknowledge, professe, testifie and declare in my conscience before God and the world, That our Soueraigne Lord King JAMES, is lawfull and rightfull King of this Realme, and of all other his Majesties Dominions and Countreyes: And that the *Pope* neither of himselfe, nor by any authority of the Church or Sea of *Rome*, or by any other meanes with any other, hath any power or authoritie to depose the King, or to dispose of any of his Maiesties Kingdomes or Dominions, or to authorize any forreigne Prince to inuade or annoy him or his Countreys, or to discharge any of his Subjects of their allegiance and obedience to his Maiestie, or to give Licence or Leave to any of them to beare Armes, raise tumults, or to offer any violence or hurt to his Maiesties Royall Person, State or Government, or to any of his Maiesties subjects within his Maiesties Dominions.

Also I do sweare from my heart, that, notwithstanding any declaration or sentence of excommunication, or depriuation made or granted, or to be made

[3] G. P. V. Akrigg, *Letters of James VI & I* (Berkeley: University of California Press, 1984), p. 204.
[4] *Ibid.*, p. 207.

or granted, by the *Pope* or his successors, or by any Authoritie deriued, or pretended to be deriued from him or his Sea, against the said King, his heires or successors, or any absolution of the said subjects from their obedience; I will beare faith and trew allegiance to his Maiestie, his heires and successors, and him and them will defend to the vttermost of my power, against all conspiracies and attempts whatsoever, which shalbe made against his or their Persons, their Crowne and dignitie, by reason or colour of any such sentence, or declaration, or otherwise, and will doe my best endeuour to disclose and make knowne vnto his Maiestie, his heires and successors, all Treasons and traiterous conspiracies, which I shall know or heare of, to be against him or any of them. And I do further sweare, That I doe from my heart abhorre, detest, and abiure as impious and Hereticall, this damnable doctrine and position, That Princes which be excommunicated or depriued by the *Pope*, may be deposed or murthered by their Subjects or any other whatsoever. And I doe beleeue, and in conscience am resolued, that neither the *pope* nor any person whatsoeuer, hath power to absolue me of this Oath, or any part thereof; which I acknowledge by good and full authoritie, to be lawfully ministred vnto mee, and doe renounce all Pardons and Dispensations to the contrarie. And all these things I do plainely and sincerely acknowledge and sweare, according to the expresse words by me spoken, and according to the plaine and common sense and vnderstanding of the same words, without any Equivocation, or mentall euasion, or secret reseruation whatsoeuer. And I do make this Recognition and acknowledgement heartily, willingly, and trewly, vpon the trew faith of a Christian, So helpe me GOD.[5]

The oath contains seven affirmations:

1. that King James is lawful and rightfull king of the realm;
2. that the pope has no authority to depose the king or to authorize any invasion of his dominions, or to discharge any of his subjects of their allegiance to him;
3. that the taker will bear true allegiance to the king and defend him against all conspiracies regardless of any sentence of excommunication or deprivation by the pope or his successors;
4. that the taker will disclose to the king all treasons or conspiracies which he knows or hears of;
5. that the taker abjures as heretical the damnable doctrine that princes excommunicated by the pope may be murdered by their subjects;
6. that neither the pope nor anybody else has power to absolve the taker from the oath;
7. that the oath was lawfully administered to the taker.[6]

---

[5] C. H. McIlwain (ed.), *The political works of James I* (Cambridge, MA: Harvard University Press, 1918), pp. 73–4.
[6] W. B. Patterson, *King James VI and I and the reunion of Christendom* (Cambridge: Cambridge University Press, 1997), pp. 79–80.

While it seems that the oath was a genuine attempt by the king to conciliate moderate Catholics by distinguishing between those who were loyal and those who were disloyal to the crown, and while he insisted on a deliberate separation of the issues of the pope's spiritual and temporal powers, the oath still contained features, in particular, points 2, 5 and 6 above, that could not have been other than problematical for Catholics. While the oath did not deny the pope's power to excommunicate a ruler, its denial of the papal power to depose a king contradicted a right long claimed by the papacy. In claiming that the deposing power of the papacy was 'impious and heretical' and a 'damnable doctrine' to boot, the oath not only censured a doctrine that was held by many reputable Catholic theologians, but effectively granted king and parliament the power to define true doctrine. Finally, the assertion that the pope had no power to absolve from the oath would not rest easy with those who recognised the pope as the supreme authority on earth in moral and spiritual matters.[7]

Robert Bellarmine wrote to the Archpriest, George Blackwell, appointed head of the English Catholic community in England by pope Clement VIII in 1598, that 'in whatsoever words the oath is conceived by, the aduersaries of the faith in that Kingdome, it tends to this end, that the Authoritie of the head of the Church in England, may be transferred from the successor of St Peter, to the successor of King Henry the eight'.[8] Pope Paul V, in two letters, expressly forbade English Catholics to take the oath. This prompted the king to write his *Triplici nodo, triplex cuneus, or an apologie for the oath of allegiance* (1607). In his response to both the pope's letters and Bellarmine, James said that it was his aim from the very beginning to distinguish between loyal Catholics and the perverse disciples of the powder treason. The king also claimed that Bellarmine had made a fundamental mistake in confusing the oath of allegiance with the oath of supremacy of the previous reign. Unlike Elizabeth's oath, the new oath did not dispute the pope's spiritual authority.

Published anonymously in 1608, James' authorship of the apology was soon suspected and Paul V asked Bellarmine to respond. His *Responsio* appeared in 1608 under the name of his chaplain, Mattaeus Tortus. Lest it be unseemly for a monarch to bandy words with a cardinal's chaplain, however, the reply was left to the bishop of Ely and Lord Almoner, Lancelot Andrewes, who answered Tortus in a cleverly titled text, *Tortura Torti*, published in 1609.

---

[7] *Ibid.*, p. 81.   [8] McIlwaine (ed.), *Works of James I*, pp. 82–3.

At this stage James decided to go public and reissue the *Apologie*, but this time containing a lengthy preface addressed to 'all most mightie monarches, kings, free princes and states of christendom'. Published in 1609, the *Praefatio Monitoria* was a warning to the leaders of Christendom that the papal claim to be able to depose rulers was a threat to European peace. In the course of the *Praefatio*, James refuted Bellarmine's accusation that he was a heretic, claiming instead to be a Catholic Christian believing in the Apostles', Nicene and Athanasian creeds. In addition he held the first four general councils of the church as 'Catholic and Orthodox'. As for the fathers of the church, for the first five centuries he reverenced them as much as, even more than, the Jesuits did. He believed the scriptures, reverencing even the apocrypha as the writings of holy and good men, despite their not belonging to the canon. As regards the saints, he honoured their memory while loath to believe all the tales of 'the Legended saints'.[9] He reverenced the Virgin Mary, confessing her to be 'in glory above both angels and men'. As regards other matters never heard of in the first five hundred years after Christ, such as private masses, communion under one kind, transubstantiation, elevation of the host, the works of supererogation, 'a thousand other trickes', and above all the worship of images, he would rather believe too little than too much. In short he confined his belief to what was contained in Scripture, the three creeds and the ancient councils. 'I may well be a Schismatike from Rome, but I am sure I am no Heretique.'[10] As regards the papal primacy, James had no problem accepting the pope as *Primus Episcopus inter omnes Episcopos* and *Princeps Episcoporum*. On the other hand he denied that the church had any earthly visible monarch 'whose word must be a Law, and who cannot erre in his Sentence, by an infallibilitie of Spirit'.[11] The section on the papal primacy was followed by a very long digression in which James gave his reasons for believing that the modern papacy was the Antichrist described in the Book of Revelation. 'And this opinion no pope can euer make me recant; except they first renounce any further medling with Princes, in any thing belonging to their Temporall Jurisdiction.'[12]

If Christianity were to be united and temporal rulers freed from the threat of deposition, it could only happen through an ecumenical council. James had expressed his views on the desirability of a general council to several Catholic rulers and to pope Clement VIII prior to the gunpowder plot, but this time it was a public expression addressed to all Christian rulers and not to the papacy. Despite the fact that the document was specifically addressed to all the rulers of Christendom, the concluding

[9] *Ibid.*, p. 124.   [10] *Ibid.*   [11] *Ibid.*, p. 127.   [12] *Ibid.*, pp. 149–50.

remarks suggest that it was aimed particularly at Catholic rulers. James' equation of the pope with the Antichrist, however, was a tactical error of judgement and unlikely to win them to his point of view.[13]

The publication of the *Premonition* awoke great interest throughout western Europe, prompting responses from both defenders and opponents of the king's views.[14] The Vatican was caught in two minds: on one hand, it encouraged intended recipients of the book to refuse to accept it; on the other hand, it sought out scholars capable of refuting the book's arguments. The issues raised by James became more urgent with the assassination of Henry IV of France in 1610. Under orders from the pope, Bellarmine responded in 1610 and the Spanish Jesuit Francisco Suarez's *riposte*, *Defensio fidei Catholicae* (1613), became a fundamental work in political theory.

Irish Catholic views on the nature of their obligations to James I should not be treated in isolation but placed in the context of the general European debate sparked by the controversy emanating from the oath of allegiance. In 1615/16 Peter Lombard, titular archbishop of Armagh (1601–25), proposed a neat solution to the difficulty in distinguishing between objective and subjective heresy. Objectively James was a heretic, but subjectively he could not be held responsible for the way he was instructed. Because of this distinction Irish Catholics could accept James as their legitimate monarch *in temporalibus*. Though Lombard was one of Hugh O'Neill's strongest supporters during The Nine Years War, he withdrew his allegiance after the treaty of Mellifont, feeling that the interests of the Catholic church in Ireland would be best served by reaching an accommodation with James. Lombard was convinced that religious toleration would follow on declarations of loyalty. From 1612 onwards Lombard did his best to minimise O'Neill's influence on Irish ecclesiastical affairs. He strove to ensure that only those of similar views to himself and of the same Old English stock as himself, were appointed as bishops. He protested strongly to the pope when the Franciscan Florence Conry was appointed as archbishop of Tuam and Owen McMahon as archbishop of Dublin, arguing that these two were strong supporters of O'Neill and not interested in reaching accommodation with James.[15] Conry, according to Lombard, 'was more eager to sustain the war than the very officers of the army itself'.[16]

---

[13] Patterson, *King James*, p. 97.   [14] *Ibid.*, pp. 97–120.

[15] J. J. Silke, 'Later relations between Primate Lombard and Hugh O'Neill', *Irish Theological Quarterly*, 22 (1955), 25, 138, 139.

[16] Lucian Ceyssens, 'Florence Conry, Hugh de Burgo, Luke Wadding and Jansenism', in The Franciscan Fathers, *Father Luke Wadding commemorative volume* (Dublin: Clonmore and Reynolds, 1957), p. 300.

In 1615–16 the Holy Office consulted Lombard about twelve questions concerning loyalty to the king that were to be put to Roman Catholics held prisoner in Wisbech castle. Lombard prepared a document for the Holy Office entitled *Ad quaestiones* in which he treated in depth the relationship between a heretical king and his Catholic subjects, and gave him the occasion to develop his earlier views on this topic. Though the king was a heretic, this was due to misfortune rather than conscious choice. Accordingly, he was still the legitimate monarch. The king would lose his royal title only if he were consciously to chose heresy. Consequently, his vassals were still bound to offer him fealty in everything that pertained to the office of the king.

As a heretic James had no right to the protection of the Catholic church – he was no longer a Christian king. Nevertheless, he still retained the right of kingship, a right he held similar to that of pagan kings, the right of Caesar. For this reason, Catholics had to recognise him as their legitimate monarch. If they refused this recognition they were guilty of *lèse-majesté*. James had authority to make laws even in matters of religion. These laws, however, had to accord with the injunctions of true religion. Otherwise, they were not to be obeyed.

Lombard's views were in advance of most Catholics of his time. Even though he believed that the pope had the right to depose a tyrannical monarch, this right existed solely on the theoretical level and Lombard was prepared to ignore it in practice. James, however, was not impressed by Lombard's distinction between theory and practice, since the theory itself was a threat to the king's concept of the divine right of kings.

In 1616 Florence Conry, one of Lombard's *bêtes noires*, published *Sgáthán an chrábhaidh* (The mirror of piety) *or Desiderius* in Louvain.[17] Conry, born into a hereditary Irish learned family around 1560, went to Spain and joined the Franciscan order, attending the university of Salamanca. In 1601 he accompanied Don Juan del Aguila as adviser to the Spanish army sent to aid Hugh O'Neill and Hugh O'Donnell. After the defeat at Kinsale he returned with Hugh O'Donnell to Spain and attended him on his deathbed. In 1606 the General Chapter of the Franciscan order appointed him provincial of the Irish Franciscan Province. At the same time he successfully petitioned Philip III of Spain for permission to open a college for Irish Franciscans in Louvain, the intellectual centre of the northern European counter-reformation. In 1607 he escorted the exiled earls from Douai to Louvain where they

---

[17] Flaithrí Ó Maolchonaire, *Desiderius*, ed. T. F. O'Rahilly (Stationery Office: Dublin, 1941).

spent the winter and accompanied them to Rome the following spring. In 1609, much to Lombard's chagrin, he was nominated archbishop of Tuam.

As far back as 1593 Conry had translated a catechism from Spanish to Irish and perhaps it was the failure of this work to make an impact that inspired him with the idea of using the Irish Franciscan college in Louvain as a centre for publishing counter-reformation material in the Irish language. Giolla Brighde Ó hEoghusa, a former professional poet, joined the Franciscans and putting his literary talents at the service of the counter-reformation, produced the first Catholic work to be published in the Irish language. This appeared in Antwerp in 1611 and a second edition was printed from the Franciscans' recently acquired printing press in Louvain in 1614–15. Conry's *Desiderius* was the second catechetical work to be published by the Irish Franciscans in Louvain. Ostensibly a translation of a Spanish religious work, the translator took considerable liberties with his original, deleting and adding sections according to his own preferences. One particular addition, almost as long as one quarter of the original work, was specifically composed with the aim of encouraging Irish Catholics to persevere in their faith. This section is of particular interest in that it contains the first recorded discussion in the Irish language on the nature of civil authority and the limits of that authority. Conry distinguished clearly between the temporal powers and the spiritual powers, and, with James I obviously in mind, he strongly affirmed that it was heresy to hold that a temporal prince could be the head of the church.

My son, dismiss this thing that the heretics say: i. that the temporal princes are the head of the Church, for that is a heresy that grew from another heresy that is at its root, ii. as to think that there are no other powers in the world apart from the civil powers, and that these are in the hands of the secular princes, and that the Church, therefore, has not powers like these to teach and guide the Christian people on the way to salvation; nor to consider, if there are spiritual powers, that they are inseparable from the civil powers and that only the civil princes possess them, who have the highest civil powers. The first part of this, that denies the existence of spiritual powers, is heresy, as it is against the Gospel and Paul, where the spiritual powers that Christ gave to Peter are clearly found, and the powers, as Paul says, that God gave to him and to the bishops to teach the Church; for Christ says to Peter in Matthew, chapter sixteen: 'I will give you the keys of the kingdom of God, and whatever you bind on earth, will be bound in the kingdom, and whatever you loosen on earth will be loosened in the kingdom of God.' And he says about that, in the thirty first chapter, when he gives him those powers: 'Feed my sheep'; and he says in the eighteenth chapter: 'whoever does not listen to the Church, consider him as a heathen and a publican'. And the second part that makes an unbreakable link between the spiritual and the temporal powers, is equally against the Gospel and Paul. And it is certain that the spiritual powers and the temporal powers originated in a different and dissimilar way for the reason that it is the people or their ancestors who gave the kings whatever power they now possess; and it is Christ himself and not the people who gave the spiritual powers to Peter and to the other apostles; through whom the same powers were given to the bishops, without any permission being sought from the people, as can be proved from Paul's epistle to Titus and from his other epistle to Timothy.

'If this be true,' said Desiderius, '(and I firmly believe it is), it is not possible to take the oaths that they are wont to ask of the poor people, .i. that the princes are head of the Church.'

'It is not possibly in any way in the world', said Simplicity, 'for those oaths would only be rash heretical falsehoods that would merit vengeance from heaven on the perjurer, and it would provoke almighty God to smite with the plague of the Philistines those heretics who would set up their prince in such a way, and bring the vengeance of Dagon, god of the Philistines, who considered himself to be the ark of the living god, on the monstrosity of a Church that would try to place itself on the right hand of Christ's Church, while trying at the same time to behead it.[18]

Conry's distinction between the temporal and the spiritual powers is based on their springing from different sources. Kings derive their powers from the people, while bishops receive their powers from Christ, through Peter and the other apostles. The Irishman, having spent many years on the continent, was very well informed of the latest forms of Catholic counter-reformation theology. Robert Bellarmine, an Italian theologian at the university of Louvain, while not the first to introduce the distinction between the temporal and the spiritual powers, was the clearest exponent of the indirect power of the pope to intervene in civil affairs. Bellarmine believed that civil authority had no right to demand absolute allegiance from its subjects, and that religious authority super-seded civil authority in what concerned religious matters. One conclu-sion emerging from this view was that the pope had authority to depose a heretical monarch and absolve his subjects of their allegiance to him.

The revolutionary view that regal authority emanated from the people, was first proposed by Suarez, a Spanish theologian from the university of Salamanca where Conry had studied. This theory, of course, was at complete variance with the divine right of kings, a theory most dear to James himself, and one on which he had written most eloquently in his *Trew Law of Free Monarchies* in 1598. Conry did not elaborate on what he meant by the people, however, though we can be sure that he was not

---

[18] Ó Maolchonaire, *Desiderius*, lines 3862–3922, pp. 127–39.

espousing twenty-first-century versions of democracy. Whether he was advocating total rejection of James' rule or not, it is difficult to decide. Could it have been a bargaining ploy, that the Irish people were free to accept or reject James, and that their allegiance was conditional on being granted religious toleration? James, of course, would have found either interpretation totally unacceptable. The reference to oaths stating that princes are head of the church can refer to nothing else but the oath of allegiance and Conry's claim, that such oaths would only be rash heretical falsehoods that would merit the vengeance of heaven on the perjurer, shows him to have been an implacable enemy of the oath, and therefore highly unlikely to have bargained allegiance for tolerance, at least on the king's terms.

Hugh McCaughwell's treatise on the sacrament of penance, *Scáthán Shacramuinte na hAithridhe* (The mirror of the sacrament of repentance), was published in Louvain in 1618, and, though ostensibly a religious work like Conry's, it too is deeply imbued with political implications. A sketch of McCaughwell's life prior to writing the *Scáthán* is instructive. Having studied in the Isle of Man, McCaughwell was employed as a tutor to the two sons of Hugh O'Neill. In 1600 when O'Neill sent his son Henry as a hostage to Spain in order to ensure Spanish military aid, McCaughwell accompanied his pupil and studied at the university of Salamanca. He joined the Franciscans and spent some time lecturing in theology in Salamanca after his ordination to the priesthood. With Florence Conry he was a cofounder of St Anthony's College in Louvain, taking up residence in June 1607. He was heavily involved in diplomatic activities between 1609 and 1614, frequently negotiating on behalf of O'Neill with William Trumbull, the English agent in Brussels. In 1612 the English spy John Bathe advised the king of Spain to turn a deaf ear to any information supplied by either Conry or McCaughwell.

McCaughwell functioned simultaneously both as a theologian and a politician, and when we take this dual role into consideration it is easier to understand the strong political dimension of the *Scáthán*. The body of this work is essentially based on the fourteenth session of the Council of Trent which dealt with the sacrament of penance from 15 October 1550 to 25 November 1551. The teaching of Trent was made available in a more pastoral form in the Catechism of the Council of Trent which appeared in 1566. Though obviously well acquainted with this work, McCaughwell does not merely reproduce it, but takes pains to adapt it to the particular circumstances of the Irish situation in the early years of the seventeenth century. Being a creative teacher, the author relieves the tedium of formal doctrine with the addition of a hundred tales drawn from the *Magnum Speculum Exemplorum* (1480). While emphasising the need for simple direct language to reach the greatest possible audience, McCaughwell was by no means indifferent to matters of style, and the treatise exhibits many of the literary traits associated with the baroque, a fashion much in vogue during the period of the counter-reformation. The author draws attention to the fact that he is writing in the year 1617, exactly one hundred years after the reformation commenced. He also uses the *Rituale Romanum* of 1614, a work that laid down guidelines for the administration of the sacraments. On line 3873 of Ó Maonaigh's edition, for example, McCaughwell refers to the *Misereatur*, a prayer which the Roman Ritual decreed should be used during the administration of the sacrament of penance. The *Scáthán* was primarily intended for a lay readership and not for clergy, as is seen from the work's *approbatio* which states that it contains all that is necessary for confession *tam confessoribus quam poenitentibus*, thus prioritising the laity. Furthermore, in the beginning of the section dealing with absolution, the author informs his readers that they too should be informed about absolution even though this feature pertains to the priest's domain.

This raises interesting questions about the level of literacy in Irish in the early years of the seventeenth century. The author's defensiveness regarding his choice of simple language indicates that, while he was aware that some of his readers would be members of the literary classes, he was nevertheless trying to reach a much wider audience. It seems that the book was intended for members of the Gaelic aristocracy to enable them to instruct their families and servants much after the fashion of English recusants, and possibly also for Irish officers serving in the Spanish Netherlands. Even allowing both for a restricted level of literacy and a small publication run, however, the contents of the work could still have percolated to a wider audience both through the manuscript tradition and through oral instruction. In this context it should be borne in mind that reading in early modern Europe was largely a social activity with books having audiences rather than readers.[19]

Deeply imbued with the polemical spirit of the Catholic counter-reformation, McCaughwell stressed from the beginning that he was writing to refute Protestants. Every other Catholic nation had produced works such as these, and they were particularly necessary for the Irish, because of the dearth of priests in their country. The reference to Ireland as a Catholic nation is of particular interest. McCaughwell uses the word 'nation' sixteen times in the course of his work and it is noteworthy that

---

[19] Robert Darnton, 'History of reading', in Peter Burke (ed.), *New perspectives on historical writing* (Cambridge: Cambridge University Press, 1995), p. 150.

the earliest examples of the description of Ireland as a Catholic nation in Gaelic sources are all associated with Louvain. Thus when Robert Chamberlain was entering the Franciscans in Louvain in 1611 he left a sum of money in his will 'for the Irish print and the publication of things that will bring honour to God, glory to our nation and to the order of Saint Francis'.[20] A few years earlier, in 1609, Tadhg Ó Cianáin's *Teicheamh na nIarlaí* (The flight of the earls), uses the words *Éireannach* and *náision* in the same context. Of further interest is the fact that he refers to Henry O'Neill as *coronél na nEirinnach a fFlonndrus* (colonel of the Irish in Flanders); and he calls the Irish college in Douai a *coláiste Eirennach*.[21] Ó Cianáin seems to be deliberately eschewing the ethnic marker *Gael* in these two cases. In similar fashion, the title page of McCaughwell's work describes him as a lecturer in theology '*a ccolaisdi na mmbráthar nÉirionnach a Lobháin*' (in the college of the Irish brothers at Louvain). Breandán Ó Buachalla has referred to the semantic shift that took place in the meaning of the word *Éireannach* in the early years of the seventeenth century. Instead of simply meaning an inhabitant of the island of Ireland, the word takes on a more restrictive application, denoting an inhabitant of Ireland either of Gaelic or Old English stock who is characterised by allegiance to the Catholic faith and to the king of England.[22] The Gaelic writers associated with Louvain seem to be deliberately playing down the ethnic rivalry associated with the terms *Gael* and *Gall* and adopting a new use of the word *Éireannach* to unite the different Catholic groupings of Ireland together.

To return to McCaughwell; in his introduction he states that he intends to deal with the sacrament of penance under the four headings of sorrow, confession, amendment and absolution, the same as those found in the Roman Ritual of 1614. The author also includes a fifth heading that treats of indulgences, and states that he intends to use the writings of James I, 'our king', to prove that the Roman Catholic church has the power to bestow indulgences, even though the king's own ministers will not even permit the topic to be discussed. Of interest is the fact that McCaughwell considers Ireland to be a Catholic nation under King James. He laments the fervour of the heretics in publishing religious material for their own followers. In their zeal to resemble the true church as closely as possible, they have produced the Book of Common Prayer in place of the Missal, though McCaughwell himself feels that the

[20] Ó Lochlainn (1939), p. 97.
[21] Tadhg Ó Cianáin, *The flight of the earls*, ed. Paul Walsh (Dublin: M. H. Gill, 1916), pp. 24, 32.
[22] Breandán Ó Buachalla, 'Cúlra is tábhacht an dáin *A leabhráin ainmnighthear d'Aodh*', *Celtica* 21 (1990), 410–13.

Heretical Book of Hell would be a much more apt title. They have even translated parts of the Bible. The Irish Franciscan criticises the accuracy of the translation, but recent scholarship has shown that he had no scruples himself about using the 1602 version of the New Testament. He has deliberately chosen a simple direct style, because when it is a matter of truth and of refuting heretics, the message is much more important than the medium. He appeals to his readers to ignore stylistic and linguistic deficiencies, and concentrate on the message, a message containing nothing new, but the old faith brought by Patrick.

After the polemical and confrontational tone of the introduction, the modern reader notes with relief that the first and second sections of the treatise, those dealing with sorrow and confession, respectively, carry no trace of controversy and concentrate exclusively on Roman Catholic teaching. One would think in fact that McCaughwell is deliberately going out of his way to avoid controversy. Regarding the obligations of Catholics to fulfil the lawful commands of the civil authorities provided that they are not in opposition to the law of God or of his church, McCaughwell cites some examples: 'If the civil authority ordered you not to frequent the sacraments, not to listen to a Catholic sermon, to attend a heretical service or sermon, not to fast, to destroy churches, to insult images, consider these to be unlawful commands that are against God or his church and that you are obliged not to obey them.'[23] Having spelt out the obligations of a Catholic in no uncertain terms, McCaughwell then leaves it up to the reader himself to decide who are the civil authorities, and the lawful commands they impose. It seems that the author is deliberately avoiding mention of the king by name in this context. Perhaps this is just normal prudence and discretion to prevent the book from being confiscated for treason, but perhaps McCaughwell had another reason for avoiding the royal displeasure. We will return to this question again.

In the third section on amendment, the sectarian element returns to the fore. McCaughwell mentions a number of places of pilgrimage associated with St Patrick such as Lough Derg, Downpatrick, Croagh Patrick and Saul, places that have been closed down through the power of 'the perverse faith'. In emphasising the importance of prayer, fasting and alms-giving as the traditional methods of atoning for sin, McCaughwell warns his readers to avoid the methods of 'the perverse clergy of the false faith'. They are enemies of the sacrament of penance

[23] Aodh Mac Aingil, *Scáthán Shacramuinte na hAithridhe*, ed. Cainneach Ó Maonaigh (Dublin: Institute for Advanced Studies, 1952), lines 3172–3179, p. 97.

with no interest in amendment. If one compares the lives of the Irish saints with those of the new clergy, one is struck by the contrast between the asceticism of the saints and the easy soft lives of the new clergy. If the saints were wont to offer the sacrifice of the Lamb of God in the mass, the new clergy are only interested in the dirty supper of corpulent Calvin, *suipér salach Chailbhin chollaigh,* the invective of the original gaining further emphasis through the use of alliteration. If these people are on the road to heaven, then Patrick was either a fool or a treacherous deceiver.

The fourth section deals with absolution, clerical jurisdiction and its accompanying pastoral problems. These were major concerns in Ireland at the beginning of the seventeenth century, with no bishop resident in the country 'except pseudobishops whose faith was erroneous'. McCaughwell's comments throw some interesting light on the state of Ireland at this time. While stressing that the power of absolution was independent of the sanctity of the confessor, the author understands the reluctance of people to confess to a priest who is living with a woman or to attend mass celebrated by such a priest. McCaughwell's solution is simple, it is better to go than not to go, especially when there is no alternative. Ignorant priests are to be avoided except in case of necessity and the author is gravely concerned about the lack of healers of souls. This is due to the persecution of the heretics, *tré phersecusion 7 inghreim na n-eiriceadh.* Wise pastors of souls have been banished and replaced with 'proud erroneous heretical bishops and deceitful ministers with no conscience who do no study at night apart from lustful questions in bed with women'. Despite the insults, dangers and threat of captivity, however, there are still sufficient young Irishmen willing to go abroad and study for the priesthood with the firm resolution of returning home and serving the spiritual needs of their flock.

Logically speaking, the treatise should come to a conclusion after completing the section on absolution, but with the addition of a fifth section on indulgences, a topic that is only indirectly related to the sacrament of penance, we come to the most controversial and contentious section of the whole treatise. McCaughwell is deeply conscious of the fact that he is composing his work in 1617, exactly one hundred years since the reformation began. He attributes the reformation to one cause and one cause only, the hurt done to Luther's pride when pope Leo X preferred the Dominican Tetzel to Luther when seeking a candidate to preach about the indulgences to be conferred on those who would finance the campaign against the Turks. When Luther failed to get the coveted position he started preaching against indulgences: 'And thus began the cursed heresy that destroyed and harrassed much of

Europe, and it is from this heresy, alas, that England, Ireland and Scotland were destroyed in matters of faith, and it is this same heresy that detains us and many more like us in foreign parts having been banished from our country.'[24]

McCaughwell then unleashes a torrent of invective against Luther, a venomous diatribe based for the most part on the infamous work of John Cochlaeus, *Commentarius de actis et scriptis Martini Lutheri* (1549). According to Cochlaeus, Luther is a monster of pride, envy, guile, hypocrisy, drollery, bestial urges and lust. His doctrine is nothing but a dirty conglomeration of heresies that have been rejected long before. He speaks an extremely foul language; he is wallowing in dirt; he breathes a diabolical spirit of revolution against all authority and incites the passions of the masses. The so-called astonishing expansion of the Protestant movement is not surprising at all; indeed, all the licentiousness of the masses was tolerated, every inconvenience of religious life was abolished, the possessions of the church were used to shock the envy of the worldly rulers. Luther has been said to have descended directly from the devil, and accused of having made a pact with the devil. While Cochlaeus did not go so far as to say that the devil also came to take Luther away, his followers will not hesitate to claim this.[25]

With Cochlaeus as his source it is easy to see how McCaughwell can call Luther 'Lúitéir mac Lucifer', Luther son of Lucifer. He adds as well that 'the devil was more frequently with him and slept more closely beside him than his own Catherine, the devilish nun he married'. Neither is Calvin spared from the venom of McCaughwell's pen – he is accused of practicing sodomy with young boys. All the heresies existing at the beginning of the seventeenth century sprang from either Luther or Calvin. By 1535 there were 128 sects, all of which originated with Luther. This number had risen to 270 by 1547. At the time of writing his treatise, McCaughwell notes that Holland, Zealand and Friesland were being torn apart by two hostile sects with nothing in common apart from the utmost abhorrence of anything that Catholics respected, a loathing for indulgences in particular.

Having used the question of indulgences as an excuse for berating Luther, Calvin and their respective followers, McCaughwell is now free to turn to matters nearer to home and closer to his heart, the religious attitude of his majesty the king. And in stark contrast to the invective heaped on Luther and Calvin, the Franciscan's attitude to the king is all

---

[24] Mac Aingil, *Scáthán*, lines 5268–5272, p. 160.
[25] Thomas Balling, *Verständigung über Luther* (Gans: Gräfelfing-Munich, 1949), pp. 17–18.

sweetness and light. For McCaughwell, James is *ár rí uasal óirdheirc*, our
noble gracious king. Despite the respect and reverence, however, it must
be acknowledged that James is not a Catholic, but has been raised in the
faith of Luther and Calvin. But the king is not to be held culpable for his
training by bad mentors. It seems that McCaughwell, while not alluding
specifically to Peter Lombard nor making use of his terminology, is
making use here of his distinction between subjective and objective
heresy, a distinction that exempts the king from personal guilt and leave
his Roman Catholic subjects free to accept him as their lawful monarch
in temporalibus.

McCaughwell, however, goes much further than Lombard. Though a
heretic giving his allegiance to the teachings of Luther and Calvin, the
views of James are totally different from 'the barbaric blasphemies they
uttered against the holy councils, the holy fathers and the wholy
apostles'. To further his argument, McCaughwell uses one of James'
own writings to good effect, the *Praefatio Monitoria* of 1609. His use of
this document, however, is highly selective, cleverly selecting passages
that suit his own argument, and conveniently ignoring the rest. He thus
avoids anything that would prove offensive to Catholics, and concen-
trates on those points on which Catholics and Protestants are in agreement. In this fashion he manages to distinguish between the views of the
king and the more extreme views of Luther and Calvin. McCaughwell
notes with favour that the king accepts the three creeds and the teaching
of the first four general councils of the church, Nicea, Constantinople,
Chalcedon and Ephesus. He also accepts any doctrine that was held
unanimously by the fathers of the church for the first 500 years after
Christ. Finally the king gives pre-eminence to scripture over all the rest.
In his efforts to avoid controversy, McCaughwell admits in an aside that
the king does not indicate which particular books of scripture he accepts,
but conveniently ignores the pointed references James makes to the
apocryphal books, deliberately declaring that he accords them reverence
without attributing canonical status to them.

McCaughwell uses the account James gives of his own faith in order to
differentiate between the king and Luther and Calvin. The Irishman
regrets James' inability to accept the other fourteen councils of the
church and the teachings of the fathers from the sixth century onwards.
Nevertheless, McCaughwell hopes to demonstrate that the church's
teaching on indulgences is already contained in the doctrines believed
by the king.

Just as he refrained earlier on in the work from naming the king when
referring to the unjust commands of the civil authorities, in no part of his
treatise does McCaughwell accuse the king of heresy. This accusation is

reserved for the ministers of the Protestant faith. These are the people who declare indulgences to be against the faith of the king. This argument is not confined to indulgences, but concerns every custom and practice of the Catholic faith. They are all based on doctrine that the king holds as firmly as the Jesuits themselves. The examples quoted by McCaughwell cover the major points of contention between Rome and the reformers. Once again it must be stressed that this is a case of rather special pleading by the Irishman. He does not inform his readers that these very disputed points are actually treated in great detail by James himself, with the king refuting Roman doctrine. It is ironic that McCaughwell uses indulgences as the springboard to prove James' Catholicity, given that the word 'indulgences' occurs only once in the *Praefatio monitoria*, and in a mere footnote at that, to explain the following sentence: 'As for Purgatorie and all the trash depending thereupon, it is not worth the talking about.'[26] The Irishman's use of James' words is thus highly selective and manipulative, calculated to give a totally erroneous presentation of the king's views, but a presentation that would make it easier for Irish Roman Catholics to accept him as their lawful sovereign. It is also worth noting that McCaughwell's zeal for indulgences is in striking contrast with the restrained measured decrees on the same topic issued by the Synod of Dublin 1614. These decrees demonstrate that the ecclesiastical authorities were well aware of the dangers involved in the abuse of indulgences and the need to curb such excesses.

Though McCaughwell seems to touch on the distinction between objective heresy and subjective heresy at the beginning of his discussion of the king's religion, though without explicitly using such terminology, he ultimately adopts a totally different approach in determining the relationship that should prevail between the king and Irish Catholics. The Irishman seems to be indicating that all Protestants are out of step except the king and that the king is a Roman Catholic in spite of himself. It was not an argument calculated to persuade professional theologians on either side of the religious divide. Indeed, it is highly doubtful if a theologian of such repute as McCaughwell himself really believed it, but he doubtless felt that it was convincing enough to appeal to Irish lay Catholics uninstructed in the niceties of theological debate and unable or unlikely to read the *Praefatio monitoria* for themselves. More importantly, it was an argument designed to help Catholics accept James as their lawful sovereign and hopefully win freedom for religion in return for their loyalty.

[26] McIlwaine (ed.), *Works of James I*, p. 125.

We have just examined two Irish language religious texts, published within a year of each other in the Irish Franciscan college of Louvain. What is most striking is that each of these texts advocates a totally different political view *vis-à-vis* the English throne, Conry holding that the king's jurisdiction depended on the will of the people and refuting the oath of allegiance, McCaughwell advocating total allegiance in temporal matters. It cannot be insignificant that Hugh O'Neill died in Rome between the appearance of these works. As long as O'Neill was alive, hope, however slender, still remained for a Spanish backed invasion, despite Philip III's deep-seated reluctance to renew hostilities with England. O'Neill's own correspondence bears testimony to these hopes and in a memorial to Philip III in March 1615, he declared that 'rather than live in Rome, he would rather go to his land with a hundred soldiers and die there in defence of the Catholic faith and fatherland'.[27] Conry himself is found pressing the case for a Spanish invasion in September of the same year, using the escape of Sir James MacDonald from Edinburgh as a pretext to seek further aid:

and now he is in arms with one thousand five hundred soldiers in his territory of the Isle. His lands are at a distance of only three hours' navigation from those of the earls, to whom the occasion of this revolt would have been of the greatest importance if the earl of Tiron had been there, for, with very little help, this gentleman could move all Scotland to revolt and they would be of great help to one another in view of their vicinity, their kinship and the strength of their territories.[28]

With O'Neill's death, however, all such hopes were dashed, and the best interests of the Catholic church in Ireland dictated that an accommodation with James was more important than ever. When placed in this context, the divergence between Conry's and McCaughwell's views is much easier to understand. The discussion of James' own religious views with the corresponding attempt to make him as much of a Catholic as makes no difference, occurs in the final section of the treatise, the section on indulgences. This section has only a tenuous link with the rest of the work. The author states that he was writing this section in 1617, one hundred years after the start of the Reformation. He makes no mention of the fact, however, that O'Neill had died a year previously – it would have hardly been politique to do so. Is it possible that this final section was an afterthought dictated by the changed political circumstances caused by O'Neill's demise? It seems that despite all the moral posturing, allegiance to James was based on pragmatic rather than theoretical

[27] Micheline Kerney-Walsh, *Destruction by peace: Hugh O' Neill after Kinsale* (Armagh: Cumann Seanchais Ard Mhacha, 1986), p. 343.
[28] *Ibid.*, pp. 385–6.

grounds. Allegiance could be offered, withheld or downright rejected, depending on changing circumstances and what was seen to be the best interests of the Irish Catholic church. The events of 1625–7 tend to confirm this view.

Because of the hostility between England and Spain during the latter part of the sixteenth century, it was only natural that the Catholic Irish should look to Spain for aid. Relations between England and Spain changed for the better, however, during the reign of James I and it was thought that this new friendship could be sealed by a marriage between the Spanish Infanta Maria and James' son, the future Charles I. It is interesting in this regard to note that in 1618 the militant Conry himself was sent from Madrid to the Archduchess Isabella, ruler of the Spanish Netherlands, to assist in the deliberations.[29] The discussions were doomed from the start, however, because of misconceptions on both sides. Matters were not helped by the fact that Philip III of Spain did not keep his councillors informed of his secret correspondence with pope Paul V. In no way would the pope grant a dispensation for the Infanta to marry a Protestant prince. Charles would have to convert to Catholicism.[30] Charles' unsolicited arrival in Madrid in March 1623 was a further complication, the prince totally failing to understand that his visit could signify only one thing to his Spanish hosts, his willingness to convert. When the marriage negotiations broke down in 1623–4, shortly before James' death, it seemed that hostilities between the two countries would break out once more. From 1625 onwards a number of Irish exiles in the Spanish Netherlands started pressing the Spanish authorities for an invasion of Ireland making use of the Irish regiment stationed in the Brussels region. Florence Conry led the pressure from the ecclesiastical point of view, Owen Roe O'Neill from the military point of view. Between the end of 1626 and the beginning of 1627 both Conry and O'Neill had to go to Madrid 'on business' and plead their case before the king in person.

Because of the deep animosity between the earls of Tyrone and Tyrconnell, the question of leadership of the campaign was a thorny issue. Joint leadership was out of the question. Brussels preferred John O'Neill while Hugh O'Donnell was the choice of Madrid, probably under the promptings of Conry. As a way out of the dilemma Madrid eventually decided to establish a republic in Ireland, with both earls acting as captains general of the said republic, one exercising his office

---

[29] Ceyssens, 'Florence Conry', p. 309.
[30] Glyn Redworth, *The Prince and the Infanta: the cultural politics of the Spanish match* (New Haven: Yale University Press, 2003), p. 16.

on land, the other at sea. To facilitate a reconciliation between the two
earls, Conry was involved in trying to arrange a marriage between Mary
Stuart O'Donnell, Hugh O'Donnell's sister, and the earl of Tyrone, but
his efforts were in vain. War failed to break out between Spain and
England, and, with Philip IV reluctant to support an Irish campaign
while the two countries were officially at peace, the proposals came to
naught.[31]

Conry, as we have seen, was one of the prime architects of the Spanish
invasion plans, but McCaughwell, if not actually involved, was at least
au fait with the proposals and well disposed towards them. In a letter
written to Propaganda Fidei on 31 July 1626, a little more than seven
weeks before his death, he complains of the slowness of the Spaniards to
get involved: 'Hispani sum tam tardi, ut vix sperari possit aliquid hoc
anno per eos effectum iri.'[32] (The Spaniards are so slow that one can
hardly hope that anything will be effected by them this year.)

McCaughwell's disillusionment is palpable. While Spanish support
was his preferred option, he was realistic enough to realise that without
military aid from the Catholic powers the interests of the Irish Catholic
church were best served by a rapprochement with the English crown.
The different and sometimes contrary points of view expressed in his
correspondence and theological work bear testimony to a man striving to
balance the best interests of Irish Catholicism against the fluctuating
political fortunes of the first twenty-five years of the seventeenth century.

[31] Tomás Ó Fiaich, 'Republicanism and separatism in the seventeenth century', *Léachtaí Cholm Cille* 2 (1971), 74–87.
[32] Brendan Jennings, *Mícheál Ó Cléirigh and his associates* (Dublin and Cork, 1936), p. 192.

9   Sectarianism: division and dissent in Irish Catholicism

Brian Jackson

Historians are predisposed to view the counter-reformation as a uniform ideology. This is clear from the descriptive canon that has been adopted generally. The counter-reformation is vigorous, rigorous and aggressive: a coherent ideology propagated with missionary fervour by a cadre of disciplined ascetic scholars spearheading the new world order. We are less inclined to view it as a complex and nuanced episode in the development of Catholicism from universal world church to denomination. This was a journey littered with internal controversy and dispute, and was characterised by a denial of an increasingly sectarian profile.

Catholic Europe may have been diverted from the realities of rejection and confessional diversity at home by the successful propagation of the faith among the native peoples of the American and Asian colonies. However, by focusing on the success of the counter-reformation as mission, historians have effectively turned their backs on the counter-reformation church as institution, and on the internal tensions and jurisdictional conflicts that are at the heart of any institution. The purpose of this chapter is to explore this tension.

The subject matter is a local dispute between the vicar general of Armagh and ordinary of Drogheda and the Franciscans based in that town. The dispute is well known and the documentation detailed. It gives us a glimpse of Catholic life in Drogheda in the period 1618–25.[1] Although unapologetically local, the dispute has a general significance for Irish Catholicism. Irish historians are familiar with the counter-reformation as the work of a hard-pressed missionary church, the beleaguered product of repression.

---

[1] The major sources for the Drogheda dispute are contained in the *Wadding papers*. The principal documents are (i) Complaints of the Franciscans at Drogheda against Balthazar Delahoyde, pp. 29–34; (ii) Answers of the Franciscans at Drogheda to the charges of the vicar general, pp. 34–46; (iii) A report of the Franciscans on the disputes at Drogheda, pp. 46–58; Balthazar Delahoyde's letter of complaint to the Congregation de Propaganda Fide, pp. 637–41; and a series of Attestations concerning the Franciscans pp. 59–69. This series of documents consists of testimonials of support from senior members of the secular clergy, principally the vicars general of various diocese.

We are less familiar with a rather more assertive face of the same institution and the manner in which it set out to re-establish its rights, privileges and jurisdictions. The dispute at Drogheda is an important symptom of this process of re-establishment that ebbed and flowed on the tide of internal dispute, tension and intermittent persecution which characterised Catholicism in Jacobean and Caroline Ireland.

Drogheda occupied an important place in the administration of the church in pre-reformation Ireland. The metropolitan maintained a residence at the manor of Termonfeckin nearby and the town was the usual site of diocesan and metropolitan councils which were usually held in the principal church, St Peter's.[2] The town was also the site of the archiepiscopal consistory court.[3] Drogheda boasted a number of religious foundations. At the dissolution, in addition to its parish churches, the town had houses of Carmelites, Dominican, Franciscan, Austin and Crutched friars, and a nunnery at Termonfeckin nearby.[4] Unusually the town straddled two dioceses: north of the river Boyne was the diocese of Armagh while the area south of the river lay in the diocese of Meath. Although this may seem a minor point of detail today, this proximity of jurisdiction had given rise to acrimonious disputes in the pre-reformation church that required the intervention and mediation of the papal chancery.[5] Indeed, it was a stated ambition of the vicar general of Armagh to unite the town under his own jurisdiction.[6] The Franciscan, Donagh Mooney, mindful of past disputes, flagged this issue as the very first point on his visitation report on the Franciscans at Drogheda in 1617.[7] Mooney's report, part of a general visitation undertaken during his term of office as provincial, sets out the extent of properties formerly held by the friars in the town.[8] Mooney noted that the Aylmer family, who were Catholic, had the use and enjoyment of the convent buildings and gardens. His chosen verb and tense (*possidebantur*) does not

---

[2] Aubrey Gwynn, *The medieval province of Armagh 1470–1545* (Dundalk: Tempest, 1946).

[3] L. P. Murray (ed.), 'A calendar of the registers of Primate George Dowdall', *Louth Archaeological Society Journal* 6 (1925–8); 7 (1929–32).

[4] B. I. Bradshaw, *The dissolution of the religious orders in Ireland under Henry VIII* (Cambridge: Cambridge University Press, 1974), pp. 121, 124, 139, 238, 239, 241, 242 and 244.

[5] A. P. Fuller (ed.), *Calendar of entries in the papal registers relating to Great Britain and Ireland: papal letters, Vol. XVII, Part I* (Dublin: Irish Manuscripts Commission, 1994), nos. 964 and 1005.

[6] *Wadding papers*, p. 5.

[7] Brendan Jennings (ed.), 'Brussels MS 3947: Donatus Moneyus, De Provinciae Hiberniae S. Francisci', *Analecta Hibernica* 6 (1934), 28.

[8] Mooney served as provincial from September 1615 to September 1618, *ibid.*, pp. 123–4; B. Jennings (ed.), 'Brevis Synopsis Provinciae Hiberniae FF Minorum', *Analecta Hibernica* 6 (1934), 172.

acknowledge full unencumbered title. This aside, Aylmer sold the property to Moses Hill, a Protestant, some time during 1612.[9] The friars clung to the notion that lay occupation was but a temporary matter. Indeed, in nearby Dundalk, Mooney had composed a conscience-easing settlement with the grandson of James Brandon, the original grantee of convent property in the town. In return for an indulgence to hold and enjoy the property in trust for the friars, Brandon undertook to pay the friars an annual income out of the property. In addition, he promised not to sell or alienate the property without the consent of the friars and that on demand he would assign his interest in the property over to them.[10] In Drogheda, where the property had been sold to a non-Catholic, there was no possibility of any such composition. Mooney's catalogue of the woes which beset the Hill family – the nightmares, the mysterious visitations, the misshapen produce from the convent garden, even the stroke suffered by Mistress Hill – are all cautionary in tone and purpose. The message was as clear as it was double edged: *caveat emptor, caveat vendor*.

A particular cause for concern was the belief, widely held in the town, that Hill had been engaged to build a residence for Sir Arthur Chichester on the riverside site occupied by the friary. Mooney's source for much of the detail surrounding the Hill family's occupancy of the convent property (and presumably of the colourful glosses on the evils of lay impropriation) was his future adversary, Balthazar Delahoyde, the vicar general of Armagh. In the space of two years these two men, who apparently had enjoyed an amicable and respectful relationship, would lead two bitterly opposing factions in an acrimonious dispute that would engulf the whole town and the clergy of two dioceses.

At around the time Aylmer sold the site of the Franciscan convent in Drogheda, four friars returned to the town and rented a house there, establishing a regular life. Each friar had a cell in the house and there was a separate refectory, a kitchen and a principal hall large enough to serve as an oratory. The oratory had a fixed altar, a raised dais for preaching and seats for hearing confession. This reference to specific '*sedes pro confessionibus audiendis*' may enhance the reputation of an order that has too often been portrayed as the last bastion of Gaelic medievalism. Beyond this public space, the friars would gather behind the altar where

---

[9] The convent had originally been granted to Gerald Aylmer, chief justice of the King's Bench. N. B. White (ed.), *Extents of Irish Monastic Possessions, 1540–1* (Dublin: Irish Manuscripts Commission, 1941), *p. 248; Fiants, Henry VIII No. 350;* Bradshaw, *Dissolution*, p. 239. Mooney dates the sale in 1612, the Brevis Synopsis of Francis Matthews gives 1610 as the date. *Anal.Hib.* 6 (1934), 30, 147.

[10] Bradshaw, *Dissolution*, p. 242; Jennings (ed.), 'Brussels MS 3947', 35.

the canonical hours were read. Inside the house the friars adopted the regular habit. Outside, in the town, they dressed in secular clothes. The main door of the house served as the door of the chapel and it was open to the public who frequented the oratory in large numbers.

The house was occasionally searched by government troops. This was a feature of the fitful persecution of Catholic clergy that shadowed events on a wider stage. When one of the older friars was captured, the towns-people surrounded the soldiers in an angry mob, attacking them with sticks and stones, and freed the prisoner. Although their 'search and seize' operation had been thwarted, the soldiers wrecked the chapel and smashed the altar.

Undaunted, the friars returned to their house and set about restoring their oratory. The Dominicans, who had also re-established themselves in the town, founded a public oratory for their own Confraternity of the Rosary. Balthazar Delahoyde had also founded an oratory. Each of these institutions existed in an apparent state of harmony until the year 1619. Delahoyde was favourably disposed towards the Jesuits. It is alleged he was inclined to take advice on diocesan matters from James Everard and Robert Bathe – two Jesuits who had come to the town. Delahoyde invited the priests to set up their own sodality and run it out of his oratory. The leading citizens of the town flocked to join it.

The Jesuits had set up sodalities in a number of towns with the support of the secular hierarchy. Daniel Kearney, the dean of Cashel, believed that the sodality promoted frequent confession and eucharistic devotion among its members. Members provided support for the poor and prayed for the souls of the departed out of their donations. The institution was judged to promote amity between friends and restored good relations where there had been dissent.[11]

An association of laity and clergy dedicated to the promotion of amity, the relief of poverty and the cure of souls sounds very much like a confra-ternity. The confraternity was a universal and characteristic feature of late medieval Christendom. Institutional fraternity was uninhibited by status, occupation or sex. Membership of more than one organisation was com-monplace. Confraternities played a major role in civic and parochial religious observances, such as Corpus Christi. In addition they served to promote peace and charity (in the sense of being at peace with and caring for one's neighbours). Charity in our contemporary sense of the word was also an increasingly important aspect of fraternal activity. This is most obviously apparent in the *scuole grandi* of Venice, which administered

---

[11] P. F. Moran *Spicilegium Ossoriense* (Dublin, 1874), p. 129.

huge reserves of funds. Charitable concern for the departed found an outlet in the institution of the chantry. Chaplains were hired confraternity servants who offered masses for the souls of the dead. Confraternities also played an active role in the parish, encouraging religious observance, funding church building and contributing to parochial life. In cases of multiple confraternities and multiple memberships, a certain jostling for position was evident and inevitable. Despite a certain fraying at the edges, the confraternity represents the embodiment of medieval religious corporatism and its clearest expression was the fraternal feast, the *prandium caritatis*.[12]

It is immediately apparent that there are a number of fundamental differences between a confraternity and the pious groups being set up in the Irish towns. The first essential point of difference is the role of the clergy. Kearney states that the group is '*moderamine Patrum Societatis Iesu*', under the control or direction of the clergy. Of equal significance is the terminology used to describe the group and its status. It is an '*aggregationem inchoatum*', an incomplete group. These two words are the key to understanding the status of Jesuit sodality organisations in early seventeenth-century Ireland and one of the substantive points of contention in Drogheda.

Aggregation of an inchoate group was a clearly defined procedure that conferred legitimate status on Jesuit sodalities. Regulations forbade the formation of a sodality outside of a properly constituted house. The original intention was to diffuse any likely jurisdictional conflict with parochial or diocesan organisations. However, it created an immediate practical problem in a missionary context: in the absence of a formal provincial structure and properly constituted houses, the Jesuits were effectively barred from forming sodalities. The problem was neatly sidestepped by informally aggregating an inchoate group to the Roman Primaria. This process of informal aggregation was effected by papal dispensation.[13] The Jesuits had been well advised to concern themselves

[12] John Bossy, *Christianity in the West 1400–1700* (Oxford: Oxford University Press, 1985), pp. 57–63.
[13] Authority for the erection of the Roman Primaria was granted by Gregory XIII (*Omnipotentis Dei*, 5 December 1584). Sixtus V allowed for the process of aggregation of sodalities in other Jesuit colleges (*Superna Dispositione*, 5 January 1587). This was extended to colleges and houses of study under the care of the Society, but not belonging to it (*Romanum Decet*, 29 September 1587). Clement VIII conferred additional authority on the general of the Society to aggregate sodalities in Jesuit residences generally. This was done by papal brief (*Cum Sicut Nobis*, 30 August 1602). John MacErlean *The Sodality of the Blessed Virgin Mary in Ireland: a short history* (Dublin: Irish Messenger, 1928), p. 5. Permanence of the residence or mission station was of the essence here and it was only after considerable lobbying that the aggregation was extended to Irish

with such procedural formalities. Other parties were also taking a keen interest. In his annual report to the Jesuit general on the events of 1620, the Irish Jesuit superior Christopher Holywood expressed concern that the friars were preaching against the Jesuits' sodalities. It was alleged that they were set up without authority (the Franciscans argued that sodalities should be confined to colleges for members and scholars of the society alone). Furthermore, the rules of the sodality, requiring members to make their confession to a Jesuit only, were held to be contrary to the Council of Trent and to canon law. Holywood asserted that the friars preached with the express authority of the Irish Franciscan provincial.[14]

A surviving register of the Sodality of the Annunciation of the Blessed Virgin founded in Dublin in 1628 gives us some understanding of how a sodality operated: a Jesuit priest acted as director of the sodality and leading members of the laity served as the prefect and officers of the sodality. These were chosen each quarter by a sophisticated process of closed nomination, shortlist and secret ballot. A surviving membership roll indicates twenty-three male lay members and forty-four female members. All the women were married but apparently not to any of the men in the sodality.[15] The rules of the sodality proclaimed its principal object to be progress in virtue and Christian piety through the sacraments. New entrants were required to make a general confession to the director. Members would make their confession and receive the eucharist on the first Sunday of each month. The six principal feasts associated with the life of Christ and the eight feasts associated with the Virgin were observed. Officers of the sodality received the sacrament on a more frequent basis. Every Sunday the sodalists met in the Oratory for an hour of reading or study. Members were expected to set an example to 'the common sort' by their piety.

A sodality was designed to direct and focus the attention of the members on the lives and example of Christ and Mary. Its organisation was disciplined and structured with the moral and devotional tone set by

sodalities, Edmund Hogan (ed.), *Ibernia Ignatiana* (Dublin, 1880), pp. 43, 49. On 6 October 1617 the pope granted an indulgence for the aggregation of sodalities at Cashel and Waterford to the Primaria (ARSI Arch. Prima Primaria Protocollo XIV Esposizione III). This concession was extended to include Clonmel, Limerick, Cork and Carrick on 28 October 1619 and copies of these were forwarded to Holywood the Irish superior on 28 December 1619) (ARSI Anglia I, fos. 89v–90r). Dispensation was also obtained permitting female membership (ARSI Anglia 1, fo. 73v). Formal aggregation could not be effected unless there was a permanent residence (ARSI Anglia I, fo. 90v).

[14] Irish Jesuit Archive, Dublin, V/N/1(1621).

[15] Clongowes Wood College MSS, 'Documents relating to the Sodality of the Blessed Virgin Mary 1628–1865', fos. 1–4r.

the priest as director, not as servant. This sets it apart as something quite distinct from its corporate precursor, the confraternity. The devotional focus was on the Eucharist and the moral tone was set by the example of the holy family: the chaste marriage of the Virgin and St Joseph was promoted as the Christian ideal.[16]

Membership of the sodality conferred considerable benefits in the form of indulgences granted on entry, on each of the major feasts, on receiving the sacrament and at death. These benefits apart, the sodality touched a popular devotional chord. The Jesuit annual letter for 1619 reported that the sodality in Kilkenny had attracted a select and pious membership. In Clonmel and Limerick, sodalities were reported to be flourishing and in Waterford the sodality had a large but prestigious membership. Another sodality was founded in Cork in 1618. It is a mark of the commitment and wealth of the members that an elaborate gilt and wooden statue of the Virgin and Child was brought from Lisbon to decorate the oratory. The statue was reported to be 3 cubits high and required eight men to carry it.[17] In Clonmel, the cult of the Jesuits Loyola and Xavier and of the novices Gonzaga and Kostkwa were also encouraged and images of all four were carried in procession through the town on feast days.[18]

This is quite a different animal from the traditional inclusive confraternity where a certain promiscuity of membership and social inclusion were characteristic. To borrow sectarian typology, the sodality exhibits characteristics of two types or points on the organisational continuum, the devotionally innovative 'collegium pietatis' and the structured protest group the 'fraternitas'. All the classic badges of a sectarian or proto-sectarian grouping are evident: voluntary association membership by proof of some special merit, self-perception of election or of special merit. There was a high level of lay commitment and participation and strong emphasis on a novel devotional regime. There was a high degree of hostility or indifference to secular society and a strong charismatic aspect to the group.[19] By this, I mean that the group was focused on an individual (the spiritual director). I also mean that the group was charismatic in the Durkhemian sense of the proximate locus of the sacred in the activity of the group.

[16] Henry Garnett, *The Societie of the Rosarie* (s.l., 1624), pp. 162–5 and p. 19.
[17] ARSI Anglia 41, fo. 195.
[18] ARSI Anglia 41, fo. 116r, Anglia 1, fo. 104v.
[19] B. R. Wilson 'An analysis of sect development', *American Sociological Review* 24 (1959), 3–15; P. L. Berger, 'Sectarianism and religious sociation', *American Journal of Sociology* 64 (1958), 41–4.

The members of the group held the priests and their sodality in high esteem. However, in common with most exclusivist groups, it was not warmly regarded by outsiders and the Jesuits encountered significant opposition in Drogheda.[20] Their opponents were not government officials or Protestant ministers, but other Catholics, regular clergy and lay people associated with other sodalities in the town.

The Franciscans alleged that the Jesuits had behaved improperly in the recruitment of members and objected volubly to what they regarded as restrictive practices. Sodality rules required members to make their confessions to a Jesuit or to a delegated priest (in Drogheda the delegates were Christopher Delahoyde, nephew of the vicar general, and Patrick Barnewall). Members were only to hear mass in the sodality oratory and members were not to miss sodality meetings. This last regulation particularly incensed the friars who held their own sodality meetings on the same days. At first it was assumed that the sodality had been set up on foot of a special grant from the pope. However, when the Franciscans demanded to see the grant it became clear that any papal concession was *viva voce* and that the Drogheda sodality had been founded on Balthazar Delahoyde's authority alone. The Franciscans noted that Delahoyde recognised no superior. In the absence of a bishop, a vicar general was empowered to perform virtually all episcopal functions throughout the diocese. This would include the conduct of episcopal visitations, admission of priests to and receiving resignations from parochial benefices, granting licences of dispensation, granting letters dimissory for clerks proceeding to ordination in another diocese and, prior to the reformation, they would receive the vows of religious and sanction the election of heads of houses.[21]

The guardian of the Franciscan house, Donagh Mooney, together with the Dominicans, made a formal complaint that the vicar general was ignoring the rights of the regular clergy.[22] Furthermore, those who had joined the Franciscan and Dominican sodalities were being drawn away from their devotions. Mooney stated that he objected to the restrictive regulations of the Jesuit sodality. He attempted to discuss

[20] Archives Generales du Royaume, Brussels, Archives Jesuitique Prov. Flandro Belgique 1451, fos. 105r–111r.
[21] A. H. Thompson *The English clergy and their organisation in the later middle ages* (Oxford: Oxford University Press, 1947), pp. 46–56.
[22] Mooney has been portrayed as an elderly, traditional cleric by historians of the order such as Meehan. He was in fact a relatively young man. Born in 1578, he saw military service before entering the friars in October 1600. He is described by contemporaries in the order as a man of great learning. He was made guardian of St Anthony's, Louvain, in 1607, and in 1611 became vicar provincial of the Irish province. He was elected provincial in 1615. Jennings (ed.), 'Brussels Ms. 3947', 13, 94, 121 and 124.

the matter with Delahoyde, Bathe and Everard, but to no avail. He offered to go to arbitration and nominated David Rothe, bishop of Ossory as arbitrator.[23] The essence of Mooney's position was that the Jesuits had no authority to erect a sodality, as there was no formal house of studies in Drogheda. This argument indicates that he was familiar with the concessions and privileges granted to the society. Bathe refused to submit papal privileges granted to the society for scrutiny and withdrew from the arbitration process.

The dispute simmered over the next nine months or so. Inevitably, the affair spilled over into the public domain. An alternative arbitrator, James Plunkett, the vicar general of Meath, was asked to intervene in the controversy. Plunkett invited Delahoyde to discuss the matter. The invitation was ignored. A year passed. Only the threat of excommunication induced Delahoyde to consent to arbitration and the offending sodality regulations were relaxed.

However, by now the dispute had developed its own momentum. The Franciscans had no public oratory in the town and so had obtained licence to say mass in the ruins of the original friary. This licence was withdrawn, allegedly at the instigation of Robert Bathe. The Franciscans were forced to share facilities with the Dominicans. Some months later, Christopher Plunkett preached to a large congregation in the Dominican oratory on the Feast of St Francis. Delahoyde and Bathe alleged that in this sermon he attacked the secular hierarchy and other regular clergy, propounding no less than twelve heretical propositions. The friars dismissed the allegation.

In Mooney's absence from the town, Delahoyde and Bathe approached leading lay beneficiaries of the Franciscan order, attempting to turn them against the friars. Four of the friars went to the vicar general, begging him not to stir up a new quarrel with the order. Delahoyde threw them out.

On the night of 26 October, Christopher Delahoyde, nephew of Balthazar, broke into the Dominican oratory chapel, destroyed the altar, stole the vessels and broke up the pulpit. The tone of the account of this incident recalls that of Mooney's earlier account of the search and seize raid of the government troops in 1611.

By 23 December the Franciscans' own oratory chapel was nearly complete. Delahoyde wrote to Mooney stating that he had not been

---

[23] Rothe's personal assessment of Delahoyde was not uncritical: 'My ancient friend Mr Balthazar Delahoid, who striving against the streame, runneth upon the rockes . . . he bewraieth such imperfections which cannot but breed a feare in his friends of his imparriengy so great a busines, and in others. . . an opinion of his weakness and insufficience for so great a chardge which hetherto was committed to him upon trust, with regard to the necessity of the hour and the want of others more able and fitt': *Wadding papers*, p. 103.

consulted about the building works, that the oratory had not been constituted with his authority and was therefore contrary to the decree *De Celebratione Missarum* of the twenty-second session of the Council of Trent. He forbade the friars to say mass there. The friars sent three prominent laymen to put their case to the vicar general. It was pointed out that the friars did not require permission to build on their own property and that the privileges of the order were well established on this point. Furthermore, the decree cited by Delahoyde (that ordinaries should not permit mass to be said in unorthodox or unconsecrated places) had not been promulgated in Ireland in the prevailing climate of persecution. It was also noted that it was a long-established privilege of the friars as a mendicant missionary order to celebrate mass on portable wooden altars. It is clear that the laity were openly questioning the role of the ordinary in persecuting the friars. Delahoyde responded by citing chapter 3 of the twenty-fifth session of the Council, prohibiting regulars from setting up new houses without the licence of the ordinary. The friars countered that they had been in Drogheda for over 300 years and their current accommodation merely reinforced an established presence.

Delahoyde was incensed and sent his nephew to the friars' chapel where, in front of a large crowd, he pronounced formal interdict on the oratory. Many citizens remained loyal to the friars in spite of Delahoyde's best efforts; he sent his nephew and Barnewall from door to door canvassing support. The vicar general excommunicated twelve of the friars' leading supporters and called on the secular clergy of the diocese to support him. These twelve citizens appealed to Rome. After five days of deliberations the secular clergy of the archdiocese rejected the interdict. The vicars general of Down and Dromore, Patrick Hanratty and Patrick Matthews, alleged the interdict had no foundation in canon law and was imposed as the result of the personal vindictiveness of Bathe and Everard. They added that the meddling Jesuits should act with greater caution: unlike the Franciscans or Dominicans they had no historical presence in the town; their position was based on a privileged relationship with the ordinary and they might just as easily lose that position of privilege and influence. Delahoyde attempted to discipline the clerics who appealed directly to Rome. Hanratty's status as a vicar apostolic, and Matthew's prestige as one of the most learned clerics in the province who had been elected to his position by the diocesan clergy and confirmed in it by the vice primate, rendered them untouchable.

At this point, Delahoyde, who was in his sixties, died. The Jesuits lobbied for preferment for his nephew Christopher, who was appointed vicar general of Meath. Allegations of Jesuit high-handed behaviour continued. It was even alleged that Mooney was threatened with arrest and told that if apprehended on the streets of Drogheda he would be handed over to the king's gaoler for trial.

The Jesuit general in Rome was disturbed that this rancorous dispute was spiralling out of control. He instructed Holywood to establish if the two Jesuits were at fault and to take appropriate action to restore harmony.[24] In another communication to Robert Nugent he advised that it was not prudent for the Jesuits to insist on their rights and privileges in disputes with other religious at this time and that it would be expedient to waive any claims for the sake of amity.[25]

Bathe and Everard chose to ignore the advice and instead obtained a favourable testimony from Thomas Dease, bishop of Meath who wrote to the general blaming the Franciscans for the events in Drogheda.[26] Dease exonerated the Jesuits from any involvement in the interdict controversy, which he saw as a justified defence of episcopal authority. Dease clearly believed in hedging his bets and he gave another equally glowing testimony to the friars.[27] The general noted that although the contentious issues between the friars and the ordinary in Drogheda seemed to have been resolved (by the latter's death) it was apparent there was little hope of restoring good relations with the Jesuits as long as Bathe and Mooney lived in the same town. Accordingly, Holywood was instructed to remove Bathe at least 5–6 miles from the town without making Bathe aware of the reason for the move. Mooney was also to be relocated.[28] In a subsequent instruction the general specified a distance of 12 miles.[29] Holywood replied that removing Bathe from Drogheda would undermine everything that had been achieved in the town. He was inclined to disregard the instruction and delayed implementing a direct order, preferring to wait for events to run their course.[30]

In the end, this paid off. Mooney died in the spring of 1625. This effectively diffused the situation in the town and a dispute that had raged for almost five years simply faded away. This of itself is remarkable. The removal of the charismatic focus (Mooney) or the legitimating force (Delahoyde) from the groups robbed them of impetus. Each group reverted to more regular patterns of religious behaviour; protest was routinised and reabsorbed into the institutional body of the church.

---

[24] ARSI Anglia 1, fo. 102v.   [25] ARSI Anglia 1, fo. 102.
[26] Irish Jesuit Archive, Dublin, MS B/17.   [27] *Wadding papers*, p. 59.
[28] ARSI Anglia 1, fos. 105r–v.   [29] ARSI Anglia 4a, fo. 1r.
[30] Irish Jesuit Archive, Dublin, MS A/61.

In its form, the dispute exhibited a number of classic sectarian features. The rhetoric employed by the protagonists in formal submissions to the Congregation de Propaganda Fide also suggests a sectarian theme. However, the substance of the dispute was jurisdictional. At its core, this was a dispute over institutional boundaries.

In his deposition, Delahoyde asserted his pre-eminent position in the local secular hierarchy as vicar general and apostolic pronotary. He argued that the friars, by their schismatic conduct, had managed to attract the attention of the magistrates to the clergy in the town and exposed them all to the risk of prison. Delahoyde also made much of the character defects of the friars who had clashed with him. Turning to the real substance of his complaint, Delahoyde attacked attempts by the friars to enforce traditional rights with regard to burials, the *ius sepulturae* and the *quarta funeralium*. He also attacked their success in securing tithes and offerings from the laity at the expense of the seculars, which he condemned as simony and alleged that the friars used the threat of civil legal action to exact their dues in full.

In response, Mooney was at pains to stress the learning and orthodox training of the friars involved in the dispute. Christopher Plunkett, a scion of a leading Pale family, was a product of Louvain. Henry Mellan, the guardian of Armagh and vicar provincial, had studied philosophy and theology at Salamanca. Mooney himself had lectured in theology and philosophy at Louvain and had served as guardian of St Anthony's College there. Equally, he was at pains to stress that allegations made by Delahoyde arose out of his want of learning and flawed textual interpretation.

Delahoyde alleged that it was the custom of the friars to entertain men and women of the town at great feasts in their house. Mooney denied the suggestion vehemently. He acknowledged that the friars did entertain local benefactors each year on the feast of St Francis, but that there was no question of clerical vows being compromised on these occasions. It is curious that of all the allegations made in this dispute, it is this one which has captured the attention of historians who have assumed, incorrectly, that they are looking at a traditional Gaelic medieval order engaged in a traditional medieval *prandium caritatis*. Mooney's *convivium* was a fundraiser.

Delahoyde also attacked the friars' assiduous defence of their traditional exemptions and privileges and alleged that they had altered the form and order of prayer offered at mass to advance the claims of the order. Mooney was quick to dismiss the charge and confirmed that as a matter of course prayers were offered for the pope, the bishops, the four mendicant orders and for the king and queen as they had always been.

Both parties to the dispute made much of government persecution. This sits rather uneasily with the suggestion made by both sides that each had resorted to the threat of the civil power to enforce their rights. When considered alongside prayers for the king and queen and loyal dedicatory epistles to the prince of Wales, it is clear that the Catholic church in the Pale had a deeply ambivalent attitude to the state.

David Roth, the first arbitrator appointed in the Drogheda controversy (and a man burdened more than most by the competing demands of clerical claims over rights and jurisdiction) struck a cautious and discordant note in his assessment of the affair to Peter Lombard:

> It greveth me that the good towne of Drogheda is nowe these fewe yeares past made the stadge of ecclesiastical outraidges, and that no sooner one debate is either ordered or abated then another sproutley arose, as it were in a circle. I have resolved not to go with anny censures . . . thinking it more secure to go on by way of persuasion than of compulsion . . . I find of more efficacie nowe a dayes, especially in this our unsettled countrey, whear a bad cause may have a fair cullour, if not of lawe at least of discretion and equitie to excuse the intention if not the woork. I will not be accusator fratrum meorum. I would rather veile over our common defects then reveale them to manny.[31]

The sequence of events in Drogheda suggests that the Catholic church occupied a semi-public position in the town. It existed in a curious 'through the looking glass' world where the actions of Catholic institutions mirrored their official Protestant counterparts. For example, the royal visitation of 1615 was matched by Mooney's visitation of 1617. Catholic sodalities were set up by the religious orders to foster piety and galvanise Catholic resistance to persecution. As persecution ebbed, these sodalities took on an institutional life of their own. Catholic solidarity in the face of persecution was displaced by disputes over rights and jurisdiction, with churchmen and the institutions they represented defending their patch. Catholicism was in effect reconstructing itself as an alternative framework for institutional religion in Ireland and in the course of this reconstruction, strong sectarian impulses had mushroomed and no amount of discretion could veil over or suppress them.

[31] *Wadding papers,* pp. 104–5.

10   Purity of blood and purity of faith in early modern Ireland

Declan Downey

In 1992, Professor Erik Midelfort, in an essay entitled 'Curious Georgics: the German nobility and their crisis of legitimacy in the late-sixteenth century', demonstrated how the attacks of prominent writers such as Sebastian Franck, Nicodemus Frischlin and Cyriakus Spangenberg, upon the legitimacy of the German aristocracy resulted in the foundation of academies for the nobility and in an increasing self-consciousness among nobles concerning the purity of their Christian ancestral blood-lines or *Ahnenprobe* as a means of proving the legitimacy of their claims to noble privilege.[1] Midelfort set this essay in the context of similar or parallel concerns for purity of blood among the nobilities of Spain and France during the same period, and began with reference to Otto Brünner's remarkable study *Adeliges Landleben und europäischer Geist: Leben und Werk Wolf Helmhards von Hohberg, 1612–1688*. Brünner's exposition of the life and work of this seventeenth-century Austrian aristocrat and poet revealed how a traditional rural-based noble culture came under threat from the increasing centralisation of power in the

---

I wish to qualify my use of words such as *race, racial and racism*. André Devyver, in his monumental study *Le Sang Épuré*, (Brussels: Éditions de l'Université de Bruxelles, 1973), argued for the use of these words to describe the growing consciousness of blood and ancestry among European nobility in the early modern period. Therefore such words should not be interpreted in the context of twentieth-century connotations of nationalist, biological racism. In the early modern period (and indeed up until the late nineteenth century), the word 'race' was used to define, describe or substitute for family, clan, lineage or a distinctive class or generation. For instance, Ferdinand Maximilian von Habsburg, ill-fated Emperor of Mexico, on the eve of his death by a revolutionary firing squad on 19 June 1867, wrote to his relatives in Vienna, '*I die in the faith, both of Holy Church and of our Habsburg race*'. (Even today, in some parts of Munster and Connacht, One can still hear at funerals, the phrase '*He/She was the last of his/her race*': in this context, the word 'race' signifies family or lineage.) See A. Wheatcroft, *The Habsburgs: Embodying Empire* (London: Viking, 1995), pp. 286–7.

[1] H. C. E. Midelfort, 'Curious Georgics : The German nobility and their crisis of legitimacy in the late-sixteenth century', in A. C. Fix and S. C. Karant-Nunn, *Germania illustrata: Essays on early modern Germany presented to Gerald Strauss, Sixteenth century studies*, XVIII (Missouri, 1992), pp. 217–42.

early modern Habsburg state and from the rise of what he called a 'bureaucratic bourgeoisie' who would later become the *noblesse de robe* and would displace or eclipse the ancient *noblesse d'épée*. Central to Brünner's and Midelfort's works is the idea of 'crisis of the nobility'.[2] The old orders in Spain, the Holy Roman Empire and France felt threatened by the pretensions of a centralising state which claimed the right to ennoble and enfranchise at will. Their sense of vulnerability was sharpened by those who had recently converted to the Catholic church (from Judaism, in particular), and who claimed through their conversion, attainments and education an entitlement to more general equality with the traditional ruling elite.

Henri Kamen and Pierre Chanu have illustrated how in Spanish territories purity of blood (*limpieza de sangre*) was qualified by proofs of Catholic ancestry, purity of faith. This became the decisive weapon of the old Castilian nobility in their exclusion from public and ecclesiastical office of potential rivals among the *conversos*. It is in this context of an ancient nobility in crisis, that this chapter will endeavour to highlight similar concerns for purity of blood and of faith among some Gaelic and Hiberno-Norman aristocrats under pressure from the politico-religious expansion of the centralising Tudor state and from the encroachments of the New English planters' acquisition of land and power. In a memorably succinct phrase Margaret MacCurtain has described this experience as 'a collision of seemingly irreconcileable cultures'.[3]

Over the last thirty years, developments in the historiography of early modern Ireland have provided a wealth of scholarly insights into the experience, mentalities and motivations of 'natives and newcomers' alike.[4] Almost forty years ago D. B. Quinn initiated the study of the colonial attitudes of the New English adventurers and planters which alienated the Gaelic, Hiberno-Norman and Old English aristocracies.[5] This approach was developed and explored more extensively by Nicholas Canny's incisive study of what may be termed 'English Calvinist

[2] *Ibid.*, 218. Also Otto Brünner, *Adeliges Landleben und europäischer Geist: Leben und Werk Wolf Helmhards von Hohberg, 1612–1688*, (Salzburg: Müller, 1949), pp. 10, 124,129–30,158–66, 315, 323, 339; For a more dramatic comparative study of the nobility in crisis see V. Press, 'Wilhelm von Grumbach und die Deutsche Adelkrise der 1560er Jähre', *Blätter für deutsche Landesgeschichte* 113 (1977), 396–431.

[3] Margaret MacCurtain, 'The roots of Irish nationalism', in Robert O'Driscoll (ed.), *The Celtic Consciousness* (Dublin: Dolmen Press, 1981), p. 371.

[4] This phrase is borrowed from the title of Ciaran Brady and Raymond Gillespie (eds.), *Natives and newcomers: essays on the making of Irish colonial society, 1534–1641* (Dublin: Irish Academic Press, 1986).

[5] D. B Quinn, 'Ireland and sixteenth century European expansion', *Historical Studies* 1 (1958), 20–32; D. B. Quinn, *The Elizabethans and the Irish* (Ithaca: Cornell University Press, 1966).

colonialism'.[6] The study of the *Mentalitätsgeschichte* of the New English colonists initiated by Quinn, developed and extended by Canny, J. P. Myers, Ciaran Brady and Andrew Hadfield has made an immense and valuable contribution to our understanding of the New English colonial viewpoint and outlook.[7] These works have touched the nerve of cultural imperialism in their examination of the self-vindicatory attitudes and writings of Elizabethan adventurers such as Fynes Moryson (Lord Deputy Charles Mountjoy's secretary), and of planters such as Meredith Hanmer and Edmund Spenser.

Hadfield makes the perceptive point that 'the supposed savage/ Scythian origins of the Irish [alleged and asserted in the writings of Geoffrey of Monmouth, Giraldus Cambrensis and Henry of Huntingdon] was given more prominence in the sixteenth century [by Camden, Moryson and Spenser inter alia] as an explanation for Irish recalcitrance as the English state sought to bend its new subjects to its will'.[8] This practice of denigration and, as Hadfield observes, 'the reliance on origin myths such as the Arthurian legends and the "matter of Britain" [an ancient imperial claim on Ireland predating Henry II and Laudabiliter] actually increased dramatically after the Reformation, namely [in] English histories of Ireland'.[9]

Authorities on the Old English colony in Ireland such as Aidan Clarke, Colm Lennon and Brady have examined and illustrated the mentality and attitudes of this elite towards the New English, the Gaelic and the Hiberno-Norman communities. During the early 1500s, the Old English (chiefly Palesmen influenced by Renaissance Humanism), urged Henry VIII to 'reform' and anglicise Ireland. According to D. B. Quinn there was 'little doubt that Englishmen regarded the attempted reassertion of English authority in Ireland in the later years of Henry VIII as being a policy of "reformation not conquest"'.[10] After the king's demise, William

---

[6] N. P. Canny, 'The ideology of English colonisation from Ireland to America', *William and Mary Quarterly* 3 (1973); N. P. Canny, *The Elizabethan conquest of Ireland: a pattern established, 1565–1576* (Hassocks: Harvester Press, 1976); N. P. Canny, 'Dominant minorities: English settlers in Ireland and Virginia, 1550–1650', in K. R. Andrews, N. P. Canny and P. E. H, Hair, The westward enterprise: English activities in Ireland the Atlantic and America (Liverpool: Liverpool University Press, 1978); N. P. Canny, *The upstart earl: a study of the social and mental world of Richard Boyle, first earl of Cork, 1566–1643* (Cambridge: Cambridge University Press, 1982).

[7] J. P. Myers (ed.) *Elizabethan Ireland: a selection of writings by Elizabethan writers on Ireland* (Hamden, CT : Archon Books, 1983); Ciaran Brady, 'Spenser's Irish crisis: humanism and experience in the 1590s', *Past & Present* 3 (1986), 17–49; Andrew Hadfield, 'Briton and Scythian: Tudor representations of Irish origins', *IHS*, 28/112 (1993), 390–408.

[8] Hadfield, 'Briton and Scythian', p. 407.

[9] *Ibid.*, p. 391.

[10] D. B. Quinn, 'Ireland and sixteenth-century European expansion', *Historical Studies* 1 (1958), 22.

Thomas wrote of his late master that 'he [Henry VIII] hath brought that nation from rude, beastly, ignorant, cruel and unruly Infidels, to the state of civil, reasonable, patient, humble and well governed Christians'.[11] Stephen Ellis noted that up until the 1570s Tudor Ireland enjoyed relative order and stability and that many English officials and writers believed that the country was about to accept the extension of English common law, order and administration.[12] This relative peace was soon broken. On 17 July 1579, a combined papal–Spanish force under the general command of James FitzMaurice-FitzGerald, landed at Dingle, Co. Kerry. The crusader standard of the holy cross was unfurled while the papal legate, Dr Nicholas Sanders, proclaimed a holy war against the 'heretic queen', Elizabeth I. The Geraldine war (1579–83) assumed the mantle of the first counter-reformation military crusade in Ireland. In 1580, Pope Gregory XIII granted the crusader's indulgence to all who took part in this cause and Gerald, the sixteenth earl of Desmond, was recognised by the papacy as '*Dux exercitus Catholicorum in Hibernia*'.[13] In both the Geraldine war and the Baltinglass revolt, the cause of counter-reformation Catholicism was invoked *inter alia,* as an ideological justification for war on the Tudor regime and its state church in Ireland.[14]

The shock that the Geraldine war gave to the Tudor regime, and the religious vehemence which characterised it, betrayed the limits of Tudor reform in Ireland and the complacency of those officials and writers who had believed that Ireland was about to embrace English law, civility and reformation. The lord deputy, Sir John Perrot, in his reaction to the defeat of the Catholic forces, identified 'popery' with the Irish and Gaelic culture with the 'Anti-Christ'.[15] In the perception of the new English, the sectarian vehemence of the war and the depraved state of affairs in Munster after 1583 was compounded further by the Nine Years War (1594–1603). For many potential new English settlers, 'Ireland resembled one of the nastier parts of the new world'.[16] It is against this

[11] *Ibid.*
[12] Steven Ellis, *Tudor Ireland, 1470–1603* (London: Longman, 1985), pp. 210–11, 250; see also Colm Lennon, *Sixteenth-century Ireland: the incomplete conquest* (Dublin: Gill & Macmillan, 1994), pp. 152–63, 190–3, 210–13, 216–21.
[13] D. M Downey, 'Culture and diplomacy: the Spanish–Habsburg dimension in the Irish counter reformation', unpublished Ph.D. thesis, University of Cambridge (1994), pp. 85–8.
[14] *Ibid.*; see also J. J. Silke, *Kinsale: the Spanish intervention in Ireland at the end of the Elizabethan wars* (Liverpool: Liverpool University Press, 1970), p. 21.
[15] Quinn, 'Ireland and European expansion', pp. 27–8.
[16] Hadfield, 'Tudor representations', p. 406 ; also see N. P. Canny, 'Protestants, planters and apartheid in early modern Ireland', *IHS* 25/98 (1986), 111–14, and Michael MacCarthy-Morrough, *The Munster plantation: English migration to southern Ireland, 1583–1641* (Oxford: Oxford University Press, 1986), pp. 279–80.

background that we can understand Spenser's description of the Gaelic and Hiberno-Norman natives as 'wilde fruit which savage soil hath bred'.[17] In *A View of the Present State of Ireland (c.* 1596), Spenser emphasised what he believed were the Scythian/savage origins and nature of the Gaelic natives (or as Fynes Moryson described them, 'the wilde Irishry'), who could only be tamed by forceful oppression.[18] This perception of degeneracy and inferiority among the Gaelic Irish may also be found in the writings of Old English Catholic writers such as Richard Stanihurst. In his *Description of Ireland,* Stanihurst asserted that the Gaelic language itself provided an obstacle to imposing order and civility on the natives: 'the verre English of birth, conversant with the savage sort of that people become degenerat, and as though they had tasted of Circe's poisoned cup, are quite altered'.[19]

Lennon and Hadfield noted that Stanihurst's criticism was not directed at the Gaelic tongue itself but against its use, since he (like many fellow Palesmen), regarded it as an obstacle to the extension of English 'civilitie' among the natives. Nevertheless, Hadfield asserts that Stanihurst's criticisms implied 'inferiority' among the Gaelic and Gaelicised communities.[20] In this regard, Stanihurst has much in common with Moryson, Hanmer and Spenser, even though his writings sought to defend the Catholic as distinct from the Gaelic culture of Ireland.[21] The perceived barbarism of Gaelic culture and the belief that Englishmen could lose their 'civilitie' through embrace of it has its source in the *Topographica Hibernica* of the medieval Cambro-Norman writer, Giraldus Cambrensis. For both old and New English writers who sought to justify English possession of Ireland and its 'duty' or 'mission' to reform the inferior and barbaric Gaelic nature and culture, Cambrensis proved to be a useful source of authority. It is against this background of an anti-Gaelic *black legend* that this chapter will focus now on its primary purpose – an exposition and examination of the concerns of Gaelic and Hiberno-Norman aristocratic writers in the context of Brünner's and Midelfort's exposition of an ancient nobility in crisis.[22]

---

[17] Quoted in MacCurtain, *Roots of Irish nationalism,* p. 371.

[18] Fynes Moryson, 'A Description of Ireland', in Henry Morley (ed.), *Ireland under Elizabeth and James I* (London, 1890), p. 426; Hadfield, 'Tudor representations', pp. 403–4, 407–8; Brady, 'Spenser's Irish crisis', pp.17–49.

[19] Quoted in Hadfield, 'Tudor representations', p. 405.

[20] *Ibid.* pp. 405–8.

[21] *Ibid.*; Colm Lennon, 'Richard Stanihurst (1547–1618) and Old English identity', *IHS* 21 (1978), pp. 121–43; Colm Lennon, *Richard Stanihurst the Dubliner, 1547–1618* (Dublin: Irish Academic Press, 1981), pp. 13–34, 70–98, 124–8, 157.

[22] On the anti-Spanish black legend, see Ricard Garcia Carcel, *La leyenda negra* (Madrid: Alianza Editorial, 1993); E. S. Arnoldsson, *La leyenda negra: estudios sobre sus origines*

For most historians, the triumph of the Tudor state machinery over Gaelic and Gaelicised Ireland after the battle of Kinsale (1601–2), and the flight of the earls (1607), heralded the demise of Gaelic and Hiberno-Norman aristocratic power and culture. As F. S. L. Lyons and Margaret MacCurtain commented, the technological and administrative superiority of a centralised Renaissance state had overcome the fragmented, anarchic, technologically and administratively underdeveloped Celtic anachronism.[23] During the reign of James I this process became evident in the confiscation of Gaelic and Hiberno-Norman Catholic estates; the plantations of New English and lowland Scottish Protestants; the abolition of Brehon Law; the creation of new boroughs and the attendant increase in Protestant representation in the Irish parliament; the imposition of draconian anti-recusant measures; the exclusion of Catholics from the administration and the establishment of a court of wards and liveries. The implications of these developments combined with the literary assaults of Hanmer, Spenser and Moryson, contributed to the crisis in which the Gaelic and Hiberno-Norman aristocracies found themselves in the early seventeenth century. Hadfield notes that 'whatever threatened Tudor sovereignty in Ireland could thus be classified as illegal'.[24] It is against this scenario that we can appreciate the ancient native aristocracies' reaction and the rise of their concern for establishing their legitimacy and identity in continental (particularly Spanish) cultural terms of purity of blood and purity of faith.

Most prominent in the literary counter-offensive against what could be termed new English Calvinist cultural imperialism was Don Philip O'Sullivan Beare, a Gaelic aristocrat exiled in Spain. As will be seen, neither he nor other high-born exiles such as Mary Stuart O'Donnell, Flaithrí Ó Maolchonaire [Florence Conry] and Richard Bermingham lacked a sense of cultural and racial superiority over the New English planters. In *Historiae Catholicae Iberniae Compendium* (Lisbon, 1621), O'Sullivan Beare made a significant distinction between 'Ghaeil' (Gaelic-Irish), 'Sean Ghaill' (old foreigners – Norman stock), and 'Nua Ghaill' (new foreigners–Elizabethan and Jacobean planters). The last group

---

(Stockholm: Statens Humanistiska Forskningsråd, 1960), chs. 2 and 3; Geoffrey Parker, *Spain and the Netherlands, 1559–1659* (London: Collins, 1979), pp. 78, 80, 160; and for echoes of its application in an Irish context see Hadfield, 'Tudor representations'; Quinn, 'Ireland and European expansion', pp. 25–8; Quinn, *Elizabethans and the Irish.*

[23] MacCurtain, *Tudor Ireland*, p. 371; F. S. L. Lyons, *Culture and anarchy in Ireland, 1890–1939* (Oxford: Clarendon Press, 1979).

[24] Hadfield, 'Tudor representations', p. 395.

(mostly Protestant), were described by the author as being 'perfidious'.[25]
O'Sullivan Beare's *Vindiciae Hibernicae contra Giraldum Cambrensem et
alios vel Zoilomastigis, liber primus, secundus, tertius . . . et contra Stanihur-
stum* (Lisbon, 1625), generally referred to as *Zoilomastix*, reveals how
some Gaelic notables regarded themselves and their race in the wider
context of European topographical, historical, cultural and political
order.

As the title suggests, it was written to vindicate the Gaelic-Irish and to
refute the claims made against them by Cambrensis and others, including Stanihurst. As Lennon explained, Stanihurst's works, especially *De
rebus in Hibernia gestis* (Antwerp, 1584), enjoyed a wide continental
readership. O'Sullivan Beare's naming of Stanyhurst in the title of his
work was meant to draw the attention of that same readership to his
criticism and refutation of Stanihurst.[26] The very word *Zoilomastix* is
derived from *zoilus* (a detractor) and *mastix* (a whip). Thomas O'Donnell
and Aubrey Gwynn have suggested that the idea of whipping or 'thrash-
ing the detractor' was to be found in the *Homeromastix*, where Homer
was attacked by Zoilus the Sophist, as related in Ovid's *Remedium Amoris*
(lines 365–6).[27] In *Zoilomastix*, O'Sullivan Beare placed very strong
emphasis on the antiquarian origin myth that the Gaelic-Irish derived
their descent through the Milesians from Spain. Apart from claiming this
notion of a common racial and blood heritage with Spain, he claimed
and emphasised the continuous loyalty of the Gaelic-Irish to the Catholic
faith since Patrician times. In this regard, O'Sullivan-Beare sought
to justify his Gaelic heritage by appealing to contemporary Castilian
Catholic sensitivities of *limpieza de sangre* whereby the purity of Spanish
blood was qualified by Iberian racial origin and continuous Catholic
ancestry and heritage since the conversion of the Visigoths.[28]

In *Zoilomastix*, O'Sullivan Beare is highly critical of Stanihurst's
mitigation of the Catholic Old English acquiescence in the Henrician
reformation and their political loyalty to a heretic regime. By highlight-
ing the negative consequences of their loyalty for the Catholic church in
Ireland, the author was giving further emphasis to the Gaelic tradition of

---

[25] M. J. Byrne (ed.), *Ireland under Elizabeth* (Dublin, 1903), pp. 50–1; Matthew Kelly
(ed.), *Historiae Catholicae Iberniae compendium* (Dublin, 1850); Jerrold Casway, *Owen
Roe O'Neill* (Philadelphia: Philadelphia University Press, 1984), pp. 3–4.

[26] Lennon, *Stanihurst the Dubliner*, pp. 117–20.

[27] Aubrey Gwynn, 'An unpublished work of Philip O'Sullivan Beare', *Analecta Hibernica* 6
(1934), 1; T. J. O'Donnell (ed.), *Selections from the Zoilomastix of Philip O'Sullivan Beare*
(Dublin: Irish Manuscripts Commission, 1960), pp. 1–11.

[28] John Lynch, *Spain under the Habsburgs*, 2 vols. (Oxford: Blackwell, 1981), I, p. 28; A.
Domínguez Ortiz, 'Los conversos de origen judío después de la expulsión', *Estudios de
Historia Social de España* 3 (1955), 223–431.

identification with Catholicism as a means of establishing Gaelic legitimacy in the eyes of Catholic Spain (and counter-reformation Europe).
In this regard, it could be said that O'Sullivan Beare was casting asper-
sions on the orthodoxy of Old English Catholics. When he attacks what
he regards as the 'treacherous' nature of the New English Protestants,
one wonders if O'Sullivan Beare is assaulting 'Englishness' itself. This
theme in *Zoilomastix* was re-echoed later in the seventeenth century by
the Hiberno-Norman exile John Lynch in his *Cambrensis Eversus* and by
the Spanish poet Jorge de Mendoza:

> The spawn of envy, the gross lies of Gerald he refutes;
> and those which the foolish Stanihurst contains.
> That work, distinguished by many interesting
> facts and by its polished style, it is called Zoilomastix. . .[29]

As shall be seen from other Irish and Spanish sources, O'Sullivan
Beare was not the first Irishman to claim that the Gaelic-Irish were of
Iberian racial origin. Indeed such claims were acknowledged by English
propagandists who used it to emphasise the 'cruel nature' of the 'Irishry'
by identifying them with the fabled cruelty of the Spanish. It was during
the Dutch Revolt that the anti-Spanish black legend gained notoriety
thanks to the Calvinist printing presses in Amsterdam, London and
Edinburgh.[30]

Since Spain was the most powerful Catholic state in Europe at this
time and was claimed to share a common racial and religious heritage
with the Gaelic-Irish, it was regarded as the best and only means of
securing Gaelic political and religious interests. Between 1529 and 1630
the appeals by various Hiberno-Norman and Gaelic notables to the
Spanish crown for political, military and cultural assistance against the
English invoked the belief in a common racial and religious identity.
Under the terms of the Habsburg–Desmond treaty of Dingle (1529), in
return for Geraldine allegiance and alliance, Charles V granted full

[29] Gwynn, 'Work of O'Sullivan Beare', p. 1; O'Donnell (ed.), *Zoilomastix*, p. 11; the poem
is printed in Kelly (ed.), *Historiae Compendium*, Introduction; Matthew Kelly (ed.), John
Lynch, *Cambrensis eversus*, 3 vols. (Dublin, 1848–52), I, p. 97. The manuscript of the
poem is in the library of the Marqués de Astorga in Madrid.
[30] B. A. Vermaseren, *Een en Ander over de Zwarte Legende betreffende Spanje en haar Onstaan
in de Nederlanden in de 16e Eeuw* (Nijmegen: Vakgroep Spaanse Taal en Letterkunde,
1984); P. A. M. Geurts, *De Nederlandse Opstand in de Pamfletten, 1566–1584* (Nijmegen:
Centrale Drukkerij, 1956), pp. 177–8; Parker, *Spain and the Netherlands*, p. 78; Hadfield,
'Tudor representations', p. 308, n. 37, where Hadfield asserts that the Irish claimed,
more specifically, a Basque ancestry and notes that the Basques, like the Irish, were
regarded as of ill repute, see John Gillingham, *Richard the Lionheart* (London: Weidenfeld
& Nicolson, 1978), p. 50.

rights, graces and privileges of citizenship in the Spanish *Monarquía* to the Irish.[31]

In 1618, the exiled archbishop of Tuam, Florence Conry, presented 'A brief relation of Ireland' to Philip III. This document provides a good example of Gaelic Hispanophilism. Having defined the different racial groups in Ireland and the terms of *Laudabiliter* Conry states:

These severall kindes of Irish agree all in one thing, to wit, in being true Catholyckes and children of the Church of Rome; yet doe they differ in . . . desires to have princes and laws over them. Every one desiring his naturall inclination and imitating his predecessors. And therefore the Auncient Irish [Gaelic], as these that are descended from the Spanyards desire allwayes to be governed by the Kings of Spayne and their successors, and bear greate affection and love to the Spanish nation. Contrarywise great hate and enmity to their enemies, and are in sharpness of wit and valour in warr, altogether like unto the Spanyard. . .[32]

Conry's observations on Gaelic affinity with Spain not only reflect a sense of cultural or ethnic identity but also indicate that the Gaelic Irish did not feel themselves isolated from the continent. Gaelic scholars had been studying in Spain since the 1400s. Furthermore, Conry's sentiments reveal a sense of identity among the Gaelic Irish which transcended the geographical distance between them and Spain – a 'pan-Iberianism'. The facility with which the Irish, especially Gaelic scholars, entered the prestigious universities of Spain and their immediate reception of Spanish citizenship may be explained by their identification

---

[31] On the treaty of Dingle (1529), see Downey, 'Culture and diplomacy', pp. 5–32; D. M. Downey, 'Irish–European integration: the legacy of Charles V', in Judith Devlin and H. B. Clarke (eds.), *European encounters* (Dublin: UCD Press, 2003), pp. 97–117; D. M. Downey, 'La Paz de Westfalia, vista desde Irlanda', in B. García García and F. Villaverde (eds.), *350 Años de la Paz de Westfalia, 1648–1998: Del antagonismo a la integracion en Europa* (Madrid: Fundación Carlos de Amberes, 1999), pp. 204–5; reference to Irish invocation of racial and religious affinity with Spain may be found in Silke, *Kinsale;* Kerney-Walsh, *Hugh O'Neill after Kinsale*; Gráinne Henry, *The Irish military community in Spanish Flanders, 1586–1621* (Dublin: Irish Academic Press, 1992), Hiram Morgan, 'Hugh O'Neill and the Nine Years War in Tudor Ireland', *Historical Journal* 36 (1993), 21–37; Roy Stradling, *The Spanish monarchy and Irish mercenaries: the Wild Geese in Spain, 1618–1668* (Dublin: Irish Academic Press, 1994); E. García Hernán, *Irlanda y El Rey Prudente*, 2 vols. (Madrid: Colección Hermes, 2000–3); Ó. Recio Morales, *España y la Pérdida del Ulster* (Madrid: Hermes, 2003).

[32] 'A brief relation of Ireland and the diversitie of Irish in the same', TCD, MS 580 (E.3.8.), ff. 49–52 a copy of an account of Irish affairs presented to Philip III in 1618 by Florence Conry, OFM. A note on the top left-hand corner of the document, in Archbishop James Ussher's handwriting states 'Presented to the Court of Spayne c.an. 1618 by Florence the pretended Archbishop of Tuam and thought penned by Philip O'Sullivan Beare.'

with Spain's culture and people. The fact that they received such privileges and sympathy reveals reciprocal fellow-feeling from their hosts. In Spain the Irish were regarded as 'Northern Spaniards' (*Nuestros hermanos irlandeses, los españoles del norte*).[33] The accommodation of the Irish in Spain was facilitated by reference to the concept of 'old ordered society'. Both Gaelic and Spanish aristocracies maintained similarly strict hierarchical structures and codes of etiquette. The hereditary professional nobilities of both elites differed uniquely from the norms of contemporary European social structures which were then in transition from feudal to early modern systems.[34] Hence the easy flow of Irish priests, scholars, professionals and military officers into important positions in Spain from the sixteenth to the eighteenth centuries.[35]

Both Conry and O'Sullivan Beare, who were of Gaelic lineage, emphasised the ancient origins of the Gaelic-Irish from Spain. Their writings placed the Gaelic-Irish and the Hiberno-Normans who had intermarried with the Gaelic aristocracy within the broader context of the Spanish nation.[36] Such a conscious and deliberate emphasis and contextualisation connected with and appealed to Spanish concerns for *limpieza de sangre,* whereby the purity of Spanish blood was identified with Iberian racial origin and Catholic heritage.[37] It was of particular

[33] Count Caracena, governor of Galicia, to Philip III, August 1602, Archivo Historico Nacional, Madrid, B. 1217.

[34] On the concept of 'Old Ordered Society' and educational institutions see R. L. Kagan, *Students and society in early modern Spain* (Baltimore: Johns Hopkins University Press, 1974); R. T. Davies, *The golden century of Spain 1507–1621* (London: Macmillan, 1964), pp. 280ff.; and for Irish professional-aristocratic structures see Ludwig Bieler, 'The island of scholars', *Revue du Moyen Age Latin* 8/3 (1952), 213; Kenneth Nicholls, *Gaelic and Gaelicised Ireland in the middle ages* (Dublin: Gill & Macmillan, 1972).

[35] In 1680 Charles II declared that 'The Irish have always enjoyed in the Spanish dominions, the same rights as Spaniards in respect of the obtaining of officers or employments. No obstacle has ever been placed in their way of their obtaining political or military appointments'; and a decree of Philip V of Spain in June 1701 confirmed that 'the privileges and graces of the Irish' would continue. These privileges included the rights 'to live, trade and acquire property in the Spanish dominions' whether 'domiciled or resident'. It was not until April 1701 that similar rights were accorded to English Catholics in Spanish territories. See John MacErlean, 'Ireland and world contact', *Studies* 8 (1919), 307–9; A. J. Loomie, 'Religion and Elizabethan commerce with Spain', *Catholic History Review* 60 (1964), 46–8; and entry 21 August 1587, *CSPI, 1586–1588*, p. 400. See also Micheline Kerney-Walsh, *Spanish knights of Irish origin*, 4 vols. (Dublin: Irish Manuscripts Commission, 1965).

[36] For Conry see above, n. 35; for O'Sullivan Beare see Byrne (ed.), *Ireland under Elizabeth*, pp. 50–1; Casway, *Owen Roe O'Neill*, pp. 3–4; and Kelly (ed.), *Historiae Compendium.*

[37] Lynch, *Spain under the Habsburgs* I, p. 28; also A. Domínguez Ortiz, 'Los conversos de origen judío después de la expulsión', *Estudios de Historia Social de España* 3 (1955), 223–431.

importance to the Spanish aristocracy and became deeply associated
with their Catholic heritage. Evidence of this racial-religious ideology
or mentality among Irish Catholic nobles is present in their various
memorials and appeals to the Spanish crown.[38] In claiming assistance
from Philip III, Philip IV, Archdukes Albert and Isabella and the papacy,
Irish noblewomen such as Catherine FitzGerald of Desmond, Elena
Countess Clancarthy, Geromma O'Connor, Eleanor O'Sullivan and
Mary Stuart-O'Donnell, stated that exile was preferable to remaining
in Ireland where they would be forced by James I or Charles I to marry
English Protestants.[39] Mary Stuart O'Donnell and Don Dualtach
O'Gallagher, in petitioning the pope, regarded such marriages with
Protestants as heretical debasement of Irish noble Catholic blood.[40]

The Salamancan graduate, Richard Bermingham OP, who was of
Hiberno-Norman origin and had adopted the Spanish style name, Fray
Ricardo de la Peña, presented Philip III with *Una breve relación de gobierno
temporal de los herejes en el Reyno de Irlanda* on 17 February 1619. This
memorial describes the persecution and plantation policy of James I:

In the new plantation of English and Scottish heretics during these times in
Ireland the king [James I] orders to leave their lands all the Catholic Irish knights
for the pure Irish and descendants of the Spanish who two-thousand years ago
won the said Kingdom . . . and governed it with justice and holy laws, adherents
to the doctrine and holiness of their many miraculous saints and learned men . . .
are now expelled from their natural properties . . . All this is done in order to
destroy the ancient Catholic and Spanish Irish.[41]

Significantly, the writer emphasises the Spanish origin of the Gaelic-
Irish and identifies this ethnicity with Catholicism. He continues with an
attack on James I's court of wards policy in Ireland, whereby on the
death of a Catholic nobleman his children were placed in the custody of

---

[38] Downey, 'Culture and diplomacy', chs. 1–4.
[39] For Catherine FitzGerald of Desmond see Archives Générales de Royaume, Brussels,
papiers d'état et de guerre, reg. 24/85; for Elena Countess Clancarty see *ibid.* reg. 27/
307, and Archivo General de Simancas, Valladolid, Estado, 44,1758; for Dona Geromma O'Connor see *ibid.*, *Estado*, 119, 843; for Eleanor O'Sullivan, *ibid.*, 119, 1751; for
other Irish noblewomen see *ibid.*, 119, 212, 219, 228, 235, 794, 2513, 2744, 2745,
2760, and *ibid.*, 235, 843, 2513 and 2744, all of whom received royal pensions; see also
Micheline Kerney-Walsh, 'Some notes towards a history of womenfolk of the Wild
Geese', *Irish Sword* 5 (1961–2); and Henry, *Military Community*, pp. 78–9.
[40] See 'Mary Stuart O'Donnell and Don Dualtach O'Galchur to the cardinal protector of
Ireland and to the pope': Archivio di Propaganda Fide, Rome, Lettere Antiche, XIV,
fols. 53 and 54. Both letters are undated but are thought to be *c.* 1627–28. They remind
the papacy that Mary Stuart O'Donnell is of royal Gaelic and Catholic blood; that she is
descended from a line of thirty kings who reigned in uninterrupted succession, and that
she resisted attempts by Charles I to have her married to a Protestant.
[41] Archivo Historico Nacional, Madrid, Monarquía de España, VI, 741–d, fols. 23, 24, 26.

an English or Scottish Protestant guardian and the revenues from their estates were assumed by the crown during their minority. On reaching the age of maturity and coming into their inheritance, these young Irish nobles were forced to marry either their guardian or their guardian's offspring. Bermingham's opinion of this practice is interesting:

the laws . . . in the said Kingdom require the said heir on his election [majority], to marry with the daughter or maid [of the guardian], or other of low fortune without lineage, nor quality of blood nor other nobility, in order that this fate will diminish the Irish nation and establish the English and Scottish heresy in the said Kingdom of Ireland. . .[42]

Again the ideology of 'purity of blood', not to mention aristocratic self-awareness, permeate Bermingham's writing. He also referred to 'the Irish nation' and identified heresy as being an Anglo-Scottish import. This is similar to the contemporary Spanish attitude which considered heresy as being foreign or alien to the natural culture and identity of Spain. Philip III took the memorial seriously enough to instruct, in his own hand, that it be read and discussed in the Council of State and that the Count Gondomar, his former ambassador in London, report on Jacobean Irish policy.[43] At that time, Spain was not in a position to assist Irish Catholics militarily, nevertheless it did help Irish refugees and made diplomatic representations on their behalf to James I.[44]

The foregoing identification by Irish Catholic clergy and nobility with Spanish racial origin, mentality and religious culture indicates a high degree of self-awareness or consciousness as a 'nation' distinct from England, in terms of race, religion and sovereignty. The fact that they identified with Spain, claimed Spanish descent and embraced Spanish religious values, intensified their alienation from England in a cosmopolitan rather than an insular nationalistic manner. Even after the defeat of the Spanish–Irish forces at Kinsale, and the flight of the earls, the Irish identification with Spain continued not only in the writings and politics of the *émigrés*, but also in the return of Spanish-educated clerics and laymen to Jacobean Ireland.[45] Yet it was during this period,

---

[42] *Ibid.*

[43] *Ibid.*; handwritten notes by Philip III on margin of fols. 23 and 24r,. See also R. Walsh (ed.), 'A memorial presented to the King of Spain on behalf of the Irish Catholics, A.D. 1619', *Archivium Hibernicum* 6 (1917), 27ff.

[44] By this time Spanish reserves were under strain, it had been forced to a twelve-year truce with the Dutch Republic and marriage negotiations with England were under way, see S. R. Gardiner, *Prince Charles and the Spanish marriage*, 2 vols. (London, 1869), II, pp. 6–8; and J. J. Silke, 'Later relations between Primate Lombard and Hugh O'Neill', *Irish Theological Quarterly* 22 (1955), 19–20.

[45] Above, notes 37, 38, 39.

particularly in the first half of the seventeenth century, that some intellectuals from the two historic communities in Ireland, the 'Gaeil' and the
'Sean Ghaill' (the Old English and Hiberno-Normans), were seeking to
forge a 'nation' of their common Irish identity, i.e. 'Éireannaigh' or
Irishmen. The Hiberno-Norman priest, Geoffrey Keating, or Seathrún
Céitinn as he was known in Irish, who was fluent in English and Irish,
was foremost in promoting this idea which he set forth in his *Foras Feasa
ar Éirinn*.[46]

What has emerged from this exploration is an appreciation of the
importance for Gaelic and Hiberno-Norman aristocratic *émigrés* of
establishing their credentials of legitimacy in Catholic Spain. As Midelfort has noted in relation to Germany and Spain, the process of
establishing purity of blood, of faith, and the exclusiveness of the noble
academies, enabled the nobility to surmount a crisis of legitimacy.[47] This
was necessary for the exiled Irish elite in terms of their self-esteem and
self-justification in the face of the New English ascendancy and the
literary assaults on Gaelic origins, nature and culture. It was also necessary for these exiles to have their native nobility recognised abroad in
order to gain acceptance in their host societies; for admission to colleges,
universities, chivalric orders, governmental, ecclesiastical and military
offices and for incorporation into the ranks of the nobility. In their
refutation of the neo-Cambrensian literary assaults of the New English
and in the establishment of their legitimacy in the context of purity of
blood and of faith, these Irish Catholic *émigré* elites contributed to the
sectarian sentiments in the denigration of Protestant planters in Ireland.

---

[46] Geoffrey Keating, *Foras feasa ar Éirinn The history of Ireland* (ed.), David Comyn and P.S.
Dineen, 4 vols. (London: Texts Soceity, 1902–14).
[47] Midelfort, 'Curious Georgics: the German nobility', pp. 217–42.

11 Concluding reflection: confronting the violence of the Irish reformations

John Morrill

I

There are plenty of reminders in this book of how gross and disfiguring were the confessional hatreds and acts of violence carried out in the name God in early modern Ireland. The rack dislocated the joints and the screw splintered the thumbs of Catholic priests and Catholic conspirators in Elizabethan and early Jacobean England (although the reign of terror lasted barely twenty-five years), and the boot splintered the shinbones of Covenanters in later Stuart Scotland (although the reign of terror was briefer still), but the intention was always to secure information that could lead to the capture of co-conspirators. And it was usually accompanied by that most chilling of all oxymorons – an instruction to the interrogators to use 'the gentler tortures' first – as in the case even of Guy Fawkes.[1] One does not suspect that the efficient collection of information was foremost in the minds of those who tortured Dermot Hurley, archbishop of Cashel, as described by Alan Ford in the toe-curling opening to this volume (above). And in Ireland torture and gross humiliation for the sake of it, resulted both from confessional self-righteousness and a desire for revenge escalating over many decades, and, again as Ford points out, is still with us. Equally unfamiliar to historians of England would be the stories of the heads of enemies being posted off coarsely packaged, or corpses being dug up and roughly reinterred in unconsecrated ground (above, pp. 00–00).[2] This was the fate at the Restoration of parliamentarian worthies interred in Westminster Abbey, but it is difficult to think of any other British examples. There are plenty of stories of sectarian atrocity one could add – several thousand of them from the Protestant depositions relating to Ulster in

---

[1] Mark Nicholls, 'Fawkes, Guy (*bap.* 1570, *d.* 1606), *Oxford Dictionary of National Biography* (2004).

[2] Cf. Clodagh Tait, *Death, Burial and Commemoration in Ireland 1550–1650* (Basingstoke: Palgrave, 2002), ch. 5 *and passim*.

the years 1641 and 1642. Then there is Cromwell's own account of how members of the Drogheda garrison were killed in cold blood long after they had surrendered (to conserve the supply of bullets, the rank and file were clubbed to death, although the governor famously was beaten to death with his own wooden leg). Indeed if we want a motto of sectarian scorn, let it be Cromwell's comment in that letter – on the man who jumped to his death, his clothes in flames, from the inferno created by the pyre of pews ignited below the church tower in which he had taken refuge – that he died crying 'God damn me, God confound me, I burn, I burn.' It is a sentence in which description and prescription are efficiently conjoined with grim satisfaction.[3]

The extreme and escalating violence that accompanied the making good of the English crown's claims to sovereign power in state and church in the two centuries after 1541 makes Irish history very different from English and perhaps British history. *Prima facie*, it makes Irish history look much more like continental European history. Ireland seems to have wars of religion that are in their confessional excesses of a type with the wars in the Netherlands and in Germany, and, to a lesser extent (because the ethnic dimension is missing) in France. And, at least on the Catholic side, there are reasons for seeing *interactions* as well as parallels. After all, by the end of the sixteenth century all Catholic priests and religious entering the fray were trained in continental seminaries, many of them at the eyes of the storm of religious conflict in the Low Countries and Paris. From the 1610s, there were great Irish lords in Spain, not reconciled to exile but dreaming of their return; and even at the height of the *Pax Hispanica*,[4] that moment (1609–21) when the superpowers took breath between the maelstroms of confessional conflict, the Spanish government was willing to give the oxygen of hope to O'Neill yearnings, and the helium of publicity too. One of the powerful and convincing moments in this book is Micheal MacCraith's demonstration that the gap between Florence Conry's *Mirror of Piety* (1616) and Hugh McCaughwell's *Mirror of the Sacrament of Penance* (1618) was not the gap between militancy and appeasement, but a consequence of the death of Hugh O'Neill which meant that an early military solution was on hold *sine die* (above).

---

[3] *The letters and speeches of Oliver Cromwell with elucidations by Thomas Carlyle* (ed. S. C. Lomas), 3 vols. (1904), letter 105, vol. I, p. 469 (Cromwell to William Lenthall, 17 September 1649).

[4] The recovery of this concept, much relied on by scholars since, can be found in Hugh Trevor-Roper, 'Spain and Europe 1598–1621', in J. P. Cooper (ed.), *The new Cambridge modern history: IV The decline of Spain and the Thirty Years War 1609–48/59'* (Cambridge: Cambridge University Press, 1970), pp. 269–71, 278–80.

But this reminder of the geopolitics is also a reminder that Irish history needs to be located in the early modern period not within a context of the three kingdoms but of the five kingdoms, with France and Spain as constantly alert players.[5] If direct military intervention was rare, it was always on the agenda, and other forms of intervention (the training of priests, the recruitment of mercenaries, the protection of radical thinkers and the publication of radical writings) were always there.

On the Protestant side, the links might seem much more British than continental. Yet James Ussher was sustained in his scholarship and in his defence of Irish identity by a web of continental contacts, and the recent rediscovery of his links to Walter Travers, long after the latter had moved on from his sojourn in Trinity College, Dublin to long exile in the heartlands of militant Protestantism on the continent, strengthens those links.[6] So there is a *prima facie* case for caution in moving too quickly from seeing the distinctiveness of Irish experience from British experience as a case for Irish exceptionalism.

However, that is to drift from where we started. The first thing this book does, is to remind us of the terrible truth of the role of sectarian violence in Irish history. It seeks to go beyond deploring it and it seeks to make sense of it. It seeks to look at the shape, pace, interconnectedness and uniqueness (or otherwise) of the Irish experience.

II

Yet if the *strongest* images conjured up by the book are of confessional violence, the most *persistent* images are of what attenuated the violence. It is not part of the received historiography to be told that 'only from the 1590s onwards is it certain that Protestantism passed Catholicism out as the religion of the newcomers' (above, p. 105). Surely the Gaelic-Irish were immovably Catholic, the Old English wobbled and then, over-whelmingly, opted for the new Catholicism that arrived from the contin-ent in and after the 1570s? The New English came with a sense of ethnic and religious superiority, and the longer they spent in Ireland, the more contemptuous they became of papists and popery, and of an Irish people besotted with popery. David Edwards' essay is a real challenge to this presumption. Not only did English Catholics flood into Ireland, they

---

[5] See Jane Ohlmeyer's exegesis of this argument in Jane Ohlmeyer (ed.), *Ireland from independence to occupation* (Cambridge: Cambridge University Press, 1995), chs. 1 and 5.
[6] See the forthcoming Cambridge Ph.D. by Polly Ha, which will reveal and explore these links (the provisional title of this thesis is 'The revival of English Presbyterianism' *1591–1641*').

came because the conditions for Catholics were easier in Ireland than they were in England. The laws against Catholic practice were milder in comparison, and enforcement was (even) more spasmodic, especially in the 1580s and 1590s when there was a zero tolerance policy in operation in England.

Furthermore, it comes as a surprise (to put it mildly) to find James Ussher conducting a long and detailed correspondence with the Catholic bishop of Ossory (David Rothe), let alone acting as a research assistant to Luke Wadding and asking him to make transcripts of documents in the Vatican archives (above, p. 151). This is, after all, the same James Ussher who (while he generally preferred to bite his tongue than to stick it out at His Grace of Canterbury) told Laud that 'whatever others do imagine of the matter, I stand fully convinced that the Pope is Antichrist', just after the repeal of the Irish article (to the satisfaction of the English primate) that had maintained that very thing (above, p. 67). And it comes as a surprise to find James Ware, a second-generation New English government official, so happily publishing, as a contribution to *Irish* history, a compendium of works by the Catholic proto-martyr of Elizabethan England Edmund Campion, the Welsh Protestant *émigré* Meredith Hanmer and the evangelical Protestant enragé Edmund Spenser, and even more of a surprise to find that it is Spenser whom he silently edits and dilutes (above, pp.141–2). And one certainly does not expect to find a bishop in the Church of Ireland stating that the reformation left the reformed church 'as much the same church as a garden before it is weeded and after is the same garden' (above).

If David Edwards' claim about the flow of English Catholics to Ireland is the most startling revelation in this book (to my mind), then the second most startling is the assertion, bolder than in his excellent book on Gaelic culture, that the 'theory that Protestant Reformation was doomed to failure because of an allegedly ingrained and reflexive bardic allegiance to Catholicism is belied by the evidence. In fact bardic poets were for the most part reticent and possibly strategically detached in their response to the rival claims of the sixteenth century reform movements' (above, p. 178). If it is important to seek out the sources of confessionalisation, it is also necessary to weigh their significance against instititutional and cultural features that hindered or limited it.

To the examples of a neat patterning offered in this book, let me add one more. Jane Ohlmeyer has demonstrated how Oliver Cromwell was willing to cut a deal with the marquis of Antrim, offering him indemnity in exchange for the use of his vessels to maintain his supply lines from England. (Otherwise they would have preyed on that same supply line.) This in itself demonstrates a pragmatism that transcended confessional contempt. It demonstrates that his primary objective was to extirpate support for the Stuarts not to extirpate papists.[7] But there is a sub-plot in Cromwell's makeshift alliance with Antrim: the negotiations secretly conducted with Irish Catholics including Patrick Crelly, abbot of Newry, to see if agreement could be reached that would allow a measure of freedom of worship for Catholics in return for a binding oath of allegiance to the English Commonwealth enforced by church leaders. Historians have recently begun to take such negotiations then, and later in the Restoration, much more seriously.[8] That there would be two confessional groups in Ireland, one geopolitically ineradicable, and one culturally ineradicable, seems certain by no later than 1590. That conflict, rather than uneasy peaceful coexistence, would characterise relations for centuries was not so inevitable.

III

If there is more going on behind the bleakly hostile rhetoric of two armed camps than meets the eye, there is more going on within the confessions too. When one thinks of violence in Drogheda, one thinks of Oliver Cromwell clubbing disarmed Catholic soldiers (as well as clergy and religious) to death, or Oliver Plunkett being hacked to pieces. So if we are told that the altar of a Dominican oratory in Drogheda was destroyed, its pulpit vandalised and sacred vessels removed, we do not expect to find out that the vandals were put up to it by a vicar general of Armagh or by the Jesuits (above, p. 211). For that matter, we do not expect to find that when bodies were disinterred and removed from their burial places, this was (except perhaps in the special circumstances of 1641–2) more likely to result from a feud between the religious orders as a cross-confessional act of terror. A great deal of the energy that one might have expected to have gone into confessional strife went into mutual recrimination amongst the Protestants and the Catholics – on the Protestant side, turf wars between English Episcopalians and Scottish Presbyterians, on the Catholic side, turf wars between Franciscans and Jesuits. And come to think of it, who suffered more persecution by the state in Ireland for religious practices in the 1630s, Catholics or

[7] Jane Ohlmeyer, *Civil war and restoration in the three Stuart kingdoms: the career of Randal MacDonnell, marquis of Antrim 1609–1683* (Cambridge: Cambridge University Press, 1993), pp. 210–39.

[8] Jeffrey Collins, 'Thomas Hobbes and the Blackloist conspiracy of 1649', *Historical Journal* 45 (2002), 305–31. See also J. Casway, 'The clandestine correspondence of Father Patrick Crelly, 1648–9', *Collecteana Hibernica* 20 (1979 for 1978), 7–20.

Presbyterians, or in the 1670s, Catholics or Protestant dissenters? It really is important to remind ourselves how little of the anti-Catholic legislation that was passed through the Elizabethan parliament was enacted in Ireland – as far as *religious* observance was concerned, there was little more than the financial penalties contained in the 1560 Act of Supremacy. As Tadhg Ó hAnnracháin points out, Ormonde in the 1640s believed it to be incontrovertible that there was no extant penalty for saying or for hearing mass (above, p. 76). And, whatever else Cromwell did, he never required anyone to attend any religious service they did not wish to attend. The *leniency* of the Irish legal system with respect to the practice of Catholicism is the first of the reasons offered by David Edwards for that hitherto unsuspectedly high level of Catholic migration from Britain to Ireland (above, p. 76). Whereas the default position in England was that Catholics were traitors, and simply to be a native-born priest in the realm of England could be taken as evidence of treason, the default position in Ireland was that a priest was guilty of *praemunire* but not of treason, without overt acts or statements derogatory to the king's title and authority. Catholic priests in Ireland were much more liable to experience acts of extra-legal violence than in England, but they were not by any means as liable to experience acts of legal violence.[9]

IV

English greed for Irish land, masked in the language of treason and reformation, left the Catholic community vulnerable to expropriation. Those excluded from control of the agencies of law and prerogative had every reason to dread the future (and all too often to detest the past). But in the conundrum about whether the English hated the Irish because they were Catholics or because they were Irish, the stories in this book of the large-scale movement of English Catholics to Ireland, and more dramatic still, of the conversions of New English Protestants to New English Catholicism, is, to put it mildly, suggestive. To think of the family of Sir Henry Bagenal (himself the son of a man of no substance who had fled to Ulster after killing a man, who provoked Hugh O'Neill in 1596 and got his comeuppance at the White Ford in 1598) as

[9] This is not to say there were fewer, especially not proportionately fewer, Irish martyrs than English ones, just that the English state held show trials before it eviscerated Catholics by 'due process', whereas in Ireland they were much more often straightforwardly murdered by those acting in the name of the state but without any show of 'justice'.

Catholic commanders in 1641 – 'in just a couple of generations from English conquerors to Catholic rebels' (above, p. 101) – is emphatically not in the usual script. The drift the other way is less startling but still too easy to overlook. In 1641 there were twelve earls born to Catholic parents in Ireland, only two of whom (the earls of Westmeath and Fingall) had Catholic wives born in Ireland. The others had English or Irish Protestant wives, or in one case an English wife who lapsed back into Catholicism at about the time of her marriage.[10] Several (including the earls of Ormonde, Thomond and Kildare) had converted to Protestantism. A court policy, adapted from James VI's policy towards the Highland lords of Scotland, of aggressive ethnic acculturation (in which religion was only one, and not the main, element) was producing results. Is it wholly foolish to think that an attrition amongst the Irish elite could have fatally weakened seigneurial Catholicism in Ireland? By 1641, nearly half of the leading Catholic families of 1601 were in exile or were Protestant, and others had adapted hybrid existences. Ulick Burke might have been an exemplary Gaelic lord when he was on the west of the Shannon, but when he was in Whitehall, Westminster, Kent or even Dublin, he was impeccably English – with an impeccably English wife (Anne Compton, the daughter of the earl of Northampton), so unthreatening in his disguised Catholicism and English raiment that he could serve as a deputy lieutenant, as a member of the English House of Lords, and, in 1641 of all years, a member of the English Privy Council. As his career over the next few years would show, he was not at the beck and call of Tridentine churchmen.

This is an important part of the story. But it would be worth pondering on whether this was the *only* period of vulnerability. From what Burke's *Irish Peerage* and *Oxford DNB* allow us to see, there is no comparable period when state action and Catholic accommodation allowed a similar haemorrhaging effect from Catholicism. In the half centuries before and after the period 1590–1640, confessionally exogamous marriage and the religious conversion of heirs was at a low level.

V

In a sense the Protestant reformation succeeded in Ireland. It succeeded in establishing itself as the religion and badge of those who governed and those who came in to settle. The English settlers of the sixteenth and

---

[10] I have based this on the information about Irish earldoms to be found in E. B. Fryde *et al.* (eds.), *Handbook of British chronology*, 3rd edn (Royal Historical Society, 1986), pp. 490–8, followed up in *The Oxford dictionary of British biography online*.

seventeenth centuries did not de-gen-erate[11] themselves in the way that so many of their Norman predecessors had in the fourteenth and fifteenth centuries. But that reformation failed in the sense that those born in Ireland before the Protestant schism and before the drive to establish uniformity of belief and practice, or those descended from those born in Ireland before that schism, overwhelmingly remained outside the church established to create that uniformity. In the sense that Ireland is unusual, if not unique in defying the principle of *cuius regio, eius religio,* the reformation failed.

In a sense the Catholic reformation succeeded in Ireland. Despite every worldly inducement to convert, a vast majority of those baptised into the Catholic faith in the early modern period in Ireland died in communion with the bishop of Rome, and out of communion with the established church. It failed in that those who embraced it were unable to acculturate those who came to settle amongst them, who systematically stripped them of any effective control of the political and legal institutions that gave them control of their own lives.

So two reformations succeeded and failed. If this book has not answered that central question in Irish historiography: why did the reformation fail?, it has at least changed the question.

In the introduction, Alan Ford explores the meaning and relevance of both confessionalism and sectarianism (above, p. 411). I would fully endorse his concerns about the application of the term confessionalisation and I am glad it is not in the title. It works best in explaining the success of reformation from above. It is least successful in explaining the failure of the reformation from above. If it is to be applied to Ireland, it will tell us little about why Protestant settlers adopted the forms of Protestantism that they did, and only a little about why (and the extent to which) the native Irish adopted/adapted to Tridentine Catholicism. It would be most helpful in explaining why so many of the Pale families of the mid century, torn between loyalty to the crown and to their faith, opted, against secular self-interest, for recusancy. But that is a dimension not focused on within this book.[12] Ford urges us instead to prefer the language of sectarianism, in the sense deployed by Brewer and Liechty (above, pp. 6–10). This places great emphasis on the symbiosis between that which is embraced and that which is rejected and (literally)

---

[11] See the discussion of the link between the Latin *gens* and the perceived process of *degeneration*, Rees Davies, 'The peoples of Britain and Ireland: I. Identities', *Transactions of the Royal Historical Society*, 6th series, 4 (1994), 1–20.

[12] Although it was explored by an excellent paper given at the conference of which this volume is a consequence, sadly that paper was not available for this collection.

demonised. When people hate one another as much as the sects here discussed, everything is likely to be contested, even time and space. At its most extreme, it means that Catholic Ireland embraced the new Gregorian calendar, Protestant Ireland, as England, the Julian calendar. They could not even agree on what day it was.

This has implications for the chronology of confessionalisation (as she prefers it; sectarianisation as Ford and McCafferty prefer it) that Ute Lotz-Heumann proposes in chapter 2. Her chronology is one that reveals how the Protestant communities perceived what was happening to them. It is an agenda driven by a failing top-down attempt to create a Protestant Ireland. Period 1 (1534–60) is a time of *uncertainty*; period 2 (1558–60) is a time of *preparation*; period 3 (1580–1603) the time of separation and *embryonic confessionalisation*; period 4 (1603–32) a time of 'confessionalisation *within* Irish society'; and period 5 (1632–49), a time of 'confessionalisation *from outside*' (above, pp. 37–8). This approach makes a great deal of sense from the Protestant perspective and she explores what they are. However, there are some problems with it. For example, as John McCafferty's chapter makes clear, the failure of Trinity College to act as the training ground for a generation of indigenous Protestant leaders meant that the process of anglicising evangelism was in full flood throughout James' reign. Between 1603 and 1625 the proportion of Irish-born Protestant Bishops fell from 60 percent to 16 percent, and of Irish-speaking bishops from 75 percent to 14 percent (above, p. 57). Behind the hollow rhetoric of a confessional state, the Protestant mission was already doomed to be the badge and trophy of a colonial elite only. I would hazard a guess that there was less expectation by 1632 that the Irish could be converted to Protestantism than there was amongst colonial bishops in 1880 that British Africa could be converted to Protestant Christianity. Irish Protestants might have been more emphatic than British Protestants that the pope was Antichrist; but they were probably also more emphatic that the empire of Antichrist would be overthrown not by their painful preaching but by the second coming.

But Lotz-Heumann's chronology fits uncomfortably with the dynamics *within* Catholicism. Certainly there was the gradual emergence of a community that was self-consciously exclusive, controlling rites of passage, sacramental discipline, self-sufficient in terms of self-help *and* the means of salvation, i.e., a community that defined itself *against* Protestantism. But while Catholics had to react to the dynamics of top-down Protestantism, it owed more to something not considered by Lotz-Heumann – the dynamic of curial geopolitics. Here the schism from Rome is important; but it is unlikely that Rome thought that 1534 had a specifically Irish resonance. The first phase would begin with the creation of the kingdom of Ireland in 1541, and the basing of English power on statute and not on papal grant, a claim that looked to the application to Ireland of the policies of appropriation of jurisdiction and of church property. But if Irish religious houses were dissolved as in England (but not to the benefit of local elites as in England and Scotland) there was no dissolution of parish guilds. An attack on the guilds and chantries was central to the fundamental challenge to that belief in the communion of saints (living and dead) which was the defining characteristic of the Edwardine reformation in England; it is not so easy to find evidence of that challenge taking place in mid-century Ireland.[13] Indeed, more generally, there was in the latter no great intensification of reformation in the early 1550s and no great Catholic Risorgimento in the later 1550s. Things were much smoother. The Acts of 1560 represented a new challenge to Rome, but no immediate change in the religious observance of most residents of Ireland. Most of the priests outside the Pale carried on much as before; and as vacancies to sees occurred, appointments were made, except in the most conspicuous of sees like Dublin and Meath. But with the beginning of the prolonged series of risings and confiscations from 1570 and especially 1580, Rome adopted a much more softly-softly approach. The key issue for Rome was whether, in defiance of the Act of Uniformity, to appoint Catholic bishops to challenge and to confront those appointed under royal mandate. Throughout Europe, Rome was hesitant to escalate tensions with schismatic Protestant rulers. In seeking to subvert rather than to confront the principle of *cuius regio eius religio*, Rome decided that to appoint and to sustain the authority of resident bishops was unwise and likely to be counter-productive. The martyrdom of Archbishop Hurley was no doubt a further spur in this direction. And so from about 1580, and especially from the pontificate of Clement VIII (1592–1605), a conscious decision was made to run the Irish church through the generals and superiors of the religious orders and through vicars general or vicars apostolic. Even where, during this phase, bishops were appointed, they remained abroad, and vicar generals exercised jurisdiction in their name (as David Rothe did for Peter Lombard, after the latter's appointment as archbishop of Armagh in 1609). What is striking is not this policy – which was standard papal policy for Protestant territories – but its reversal in 1618 (the year in which Tadgh

---

[13] Colm Lennon, 'The chantries in the Irish reformation; the case of St Anne's Guild, Dublin, 1550–1630', in R. V. Comerford *et al.* (eds.), *Religion, conflict and coexistence in Ireland* (Dublin: Gill and Macmillan, 1990), pp. 6–25.

Ó hAnnachrain's chapter suggestively begins) when progress was rapidly made towards filling many, though not all sees, with resident Catholic episcopate. Only in the 1640s, and specifically with the round of appointments made at the height of the nunciature of GianBattista Rinuccini in 1647 was the hierarchy fully restored, just in time for the Cromwellian Armageddon. The murder of many bishops and abbots and a significant number of priests (and the transportation to Barbados of many more) marks a clear departure from previous English and Irish Protestant practice in Ireland, and coincided with an abandonment of priest-killing in England. A chronology based on the experience of the Catholic community would thus run not as 1534–60, 1560–80, 1580–1603, 1603–32 and 1632–49 but 1541–80, 1580–1618, 1618–41 and 1641–60 and 1660–1721. One could add that both these chronologies would be different again if one were not trying to make broad sense of the Irish experience but of the experience of the Pale or of Ulster. But I only have space to throw that out, not to develop it – just think (in the case of Ulster) of the Gaelic links between south-west Scotland and north-east Ireland, the concentration of Scottish settlers alongside English, of the distinctive patterns of plantation and ethnic cleansing.

VI

This is, then, a welcome for this book as a contribution to the longitudinal history of Ireland and a contribution to understanding how it came to be as it is. It is a book that locates the religious divisions within their archipelagic and their continental contexts, and it recognises and fitfully explores the moral economy of violence and sectarian detestation. I will confide in the reader that when I first read the collection, I suggested that the title of the volume should not be about the origins of sectarianism but *Papists and Heretics: debates within and between the Churches of Ireland 1540–1660*. Having written this concluding reflection, I do not shift from thinking that mine is the more accurate title; but that there is more to the volume than my safe restatement makes clear. Alan Ford writes (above, p. 23) about 'the mysterious transition from peaceful coexistence to brutal hostility' as the true subject of this volume. It is a little less mysterious once you have read the book, and a little less a movement from white to black. Above all, it is a salutary reminder to all who approach the subject that the uniqueness of the Irish experience needs an archipelagic and continental context to make sense. Let those dialogues continue to grow. . .

Index

Á Becket, Thomas 135
Act for English order habit and
    language 139
Act of Attainder of Shane O'Neill 132
Act of Supremacy 76, 105–106, 122, 234
Act of Uniformity 238
Adair, Archibald 63, 71
Adams, Bernard 64
Alen, Sir John 104, 122
Allegiance, oath of 184–186, 200
Allen, John 126
Almond, John 107
Althone 92, 125
Andrews, George 17
Andrews, Lancelot
    Tortura Torti 186
Ann of Denmark 183
Antrim, Randall MacDonnell, marquess
    of 232
apocalyptic
    absence in Hanmer 144
    application to Ireland 147, 148,
        149, 152
    Hooker's writings 136
    Spenser's *View* 139, 154
    Ussher 149
Archbold, Matthew
Ardagh 116
Armagh, Synod of 88, 171
Arthur, king of England 132, 138
Arundel, Sir John 110
Atherton, John 56, 71
Audley family 109, 116
Augsburg, Peace of 25, 49, 183
Aylmer family 204, 205

Babington, Brutus 62, 69
Bagenal family 100–101, 126
Bagenal, Walter 101, 113, 125, 126
Bagenal, Sir Henry 234
Bale, John 134

Balkans 77, 78
Ballinasloe 118
Ballyadams 125
Ballyleman Castle 125
Baltinglass revolt 219
baptism 19
Barlow, William 84–85
Barnewall, Patrick 210, 212
Barnewall, Richard 92
Barnewall, Sir Christopher 121
Barnwall family, barons of
    Trimleston 92
Barrington family 104
Barrington, Francis 125
Baskerville family 116
Bassett, Philip 113
Bathe, John 192
Bathe, Robert 206, 211, 212, 213
Bedell, William
    ecclesiastical courts 69
    linguistic ability 57
    nodel bishop 68
    policy in Kilmore 19
    resigns Ardagh 59, 62
Bellarmine, Robert 73, 186, 188, 191
    Responsio 186
Bermingham, Richard 221, 226, 227
Best family 112–114
Binchy, D.A. 150
Blackwell, George 186–187
Boece, Hector 142
Book of Common Prayer 194
Borromeo, St Charles 73–74
Bottigheimer, Karl 6
Bowen family 119, 120
Bowen, Sir John 125
Boyne, Battle of 157
Brabazon, Antony 118, 125
Bradshaw, Brendan 32, 35
Brady, Ciaran 218
Brandon, James 205

Bramhall, John
  Anglican identity 55
  church property 70
  High Commission 52, 71
  secular office 58
  religious controversy 65
  religious policy 59
  Wentworth's ally 71
Brewer, John 9, 236
Brigid, St 164, 170
  Brigid's Bell 143
Brittans of Lyons 114
Brooksbury, Mr 112
Brouncker, Sir Henry 113
Browne, Nicholas 120
Brownes of Kerry 117
Brünner, Otto 216–217, 220
Burghley, William Cecil, 1st baron 141
Burke see Clanrickard
Burke, Ulick 235
Butler, Edmund 116
Butler family of Callen 109
Butler family of Kilcash 109
Butler family of Ormond 109, 115
  see also Ormond, Mountgarret
Butler, Pierce 116

Caball, Mark 16, 232
Cahill, Patrick 78
Calvert, Sir George 115
Calvin, John 196, 197–198
Cambrensis, Giraldus
  as historian 127, 130, 131, 132, 135,
    136, 139, 142, 144, 146
  attitude to Irish 136, 142–144, 150, 156,
    157, 218, 223, 222
  Expugnatio 131, 132, 133, 135, 136, 142
  historiography 130, 146
  Topographia 131, 168, 154, 220
Camden, William 144–146, 150, 218
  Britannia 144
Campion, Edmund
  as historian 131, 132, 136, 142, 144, 152
  Two bokes 130, 154, 232
  in Ireland 129
  martyr 133
  religion 132–133, 139, 141
Canny, Nicholas 217, 218
Caraffa, Vincent 68
Carew family 133
Carew, Sir Peter 133
Carlow, Co. 115, 125, 126
Casey, Donal 78
Castlehaven, James Tuchet,
    3rd earl of 126
Castlemartin 114

Catholic church in Ireland
  episcopate 74, 75, 78
  reorganization 79–80
Catholic reformation see counter-reformation
Cavan 119
Celestine I, Pope 139, 145
Chamberlin, Robert 84, 86, 194
Chandler, John 115
Chanu, Pierre 217
Charles I
  appointment of bishops 63, 67, 72
  church property 58, 69, 70
  Malone's appeal to 84–88
  marriage 107, 201
Charles V 223
Chichester, Sir Arthur 60, 62, 112, 205
Church of Ireland
  1615 Articles 66–59, 70, 232
  church and state 58
  Convocation 67, 71
  ecclesiastical courts 69–71
  high commission 52, 71
  number of dioceses 58–61
  poverty
Clancarty, Eleanor Countess 226
Clanrickard, Richard Burke, 4th earl
Clanrickard, Ulick, 5th earl 118
Clarke, Aidan 218
Clarke, Hugh 115
Clarke, William 122
Claudian 155
Clement VIII, Pope 73, 186,
    187, 238
Clere family 120
Clere, Katherine 120
Clinton family 120
Clones 119, 120
Cochlaeus, Johannes 4, 197
Colclough family 126
Colcough, Antony 126
Colgan, John 127
Collum, William 125
Colm Cille 164, 170
Colton, John 171
Compton, Anne 235
confessionalization
  definition 6, 25, 37–53
  historiography 25, 35–37
  in Ireland 5–8, 13, 22
  problems with 7–8, 13, 236–237
confirmation 67, 79, 80
Confraternity 206–207, 209
Congregation de Propaganda Fide 214
Conry, Florence
  appointment as archbishop 188
  biography 189–191

Conry, Florence (*cont.*)
  Brief relation 224
  cultural superiority 221, 225
  and Hugh O'Neill 192
  political thought 192, 200–202
  Sgáthán and chrábhaidh 189,
    190–191, 230
  St Anthony's College 192
Cooke family 116
Cooke, Sir Walsingham 115
Corby, Ralph 107
Corish, Patrick 50, 74, 79
Cork, Co. 116, 117, 126
Cork, Richard Boyle, 1st earl 18, 19, 49
Cosby family 104
Cosby, Francis 119
Cosby, William 125
counter-reformation
  definition of 26–29, 32–34, 203
  European 189, 190, 191, 223
  impact in Ireland 39, 80, 105, 203, 219
  and Irish language 190
  native Irish response 158, 162, 181, 182
  success 236
Cox, Richard 157
Crelly, Patrick 233
Crispe family 116
Croagh Patrick 195
Cromwell, Oliver
  Drogheda massacre 229–230, 233
  Irish policy 78, 234
  and marquess of Antrim 232–233
Cuffe, Hugh 117
Cullum family 117
Cullum, Robert 116

Daniel, William 57, 64, 65
Davells family 108
Davells, Henry 119
Davells, Thomas 120, 125
De La Pole, Henry 111, 119
De Mendoza, Jorge 223
De Voragine, Jacobus, *Legenda aurea* 165
Dease, Thomas 81, 213
Del Aguila, Don Juan 189
Delahoyde, Balthazar 203–215, 233
Delahoyde, Christopher 210, 211
Delumeau, Jean 161
Dempster, Thomas 151
Derg, Lough 160, 168–170, 195
Desmond risings, 41, 109, 110, 134, 135
Desmond, Gerald Fitzgerald,
    16th earl 219
Digby, Sir Kenelm 90
Dillon family 109
Dillon, Thomas, 4th viscount 92

Dingle 219
  Treaty of 223
divine rights of kings 134, 189, 192
Dominican order, in Drogheda 204, 206,
    210, 211, 233
Douai 189, 194
Dowdall family 121
Dowdall, Sir John 21
Downey, Declan 3
Downham, George 62, 66, 67
  Papa Antichristus 65
Downpatrick 195
Draycott, Henry 104, 121
Drogheda 204–215, 231, 233
Dublin, city 124
Dublin, Co. 98, 123, 126
Dublin, Synod of 206, 199
Duffy, Eamon 39, 177
Dundalk 123
Dundas, James 63
Dungan, Edward 78
Dungan, Walter 92
Dunnaman 116
Dutch revolt 223

earls, flight of 221
education 20–22, 41, 43, 45–46, 57–58
Edward VI 38, 104
Edwards, David 3, 231–232, 234
Elizabeth I
  church settlement 90, 101, 104
  death 184
  heresy of 83, 106, 219
  plantation 100, 103
Elllis, Stephen 219
emigration 98–109
English, Richard 11
Eniskeane 119
Enos, Walter 89, 90, 91, 93
Eusebius, *Ecclesiastical history* 141
Everard, James 206, 211, 212, 213
Everson family 116

Ferdinand II, Holy Roman
    emperor 99
Fermanagh, Co. 1
Fitzgerald *see* Desmond
Fitzgerald family 109, 135
Fitzgerald, James Fitzmaurice 110, 219
FitzGerald, Catherine 226
FitzGerald, Sir Luke 92
Fitzharris family 109
FitzRalph, Richard 171
Fitzsimon, Henry 20, 44, 146–147
Fleetwood family 117
Fleetwood, Sir Richard 117

Fleetwood, Thomas 117
Fleming family of Slane 109
Fleming, Thomas 73, 78
Flower, Robin 164
Four Masters, Annals of the 54, 70
Foxe, John 134
    Actes and monuments 135
Francis, St 194, 211, 214
Franck, Sebastian 216
Franciscan order
    bishops 188
    Colleges 189, 192, 214
    Drogheda dispute 203–215, 233
    hagiography 127
    and Irish language 190–191
    Irish provincial 189
    Observant reform 172
    and William Malone 78, 84–85
Fraser, Antonia, 183
French, Nicholas 82, 91, 93
Frend family 114
Freshford 107
Frischlin, Nicodemus 216
funerals 19–20

Gaelic Irish
    historiography 127, 131
    language and culture, 122, 139, 140,
        141–146, 178
    literati 158–159, 183
    national feeling 193–194, 228
    racial identity 220, 226
    and reformation 232
    religious commitment 231
Galway, Co. 118
Gathelus 143
Geneva 98
George, St 140, 146
Geraldine War 219
Gerard, Lord William 139
Gilles, William 167
Gillespie, Raymond 32
Ginzburg, Carlo 178
Giraldus *see* Cambrensis, Giraldus
Glascock, Richard 125
Glaslough 119
Godwin, Francis, *Catalogue of bishops* 153
Gondomar, Diego Sarmiento de Acuña,
    Count 227
Gordon family 119
Grace family 120
Graces, the 123
Graiguenamanagh 125
Green, George 126
Greene family 116
Gregorian Reform movement 171

Gregory XIII, Pope 219
Gunpowder plot 107, 109, 112, 184, 187
Gurguntius, king of Britain 131, 132, 138
Gwynn, Aubrey 222

Hadfield, Andrew 218, 220, 221
hagiography, Irish 127, 128, 158–161, 167
Haigh, Christopher 39, 102
Hamilton familiy 118
Hampton, Christopher 66
Hampton, William 112
Hanmer, Meredith
    Chronicle of Ireland 142
    colonial attitudes 218, 221
    as historian 141–144, 146, 152, 220, 232
Hanratty, Patrick 212
Harington, Sir John 181
Harpole family 108
Harpole, Robert 119, 126
Harpole, William 125
Harris, Paul 78
Harris, Walter 152, 153
Hayden, Mary 5
Hayward, John 125
Heatherington family 125
Hedwich family 114
Henly, Mr 117
Henry II 218
Henry IV of France 188
Henry VIII
    apostacy 83
    historiography 130, 133
    Irish policy 102, 103, 218–219
    Irish reformation 38
Heygate, James 63
Higden, Ranulf, *Polychronicon* 142
Hill family 205
Hill, Moses 205
historiography, German 16
Holinshed, Raphael 132, 133
    Chronicles 127, 130–136
Holy Cross abbey 108
Holy Roman Empire 49, 217
Holywood, Christopher 208, 213
Hooker, John 133–136, 156
Hovendon family 107, 111
Howe, Thomas 112
Huguenots 98, 99, 184
humanism 127, 133, 136, 137, 138, 142,
    145, 157, 218
Huntington, Henry of 218
Hurley, Dermot 1, 43, 238

Inchiquin, Murrough O'Brien, earl
    of 82, 91
Ingoli, Francesco 79

intermarriage 15, 17–19, 120–121, 201, 225, 235

Jackson, Brian 3
James VI & I
  accession 101, 155
  Apologie 186–187
  appointment of bishops 55–58, 61–63, 72
  church property 58, 69
  Irish parliament 141
  king of Ireland 183–195
  king of Scotland 176
  plantation 100, 221, 226
  political thought 197–202
  Praefatio monitoria 187, 198, 199
  religious policy 55–59, 67, 183
  Trew law 191
  Triplici nodo 186
Jans, James 121
Jedin, Hubert 27
Jefferies, Henry 34
Jenison, Thomas 110
Jesuits, Society of Jesus 22
  in Drogheda 206, 1573, 1826, 233
  general 208, 213
  historians 145–146
  missionaries 77, 96, 107
  religious controversy 50, 65, 83, 84, 188, 199
  superior of 91
Jones, Lewis 60
Jones, Thomas 21, 58, 64
Juxon, William 58

Kamen, Henry 217
Kaplan, Benjamin 30
Kavanagh family 119, 121
Kearney, Daniel, dean of Cashel 206, 207
Keating, Geoffrey 128, 144, 146, 228
Kells, Book of 150
Kells, Synod of 81
Kilcolman 116
Kildare Rebellion, The 38
Kildare, earls of 235
Kilkenny city 108, 120
Kilkenny, Co. 115, 116, 123, 125
Kilkenny, Confederation of
  confessionalization 52
  disagreements within 52
  General Assembly 126
  loyalty to Stuarts 86–88
  New English in 126
  role of bishops 82–94
  Supreme Council 82, 91

Kilkenny, statutes of 139, 156
Kilkenny, synod of 81
Kilmore, Co. Cork 117
King, William 181
Kinsale, battle of 189, 221, 227
Knatchbull family 109, 112, 113, 116
Knox, Andrew 63, 64, 69, 71

Lake, Arthur 67
Lancaster, John 64
Lane, Sir Parr 140
  The holy ile 140
Lateran Council, fourth 135
Laud, William 58, 59, 63, 67, 70, 232
Leabhar Gabhála 130, 138, 144
Leinster 114, 119, 120
Leke family 114
Leland, Thomas 157
Lennon, Colm 18, 41, 33, 218, 220, 222
Leo X, Pope 196
Leslie, Henry 71
Liechty, Joseph 9, 10, 236
Limerick, Co. 116, 125
Lithgow, William 14
Loftus, Adam, viscount Ely, 58
Lombard, Peter
  Ad quaestoines 189
  appointment of bishops 60, 188, 190
  as archbishop 238
  church–state relations 79, 83
  death 79
  definition of heresy 188–189, 198
  Drogheda dispute 215
Lotz-Heumann, Ute 6, 237
Louvain 189–190, 192, 194, 214
Luther, Martin 4, 11, 134, 147, 181, 196–198
Lynch, John 89–90, 93, 223
Lynch, Roland 64, 66
Lynch, Walter 91
Lyons, F. S. L. 221

Mac an Bhaird, Fearghal Óg 170, 176, 177
Mac Bruiadeadha, Domhnall 176, 177
MacBruiadeadha, Maoilín Óg 175, 181
MacCarthy-Morrogh, Michael 117
MacCawell, Edmund 168
Mac Con Midhe, Giolla Brighde 171–172
MacCraith, Micheál 3
MacCurtain, Margaret 217, 221
MacDonald, Sir James 200
MacEgan, Boethius 75
MacFirbisigh, Dubhaltach 154
Mac Niocaill, Aonghus 168
McCaughwell, Hugh 4

Scáthán Shacramuinte na hAithridhe 4,
    188–189, 192–202, 230
McGrath, Miler 56, 60, 64, 66, 97
McKenna, Lambert 165
McMahon, Owen 188
Magennis, Hugh 19
Maguire, Lord Connor 124
Malone, William 85–86, 91
    Reply to Ussher 83–84
Madrid 201
mandates controversy 47, 112–113
Maria, Infanta 201
Marian exiles 98
marriage *see* intermarriage
Marriott, Luke 124
Marshall family 116
Marshall, Francis 113
Marshall, Robert 113
Mary, Queen 39
Mary, queen of Scots 183
Mary, Virgin 162–165, 165–166,
    168, 170, 173, 187
Masterson family 115, 120
Masterson, Sir Richard 115, 120
Masterson, Sir Thomas 119, 120, 121
Matrix, Castle 125
Matthews, Patrick 212
Maurenbrechter, Wilhelm 26, 27
Maxwell, John 67
Meath, Co. 121
Meigs, Samantha 34, 35, 158–161,
    178–179
Mellan, Henry 214
Mellifont, treaty of 188
Midelfort, Erik 220, 228
Molyneux, Daniel 142
Monaghan town 119
Monaghan, Co. 119
Monaghan, Seán 2
Monahincha 108
Monck, Sir George 92
Monmouth, Geoffrey of 132, 138, 218
Montgomery, George 59, 60, 64
Mooney, Donagh 204–215
Morduant, Lord Henry 95–96
Mörke, Olaf 30
Mornington 121
Moryson, Fynes 218, 220, 221
Mountgarret, Edmund Butler,
    4th viscount 116
Mountgarret, Richard Butler,
    3rd viscount 116
Muirchú 130
Mullaghmast, Massacre of 119
Mullingar 114
Mulvaney, Patrick 78

Munster
    condition in 1580s 219
    English Catholics in 113, 116–118, 120
    poetry in 174, 177
Muskerry, Donough McCarthy, 2nd
    viscount 92
Myers, J. P. 218

Netherlands 197, 230
Newcastle, Co. Dublin 114
'New English'
    colonial mentality 217–218, 220, 221
    and native Irish 140
    Protestants 99, 100, 110
    religious identity 231
    replacement of Catholics by 100
    sectarianism 219
    treachery of 223
Nine Years War 43, 103, 109, 144,
    188, 219
Northern rebellion 110
Northumberland, Henry Percy,
    9th earl 184
Norton, Henry 107–108
Nugent, Robert 213

Ó Buachalla, Breandán 194
Ó Cianáin, Tadhg 194
Ó Cearnaigh, Seaán 180–181
Ó Dubhthaigh, Eoghan 173
Ó Maolchonaire, Tuileagna 169–170
O'Brennan family 120
O'Brien family, *see* Thomond
O'Brien, Diarmaid 172
O'Byrne family 121
O'Connor, Geromma 226
O'Cullenan, John 78
Ó'Dálaigh, Aonghus Fionn 160, 162–167,
    168, 170, 173
O'Devany, Cornelius 47, 60
O'Donnell, Hugh, earl of Tyrconnell
    201, 202
O'Donnell, Thomas 222
Ó Duinn, Lord Tadhg 167
O'Ferrall, Richard 92
O'Gallagher, Don Dualtach 226
Ó hAnnracháin, Tadhg 3, 234, 238
Ó hEughusa, Giolla Brighde 190
Ó hOireachtaigh, Dáibhidh 171
Ó hUiginn, Aonghus 170
Ó hUiginn, Domhnall Óg 181
Ó hUiginn, Fearghal Óg 170
Ó hUiginn, Pilib Bocht 172, 180
Ó hUiginn, Tadhg Dall 169
O'Lawlor family 120
O'Lonegan family 120

O'Mahoney, Conor 87
O'Meagher family 120
O'Meara, Tadhg 179
O'Neill family 144, 201
O'Neill, Henry 194
O'Neill, Hugh, earl of Tyrone
  and Florence Conry 192
  death 200, 230
  in exile 200, 230
  fosterage 111
  and Peter Lombard 188
  and Hugh McCaughwell 192
  Nine Years War 43, 189, 234
O'Neill, John 201, 202
O'Neill, Owen Roe 91, 92, 201
O'Neill, Shane 132
O'Queely, Malachy 81
O'Reilly, Hugh 78
O'Sullivan, Eleanor 226
O'Sullivan Beare, Philip
  Gaelic Irish origins 225
  Historiae Iberniae compendium 221–223
  historian 5
  marriage alliance 120
  Vindiciae Hibernicae 222–223
O'Toole, Felim 173
O'Tooles 125
Ohlmeyer, Jane 232
Old English 15
  as colonists 220, 222
  and English Catholics 100
  humanist reform 218
  in parliament 53
  relations with native Irish 78, 81, 220, 223, 228
  religious commitment 231
  and Wentworth 52
Orde family 114
ordination, 79
Ormond, earls of 235
Ormond, James Butler, 12th earl
  peace negotiations 81, 82, 94
  lord lieutenant 76, 83
Ormond, Walter Butler, 11th Earl 113
Owen, Henry 111

Paget, Lord Charles 111
Paisley, Ian 11
Palladius 139, 145
Parker family 114
Parker, Edward 125
Paul, St 54, 55, 190–191
Paul V, Pope 186, 201
Peerce, John 112
penal laws 221
  under Chichester 112–114

  impact on English Catholics in Ireland 122–123
  less severe than England 76–77, 105, 106, 107, 231–232, 234
  Praemunire, statutes of 77
  see also Act of Supremacy
Periodisation 4–5, 24–25, 32–35, 37–53, 237, 239
Perrot, John 219
Philip III of Spain 189, 200, 201, 224, 226, 227
Philip IV of Spain 202, 226
Piggott family 104
Pilgrim Fathers 99
pilgrimage 168, 169, 195
pilgrims 108
plantation 3, 117, 221
  Connacht 52
  Ely O'Carroll 120
  Longford 120
  Munster 99, 103
  Ulster 99, 100, 118–119
  Wexford 115, 120
Plunkett, Christopher 211, 214
Plunkett, James 211
Plunketts, lords of Louth 121
Po-Chia Hsia, Ronald 35
Pointz family 116
Pointz, Elizabeth 109
pope, papacy
  as Antichrist 4, 65, 66–67, 68, 72, 135, 147, 187–188, 219, 232, 233, 237
  deposing power 191
  papal primacy 187
  petition to 226
Prater, Thomas 113
Preston, Thomas 92
Privy Council, English 95, 97
Propaganda Fide 79
Protestant reformation
  native Irish response 158, 161, 173–174, 176–177, 178–179, 180–182, 232
  in sixteenth century 38, 105, 222, 238
  success and failure 235–236
Purcells of Kilkenny/Tipperary 120
Puritans
  in America 99
  Protestants labelled as 89–93, 123, 147
Pym, John 108

Queen's Co. 119, 120
Quinn, D. B. 217, 218

Raleigh, Sir Walter 133
Rathbride, 114

Readen, William 112
reformation see *Protestant reformation*
Reinhard, Wolfgang 24, 25, 28,
    29–30, 35
Restoration 233
Rich, Barnaby 139, 140
Richardson, John 58, 59, 62, 67
Rider, John 146–147
Rinuccini, GianBattista 92–93
    Catholic hierarchy 239
    Confederate divisions 82
    confessionalisation 52–53
    in Ireland 38, 79, 81, 92–93
    Stuart monarchy 87
    Supreme Council 82
    treatment of Protestants 90–91
Rising, of 218
    depositions 122, 124, 125
    English Catholics in 116, 117,
        123–126, 235
    leaders of 100–101
    origins 14, 52, 76
    sectarianism 155
Ritter, Moriz 26
Robinson-Hammerstein, Helga 21, 45
Roche, David, 7th viscount
    of Fermoy 117
Roche, John 86, 91
Rochford, Luke 78
Rochfort, Robert 146
Roscommon, Co. 125
Rothe, David
    as bishop 238
    church–state relations 81
    dispute with Thomas Fleming 73
    Drogheda dispute 211, 215
    historian 5, 140, 146
    and Ussher 151, 232

Salamanca 192
Sanders, Nicholas 110, 219
Saul 195
Schilling, Heinz 25, 28, 35
Scotland 176–177, 182, 235
sectarianism
    atrocities and violence 1–4, 219,
        229–230, 231
    bardic poetry 16, 173, 177, 181
    and Catholic church 195, 203, 214
    definition 4, 8–11, 209, 236–237
    emergence 22–23
    in historiography 132, 155–156, 239
    peaceful coexistence 13
Shelford, Robert 67
Sherwood, John 113
Shrule 119, 125

Sibthorp, Christopher 148
Silken Thomas, The revolt of 135
Simms, Katherine 171
Slingsby family 117, 126
Slingsby, Henry 126
Slingsby, Sir Francis 117
Smyth family 116
Smyth, Thomas 125
sodalities 206, 207–209, 210–211
Spain 201
Spangenberg, Cyriakus 216
Spenser, Edmund
    as historian 140, 141, 143, 144, 146,
        152, 154
    in Ireland 117
    and Irish culture 144, 154, 156,
        220, 221
    Protestant planter 116, 218
    View of Ireland 136–139, 140, 154–155,
        220, 232
Spenser, Peregrine 117
Spenser, Silvanus 117
Spensers of Cork 117
Springs of Kerry 117
St Lawrence family of Howth 109
St Patrick
    Catholic saint 195, 196
    conversion of Ireland 130, 139, 145
    historiography 130, 142, 143–144, 145,
        146–147, 150
    and Irish identity 140, 147, 148
    in Irish poetry 164, 168–170, 171
    writings 152
St Patrick's purgatory 48, 143, 160, 168
Stanihurst, Richard
    and Campion 129
    De rebus gestis 222
    Description of Ireland 220
    as historian 128, 130, 131, 132, 133,
        142, 144
    attitude to Irish 135, 136, 222, 223
    political loyalty 222
    religion 132–133, 139
Stanley, Sir William 104, 110, 111
Stephenson family 117, 126
Stephenson, Oliver 120, 125
Stilcho 155
Stillorgan 120
Strabane 118
Stradbally 119
Strange, Thomas 151
Stuart O'Donnell, Mary 221, 226
Stuart monarchy 58, 108, 229, 233
    Catholic attitudes to 84–88, 89
Suarez, Francisco 191
    Defensio fide 173

Sweetman family 112
Synge, George 65

Talbot, Robert 92
Tanner, John 62
Temple, Sir William 1
Templeogue 114
Termonfeckin 204
Tetzel, Johann 196
Thirty Nine Articles 67
Thirty Years War 25
Thomas, William 218
Thomond, earls of 235
Thomond, Barnabas O'Brien, 6th
  earl of 90
Thomond, Conor O'Brien, 3rd earl
  167, 175
Thornton, Sir George 116, 119–120
Thorntons of Limerick 117
Tipperary, Co. 108
Tirechán 130
Tirry, William 81
Tobbersool 121
Todd, John 60
Tortus, Mattaeus 186
Tractus de Purgatorio Sancti Patricii 168
Travers, Walter 231
Trent, Council of
  Balkans 77
  closure 105
  confessionalisation 45
  decrees 61, 68, 75–76, 192, 208, 212
  in Gaelic poetry 176, 177, 179
  Tridentine Catholicism in Ireland
    49–50, 53, 73–8, 162, 236
Tresham, Sir Thomas 95, 96
Trinitarian order 5
Trinity College, Dublin
  confessionalisation 20, 21, 45–46
  education of clergy 57, 62, 231
  failure of 237
  Irish language 181
  students and graduates 22, 152
Troeltsch, Ernst 8
Trumbull, William 192
Turvey 121
Tyrone 119
Tyrone, earl of see O'Neill, Hugh

Ulster Freedom Fighters 2
Urban VIII, Pope 80
Ussher, Henry 64
Ussher, James
  Answer to challenge 150
  anti-Catholicism 64, 66
  Antichrist 67

Britannicarum ecclesiarum antiquitates
  150–151
  and Catholics 4, 13, 232
  Discourse of religion 148, 149
  ecclesiastical courts 70
  education 58
  as historian 142, 145, 147–151,
    153–154
  the Graces 48
  and Irish culture 154, 156–157
  lord chancellor 58
  puritan links 67
  Reduction of episcopacy 67
  religious controversy 65, 83–84, 85
  Veterum epistolarum sylloge 150
  and James Ware 152
Ussher, Robert 58

Verstegen, Richard 97, 107
von Pastor, Ludwig 27
von Ranke, Leopold 26

Wadding family 120
Wadding, Luke
  defence of Malone 85, 86–87
  and Ussher 151, 232
Waddington, Ralph 115
Waldensians 148
Wale family 120
Wales 182
Wall, Gerard 92
Wandesford, Christopher 116
Ward, Maurice 78
Ware, Sir James
  as historian 16–17, 142, 152–155, 232
  and Irish culture 156–157
Waterford, Synod of 81
Weber, Max 8
Welsh language 143
Wentworth, Thomas, Lord Deputy
  appointment of bishops 62, 63
  British dimension 38
  and church property 58, 70
  downfall 123
  policy in Ireland 50–52, 63, 71, 76,
    123, 155
Westmeath, Co. 114
Westminster Abbey 229
Westmorland, Lord 111
Westphalia, Treaty of 7
Wexford 108, 119
Wexford, Co. 123, 126, 115
White, Stephen 146, 151
Wicklow, Co. 126
Williams, Griffith 93
Wisbech 189

Wolverstone, Francis 126
Wolverstones of Stillorgan 120, 126
Woodfen, John 125
Woodfield family 114
Woodfield, John 125
Worrall, Christopher 113

Wright, Frank 12

Youghal 118
Young, William 126

Zeeden, Ernst Walter 27, 28

Is There Peace?

Is There Peace?

AN OVERVIEW OF THE WINNING POEMS AT THE LIVERPOOL NATIONAL EISTEDDFODAU

by

PATRICIA WILLIAMS

MODERN WELSH PUBLICATIONS

2019

First Impression - March 2019

ISBN : 978-1-9996898

Copyright with Modern Welsh Publications

To

Elisabeth

ACKNOWLEDGEMENTS

I am very grateful to Dr John Williams for supplying the pictures that accompany this book and suggesting suitable captions. I am also grateful to my two daughters, Lowri and Carys, for their encouragement and constructive criticism, and Lowri for proofreading the text. Finally I owe particular thanks to Rev. Dr. D. Ben Rees for taking an interest in the work and being prepared to publish it. Without his help and encouragement it would not have seen the light of day.

THE AUTHOR

Patricia Williams is a native of Bwlchgwyn/Gwynfryn, near Wrexham. She was brought up in an English speaking home but had the benefit of attending Gwynfryn Primary School, where the enlightened headmaster, Mr E D Parry, taught Welsh as a second language at a time when it was not compulsory or even fashionable to do so. She then attended Grove Park Girls' Grammar School, Wrexham, where she was further motivated to continue her Welsh studies by the inspired teacher Miss Menai Williams. She has spend most of her life in Liverpool, first of all teaching Latin at Merchant Taylors School for Girls, before being appointed lecturer in the Celtic Department of Liverpool University and subsequently the University of Manchester. Her main research interest is Welsh Medieval Literature, particularly works translated from Latin.

PREFACE

I was motivated to read the winning poems in the National Eisteddfodau held in Liverpool in 1884, 1900 and 1929 by the following occurrences: first of all the festivals held under the auspices of The Merseyside Welsh Heritage Society to commemorate two nationally acclaimed poets, and secondly the discovery that two bardic chairs are housed in the Liverpool Town Hall. Furthermore, when I saw that the winners of the chair in the above mentioned eisteddfodau were Dyfed, Pedrog and Dewi Emrys, the bardic names of Evan Rees, John Owen Williams and David Emrys James respectively, all well-known poets, and two of them non-conformist ministers in Liverpool, I felt compelled to read their odes. Likewise two of the poets who were awarded the crown are also well-known and their works have stood the test of time. Consequently I felt the urge to read their crown winning poems too and re-introduce them to the modern reader.

These poems are not an easy read. They are far too long and require perseverance to peruse them to the end, but they are part of the Liverpool Welsh Heritage and I believe it is important that those of us who live here should realise that poets of distinction, like the ones named above, are part of it. For that reason I have tried to give a brief synopsis of the content of the poems and present them in a more reader friendly style, in the hope that the modern reader will be able to have some appreciation of them.

AN ANALYSIS OF THE ODES AWARDED A CHAIR AT THE LIVERPOOL NATIONAL EISTEDDFODAU OF 1884, 1900 AND 1929

The earliest reference to a chair being awarded as a prize to the chief poet (*pencerdd*) was in *The Chronicle of the Princes* in 1176.[1] Nowadays the term used in Welsh for an ode which is entered for the chair competition at an eisteddfod is an *awdl*. This is a long poem which must be composed in one or more of the 24 strict traditional metres dating back to the Middle Ages and containing *cynghanedd*, an intricate system of rhyme and alliteration.

On reading an article on missing eisteddfod chairs[2] and realising that two of them were in Liverpool Town Hall, I decided to research the three national eisteddfodau that were held in the city in 1884, 1900 and 1929. During that period hundreds of Welsh people emigrated to Liverpool, many of them making a substantial contribution to the prosperity of the city.[3] Nevertheless they did not forget their roots and they transferred the religious and cultural traditions of their homeland to their new environment.

As part of their endeavours to promote Welsh culture, eisteddfodau were held before 1884 but not on a national scale. However, in a meeting of

---

1   Thomas Jones, *Brut y Tywysogion Peniarth 20 version* (Cardiff, 1952), p. 127.

2   Emyr Gruffudd, 'Dewi Emrys a'r Cadeiriau Coll' in *Barddas* Spring 2014, No. 322 (Lolfa, Talybont), p. 46-7.

3   For further information in English, see D Ben Rees, *The Welsh of Merseyside* Vol 1 (Liverpool 1997) and *Labour of Love in Liverpool* (Liverpool, 2008).

the National Eisteddfod Committee[4] held at Denbigh in August 1882 Liverpool was chosen as the prospective host town for the 1884 National Eisteddfod, to the astonishment of the vast majority of the Liverpool Welsh, who feared it was too ambitious a project for them to undertake. Nevertheless a meeting was held in the Concert Hall, Lord Nelson Street,[5] on 31 August, to consider the matter. Nothing was decided on that evening but after several subsequent informal meetings it was decided to accept the challenge and invite the eisteddfod to the city.

It was reported in the editorial of *Transactions of The Royal National Eisteddfod of Wales 1884* (p. xxii), that the bid to invite the eisteddfod to Liverpool contained 'the names of about 300 Liverpool gentlemen, including the Mayor, 29 City Councillors and the leading Welsh inhabitants of the district.' In the light of modern practice this statement is astonishing on two counts; firstly, only men signed the document, and secondly it was reported through the medium of English, but this would have been in keeping with the spirit of the age, when the language was not an issue. In the 19th century the doyens of the eisteddfod were more interested in proving that they had a culture which was equal to that of any other country than in using the eisteddfod as a means of preserving the Welsh language.[6] It is also possible that this attitude was a result of the hostile reaction of the press to the eisteddfod as a cultural establishment. In an article about the Chester Eisteddfod in *The Times* 8 September 1866 the Welsh language was described as 'the curse of Wales' and it concluded that it was a defective knowledge of the English language that deprived Welsh people of the culture and material success enjoyed by their English neighbours. It also maintained that the sooner the eisteddfod tradition died out, the better, as it was 'a foolish interference with the material

---

4   Established in 1880 as the ruling body, it is now known as *Llys yr Eisteddfod Genedlaethol* (The Court of the National Eisteddfod).

5   Now a block of luxury flats.

6   Hywel Teifi Edwards, *Yr Eisteddfod. Cyfrol Ddathlu Yr Eisteddfod 1176-1976* (Llys yr Eisteddfod Genedlaethol, 1976), pp. 42, 65, 86.

progress of civilization and prosperity'. A more balanced viewpoint was stated in *The Times* 20 September 1884, but it still revealed a somewhat patronising attitude to eisteddfodau, which, it claimed, 'may be freely conceded . . . the praise of having furthered national education and having aided in the piercing of a thick cloud of mental darkness'. In the light of such an attitude, it is understandable why so many of the activities in the 1884 Eisteddfod were conducted through the medium of English.

The Eisteddfod was proclaimed on 10 November 1883[7] with much pomp and circumstance but the gilt was taken off the celebrations by the news of Gwilym Hiraethog's death.[8] It was decided to commemorate his enormous contribution to Wales in general and the eisteddfod in particular by making 'Gwilym Hiraethog' the subject of the ode for the chair competition, that is a long poem in one or more of the 24 traditional Welsh metres.[9] Nevertheless the original subject, 'The Last Druid' was retained for another poetry competition, carrying a prize of the same monetary value and a golden trophy in place of a chair. The change of title was justified by the fact that whereas there were 13 entries for an ode to Gwilym Hiraethog, there were only two for 'The Last Druid', neither of which was deemed worthy of a prize.

The adjudicators of both odes were Richard Parry (Gwalchmai),[10] Richard

---

7 It was, and still is, common practice to hold ceremonies to proclaim the eisteddfod a year in advance.

8 Gwilym Hiraethog was the bardic name of Rev. William Rees (1802-83). Independent minister, writer, editor and political leader. See *Dictionary of Welsh Biography on line*, (s.v.) and D Ben Rees, *The Polymath: Reverend William Rees (Gwilym Hiraethog: 1802-1883)*, (Liverpool, 2002).

9 This was not the first time that a member of this family had been the subject of an ode. In the 1869 Liverpool Eisteddfod Richard Foulkes Edwards (Rhisiart Ddu o Wynedd) had won a chair for his elegy to Gwilym Hiraethog's brother, Rev. Henry Rees, an eminent Calvinistic Methodist minister in Liverpool.

10 Poet and minister with the Welsh Independents, although his family were Methodists. He won ten chairs and numerous other prizes but little of his work has stood the test of time. See *Dictionary of Welsh Biography on line* (s.v.)

Davies (Tafolog)[11] and Morris Owen (Isaled).[12] Some very scathing criticisms were made of 'The Last Druid'[13] but they unanimously agreed that the memorial ode to Gwilym Hiraethog had reached a satisfactory standard and awarded the chair to Rev. Evan Rees (Dyfed).[14]

The ode is divided into five parts with a synopsis of the contents in an introductory paragraph. This is followed by a note to the reader, explaining that the fame of Gwilym Hiraethog obviated the necessity for explanatory notes on his life history.

The first section, 'The Shepherd', opens with an appeal to the nation to weep for the loss of so great a man. This is followed by a eulogistic description of his religious upbringing, with references to his boyhood haunts. In mentioning his success in educating himself in spite of the lack of formal schooling, the poet uses an interesting phrase *hunan ddiwyllydd* (self cultivator), a farming term employed metaphorically here to refer to education. The phrase is also italicized, together with many others in this ode, as a means of attracting the reader's attention to a particular point or arcane observation, but oftener than not the practice is unnecessary. In the lines below the reader can understand without the added aid of italicization that the poet is playing on words. *Hiraeth* means 'longing' but is also the first part of the subject's name:

> Awch hiraeth o'i ol sy'n chwerw, - *hiraeth*
> Erys yn ei *enw*.

---

11   Poet and literary critic; a farmer's son who spent most of his life in Cwm Tafolog, near Cemais, Montgomeryshire, becoming well-known after winning several prizes in local eisteddfodau. See *Dictionary of Welsh Biography* (s.v.)

12   Lawyer, poet and literary critic about whom little is known. He died in 1916. See *Goleuad*, 24 March, 1916, 8-9.

13   William R Owen (ed.), *Transactions of the Royal National Eisteddfod of Wales* (Liverpool, 1884), p. 633.

14   Calvinistic Methodist minister and subsequently archdruid. See *Dictionary of Welsh Biography on line* (s.v.)

(The pain of longing for him is bitter - longing
Continues in his name, i.e. Hiraethog).

Similarly in the following line readers can see the contrast for themselves:

Caru'r *dynol*, cael y *dwyfol*
(Loving *humanity*, obtaining the *divine*.)

Because of the unique nature of poetry, particularly poetry in the strict, metres, translation cannot do it justice. Therefore I will keep translations of the quotations to a bare minimum and give a synopsis of the content instead. In another stanza it is not obvious why the poet underlines *barddoniaeth* (poetry) and *iachawdwriaeth* (salvation). Perhaps he is suggesting that it is through poetry, and the poetry of Gwilym Hiraethog in particular, that one achieves salvation.

In the second section, 'The patriot', the poet expresses Gwilym Hiraethog's desire to do his best for his country and his language. He describes how he employs various aspects of his character to achieve his vision of improving the lot of his fellow-countrymen, sometimes as gentle as a lamb, sometimes as strong as a lion. He refers to his launch of a Welsh newspaper *Amserau* (Times) in Liverpool and publications of his such as *Llythyrau'r Hen Ffarmwr* (Letters of an Old Farmer) in which he discussed injustice at home, comparing it with similar injustices abroad in countries like Hungary, which was at that time under the domination of Austria. Then the poet loses all sense of proportion and compares the journalistic attempts of his hero to improve society to that achieved by Jesus Christ in saving the world.

In the third section, 'The Poet', Gwilym Hiraethog is named as the 'favourite of the Muses'. As a poet he had the ability to influence the feelings of his readership or audience, he could also inspire congregations with his hymns and educate many through his wise adjudication, but says Dyfed, we should not judge his poetic qualities but enjoy and treasure them.

In the fourth section, 'The Preacher', we are presented with a portrayal of Gwilym Hiraethog as a shepherd of sheep becoming a shepherd of souls. The poet emphasises his theological knowledge and refers to him as *Koheleth*, the alleged author of *Ecclesiastes*. He praises his oratorical powers and the meaningful gesticulations he would make to emphasise his point and to which his audience would react positively. Nevertheless his eloquence was not merely aimed at stirring up emotions but to win souls. This section concludes with references to his success as a minister in Mostyn, Denbigh and Liverpool.

The fifth section, 'The Complete Character', deals with the influence of his home, which was also the font of his success. A magnanimous man, unrestricted by any specific party, he was widely read in a vast number of subjects, Science, Astrology, Philosophy, Geography, History, Natural Sciences and Rhetoric. The section concludes with a stanza on his death and the sad loss to society. His memorial would be his life's work.

In his adjudication on this ode, Gwalchmai said that the style was impressive, although there were occasional lapses of expression, when the poet reverted to colloquial language. His chief objection, however, was the inadequate treatment of the political side of Gwilym Hiraethog's character. Isaled too was opposed to the use of dialectal words or phrases and claimed that the meaning was sometimes obscured by the poet's ingenious use of language and metre. Tafolog was full of praise for the style and masterly use of the strict metres but felt that the description of the nation's grief at the loss of so great a man was restrained, to the extent of losing its intensity. Nevertheless he considered the ode to be worthy of the chair.

The next National Eisteddfod to be held in Liverpool was in 1900 and like the 1884 eisteddfod, was considerably shorter than those of today. It began with an inaugural meeting on the Monday evening in the council Chamber of the Town Hall where a lecture entitled 'The defects of Technical Education in Wales' was given by Harry Reichel (1884-1927), Principal of the University College of Wales, Bangor. Following the lecture an 'at home' was hosted by the Lord Mayor, Louis Cohen, 'attended by the general committee and other prominent officials of the Eisteddfod together with their lady friends'. This confirms that there were no women among the officials, as in 1884. It was recorded in the *Cofnodion* (Transactions):

> The gathering was one of the brightest and most successful of the social
> events that have ever taken place in connection with the Eisteddfod and it
> was the thoughtfulness and generosity of the Lord and Lady Mayoress that
> enabled the Eisteddfod to be inaugurated with such *éclat*.

Little wonder therefore that the Lord Mayor was inaugurated as a member of the Gorsedd of Bards in a ceremony held at Whitely Gardens, Everton, the next morning. Louis Cohen chose *Cohenydd* as his bardic name and his wife Mai Cohenydd, from which nomenclature one can assume that her name was May Cohen. The Lord Mayor made a speech in the Gorsedd ceremony and later that morning another oration in the pavilion that had been erected in North Haymarket. Lord Mostyn too delivered a speech in that session. In fact, speeches were delivered in every session of the eisteddfod, morning, afternoon and evening, all of which are recorded in the *Transactions*.

That is the background of the eisteddfod in which John Owen Williams (Pedrog) won his chair, now housed in the Liverpool Town Hall. The subject of his ode was 'The Shepherd', described thus in the *Transactions*:

> The shepherd was recognised as an ideal subject for the chair ode, the most

eloquent testimony to this being the fact that it attracted no fewer than 20 competitors. The chair was a beautifully designed piece of oak furniture, valued at £15, to which was added a money prize of £25.

The adjudicators were Professor (later Sir) John Morris-Jones,[15] Richard Davies (Tafolog,)[16] and Rev. R A Williams (Berw).[17] The adjudication was delivered by John Morris-Jones but the panel was not unanimous. Morris-Jones and Berw wanted to award the chair to Pedrog but Tafolog was in favour of another poet whose nom-de-plume was Alun Mabon. The author of that ode was Eliseus Williams, better known by his bardic name Eifion Wyn. Ironically, although Pedrog was a prolific and highly regarded writer in his day, it is Eifion Wyn who has stood the test of time. Sections of his works are quoted nowadays by people who have never even heard of Pedrog, let alone read his work. Morris-Jones's objection to Eifion Wyn's ode was that he had confined himself to writing about the shepherd in the literal sense of the word, but his greatest sin was that he had confined himself to writing about a shepherd in Wales alone. He also criticised the ode for being too short, containing only 500 lines as opposed to the 1800 lines in Pedrog's composition.

Pedrog's nom-de-plume for the competition was Hesiod, a Greek poet dating to the eighth century BC. Hesiod used to refer to himself as a farmer from Boetia, but whether he was a shepherd as well is not clear. Certainly none of his pastoral poems have survived, although he wrote on the techniques of farming but Pedrog clearly admired his work and referred to him as a shepherd and a poet.

The ode opens with a discussion about the meaning of shepherding and pronounces it to be the care of the wise for the unwise. One example

15   Professor of Welsh at the University College of Wales, Bangor, and a notable Celtic scholar.
16   See note 11 above.
17   From Pentre Berw, Anglesey. Anglican priest, who served for a while at Waunfawr. He won the chair at the London Eisteddfod of 1887 with an ode to Queen Victoria.

of this is the care of God for his universe and another, expressed in an uninspiring stanza, the care of the shepherd for his flock with the aid of his dog. The poet continues by giving a portrayal of the shepherd searching for his flock in the midst of a snow storm and rescuing those which had fallen beneath a cairn. In contrast is a description of the shepherd in his poor cottage enjoying the pleasures of nature as he sets out early on a summer morning.

In the next section the poet discusses the old biblical shepherds – Abel, Moses, David and the prophets of Israel. He then mentions a Welsh prophet who had graduated from the college of shepherds, namely Gwilym Hiraethog, the subject of the winning ode in the 1884 Eisteddfod. This leads to the shepherds of Bethlehem and the Good Shepherd calling the nations of the world to his fold. In this section he tries to create *cynghanedd* (a form of precise alliteration required in the strict) from the names of various nations, a technical device heavily criticised by Morris–Jones.

> Iesu swyna'r Caucasiaid, - i'w ddedwydd
>   Ddiadell daw Persiaid;
>   A gorwibiog Arabiaid; - ac mae'r don
>   Gan Iuddewon (sic) a duon Hindwiaid.
> (Jesus entices the Caucasians, – to his blessed
>   flock come the Persians;
>   And nomadic Arabs answer his call
>   And Jews and black Hindus.)

Nevertheless in spite of its faults the ode was deemed to be more substantial than any other in the competition. Below is the account of the chairing ceremony given in the *Transactions*:

> The winner was, as is generally the case, discovered to be sitting in the middle of the audience. The tall gentlemanly figure of the Rev. J O Williams

(Pedrog) was instantly recognised, and as he made his way to the platform he met with a most cordial reception. The ceremony observed in installing the successful bard was, in almost every particular, the exact replica of the crowning ceremony, but additional effect was given to it by the singing of 'See the Conquering Hero comes'.

The *Transactions* of the Liverpool Eisteddfod of 1929 was very different from those of the two previous eisteddfodau held in the city, in as much as it was a slimmer volume and written in Welsh. The ode was also shorter than the lengthy compositions presented at the eisteddfodau of 1884 and 1900. The title was 'Dafydd ap Gwilym'[18] and the adjudicators Rev J T Job,[19] R Williams Parry,[20] and Rev. J J Williams.[21] The winner of the chair in the Liverpool Eisteddfod of 1929 was Rev. D Emrys James (Dewi Emrys).[22]

The ode divides into three; the first part, in the style of a promising apprentice, according to R Williams Parry, opens with the question: 'Who goes at the end of the day to the tranquillity of the meadows?' The answer is a poet called a troubadour with a guitar in his hand singing outside a convent, disturbing the prayers of the nuns. We are told that one novice hears the sweet song of the poet in the midst of her worship. The word used for worship here is *adolwyn*, which can also mean desire. The implication is that the nun would prefer to be outside listening to the poet's love song than chanting her prayers. She later feels ashamed and repents. The birds too are affected by the poet's singing but he himself

---

18   Best known court poet of the 14th century. See *Dictionary of Welsh Biography online*, s.v.

19   Calvinistic Methodist, minister, hymn-writer and poet. He won the chair at the Newport Eisteddfod 1897 on the title 'Brotherly Love' and the crown in the Liverpool Eisteddfod of 1900 on the title 'Williams Pantycelyn'. See *Dictionary of Welsh Biography*, s.v.

20   Lecturer in Welsh at the University College of Wales, Bangor and chaired bard at the Colwyn Eisteddfod of 1910 for his ode 'Summer', one of the best known odes of the 20th century.

21   Minister with the Welsh Independents and winner of the chair at the Caernarfon Eisteddfod of 1906 on the title 'The Moon' and the Llangollen Eisteddfod of 1908 on the title 'Ceiriog', a well-known poet of the area.

22   He was the winner of more chairs than any other poet, except the one time archdruid Dyfed.

sleeps soundly under the shade of the tree.

The scene changes in the second part to Strata Florida, the alleged burial place of Dafydd ap Gwilym, although no grave of the 'green forest's bishop', as the author of this ode refers to the poet, has been found there. Although he may have been forgotten by the modern generation, he maintains his memory still survives in the world of nature. As Dewi Emrys bemoans the lack of visual traces of Dafydd ap Gwilym's presence, he sees a seagull, subject of one of poet's best known nature poems, flying past. This and the birdsong around him, as well as the sight of other natural objects, once praised by the poet, bring back memories of Dafydd ap Gwilym and secure his immortality.

The third part deals with the decline in cultural and religious values since the days of Dafydd ap Gwilym. Dewi Emrys regrets the loss of natural beauty as industry encroaches and everything is defiled as a result of greed. He then uses pulpit oratory to condemn the evils of his age. He describes city life where people live in dirty hovels, rearing children unable to appreciate the scent of flowers nor the sound of the cuckoo. He longs for a return of the civilised age of the noblemen who used to patronise poets, an age when it was possible to enjoy the verdant meadows and the 'old religion' of nature, an age which was defiled only by the jealous husband of Morfydd, Dafydd ap Gwilym's beloved. She was the epitome of female beauty with her red lips, her white hands, her fair hair and her pleasant voice in contrast to the image of a modern woman.

In the opinion of Rev J T Job this long section of 274 lines contained much superfluous matter with the poet allowing himself to be carried away by his own rhetoric.[23] On the other hand Rev J J Williams considered this section to be the jewel in the crown.[24] Nevertheless, in spite of their differences of opinion in evaluating the ode, the three adjudicators

---

23   *Cofnodion a Chyfansoddiadau Eisteddfod Genedlaethol Lerpwl 1929* (Caerdydd, 1929), p. 22.

24   *Ibid.* p. 22.

deemed it worthy of the chair. To sum up, it is a highly readable ode, containing many memorable lines, giving a vivid portrayal of Dafydd ap Gwilym in a style not dissimilar to the great poet's own.

By modern standards, these odes are dated, largely because of their excessive length and repetition of ideas, but they reflect the literary taste of their age and as such deserve to be presented to a modern readership.

AN ANALYSIS OF THE POEMS AWARDED A CROWN AT THE LIVERPOOL NATIONAL EISTEDDFODAU OF 1884, 1900 AND 1929

A composition entered for the crown competition at an eisteddfod is called a *pryddest*, a long poem in free metre, sometimes, but not necessarily, containing *cynghanedd*, a complex system of rhyme and alliteration. This technical term, therefore, will be used throughout this article to refer to the poems analysed below. The designated title for the *pryddest* in the Liverpool National Eisteddfod of 1884 was 'Egypt' and the adjudicators were Rev. D Howell (Llawdden),[1] John Hughes, better known by his bardic name Ceiriog[2] and Rev. J Cynddylan Jones.[3] The winner was Mr E Ffoulks, Llanberis, manager of the Dinorwig Quarry, scholar and poet. Little is known of him but he contributed several articles on antiquarian themes to English and Welsh periodicals and newspapers such as the *Welsh Outlook* and *Manchester Guardian*.[4]

The winning *pryddest* contains more than 2000 lines, preceded by a prose introduction dealing with Egypt, its landscape, its ruins, its history and culture. The *pryddest* is divided into seven sections:

---

1   Anglican priest and poet. See *Dictionary of Welsh Biographay online*, s.v.
2   Clerk in the London Road goods station, Manchester, later station master on the Cambrian railways at Llanidloes and superintendent of the newly opened line from Caersws to the Van lead mines. One of the most popular poets of the 19th century. See *ibid.*, s.v.
3   Poet and one time minister with the Independents in London, later returning to Wales to serve with the Calvinistic Methodists. See *ibid.*, s.v.
4   'Notes of the Month', *Welsh Outlook* Vol. 4 No. 12, Dec. 1917, p. 418.

1. Introduction, in which the poet describes Egypt using laudatory adjectives and phrases such as 'magical' and 'hallowed land'.

2. *The beginnings of Egypt.* In this section he describes the river Nile and the blessings it brings. He also describes the two great lakes which were the source of the Nile and its tributaries, lakes which were discovered by Livingstone and Baker and renamed Victoria and Albert in honour of the Queen and her consort. The influence of the British Empire can be seen clearly here. No poet in a modern eisteddfod would refer to the royal family in such adulatory terms.

3. *Memphis.* This was the capital of Lower Egypt in the pre Christian era, but now in ruins. The same respect towards kings can be seen in this section too. The poet tells of the establishment of the ancient city by its first king Menes in a passage of prosaic lines, which can only be regarded as poetry because of their arrangement in the form of verse. He then takes an imaginary 'look' at Memphis in the days of its glory and describes the welcome received by the Pharoah when he returned from his campaign in Ethiopia, bringing a host of slaves with him, while the fair skinned ladies of the court watched with a contemptuous smile as the foreign troop of Ethiopians passed by. Political correctness would prevent such a racist comment nowadays. This section of the *pryddest* concludes with a reference to the magnificent temples of yore, now in ruins.

4. *The first Empire of Thebes.* In this section the poet laments the destruction of Memphis but rejoices in the fact that the ruins of Thebes, on the east bank of the river Nile within reach of the city of Luxor, bear witness to the glory that existed once in Egypt and illustrate how the country rose from its ruins after occupation by Greece and Rome. He refers to the castles of Wales and compares them unfavourably with the splendour of the Egyptian temples. He concludes with a eulogy to the emperor Amenemhat praising

his military achievments and his contribution to the fine arts, particularly the fine buildings that were erected in the city of On.[5] Throughout the *pryddest* the poet shows his detailed knowledge of Egyptian history and wonders at the excellence of their art in a primitive era. The splendid buildings remind modern tourists of the famous people who had once sojourned there, such as Joseph, Moses, Plato and Usertesen (or Senusret), who was probably the Pharaoh who elevated Joseph to a position of authority.

5. *The Shepherd-princes and the Coming of Israel.* In this section the poet explains that the monarchy of Thebes had been overthrown and that foreign regimes had sought to usurp it because of the mildness of its climate and the fertility of its land. However he did not know whether they had achieved their goal by armed force or by taking diplomatic advantage of circumstances. He then writes about Abraham's arrival in Egypt and his dissatisfaction with its amazing temples and outstanding culture. This is followed by a lengthy account of Joseph in Egypt. Cynddylan Jones was very critical of this passage and said that no-one should elaborate on well-known scriptural stories, as the original was always better than the adaptation.

6. *The Second Empire of Thebes and the Departure of Israel.* The poet describes the victory of Thothnes[6] over Thebes and its restoration to its former glory. Nevertheless the new situation was not ideal, as it involved man's inhumanity to man, a consequence of conquest in every age but in this context a reference to the captivity of the Israelites in Egypt until they were led to freedom by Moses.

---

5   Joseph was married to the daughter of the priest of On (Gen 41:45), one of the most sacred places in Egypt. It was named Heliopolis by the Greeks and El Minah by the present government of Egypt.

6   This was probably Thothnes III. http://www.forgottenbooks.com/readbook_text/The_Truth_of_the_Bible_1000647301/259, p 249.

7. *Degeneration*. The poet repeats his eulogistic account of the indigenous rulers' achievements before rebuking Britain for not attempting to repel their conquerors. This is an unexpected comment in the days of the British Empire, when the occupation of other lands was generally accepted, but the poet makes similar comments about freedom, which could be adapted to today's political climate. 'Better to live freely in a barren land than to live in captivity in the most magnificent country in the world.' His observations on the ancient Egyptian language are also interesting. He writes about two young lovers of the ancient world speaking to each other in the old language which is now only used on memorials. Perhaps this was a veiled reference to the state of the Welsh language.

This *pryddest* is not bedtime reading and perseverance is required to read it in its entirety. It is far too long and many sections are prosaic, but it shows evidence of extensive research and the poet's knowledge of Egyptian history and art, not to mention his knowledge of the Bible, is phenomenal.

The subject of the *pryddest* for the 1900 Eisteddfod was 'Williams Pantycelyn', the most famous hymnwriter of the 18th century Methodist Revival and the only one who is frequently referred to by the name of his home, Pantycelyn.[7] There were eleven entries, the winner being Rev. John T Job.[8] The adjudicators were J J Roberts (Iolo Caernarfon)[9], Ben Davies[10] and John Hughes (Glanystwyth)[11] but only the adjudication of Iolo Caernarfon

---

7 William Williams of Pantycelyn was the most famous hymn writer of the 18th century Methodist Revival. He wrote over 1000 hymns in English and Welsh, his best-known English hymn being "Guide me oh thou Great Redeemer". See *Dictionary of Welsh Biographay online* , s.v.

8 John Thomas Job (1867-1938) was a Calvinistic Methodist minister and poet. In addition to this crown, he won the chair three times at the national eisteddfodau of 1897, 1903 and 1918. See Meic Stephens, *The Oxford Companion to the Literature of Wales* (Oxford, 1986), s.v.

9 Methodist minister and one of the 'new poets' discussed by Thomas Parry. See I Bell (trans.) *History of Welsh Literature* (Oxford, 1955), 359-61.

10 Welsh Independent minister and another of the so-called 'new poets'. See n.9 above.

11 Wesleyan Methodist minister, litterateur and poet.

which forms the core of 'The Song that was not Sung', as an attempt by the poet to rationalise his mother's stay in the asylum.[28] In other words the poet equates the refuge of the wilderness to the refuge of the asylum.

This *pryddest* is challengingly imaginative and difficult to interpret at times. It has to be read several times to make any sense of it at all, but in spite of its arcane qualities, it compels the reader to think long and hard about the meaning of it and the effort to find an answer is in itself a valuable experience. As in the case of the odes in the strict metres, which were entered for the chair competition, these *pryddestau* are not light or compulsive reading but they are part of Wales' literary history and as such are worthy of our attention.

---

28   *Yng Ngolau'r Lleuad*, 306.

The Northern Haymarket site for the 1884 and 1929 Eisteddfodau.
Picture shows its transition to a munitions factory by 1915.
Lleoliad Eisteddfodau 1884 a 1929, wedi ei droi'n ffatri arfau erbyn 1915.

Hwfa Môn,
The Archdruid / Yr Archdderwydd,
Eisteddfod 1900

Advertisement
Hybyseb ar gyfer Eisteddfod 1900

PRELIMINARY NOTICE.

£ THE ℈

1929 EISTEDDFOD

WILL BE HELD IN

LIVERPOOL

(SEFTON PARK)

AUGUST 5th to 10th, 1929.

The "LIST OF SUBJECTS" is Now Ready

AND MAY BE OBTAINED FOR 1/3 (POST FREE) FROM

The General Secretaries,
THE ROYAL NATIONAL EISTEDDFOD OF WALES, 1929
43, Renshaw Street, Liverpool.

Preliminary Notice
Rhaghysbysiad Eisteddfod 1929

Crowds attending a Bardic Ceremony at the Gorsedd Circle, 1929
Cynulleidfa wrth Gylch yr Orsedd, 1929

AT THE CIRCLE OF STONES : THE ARCHDRUID IN PRINCE'S PARK.

The Archdruid at the Logan Stone, Prince's Park - 1929 Eisteddfod
Yr Archdderwydd wrth y Maen Llog, Parc y Tywysog.

Côr Eisteddfod Choir 1929

The current gates at Prince's Park where the Bardic Ceremonies took place
Mynedfa Parc y Tywysog lle y cynhelid seremonïau'r Orsedd yn 1929

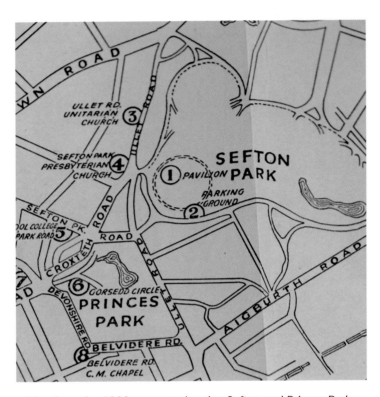

Map from the 1929 program showing Sefton and Princes Parks
Map o raglen 1929 yn dangos lleoliad Parc Sefton a Pharc y Tywysog

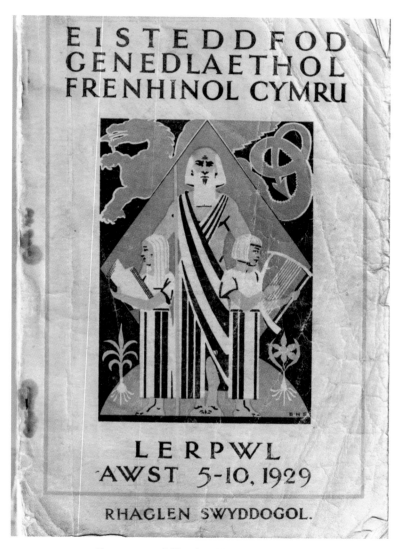

Programme / Rhaglen Eisteddfod 1929

Commemorative Plate / Plât Coffa
Eisteddfod 1929

David Griffith (Clwydfardd) 1800-1894
The First Archdruid / Yr Archdderwydd cyntaf

William Rees (Gwilym Hiraethog) 1802-83
Subject of Ode / Testun Yr Awdl, Eisteddfod 1884

Rowland Williams (Hwfa Môn) 1823-1905 Archdderwydd / Archdruid 1895-1905
Portrait by Christopher Williams (1905)

J T Job in/yn 1904
Crowned Bard / Bardd Coronog Eisteddfod 1900

Evan Rees (Dyfed) 1850-1923
Chaired Bard / Bardd Cadeiriol 1884, Archdruid / Archdderwydd 1900
Frontispiece of *Gwaith Barddonol Dyfed* (vol. 2 1907)

John Owen Williams (Pedrog) 1853-1932
Chaired bard / Bardd Cadeiriol Eisteddfod 1900
Archdruid / Archdderwydd Eisteddfod 1929

Caradog Prichard (1904-1980)
Crowned Bard / Bardd Coronog Eisteddfod 1929

David Emrys James (Dewi Emrys) 1881-1952
Chaired Bard / Bardd Cadeiriol
Eisteddfod 1929

The Chair for the 1884 National Eisteddfod in the Liverpool Town Hall.
On the main panel is the coat of arms of Owain Gwynedd with a Liver Bird, the symbol of the city of Liverpool on top.
Cadair Eisteddfod 1884 yn Neuadd y Dref Lerpwl.
Arfbais Owain Gwynedd ar y prif banel gyda'r Liver Bird, symbol o Lerpwl uwchben.

The Chair for the 1900 National Eisteddfod in the Liverpool Town Hall.
Cadair Eisteddfod 1900 yn Neuadd y Dref Lerpwl.

Druidic scene on main panel of the 1900 chair
Golygfa dderwyddol ar y prif banel

This book was designed and printed
by Melita Press, Malta

and

Published by Dr. D. Ben Rees of Modern Welsh Publications
32, Garth Drive, Allerton, Liverpool L18 6HW
a Publishing House which has been in existence since 1963

A Oes Heddwch?

A Oes Heddwch?

AROLWG AR AWDLAU A PHRYDDESTAU BUDDUGOL EISTEDDFODAU CENEDLAETHOL LERPWL

gan

PATRICIA WILLIAMS

CYHOEDDIADAU MODERN CYMREIG

2019

Argraffiad - Mawrth 2019

ISBN : 978-1-9996898

Hawlfraint gyda Cyhoeddiadau Modern Cymreig
32, Garth Drive, Allerton, Lerpwl/Liverpool L18 6HW

I

Elisabeth

CYDNABYDDIAETH

Mawr yw fy nyled i Dr John Williams am dynnu rhai o'r lluniau ac am droi rhai eraill i ffurf gymeradwy ar gyfer eu hargraffu. Rhaid diolch hefyd i fy nwy ferch, Lowri a Carys am eu cefnogaeth a'u beirniadaeth adeiladol, a Lowri am brawfddarllen y gyfrol. Diolch arbennig i'r Parchedig Ddr. D. Ben Rees am gymryd diddordeb yn y gwaith a'i gyhoeddi. Heb ei gymorth ef, ni fyddai byth wedi gweld golau dydd.

AM YR AWDUR

Brodor o Fwlchgwyn/Gwynfryn, ger Wrecsam, yw Patricia Williams. Cafodd ei magu ar aelwyd Saesneg ond cafodd y fraint o fynd i Ysgol Gynradd Gwynfryn lle roedd y Prifathro dawnus E D Parry yn dysgu Cymraeg fel ail iaith, pan nad oedd hi'n orfodol nac yn ffasiynol i wneud hynny. Bu'n ffodus i gael hyfforddiant pellach yn y Gymraeg yn Ysgol Ramadeg y Merched Grove Park Wrecsam gan yr athrawes ysbrydoledig, Miss Menai Williams, a gododd awydd ynddi i barhau gydag Astudiaethau Cymraeg a Chelteg. Mae wedi treulio'r rhan fwyaf o'i hoes yn Lerpwl, gan ddysgu Lladin yn Ysgol y Merched Merchant Taylors yn ei dyddiau cynnar yn y ddinas, cyn ei phenodi'n ddarlithydd yn Adran Geltaidd Prifysgol Lerpwl ac wedyn Prifysgol Manceinion. Llenyddiaeth yr Oesoedd Canol yw ei phrif ddiddordeb ymchwil, yn enwedig cyfieithiadau o'r Lladin.

RHAGAIR

Fe'm hysgogwyd i ddarllen yr awdlau a'r pryddestau buddugol yn eisteddfodau Lerpwl 1884, 1900 a 1929 gan ddau ddigwyddiad. Yn gyntaf dwy ŵyl o dan nawdd Cymdeithas Etifeddiaeth Cymry Glannau Mersi i goffâu Pedrog (2010) a Hedd Wyn (2017) ac yn ail gwylio rhaglen deledu am gadeiriau eisteddfodol na wyddai neb am flynyddoedd ble yr oeddent a gweld bod dwy ohonynt wedi eu darganfod yn Neuadd y Dref yn Lerpwl. Yn ogystal â hyn, pan welais fod beirdd mor adnabyddus â Dyfed, Pedrog a Dewi Emrys wedi ennill y gadair, a bod pryddestau J T Job a Caradog Prichard wedi dod i'r brig yn y gystadleuaeth am y goron (yn wir enillodd Caradog Prichard ei drydedd goron yma yn Lerpwl), teimlais yr awydd i ddarllen eu cyfansoddiadau a'u hail gyflwyno i ddarllenwyr heddiw.

Nid yw'r cerddi yn rhai hawdd eu darllen. Maent yn llawer iawn rhy hir ac mae gofyn am ddyfalbarhad i'w gorffen ond maent yn rhan o etifeddiaeth Cymry Lerpwl ac rwy'n credu ei bod yn bwysig i ni sydd yn byw yma sylweddoli bod beirdd safonol fel y rhai a enwyd uchod yn rhan ohoni. Oherwydd hynny rwyf wedi ceisio rhoi crynodeb syml o gynnwys y cerddi, eu dadansoddi a'u cyflwyno mewn ffordd ddarllenadwy, yn y gobaith y caiff y darllenydd modern flas arnynt. Mae'r dyfyniadau yn orgraff yr oes ac nid wyf wedi ceisio eu cywiro. Os gwelir gwall, nid esgeulustod yw hynny ond ymdrech i'w cyflwyno yn union fel y maent.

AWDLAU EISTEDDFODAU CENEDLAETHOL LERPWL 1884, 1900 A 1929

Ar ôl darllen yn *Barddas*[1] am y cadeiriau eisteddfodol a aeth ar goll a sylweddoli bod dwy ohonynt yn Neuadd y Dref yn Lerpwl, fe'm hysgogwyd i ymchwilio i hanes yr eisteddfodau cenedlaethol a gynhaliwyd yn y ddinas honno yn 1884, 1900 a 1929. Yn y cyfnod hwnnw roedd cannoedd o Gymry wedi ymsefydlu yn Lerpwl, gan gyfrannu'n aruthrol i ffyniant y ddinas a rhai ohonynt wedi ymgyfoethogi eu hunain yr un pryd.[2] Serch hynny, nid anghofiasant eu gwreiddiau a cheisiasant gadw hen draddodiadau crefyddol a diwylliannol yr hen wlad, gan gynnwys cynnal eisteddfodau.

Fe fu eisteddfodau mawr eraill yn Lerpwl yn gynharach na 1884 er nad ar raddfa genedlaethol, ond yn Awst 1882 mewn cyfarfod o Gymdeithas yr Eisteddfod Genedlaethol[3] yn Ninbych dewiswyd Lerpwl gyda mwyafrif teilwng fel mangre i gynnal Eisteddfod Genedlaethol 1884. Bu'n syndod i'r rhan fwyaf o Gymry Lerpwl fod eu dinas yn cael ei hystyried fel lleoliad i gynnal yr eisteddfod genedlaethol a bu ganddynt ofn fod y fenter yn rhy uchelgeisiol. Eto i gyd, cynhaliwyd cyfarfod yn y Neuadd Cyngherddau, Lord Nelson Street[4] ar Ddydd Iau 31 Awst i ystyried y mater. Fe'i mynychwyd gan tua dau ddwsin o bobl ond ni chytunwyd ar ddim byd y diwrnod hwnnw. Serch hynny, ar ôl cynnal nifer o gyfarfodydd anffurfiol eraill, penderfynwyd

---

1   Emyr Gruffudd, 'Dewi Emrys a'r Cadeiriau Coll' yn *Barddas* Rhifyn Gwanwyn 2014, Rhif 322 (Lolfa, Talybont), t. 46-7.

2   Am wybodaeth fanwl, gweler D Ben Rees, *Cymry Lerpwl a'r Cyffiniau* (Lerpwl, 1996) a *Codi Stêm a Hwyl yn Lerpwl* (Lerpwl, 2008).

3   Cymdeithas yr Eisteddfod, a sefydlwyd yn 1880, oedd y bwrdd rheoli. Wedyn yn 1937 unwyd y Gymdeithas gyda'r Orsedd i ffurfio Cyngor yr Eisteddfod Genedlaethol ac yn 1952 fe'i diwygwyd ymhellach a'i alw yn Llys yr Eisteddfod Genedlaethol.

4   Erbyn hyn mae'n safle fflatiau moethus.

gwneud cais swyddogol i wahodd yr Eisteddfod Genedlaethol i Lerpwl yn 1884.

Dywedodd ysgrifennydd y pwyllgor llên, William R Owen, yn ei ragymadrodd golygyddol i *Transactions of The Royal National Eisteddfod of Wales 1884*, (t. xxii), fod y ddeiseb i wahodd yr eisteddfod yn cynnwys *'the names of about 300 Liverpool gentlemen, including the Mayor, 29 City Councillors and the leading Welsh inhabitants of the district.'* O safbwynt arferion cyfredol, mae yna ddau ryfeddod ynglŷn â'r gosodiad hwn: yn gyntaf, dynion yn unig oedd wedi arwyddo'r ddeiseb ac yn ail, defnyddid yr iaith Saesneg yn y trafodaethau, ond roedd hyn yn unol ag ysbryd yr oes. Prif amcan Cymry deallus y bedwaredd ganrif ar bymtheg oedd defnyddio'r Eisteddfod i brofi bod ganddynt hwy ddiwylliant mor ogoneddus ag eiddo'r Saeson, yn hytrach na'i gwneud yn offeryn i gadw'r iaith.[5] Efallai hefyd mai ymateb oedd hyn i adroddiadau sarhaus yn y wasg Saesneg am yr Eisteddfod fel sefydliad diwylliannol. Mewn erthygl am Eisteddfod Caer yn *The Times* 8 Medi 1866 disgrifiwyd yr iaith Gymraeg fel *'the curse of Wales'* a thaeru mai eisteddfodau ac anwybodaeth o'r iaith Saesneg oedd wedi amddifadu'r Cymry o'r diwylliant a'r llwyddiant materol yr oedd eu cymdogion dros Glawdd Offa yn ei fwynhau. Aethpwyd ymlaen i ddweud mai gorau po gyntaf y deuai tranc eisteddfodau am nad oeddent ddim amgen nag *'a foolish interference with the material progress of civilization and prosperity'.* Datganwyd barn ychydig mwy goddefgar at eisteddfodau yn *The Times* 20 Medi 1884, ond hyd yn oed wedyn roedd yna dinc nawddoglyd yn yr adroddiad: *'They* (eisteddfodau) *may be freely conceded moreover the praise of having furthered national education and having aided in the piercing of a thick cloud of mental darkness'.* Yng ngoleuni agwedd o'r fath gellir deall paham y cafwyd cymaint o Saesneg yn Eisteddfod 1884.

Cyhoeddwyd yr Eisteddfod ar 10 Tachwedd 1883 gyda llawer o rwysg a rhodres, ond fe ddifethwyd yr hwyl gan y newyddion trist fod Gwilym

---

5   Hywel Teifi Edwards, *Yr Eisteddfod. Cyfrol Ddathlu Wythganmlwyddiant Yr Eisteddfod 1176-1976* (Llys yr Eisteddfod Genedlaethol, 1976), tt. 42, 65, 86.

Hiraethog wedi marw ddeuddydd ynghynt. Penderfynwyd coffâu ei gyfraniad aruthrol i'r Eisteddfod a'i wlad drwy wneud 'Gwilym Hiraethog' yn destun awdl y gadair.[6] Serch hynny, cedwid y dewis cyntaf 'Y Derwydd Olaf' ar gyfer cystadleuaeth farddonol arall a chynnig i'r enillydd wobr ariannol o faint cyfartal ynghyd â thlws aur yn lle cadair. Cyfiawnhawyd y newid oherwydd cafwyd tri ar ddeg yn cystadlu ar 'Gwilym Hiraethog' a dau yn unig ar 'Y Derwydd Olaf', ond nid oedd yr un o'r ddau yn deilwng o'r wobr.

Beirniaid y ddwy awdl oedd Richard Parry (Gwalchmai),[7] Richard Davies (Tafolog)[8] a Morris Owen (Isaled).[9] Roedd Tafolog yn llym iawn ei sylwadau ar 'Y Derwydd Olaf'. Dywedodd fod un ymgeisydd yn deall y gynghanedd yn eithaf da,

> Ond y mae'n anhawdd darllen llawer dernyn o'r Awdl hon heb deimlo mai anffawd yn hytrach na ffawd oedd iddo ef a hithau erioed gwrdd â'u gilydd, gan mai ei hadnabod fel meistres fympwyol a gormesol yn hytrach nag fel morwyn ostyngedig ac ufudd a gafodd.'[10]

Er hynny, roedd y tri yn credu bod teilyngdod i awdl goffa 'Gwilym Hiraethog' a dyfarnwyd bod y Parch. Evan Rees (Dyfed)[11] yn deilwng o'r

---

6   Nid dyna'r tro cyntaf i aelod o'r teulu fod yn destun awdl - yn Eisteddfod Lerpwl 1869 enillodd Richard Foulkes Edwards (Rhisiart Ddu o Wynedd) gadair am ei farwnad i frawd Gwilym Hiraethog, Y Parch. Henry Rees. Os am hanes Gwilym Hiraethog, gweler D Ben Rees, *Y Polymath: Parchedig William Rees (Gwilym Hiraethog : 1802-1883)* (Lerpwl, 2002).

7   Bardd a gweinidog gyda'r Annibynwyr, er bod ei deulu i gyd yn Fethodistiaid. Enillodd ddeg o gadeiriau eisteddfodol a nifer o wobrau eraill, ond ychydig o'i waith sydd o werth barhaol. Gweler *Y Bywgraffiadur Cymreig ar lein* (s.v.) yba.llgc.org.uk

8   Bardd a beirniad llenyddol; mab ffarm a dreuliodd ei blentyndod yng Nghwm Tafolog, ger Cemais, Sir Drefaldwyn ac a ddaeth yn adnabyddus fel bardd ar ôl ennill amryw o wobrau mewn eisteddfodau lleol. Gweler *Y Bywgraffiadur Cymreig ar lein* (s.v.).

9   Cyfreithiwr, bardd a beirniad llenyddol; bu farw yn 1916. Gweler *Goleuad*, Mawrth 24, 1916, 8-9.

10   William R Owen (ed.), *Transactions of the Royal National Eisteddfod of Wales* (Liverpool, 1884), p. 633.

11   Gweinidog gyda'r Methodistiaid Calfinaidd, bardd ac archdderwydd yn ddiweddarach; gweler *Y Bywgraffiadur Cymreig*, (s.v.) yba.llgc.org.uk

gadair. Wrth ddyfynnu o'r testunau ni wneir unrhyw ymdrech i ddiwygio'r orgraff i Gymraeg fodern na chywiro'r iaith; felly, fe fydd ambell air neu gymal yn ymddangos yn ddieithr i ni heddiw.

Rhennir yr awdl yn bum rhan a cheir crynhoad o'r cynnwys mewn paragraff rhagarweiniol a elwir 'Y Cynwysiad'. Dilynir hyn gan nodyn at y darllenydd yn egluro absenoldeb nodiadau eglurhaol, am fod hanes Gwilym Hiraethog yn hysbys i bawb.

Egyr y rhan gyntaf, 'Y Bugail Defaid', drwy erfyn ar y genedl i wylo oherwydd colli dyn mor fawr. Yna pentyrra ddisgrifiadau canmoliaethus o'i fywyd cynnar ym mro ei febyd, gan gyfeirio at Lansannan, 'Y Chiwlbren Isaf', (y tŷ lle y'i ganed), Mynydd Hiraethog a'r afon Aled. Canmola'r fagwraeth dduwiol a gafodd a dweud sut y llwyddodd i addysgu ei hunan er gwaethaf diffyg addysg ffurfiol.

> Daliodd a gafodd, gwenodd trwy ganol
> Ei bwnc i ryddid ei ben cyrhaeddol;
> *Hunan ddiwyllydd* yn ddinawdd hollol
> A'i anfanteision yn fintai oesol.

Gwelir o'r dyfyniad uchod mai nodwedd anghyffredin yn yr awdl yw bod ambell air ac ymadrodd wedi eu hitaleiddio fel ffordd o dynnu sylw'r darllenydd at ryw bwynt arbennig neu at ryw synnwyr awgrymog o dan yr wyneb, ond gan amlaf ymddengys yr arfer yn ddiangen. Yn y llinellau isod, go brin fod angen tanlinellu er mwyn i'r darllenydd sylweddoli bod y bardd yn chwarae ar eiriau:

> Awch hiraeth o'i ol sy'n chwerw, - *hiraeth*
> Erys yn ei *enw*:
> A than yr hiraeth hwnnw, - Cymru rydd,
> Am law ei noddydd ymdeimla'n weddw.

Nid oes angen tanlinellu yn y llinell isod chwaith i weld bod yna wrthgyferbyniad:

> Caru'r *dynol*, cael y *dwyfol*

Nid yw mor amlwg paham y tanlinellwyd 'barddoniaeth' ac 'iachawdwriaeth' yn y llinellau isod, oni bai ei fod yn gweld dolen gyswllt rhwng y ddau.

> Heibio arddunedd a swyn *barddoniaeth*,
> Esgynnwn, gyrwn at uwch ragoriaeth;
> I wel'd Hiraethog ar bell diriogaeth
> Oesol ddihalog sylweddau helaeth;
> Uchderau *Iachawdwriaeth*, - lle mae Duw
> Yn bwrw diluw o ysbrydoliaeth.

Dywed yn ddibetrus fod ysbrydoliaeth yn dod o Dduw; efallai ei fod yn awgrymu mai drwy farddoniaeth yn gyffredinol a barddoniaeth Gwilym Hiraethog yn arbennig, y ceir iachawdwriaeth yn y pen draw.

Yn yr ail ran, 'Y Gwladgarwr', mynega'r bardd awydd Gwilym Hiraethog i wneud ei orau dros ei wlad a'i iaith. Disgrifia wahanol agweddau o'i gymeriad i gyflawni ei freuddwyd o wella cyflwr ei gydwladwyr:

> Llariaidd a *gwylaidd* o galon, - fel *oen*,
> Heb flas ar ddichellion;
> Ond i yrru blinderon - o'i fro dlawd,
> Daw holl anianawd y *llew* yn union.

Cyfeiria wedyn ato'n creu y papur *Amserau* ac at ei gyhoeddiadau fel *Llythyrau'r Hen Ffarmwr* a oedd yn tynnu sylw at anghyfiawnder gartref ac yn ei gymharu ag anghyfiawnder tebyg mewn gwledydd tramor fel Hwngari, a oedd o dan reolaeth Awstria. Yna mae'r bardd yn mynd dros ben llestri ac yn cymharu ymdrechion newyddiadurol ei arwr i wella'r gymdeithas gyfoes

â'r hyn a wnaeth Iesu Grist i achub y byd yn gyffredinol:

> Y bywiog awdwr! Mor debyg ydoedd
> Yn hyn, i'r Iesu ar ran yr oesoedd.

Yn y drydedd ran, 'Y Bardd', cyfeirir at Gwilym Hiraethog fel 'anwylyd Awen', a rhestrir ei nodweddion fel bardd. Roedd y ddawn ganddo i ddylanwadu ar deimladau ei ddarllenwyr neu ei wrandawyr;

> Gwnai i wyneb gain wenu, - eto'n deg
> > Tynai dant *galaru;*
> Llwyddiannus gallai ddenu - o'n henaid,
> Dawel *ochenaid, wylo a chanu.*

Ysbrydolodd gynulleidfaoedd gyda'i emynau ac addysgu llawer gyda'i feirniadaethau doeth, ond, meddai Dyfed, ni ddylem ni ei feirniadu ef:

> Nid ein swydd yw *dadansoddi* - arddunedd
> > Ei farddonol deithi
> *Aros, mwynhau, trysori,*
> O fewn ei nef a wnawn ni.

Yn y bedwaredd ran, 'Y Pregethwr', cawn bortread o'r bugail defaid *'gwladaidd'* yn troi'n fugail eneidiau dirodres. Pwysleisir ei wybodaeth diwinyddol a chyfeirir ato fel *Koheleth,* sef awdur honedig *Llyfr y Pregethwyr.* Disgrifir ei ddawn areithio a'r ffordd y defnyddiai osgo ei ben, ei law a'i fys i bwysleisio rhyw bwynt neu'i gilydd, ond nid ystumiau ofer oeddent: 'Roedd *enaid* yn *amnaid* hwn'. Sonnir am ymateb ei gynulleidfa i'w huodledd:

> Ei bur lais rhinfawr barlysai'r ynfyd,
> Y mwya'i ryfyg lesmeiriai hefyd.

Ond

Nid gweinidog y *nwydau* - oedd William
I ddal ar *deimladau*
Ond gweinidog *eneidiau* - truenus
Yn deyrn soniarus i *drin* synwyrau.

Diweddir y rhan hon gyda chyfeiriadau at ei lwyddiant fel gweinidog ym Mostyn, Dinbych a Llynlleifiad (Lerpwl).

Yn y rhan olaf, 'Y Cymeriad Cyflawn', sonnir am ddylanwad ei aelwyd fel ffynhonnell ei holl lwyddiant. Dyn eangfrydig ydoedd na chafodd ei gyfyngu gan blaid arbennig. Disgrifir ef fel *'Tad darlithwyr Cymru'* a oedd yn hyddysg mewn pynciau niferus fel Gwyddoniaeth, Seryddiaeth, Athroniaeth, Daearyddiaeth, Hanesiaeth, Anianyddiaeth ac Araethyddiaeth. Ond

O dir *gras* y deuai'r grym - gynaliodd -
A dda fugeiliodd gyneddfau Gwilym.

Yn olaf sonnir am ei farwolaeth a'r golled enbyd ar ei ôl. Ei gyfraniad fydd ei goffadwriaeth yn anad dim:

Ni raid i feddrod Gwilym wrth flodau,
Erys ei *hanes* yn llawn rhosynau;
Peraidd ddylanwad eu pur ddalenau
A ddaw a llesiant i weddill oesau;
A'u gloewon emog liwiau - mor ddilyn*
Heb weled gwyfyn - heb lid gauafau.

*dilin = coeth, euraid, disglair

Yn ei feirniadaeth ar yr awdl hon, dywedodd Gwalchmai fod y mynegiant 'yn feistrolgar a tharawiadol', er bod y bardd yn dangos diffyg chwaeth weithiau drwy ddefnyddio ymadroddion fel 'dyn a'i lon'd o uniondeb' a 'domen ludw'.

Ceir yr un fath o sylw gan Isaled a'i beirniadodd yn llym am ddefnyddio 'geiriau ac ymadroddion gwerinol ac estronaidd', megis 'hidliai' a 'melodion' – sylwadau a fyddai'n gwbl anghymeradwy i feirniaid llenyddol heddiw. Dywedodd Isaled hefyd nad oedd y bardd bob amser yn mynegi ei hun yn eglur ac yn cuddio'r ystyr o dan gywreinrwydd yr iaith a'r gynghanedd:

> Er hir bendronni uwchben rhai breichiau o benillion, rhaid i mi addef fy mod yn bur amheus pa un a gefais afael ar eu gwir ystyr. Wrth ddarllen y cyfansoddiad, yr oedd yr aneglurder hwn yn lladd llawer ar y mwynhad a gefais wrth ddarllen y cyfansoddiad.[12]

Er ei fod yn cymeradwyo'r cyfansoddiad ar y cyfan, prif gŵyn Gwalchmai yn ei erbyn oedd ei bod 'yn ddiffygiol yn ei gynwysiad oherwydd nad yw'r elfen wleidyddol a rhyddfrydol oedd yng nghymeriad y gwrthrych yn ddigon amlwg.' Roedd Tafolog yn canmol y cynllun a'r cynganeddu ond o ystyried poblogrwydd gwrthrych y canu a'r hiraeth genedlaethol ar ei ôl, tybiai 'fod y bardd wedi taro cyweirnod rhy ddieithr-uchel i gordio yn dda â miwsig hiraeth calon y genedl'. Ond, er gwaethaf hyn, dywedodd fod yr awdur wedi dadansoddi ffeithiau'r hanes yn fwy trwyadl na'r un o'r cystadleuwyr eraill ac wedi eu mynegi mewn dull barddonol. Yn y diwedd, er bod yna wendidau yn y canu ac er nad oedd y beirniaid yn credu y byddai hon yn un o'r awdlau eisteddfodol mwyaf nodedig, nid oedd ganddynt betrusder yn ei dyfarnu'n orau ac yn deilwng o'r gadair.

Yr eisteddfod genedlaethol nesaf a gynhaliwyd yn Lerpwl oedd yn 1900 ac fel eisteddfod 1884 roedd hi'n dipyn cwtocach nag eisteddfodau heddiw. Doedd hi ddim yn dechrau o ddifrif tan y Dydd Mawrth ac yn gorffen ar y dydd Sadwrn ond digwyddodd yr hyn a gofnodir fel *an inaugural meeting* ar y Nos Lun. Cynhaliwyd hwnnw yn Siambr y Cyngor yn Neuadd y Dref, lle y traddodwyd darlith ar y testun: '*The defects of Technical Education in Wales*' gan Harry Reichel, Prifathro Coleg Prifysgol Bangor 1884-1927. Ar ôl y ddarlith rhoddwyd yr hyn a ddisgrifir fel *at home* gan Yr Arglwydd

---

12   *Transactions of the Royal National Eisteddfod of Wales* (Liverpool, 1884), p. 19.

Faer, Louis Cohen, – ac i ddyfynu o'r *Transactions*: *'It was attended by the General committee and other prominent officials of the Eisteddfod together with their lady friends'.* Mae hyn yn cadarnhau nad oedd yna ferched ymhlith y swyddogion, fel yn 1884. Fe gofnodir yn y *Cofnodion*:

> The gathering was one of the brightest and most successful of the social events that have ever taken place in connection with the Eisteddfod and it was the thoughtfulness and generosity of the Lord and Lady Mayoress that enabled the Eisteddfod to be inaugurated with such éclat.

Dim rhyfedd i'r Arglwydd Faer gael ei dderbyn y bore canlynol i'r Orsedd a gynhaliwyd yn Whitely Gardens, yn Everton, gan yr Archdderwydd, Hwfa Môn. Yr enw barddol a ddewiswyd ar gyfer Louis Cohen oedd Cohenydd. Mae'n debyg mai May Cohen oedd enw ei wraig, oherwydd yr enw a roddwyd arni hi oedd Mai Cohenydd. Rhoddodd yr Arglwydd Faer araith yn seremoni'r Orsedd ac yn ddiweddarach y bore hwnnw un arall yn y pafiliwn, a godwyd yn North Haymarket. Cafwyd araith hir arall yn y sesiwn hwnnw hefyd gan yr Arglwydd Mostyn. Yn wir ceid araith ym mhob sesiwn o'r Eisteddfod, fore, p'nawn a hwyr, a chofnodwyd hwy i gyd yn y *Transactions*.

Dyma felly oedd cefndir yr eisteddfod yr enillodd Y Parchedig John Owen Williams (Pedrog) ei gadair ynddi. Testun yr awdl oedd 'Y Bugail' a dyma a ddywed y *Cofnodion* amdani:

> The shepherd was recognised as an ideal subject for the chair ode, the most eloquent testimony to this being the fact that it attracted no less than 20 competitors. The chair was a beautifully designed piece of oak furniture, valued at £15, to which was added a money prize of £25.

Ac mae'r gadair honno yn cael ei chadw yn Neuadd y Dref, yn Lerpwl.

Y beirniaid oedd Yr Athro (yn ddiweddarach Syr) John Morris-Jones,[13] Tafolog,[14] ac yn drydydd Berw.[15] Syr John draddododd y feirniadaeth, ond nid oedd y tri yn gytûn. Roedd ar Syr John a Berw eisiau gobrwyo awdl Pedrog ond Tafolog yn ffafrio awdl bardd â'r ffug enw Alun Mabon. Awdur yr awdl honno oedd Eliseus Williams, sy'n fwy adnabyddus o dan ei enw barddol Eifion Wyn. Yr eironi yw bod Eifion Wyn wedi parhau yn boblogaidd fel bardd ar hyd y blynyddoed ac 'Y Bugail' yw ei gyfansoddiad mwyaf adnabyddus yn y mesurau caeth, ond, er gwaethaf y ffaith iddo fod yn ei ddydd yn un o gyfansoddwyr mwyaf toreithiog ei genhedlaeth, ychydig iawn o bobl heddiw sydd wedi clywed am Pedrog, heb sôn am ddarllen ei waith. Yr hyn a oedd gan Morris-Jones yn erbyn awdl Eifion Wyn oedd iddo gyfyngu ei hun yn ormodol i ystyr lythrennol ei destun. Ychwanegodd, 'Mae ei awdl yn fwy cyfyng na hynny – mae wedi cyfyngu ei hun i draethu am fywyd bugail yng Nghymru.'

Ffug enw Pedrog ar gyfer y gystadleuaeth oedd Hesiod, bardd Groeg o'r wythfed ganrif cyn Crist. Cyfeiriai Hesiod ato ei hun fel ffarmwr o Boetia, ond dwn i ddim ai ffarmwr o fugail oedd ef ai peidio; yn sicr does dim bugeilgerddi o'i eiddo wedi goroesi, er iddo ysgrifennu ar dechnegau ffarmio. Roedd wedi apelio at Pedrog, mae'n amlwg, ac mae'n cynnwys englyn iddo yn ei awdl:

> Hesiod gynt, yn ystig oedd, - a'i ddefaid
> Hyd ddifyr fynyddoedd;
> Yno i galon gai olud
> Bröydd hud, a bardd ydoedd.

Dywedodd Syr John am awdl Pedrog: 'Os yw awdl Alun Mabon yn fer y mae

---

13 Athro'r Gymraeg yng Ngholeg Prifysgol Bangor, fel y gelwid ef bryd hynny, ysgolhaig Celtaidd o fri a bardd nodedig,

14 Richard Davies, gw. nodyn 8 uchod.

15 Y Parch. R A Williams o Bentre Berw, Sir Fôn, offeiriad yn eglwys Loegr ac a wasanaethodd am gyfnod yn Waunfawr. Enillodd y gadair yn Eisteddfod Llundain 1887 ar awdl i'r Frenhines Fictoria.

awdl Hesiod yn rhy faith'. Pum can llinell oedd yn y naill ond mil saith gant o linellau yn y llall, yn ymestyn dros dri deg saith o dudalennau. Pan ystyrir mai mil tri chan llinell oedd holl gynnyrch Cynddelw Brydydd Mawr, mae'n anhygoel fod un gerdd yn cynnwys cymaint o linellau. Nid oes rhyfedd fod yna 'gamgopïo a diofalwch' ynddi weithiau. Meddai Syr John:

> Mae'r arddull weithiau'n drwsgl ac afrwydd ac mewn mannau hyd yn oed yn
> ddrwg; ond yn ei fannau gorau y mae rhyw nerth a mawrhydi'n perthyn i'r
> bardd hwn na pherthyn i'r un o'i gyd-ymgeiswyr.

Mae'r awdl yn dechrau drwy ymholi ynghylch egwyddor bugeiliaeth a dod i'r canlyniad mai gofal y deallus am yr anneallus ydyw. Yna mae'n sôn am ofal Duw am ei fydoedd ac enwa enghreifftiau eraill o'r un egwyddor nes dod at y bugail ei hun a'i ofal am ei braidd gyda chymorth ei gi. Mewn ychydig o gwpledi cywydd, na ellir eu rhestru ymysg y rhai mwyaf disglair yn yr awdl, dywed:

> Bugail; - ni nyddid ini
> Gan neb ei gân heb ei gi;
> Hwn, erioed, sydd fel yn rhan
> Ohono ef ei hun.

Yna ceir darlun o'r bugail yn chwilio am ei braidd yng nghanol storm o eira ac yn achub rhai a 'ddisgynodd is y gaenen':

> Yn fyw dan eu hanfad do
> 'Roedd ei annwyl braidd yno!
> Ac o nerthol gynorthwy
> O'u bedd oer achubodd hwy.

Yna daw'r haf ac y mae'n creu darlun o'r bugail yn ei fwthyn tlawd; disgrifia ei brofiadau a'i bleser ym myd natur fel y cychwyna allan gyda'r wawr:

O gresyn i'r wawr groesi - y gorwel
    Heb i garwyr tlysni
   Yma weled, a moli
   Awdur hael ei cheinder hi.

Yna mae'n traethu am yr hen fugeiliaid beiblaidd –Abel, a Moses a Dafydd a hen broffwydi Israel. Crybwylla broffwyd a gaed o Gymru oedd wedi graddio, 'o goleg y bugeiliaid'. Gan ei fod yn cyfeirio fan hyn at Lansannan a Hiraethog mae'n amlwg ei fod yn cyfeirio at Gwilym Hiraethog, y trafodwyd yr awdl fuddugol amdano yn Eisteddfod 1884 uchod. Yna try Pedrog at fugeiliaid Bethlehem ac arwain at y Bugail Da yn galw'r cenhedloedd ato. Gweler fel y mae'n ceisio cynganeddu rhestr hir o enwau'r cenhedloed:

Mae'n galw y Mongoliaid, - ei nodau
    A edwyn Tartariaid;
   A byw yw ei swyn heb baid
   Yn awyr y Chineaid.

Hylon eilw anwyliaid, - yn lluoedd,
    Trwy'r gorllewin telaid;
    Yn rhin i lawer enaid – hwnt i'r don
    Mae'r acenion ar Americaniaid.

Ei hiaith wypu Ethiopiaid, - troi o'r nen
Hon ni phair cynhen yr Affricaniaid.

Muda gwsg Madagasgar, - yn awyr
    Barneo mae'n seingar;
   Trwy awelon Australia'r – seinia hi,
    "Daeth yr addewid i eitha'r ddaear."

Iesu swyna'r Caucasiaid, - i'w ddedwydd
    Ddiadell daw Persiaid;

A gorwibiog Arabiaid; - ac mae'r don
Gan Iuddewon a duon Hindwiaid.

Nid yw'n rhyfedd i Syr John ddweud, 'Dylai bardd cystal â hwn wybod nad barddoniaeth ydyw cynganeddu rhyw rhestr o enwau dieithr'. Ond i ddiweddu ei feirniadaeth mae'n dweud: 'Wedi rhoi holl feiau'r awdl hon yn ei herbyn yn y glorian, nid oes amheuaeth yn fy meddwl i nad yw'n drymach o ddigon na'r un arall yn y gystadleuaeth'. Ni wyddys paham fod Syr John yn credu bod 'trymder' yn rhinwedd. Efallai ei fod yn golygu bod yr awdl yn fwy 'sylweddol' nag eiddo ei gystadleuwyr.

Dyma'r adroddiad ar y cadeirio a geir yn y *Cofnodion* - yn yr iaith Saesneg, wrth gwrs, yn ôl arfer yr oes:

> The winner was, as is generally the case, discovered to be sitting in the middle of the audience. The tall gentlemanly figure of the Rev. J. O. Williams (Pedrog) was instantly recognised, and as he made his way to the platform he met with a most cordial reception. The ceremony observed in installing the successful bard was, in almost every particular, the exact replica of the crowning ceremony, but additional effect was given to it by the singing of 'See the Conquering Hero comes'.

Roedd popeth a ddigwyddodd ar ôl hyn braidd yn fflat. Fel y dywed y *Cofnodion* am y cyfarfod cyntaf yn y pafiliwn y bore wedyn:

> The attendance was small and subdued as if the exciting events of the previous 3 days had for the moment dulled the keen edge of even the most enthusiastic.

Ond roedd y pafiliwn yn llawn erbyn cystadleuaeth y corau meibion yn y prynhawn. Cafwyd dau gyngerdd ar ôl hynny – un ar y Nos Wener a'r llall ar y Sadwrn. A dyna ddiwedd Eisteddfod Genedlaethol Lerpwl 1900, lle y cyflawnodd Pedrog ei gamp fawr.

Mae cyfrol *Cyfansoddiadau Eisteddfod Lerpwl 1929* yn wahanol i rai y ddwy eisteddfod flaenorol a gynhaliwyd yn y ddinas, yn gymaint â'i bod yn llai swmpus a'r iaith Gymraeg yn gyfrwng mynegiant ynddi. Roedd yr awdl hefyd yn fyrrach na'r rhai hirfaith a gynigwyd ar gyfer cystadleuaeth y gadair yn eisteddfodau 1884 a 1900. Y teitl oedd 'Dafydd ap Gwilym' a'r beirniaid Y Parch. J T Job,[16] R Williams Parry,[17] a'r Parch. J J Williams.[18] Yn fuddugol yn Eisteddfod Lerpwl 1929 oedd Y Parch. D Emrys James (Dewi Emrys).[19] Mae'r awdl yn ymrannu'n dair. Agorir y rhan gyntaf 'yn null prentis addawol', chwedl R. Williams Parry, drwy ofyn y cwestiwn, 'Pwy sy'n mynd ar derfyn dydd / I dawelwch y dolydd?' Yr ateb yw bardd a elwir yn drwbadŵr a gitâr yn ei law yn canu y tu allan i leiandy, gan aflonyddu ar baderau y lleianod:

> Wrth droed Iôr plyg y forwyn – yn lili
> Welwlwyd yn ei gwanwyn;
> Ond ar ganol adolwyn
> Tery mawl y cantor mwyn.

Gwelir defnydd clyfar iawn o'r gair 'adolwyn' yma. Mae iddo ddwy ystyr: 'dymuniad', ond mewn ystyr grefyddol 'gweddi'. Yr awgrym yw y buasai'n well gan y lleian fod allan yn gwrando ar serchgan Dafydd na bod wrth ei phaderau. Caiff ei swyno gan ddawn y bardd ac wedyn cywilyddio:

---

16 Gweinidog gyda'r Methodistiaid Calfinaidd, emynydd a bardd. Enillodd y gadair yn Eisteddfod Casnewydd 1897 ar y teitl 'Brawdgarwch' a'r goron yn Eisteddfod Lerpwl 1900 ar y teitl 'Williams Pantycelyn'. Gweler *Y Bywgraffiadur Cymreig hyd 1940* (Llundain, 1953).

17 Darlithydd yng Ngholeg Prifysgol Bangor a bardd cadeiriol Eisteddfod Colwyn 1910 am ei awdl, 'Yr Haf', un o awdlau eisteddfodol mwyaf adnabyddus yr ugeinfed ganrif.

18 Gweinidog gyda'r Annibynwyr ac enillydd y gadair yn Eisteddfod Caernarfon 1906 ar y teitl 'Y Lloer' ac yn Eisteddfod Llangollen yn 1908 ar y teitl 'Ceiriog'.

19 Enillodd Dewi Emrys fwy o gadeiriau na'r un bardd arall heblaw Dyfed ac yn ôl Twm Morys, collodd fwy hefyd!

Hi'r dlos drwy'r nos yn glanhau
Euogrwydd â llif dagrau.

Mae'r adar hefyd yn cael eu deffro a'u hudo gan ei gân:

Deffry'r adar ac aros – yn dawel;
Gwrandawant rhwng deilios
Ei gywydd, a dysg eos
Serenâd gormeswr nos.

Ond mae'r bardd ei hun yn gallu cysgu'n dawel 'dan gysgod gwŷdd . . .ym mhlas y gôg'.

Symudir yr olygfa yn yr ail ran i Ystrad Fflur, y mynachdy lle y tybid i Dafydd ap Gwilym gael ei gladdu, er nad oes ôl o fedd 'esgob y glascoed' i'w weld yno heddiw:

Dyma'i lwch, hardd brifardd bro, - eos tir
Heb dyst arwyl iddo,
Hen ywen syn er cyn co',
A daen drist adain drosto.

Ond er i Dafydd ap Gwilym gael ei anghofio gan y genedl, mae byd natur yn dal i ddwyn atgofion amdano. Wrth i Dewi Emrys ofidio am absenoldeb olion gweladwy ohono, gwêl wylan, testun un o gywyddau mwyaf adnabyddus Dafydd, yn hedfan heibio, gan ddwyn atgofion yn ôl iddo:

Daw heibio wylan lanwedd,
A'r ewyn gwyn yn ei gwedd,
Ffy dros y berth tan chwerthin,
A miri môr ar ei min.

Mae hon a'r côr o adar a glywir o'i gwmpas yn canu, yn ogystal ag elfennau

eraill o fyd natur a folodd Dafydd yn ei gywyddau yn sicrhau ei goffadwriaeth.

Mae'r drydedd ran yn ymwneud â'r newid sydd wedi digwydd ers dyddiau Dafydd ap Gwilym, a'i ysbryd yn condemnio dirywiad yr oes bresennol mewn diwylliant a chrefydd:

> Uwch hen garnedd y salm a'r weddi
> Oedai distawrwydd didosturi.
> Daearwyd hen broffwydi – yn llwch hon,
> Rhoi hedd mawrion dan wraidd mieri.

> Ciliodd llawenydd dolydd deiliog,
> Tawodd llonder y fin chwerthinog,
> Niwl a glaw roed yn welw glôg – am y byd,
> Ail i dristyd nychlyd fynachlog.

Hiraetha'r bardd am hyfrydwch y dyddiau a fu, ond gwêl ddim ond hagrwch o'i gwmpas wrth i ddiwydiant ennill tir:

> Daeth nwyon creulon i faes carolau,
> Rhaib llosnur a dur i lawnt mwynderau,
> Lle bu glendid sêr, ryfyg ffumerau,
> A goruwch y tir ysgrech hwterau,
> Poer anwedd safn peiriannau – a chwŷs dyn,
> Uffernau iaswyn tân y ffwrneisiau.

Mae popeth wedi ei halogi oherwydd Mamon, 'gwreiddyn drygioni' ac mae Dewi Emrys yn mynd i hwyl bregethwrol wrth gomdemnio ffaeleddau'r oes:

> Oes rhith llawenydd a dwys eglwysi,
> Asbri tant cywir ni roddir iddi;
> Oes nwydus heb ddeunydd gwynddydd ganddi,
> A nos rhialtwch yn dristwch drosti;

Oes Famon, oes gwirioni – corn a chrwth,
Oes lwth, oes fodrwth, nid oes sifalri.

Oes peiriant a dyfais barod, - oes ffals,
A'i phaent yn gydwybod;
Oes euro clai, oes rhoi clôd
I saer a harddio sorod.

Oes ffugwyr, treiswyr trawsion – a'u rhysedd,
Oes y croesau trymion.
Tardd sŵn gwae i'w chwaraeon,
Ochain lleddf i'w chanu llon.

Mae'n disgrifio bywyd y ddinas lle mae pobl yn byw mewn hofelau budr a phlant heb allu mwynhau arogl blodau na chlywed sŵn y gôg. Mae'n hiraethu am adfer bywyd gwaraidd yr hen ddyddiau megis yn llys Ifor Hael, noddwr Dafydd, a dychwelyd i fwyniant y 'dolydd deiliog' a 'hen grefydd y gwŷdd a'r gôg', oes a surwyd yn unig gan Eiddig, sef llys enw Dafydd ar ŵr ei gariad Morfydd. Hi oedd yr ymgorfforiad perffaith o brydferthwch merch gyda'i gwefus 'lliw'r mefus a'r mafon', ei llaw wen, ei gwallt hir melyn a'i llais mwyn o'i chymharu â'r ddelwedd o ferch yr oes fodern:

A'i min yn megino mwg;
Llygaid llesg a lliw gwaed llwyd,
Gwallt byr fel gallt a borwyd;
Gwefus gochlyd, graslyd, grin,
Gwêr deifiog ar ei deufin.
I'w gweld ni fyn rosyn rhudd
Ond eira ar ei deurudd;
Nid gwrid, ond cwrlid carlwm,
Lliw calch trwch, lliw tristwch trwm.

Mae'r Parch. J T Job yn gweld y rhan hir hon (274 o linellau) yn cynnwys pethau amherthnasol a'r awdur yn gadael i'w hwyl ei gario ymaith yn rhy bell.[20] Ar y llaw arall credai'r Parch J J Williams mai'r rhan hon oedd 'coron y gerdd'[21]. Bid a fo am hynny, mae'r awdl yn ddarllenadwy iawn a llawer o linellau cofiadwy ynddi. Yn anad dim, mae wedi rhoi darlun bywiog o Dafydd ap Gwilym i ni ac wedi ceisio dynwared arddull y bardd mawr ei hun. Fel y dyfarnodd y tri beirniad, roedd yn llawn deilwng o'r gadair.

Yn ôl safonau modern nid yw'r awdlau hyn yn ddeniadol; maent yn rhy hir, yr iaith yn hynafol a'r syniadau yn ail-adroddus, ond fel adlewyrchiad o chwaeth llenyddol eu hoes ac o'r traddodiad barddonol drwy'r oesoedd, maent yn werth eu cyflwyno i bawb sydd â diddordeb yn hanes llenyddiaeth Cymru.

---

20   *Cofnodion a Chyfansoddiadau Eisteddfod Genedlaethol 1929* (Caerdydd, 1929).
21   *Ibid.* t. 22.

PRYDDESTAU EISTEDDFODAU CENEDLAETHOL LERPWL 1884, 1900 A 1929

Testun y bryddest yn Eisteddfod Lerpwl 1884 oedd 'Yr Aipht' a'r beirniaid oedd Y Parch. D Howell (Llawdden),[1] John Hughes, sy'n fwy adnabyddus wrth ei enw barddol Ceiriog[2] a'r Parch. J Cynddylan Jones.[3] Yr enillydd oedd Mr E Ffoulks, Llanberis, rheolwr Chwarel Dinorwig, ysgolhaig a bardd, gŵr a garai'r encilion. Cyfrannai Mr Ffoulks erthyglau ar themáu hynafiaethol a llenyddol yn Saesneg a Chymraeg i gylchgronau a phapurau newydd fel y *Welsh Outlook* a'r *Manchester Guardian*.[4]

Mae'r bryddest fuddugol yn cynnwys dros 2000 o linellau sy'n cael eu blaenori gan ragymadrodd mewn rhyddiaith yn ymdrin â'r Aifft, ei thirwedd, ei hadfeilion, ei hanes, a'i diwylliant. Rhennir y bryddest yn saith rhan:

(1) *Blaengerdd*, lle mae'r bardd yn disgrifio'r Aifft ag ymadroddion canmolaethus megis 'tir cysegredig' a 'chyfareddol';

> Yn arglwydd ar y ddaear, nid oes un
> > Yn fwy ardderchog na'i awyddfryd lem
> I dreiddio drwy y myrdd dirgelion trwch
> > Caddugawl sydd o'i amgylch ol a blaen.

(Ni wneir unrhyw ymdrech wrth ddyfynnu o'r testunau i ddiwygio'r orgraff i Gymraeg fodern na chywiro'r iaith; felly, fe fydd ambell air neu gymal yn

---

1   Offeiriad Anglicanaidd a bardd. Gweler hefyd Y *Bywgraffiadur Ar-lein*, s.v.

2   Gweler *ibid.*, s.v.

3   Bardd a gweinidog gyda'r Annibynwyr yn Llundain ar un cyfnod, cyn dychwelyd i Gymru a gweinidogaethu gyda'r Presbyteriaid. Gweler *ibid.*, s.v.

4   'Notes of the Month', *Welsh Outlook* Vol. 4 No 12, Dec 1917, p. 418.

ymddangos yn ddieithr i ni heddiw.)

(2) *Boreu yr Aipht*. Yn y rhan hon disgrifia'r afon Nilus a'r bendithion a ddaw i'r wlad yn ei sgil:

> Flwydd ar ol blwydd, fe lifa'r rasol afon,
> Rho'i ar ei newydd diroedd newydd haen;
> Oes ar ol oes, gadawai ei dylifon
> Ffrwythlonach gweryd dros y tir ar daen

Gwelir hefyd ddylanwad yr Ymerodraeth Brydeinig ar y bardd pan sonnir am y llynnoedd mawr y tardda'r Nilus ohonynt:

> Llithra'r dyfroedd hyn
> Nes cyd-grynhoi mewn dau ardderchog lŷn, -
> Y llynau sydd yn adlewyrchi bri
> Brenhines Prydain Fawr, a'i Dewrion hi.

Y 'Dewrion' oedd Livingstone a Baker, a ddarganfu'r llynnoedd hyn a newid eu henwau i Victoria ac Albert. Ni fyddai'r un bardd mewn eisteddfod fodern yn cyfeirio at deulu brenhinol Lloegr yn y modd taeogaidd hwn.

(3) *Memphis*, sef prifddinas Is Aifft yn y cyfnod cyn Crist, ond bellach yn adfeilion. Gwelir yr un parch at frenhinoedd yma eto. Edrydd y bardd hanes sefydlu'r ddinas hynafol hon gan ei brenin cyntaf Menes mewn dilyniant o linellau rhyddieithol dros ben - yn wir yr unig hawl sydd ganddynt i fod yn farddoniaeth yw eu bod wedi eu gosod ar ffurf prydyddiaeth:

> Ond wele! Allan o'r cysgodion gwyll,
> O fysg ei ragflaenoriaid sydd yn ngholl
> Yn ngoror anghof, - deua un ymlaen
> A saif ar ddaear eglur hanesyddiaeth
> Y cyntaf o frenhinol enwau'r byd

Ar restr hanes. Menes ydyw ef.

Yna mae'n cymryd trem (dychmygol) ar Memphis 'pan oedd dydd / Ei mawredd yn ei anterth' ac yn disgrifio'r croeso mawreddog a gafodd y Pharaoh pan ddychwelodd o'i ymgyrch yn Ethiopia, gan ddwyn myrdd o gaethion gydag ef, a merched y llys yn edrych arnynt:

> A'r Aiphtesau cain
> Yn malchder eu melynaidd brydwedd hwy
> A fflachient ddirmyg-wên, tra'r Ethiop lu
> Estronol a ânt heibio.

Byddai cywirdeb politicaidd yn gwrthod caniatáu y fath sylwadau hiliol heddiw. Mae'r rhan hon o'r bryddest yn gorffen gyda chyfeiriad at y temlau mawreddog gynt nad ydynt bellach yn ddim ond adfeilion.

(4) *Ymherodraeth Gyntaf Thebes*. Yn y rhan hon, gofidia'r bardd am ddirywiad Memphis ond ymhyfryda yn y ffaith fod adfeilion Thebes (ar lan ddwyreiniol yr afon Nilus o fewn terfynau dinas Luxor) yn dyston i'r gogoniant a fu unwaith yn yr Aifft ac yn adlewyrchu'r ffordd y cododd y wlad o'i hadfeilion ar ôl goresgyniad Groeg a Rhufain. Cyfeiria at gestyll Cymru a'u cymharu yn anffafriol â gwychder temlau'r Aifft:

> Cestyll a chaerau hen Gymru anwylaf
> > Gadwant orchestion y Brython mewn bri;
> Dygant o bellter ein hoesoedd boreuaf
> > Ysbryd ein dewron gyndadu i ni.

> Ond, mae eu hurddas yn cilio mewn gwylder
> > Wrth hen adfeilion yr Aipht, sydd a'u rhawd
> Wedi parhau o eithafion pell amser,
> > Wedi goroesi pob anrhaith a ffawd. . .

Mae'n canmol yr 'ymherawdwr Amenemhat' am ei orchestion milwrol ac am ei gyfraniad i'r celfyddydau cain, yn enwedig yr adeiladau gwych a godwyd yn ninas On.[5] Mae'n debyg mai Amenemhat IV a olygir yma, ymerodr y cysylltir ei enw â Moses; yn wir mae'n bosibl mai Moses ei hun a olygir.[6]

Drwy'r bryddest mae'r bardd yn dangos gwybodaeth fanwl o hanes yr Aifft ac yn rhyfeddu at orchest eu celf mewn oes gyntefig:

> Pwy sydd all ddweyd
> Pa ddyfais goll a feddai'r gweithwyr hen
> I gloddio, cludo, codi'r meini hyn?
> Dirgelwch yw; ond gorchest oedd a'u gwna
> Yn hafal i'n celfyddwyr clodfawr ni
> Sy'n feilchion etifeddion oesau fil!

Yna mae'r bardd yn dweud y byddai'r adeiladau ysblennydd hyn yn atgoffa teithwyr modern o enwogion eraill a fu yno, megis Joseph, Moses, Plato ac Usertesen (neu Senusret). Efallai mai hwn oedd y Pharaoh a ddyrchafodd Joseph i fri.

(5) *Y Bugail-frenhinoedd a Dyfodiad yr Israel.* Yn y rhan hon mae'r bardd yn egluro bod brenhiniaeth Thebes wedi ei dymchwel a 'llu yr estron' yn ceisio cipio'i choron 'oherwydd mwynder ei thywydd a braster ei thir, ond ni wyddys sut yr enillasant hi:

> Ai gydag arfog ymgyrch, ynte drwy
> Fedrusrwydd parod, hyf, i neidio i fewn
> I adwy amgylchiadau.

---

5   Priodwyd Joseph â merch offeiriad On (Gen 41:45), un o'r lleoedd mwyaf cysgredig yn yr Aifft. Fe'i henwyd yn Heliopolis gan y Groegiaid ac El Minah gan lywodraeth bresennol Yr Aifft.

6   Ashton, John F and Down, David, *Unwrapping the Pharoes: How Egyptian archaeology Confirms the Biblical Timeline* (Green Forest, AR: Master Books, 2006), p. 92.

Yna sonnir am Abraham yn dyfod i'r Aifft a gweld ei themlau rhyfeddol a'i holl gelfyddydau gorchestol, ond nid oeddent yn rhyngu ei fodd:

Ond trist ac adgas ganddo oeddynt oll,
A thrôdd ei wyneb tua Chanaan draw,
Tir yr addewid ddwyfol.

Wedyn ceir adroddiad hirwyntog am Joseph yn yr Aifft. Mae Cynddylan Jones yn feirniadol iawn o hyn ac yn dweud na ddylid ymhelaethu ar hanes ysgrythyrol sy'n adnabyddus i'r darllenwyr: 'digon yw *touch* neu ddau i ddeffro'r côf a'r dychymyg. Mor *flat* yw Joseph y Bryddest hon o'i gymharu â Joseph Genesis!'

(6) *Ail Ymherodraeth Thebes ac Ymadawiad yr Israel*. Disgrifir buddugoliaeth Thothnes[7] dros Thebes a'i hadfer i'w hysblender cynt. Er canmol gorchestion ymerodraeth Thebes i'r cymylau, gwêl y bardd nad yw'r sefyllfa yn ddelfrydol o bell ffordd:

Mor drist yw edrych drwy ddirif gofnodion
Teyrnasoedd byd, a gweled yn mhob oes
Greulonder dyn at ddyn, gorthrymder, llid,
Yn nodi â chyhuddol olion gwaed
Holl uchel rwysg cenhedloedd.

Gellid gwneud yr un feirniadaeth ar y byd heddiw, ond cyfeirio mae'r bardd yn y cyswllt hwn at yr Israeliaid yn cael eu trin fel caethweision yn yr Aifft nes i Moses eu harwain i ryddid.

(7) *Y Dirywiad*. Mae'r bardd yn ail-adrodd gorchestion yr hen lywodraethwyr brodorol cyn mynd ymlaen i sôn am y goresgynwyr. Diwedda'r bryddest

---

7   Mae'n debyg mai Thothnes III oedd hwn. http://www.forgottenbooks.com/readbook_text/
     The_Truth_of_the_Bible_1000647301/259, p 249.

gyda cherydd i Brydain am beidio â mynd i helpu'r Aifft i adfer ei hen ogoniant ac yn bwysicach byth ei rhyddid.

> Frydain! (sic) pan welaist genedl hen yr Aipht
> Yn sefyll ger ei Phyramidau bàn
> A'i themlau heirdd, gan gofio uchel fri
> Ei hen gyndadau, - pa'm na ddaethost ti
> I erchi i'w gormeswyr gilio draw,
> A galw'r orthrymedig genedl hon
> I rodio ei godidog wlad - *yn rhydd*!

Mae hyn yn sylw annisgwyl yn nyddiau'r ymerodraeth Brydeinig, ond ceir sylwadau eraill ganddo y gellid eu cymhwyso i'n byd ni heddiw:

> Fendigedig Ryddid! Gwell oedd byw yn rhydd
> Mewn anial dir, neu newydd wlad ddi-nawdd
> Na bod yn gaeth yn ngwychaf wlad y byd.

Diddorol hefyd oedd ei sylw am iaith yr hen Eifftwyr. Disgrifia ddau gariad dychmygol o'r hen oesoedd yn sgwrsio â'i gilydd:

> Murmur wnaent
> Eu tyner ymgom yn yr hen, hen iaith
> Nad oes yn awr ond cofgolofnau'r Aipht
> Yn dweyd ei hanngofiedig eiriau hi!

Tybed a oedd yn meddwl am dranc yr iaith Gymraeg?

Nid yw'r bryddest hon yn un i ddarllen yn y gwely ac mae angen dyfalbarhad i'w darllen i'r diwedd. Mae'n llawer iawn rhy hir ac yn rhyddieithol iawn mewn mannau, ond mae ôl ymchwil eang arni ac mae gwybodaeth y bardd o hanes a chelfyddyd Yr Aifft yn rhyfeddol, heb sôn am ei wybodaeth o'r Beibl.

Testun y bryddest yn Eisteddfod 1900 oedd 'Williams Pantycelyn'. Cafwyd un ar ddeg o gyfansoddiadau a'r enillydd oedd Y Parch. John T Job. Y beirniaid oedd Iolo Caernarfon,[8] Ben Davies[9] a Glanystwyth,[10] ond beirniadaeth Iolo Caernarfon yn unig a gyhoeddwyd. Canmolodd y pwyllgor am eu 'penderfyniad doeth a phrydferth' wrth ddewis testun cystadleuaeth y goron, am fod Williams Pantycelyn yn un o'r dynion mwyaf mewn athrylith a gras a welodd Cymru erioed. Am yr un bryddest ar ddeg a dderbyniwyd, dyfarnodd rai yn rhagorol iawn, eraill yn ganmoladwy a rhai yn dra chyffredin ond 'nemawr un ohonynt yn ddifrycheulyd' oherwydd gwallau iaith a mesur. Priodolai'r diffygion hyn i'r prinder amser a ganiateid ar gyfer y cyfansoddi, ond roedd iaith y goreuon yn rhydd o'r beiau hyn - 'yn goeth a seml a'i fydryddiaeth yn esmwyth a pherorol'.

Mae'r bryddest hirfaith hon (1267 o linellau) wedi ei rhannu'n chwe rhan:

(i)   *"A hi eto yn dywyll"* - *Toriad Dydd y Diwygiad*.
       Sonnir am gyflwr di-grefydd Cymru cyn i dri o ddiwygwyr ifanc, sef
       Howell Harris, Daniel Rowland a Griffith Jones, weld eu cyfle i efengylu.

(ii)   *Odfa* (sic) *Talgarth: "Dyma'r boreu, fyth mi gofia".*
       Mae'r rhan hon yn ymwneud â'r oedfa lle y cafodd Pantycelyn
       droedigaeth ar ôl clywed llais Howell Harris yn tarannu fel barnwr yn
       erbyn drwgweithredoedd yr oes, a'r gynulleidfa yn cael ei dwysbigo gan
       ei huotledd:

       Gwelwant, wylant, a llewygant o dan ruthr ei daran-eiriau:
       Annioddefol yw eu hingoedd - cerdda'r Farn drwy'u cydwybodau.

---

8   J J Roberts, gweinidog gyda'r Methodistiaid ac un o'r 'beirdd newydd' y sonnir amdanynt gan
     Thomas Parry yn ei *Hanes Llenyddiaeth Gymraeg hyd 1900* (Caerdydd, 1944), 282-88. Gw.
     hefyd I. Bell (cyf.), *History of Welsh Literature* (Oxford, 1955), 359-61.
9   Gweinidog gyda'r Annibynwyr ac un arall o'r 'beirdd newydd'.
10   Y Parch. John Hughes, llenor a gweinidog gyda'r Wesleaid.

Ond pwysleisiodd fod yna achubiaeth i'r rhai edifeiriol drwy'r aberth ar Ben Calfaria. Yna ceir disgrifiad o ymateb y Pantycelyn ifanc i'r bregeth rymus hon a'r bardd yn gweu ymadroddion o emynau'r pêrganiedydd i gyfleu'r effaith a gafodd neges Howell Harris arno:

> Hynod foreu! Dyma "ymffrost" Williams, mwyach, clywch ei lef:-
> "Dyma'r boreu, fyth mi gofia, clywais inau Lais y Nef;"
> Daethai yma'n "ddi-baratoad". Ond ca'dd ddychwel idd ei fro
> Gyda'r byrdwn *"Pen Calfaria, - nac aed hwnw byth o'm co' ".*

(iii) *Ar y Rhiwiau: "Gwialen" Williams "yr hon a flodeuasai".*
Sonnir am y diwygwyr yn torri allan o'r 'eglwys rewllyd, lawn ffurfioldeb' a mynd ar hyd 'ffordd ddi-dramwy' i arwain eu cynulleidfaoedd o gaethiwed pechod drwy rym eu pregethu, fel yr arweinodd Moses â'i wialen yr Israeliaid o'u caethiwed hwythau. 'Gwialen' Williams yw ei awen.

(iv) *Apolos yr Eglwysi.*
Duw yr haul a goleuni, duw'r gwirionedd a darogan, duw cerddoriaeth a barddoniaeth a duw iachâu yw Apolos. Gellir gweld ei fod yn drosiad amlwg ar gyfer Pantycelyn, a feddai ar yr un priodoleddau, er efallai yn amhriodol o anghristionogol! Yn yr isadran gyntaf disgrifir ei ddawn fel pregethwr a'i eiriau 'megis Mai-gawodydd tirion - / Peraidd wlithwlaw efengylaidd geidw'r seintiau fyth yn irion'. Yn y tair isadran nesaf canmolir ei arbenigedd yn arwain seiadau, er mwyn i'r gynulleidfa fynegi eu profiadau ysbrydol, ei lwyddiant fel heddychwr yn uno'r pleidiau a'i deithiau o gwmpas Cymru yn pregethu'r efengyl. Sonnir am ei adnabyddiaeth o'r natur ddynol a gorffen drwy gymharu ei ddawn emynyddol â 'miwsig telyn' Orpheus, a oedd yn denu hyd yn oed bwystfilod â melsyter ei gerdd. Yn wir, cyfeirir ato fel 'Opheus eneiniedig Cymru'.

(v) **Duwinydd a Llenor y Diwygiad.**
Mae'r rhan hon yn ymwneud ag athrylith Williams i wrthbrofi heresïau megis Sabeliaeth,[11] Sandemaniaeth[12] ac Antimoniaeth.[13] Yna mewn llinellau digon rhyddieithiol, rhestra'r bardd nifer o'i weithiau:

> Dacw *"Grocodeil yr Afon!"* Os rhaid dal ei hagr-drem anferth! -
> Daw'r *"Aurora Borealis"* ar y byd i wenu'n brydferth;
> Dacw *"Ddrws y Seiat Brofiad"* yn croesawu'r miloedd ato;
> Dyna adlais Gwestwr Cana ar *"Briodas"* yn egluro.
> Llithrig-beraidd *"Ymddiddanion!"* Ynddynt erchir i'r ysbrydoedd
> O'r dyfnderoedd ddwweyd eu cyffes i Wirionedd teyrnas Nefoedd.

(vi) *"Pêr Ganiedydd Cymru"*. Mae'r rhan hon yn hir iawn, yn wir gyhyd â phum adran gyntaf y bryddest gyda'i gilydd ac y mae iddi saith is-adran.
(a) Yn yr is-adran hon cyfeirir at Bantycelyn fel 'brenhin-bren cysgodfawr Awen Cymru'. Y pren mwyaf yn y goedwig yw'r brenhinbren ond fe'i defnyddir hefyd yn drosiadol am uchelwr.

(b) Cyfeirir yma at ei waith *Golwg ar Deyrnas Crist*. Mae'r bardd yn dweud bod bywyd bucheddol Williams yn esiampl i bechaduriaid a'i gerdd yn dangos y ffordd i iachawdwriaeth a gras Duw yng Nghrist. Isod gwelir rhai o linellau mwyaf teimladwy'r bryddest:

> Ha! Nid rhyfedd Bantycelyn, iti lonni'th genedl drist
> A'th ddihalog gerdd anfarwol, "GOLWG" gest "ar DEYRNAS CRIST".
> Chwi awennau beilch y ddaear! Ymwyleiddiwch yn gytûn!
> Yfwch fiwsig Pantycelyn, ddaeth o Delyn Mab y Dyn.
> "CRIST YN BOB-PETH, CRIST YN MHOB-PETH- drachtiwch o'r

---

11 Athrawiaeth a ddaliai nad yw y Drindod ond yn agweddau ar y Bod Dwyfol.
12 Sect a sefydlwyd tua 1730 gan John Glas, gweinidog Presbyteraidd yn Eglwys yr Alban. Taera nad oedd cefnogaeth i eglwys genedlaethol yn y Testament Newydd am fod teyrnas Crist yn ysbrydol.
13 Golyga 'yn erbyn y gyfraith'. Y gred fod cyfiawnhad drwy ffydd a gras dwyfol yn golygu nad oes rhaid i'r rhai sydd wedi eu hachub ufuddhau i'r ddeddf foesol.

Ffynhonau hyn:
Gwin neithdarol Beirddion Nefol ydyw Gwaed Calfaria Fryn!

(c) *Theomemphis.*

Mae'r rhan hon yn ymwneud â cherdd hir Pantycelyn lle mae'n olrhain taith bywyd dyn o'i gyfnod pechadurus i'w droedigaeth a'r iachawdwriaeth a ddaeth iddo drwy hynny.

Gwelaist lygaid Theo'n gloywi pan "yn nyfnder angau loes",
Gwelaist hwy yn cau'n fuddugol - yn llawn o'r Weledigaeth Nefol -
Gweledigaeth angau'r Groes.

(ch) *Rhwng y deufyd - Galarnadwr y Diwygiad*

Canmolir Williams am ei ddawn i gysuro'r rhai sydd yn dioddef profedigeth, megis ei alarnadau i Griffith Jones, Llanddowror, George Whitfield ac eraill, yn bregethwyr ac yn wragedd. Ymhelaetha ar ei farwnad i'w gyfaill Daniel Rowland a'i gymharu â Dafydd yn gofidio am Jonathan. Gelwir ef yn 'gysurwr anwyl Seion, a ddysgodd Eglwys y Diwygiad / I dawelu mewn cymundeb gyda saint y Gogoneddiad'.

(d) *Tywysog Emyn Cymru. Ei Emynau*

Yn yr is-adran hon mae'r bardd yn cyfarch Williams: 'Bantycelyn orfoleddus! Tal Dywysog Emyn Cymru'. Mae'n ei ganmol yn arbennig am fynegi 'gwironeddau dwyfol' a 'sicrwydd byth am gadwedigaeth' yn 'iaith y werin', a swynid gan ei eiriau. Yna mae'n rhoi braslun o gynnwys rhai o'i emynau gan ddyfynnu llinellau ohonynt i gadarnhau ei bwynt. Gorffenna drwy fynegi ei ymateb personol i'r emynau, sydd yn 'gynnyrch Ysbryd Duw'. Mae'n cyfarch yr emynau eu hunain a dweud, 'Gwelaf yn eich calon chwi / Ryw ddarluniau sydd yn darllen hanes llawn fy nghalon i'.

(dd) *Prif gyfrwng Mawl y Goruchaf i Genedl gyfan. Ei le yn Mywyd y Genedl.*

Mae'r bardd yn trafod y briodas rhwng yr emyn a'r dôn y cenid ef arni, a'r effaith a gafodd ar y gynulleidfa. Mewn gormodiaith ddiffrwyn mae'n sôn

am ddylanwad y canu ar wahanol garfannau o gymdeithas: y pregethwr, y bugail ar y bryniau, y llaethferch, y gôf, y glowr a'r morwr, wrth eu gwaith ac mewn angladdau, hyd yn oed yn angladd Williams ei hun. Ond, meddai'r bardd:

> Chlywi *di* mohonynt *byth*:
> Hoelia'th glust i wrando'n ddyfal heddyw ar eu cân ddilyth;
> Gwelaf fyrdd o Gymry disglair draw yn eistedd ar dy fedd,
> Wedi eu gwisgo â Gorfoledd - gwisg y Briodasol Wledd.

Mynega ei adwaith personol hefyd mewn llinellau cocosaidd:

> Minau âf i'r "Babell" acw, yn unigedd pêr y wlad -
> Ddistadl gapel bach di-addurn, lle addolai Mam a Nhad.

Mae emynau Pantycelyn yn cael eu defnyddio gan y teulu gartref hefyd; disgrifir rhieni ifainc fel 'engyl ar eu hedyn' yn suo-ganu'r plentyn i gysgu gydag emynau Pantycelyn - 'pur lenyddiaeth Arall Fyd' sy'n cael ei chymharu i gân Adar Rhiannon y byd paganaidd - adar, meddai'r bardd, sydd 'wedi eu magu yn nghoedwigoedd Seion Fryn'.

(e) *Buddugoliaeth Bardd y Groes*

Bydd ysbryd Pantycelyn yn gorchfygu - 'yspryd gafodd ei fedyddio / Gan yr Ysbryd Glân Ei Hunan'; a bydd y gwirionddau a bregethodd a chanu amdanynt yn goroesi i ddylanwadu ar ddiwygwyr y dyfodol.

> Ynddynt hwy y gwreiddia'r cedyrn - cedrwydd cryfion trag'wyddoldeb
> Sydd a'u cangau, - megis dithau -'n llawn o fiwsig anfarwoldeb.

Ar ôl diferlif o iaith flodeuog, rodresgar mewn darnau, mae'r bryddest yn terfynu ar nodyn distaw:

> O Bantycelyn! Fab y Gân! -

Dych'mygaf glywed dy Emynau

Fel gwyrthiau'n gwau yn Moliant glân

Cerddorfa'r Nef a'i myrdd delynau!

Oes yno Emyn mwy ei fri? -

Eill ganu'n uwch am Galfari?

Dywedodd Iolo Caernarfon am y bryddest hon, 'Gall gwerinwr ei deall, a gall ysgolhaig ei mwynhau',[14] ond oherwydd ei hyd a'r duedd i ailadrodd yr un syniad mewn diwyg newydd, mae angen dyfalbarhad i ddarllen drwyddi.

Os oedd pryddest fuddugol Eisteddfod 1900 yn gyffredinol ddealladwy, fel arall oedd pryddest Eisteddfod 1929, 'Y Gân ni Chanwyd'. Roedd hon yn gyfansoddiad eithriadol o anodd, a hyd yn oed beirniaid mor ddeallus â'r Parch. William Evans (Wil Ifan),[15] Yr Athro W J Gruffydd,[16] a'r Parch. John Jenkins (Gwili)[17] yn cyfaddef hynny.[18] Y buddugol oedd Caradog Prichard a hynny ar ddyfarniad dau o'r beirniaid yn unig. Er bod Wil Ifan yn gwerthfawrogi coethder ei farddoniaeth, nid oedd am roi'r wobr gyntaf iddo am nad oedd yn teimlo ei fod wedi canu 'cân i'w destun'. Wrth gwrs ni wyddai pwy oedd yr awdur; nid oedd ganddo fantais beirniaid diweddarach, a gaent synhwyro drwy ddarllen gweithiau eraill Caradog Prichard, megis *Afal Drwg Adda* ac *Un Nos Ola Leuad*, beth oedd cefndir y bryddest a beth oedd y cymhellion a'i ysgogodd i'w chyfansoddi. Hon oedd ei drydedd goron mewn tair blynedd[19] a'r ysbrydoliaeth i lunio'r pryddestau ar gyfer y cystadlaethau hyn oedd salwch meddyliol ei fam. Roedd y thema hon yn amlycach yn y ddwy gyntaf sef 'Y Briodas' a 'Penyd', ond gwelir yr un thema mewn diwyg gwahanol a llai amlwg yn y drydedd hefyd, sef 'Y Gân

14 E Vincent Evans, (gol.) *Cofnodion a Chyfansoddiadau Eisteddfod Genedlaethol 1900* (Caerdydd, 1929), t. 55.

15 Y Parch William Evans, gweinidog gyda'r Annibynnwyr a chyn-archdderwydd.

16 Pennaeth Adran y Gymraeg yng Ngholeg Prifysgol Caerdydd, fel y'i gelwid bryd hynny, beirniad llenyddol a bardd.

17 Y Parch. John Jenkins, diwinydd, ysgolhaig a bardd.

18 *Cofnodion a Chyfansoddiadau Eisteddfod Genedlaethol 1929*, tt. 43, 60, 70.

19 Caergybi 1927, Treorci 1928 a Lerpwl 1929. Enillodd y gadair yn Eisteddfod Llanelli 1962.

ni Chanwyd'.[20] Rhennir y bryddest yn dair rhan ac egyr y rhan gyntaf gyda'r bardd yn dweud bod hen ŵr yn cael ei wawdio gan ieuenctid natur:

> "Hen ŵr, Hen ŵr!" Llafar yw'r ddaear werdd
> Gan wawd yr egin gwirion yn ei thwf.

Mae'r hen ŵr yn gweld yr un peth yn digwydd ym myd Natur hefyd:

> Chwerddwch. O flagur gwan,
> Gwatwarwch fwyfwy can y daw eich tro;
> Cewch deimlo min y bladur yn y man
> A thewi'n isel a diflannu o go'.

Yna mae'n cyfarch y dderwen sy'n rhannu'r un profiad ag yntau ac yn cyfeirio at y chwaoedd gwynt yn ei dail fel cerddi sy'n mynegi atgofion a rydd ystyr i fywyd, ond sydd mewn perygl o fynd yn angof. Serch hynny, mae'r ddaear yn trugarhau wrth y ddau am eu hanfodlonrwydd,

> Dderwen, yr ing a wyddom ni ein dau
> Heddiw, fe'i gwybu'r ddaear hen erioed.
> Fe'i gwybu, a dysgodd drwyddo drugarhau
> Wrth flin hen ddynion a chwynfannus goed.
> A phan fo'i braich amdanom ninnau'n cau
> Cyn hir yn y dawelaf, olaf oed,
> Odid mai yn y cymun hwnnw y daw
> Nodau'r gynghanedd berffaith oddi draw.

Ond hyd yn oed os ceir ystyr i fywyd pan ddêl y diwedd, sylweddola mai ynfydrwydd yw priodoli i elfennau byd natur yr un emosiynau ag a deimla ef ei hun.

---

20 I ddeall Caradog Prichard yn iawn, dylid darllen astudiaeth drylwyr Menna Baines, *Yng Ngolau'r Lleuad. Ffeithiau a Dychymyg yng Ngwaith Caradog Prichard* (Llandysul, 2005).

Ynfytyn wyf! Nid oes i'r dderwen hon
    Lygad na chlust na chalon i ddyheu.

Serch hynny, dymunai 'fantellu'r pren â drylliog wisg' ei henaint ei hun

A chwythu arno anadl einioes tad
Fel y gwybyddai boen f'anniddig stad.

Byddai'r hen ŵr yn mynd am dro dychmygol o'r gwely at lyn o dan yr Allt;[21] yn y fan honno daw gweledigaethau iddo ac wedyn byddai'n chwerthin yn ei gwsg 'fel claf na ŵyr mai twymyn ydyw haul ei haf'. Yna mae'n datgelu fel y byddai'n arfaethu cau amdano gaer o waith athronwyr a llenorion y byd er mwyn chwalu'r hen atgofion a ddeuai i aflonyddu arno. Dyna oedd ei ddymuniad, meddai, pan oedd yn 'benllywydd' yn ei lys a'i 'weision lifrai'n diwyd fynd a dod', ond bellach ni allai roi gorchmynion iddynt ac roedd ei grythor wedi peidio â chanu. Yn lle morynion llys ei ieuenctid, daw Plato a'i fintai i ymweld ag ef. Mae'n anodd deall paham y mae'n troi at Plato – efallai am fod yr athronydd hwnnw yn credu yn anfarwoldeb yr enaid. Diwedda'r rhan hon gyda'r bardd yn dringo'r Allt eto a mynd at y llyn; nid yw ots ganddo a siaradai neb ag ef ai peidio, ond cred y byddai'n iach hyd wawr, pan fydd 'y crythor fyth yn curo am ei grwth'.

Dechreua'r ail ran drwy gyfeirio at brofiadau a gawsai'r hen ŵr unwaith:

Pob wylo dagrau, pob rhyw lais a chwardd,
    Pob nwyd a diwniwyd yn anfarwol gân,
Pob gair a fu'n blaguro yng nghalon bardd
    I wywo'n llwch ac i flodeuo'n dân.

Ond fe fyddai'n fodlon gadael y byd hwn pe bai'n gallu ail-fyw yr egni a oedd iddo gynt:

---

21   Roedd delwedd y llyn yn chwarae rhan bwysig yng ngweithiau Caradog Prichard; cafodd ei eni mewn tŷ ar Allt Pen y Bryn ac wedyn bu'n byw mewn tŷ arall ar Allt Glanrafon.

Awn at fy nhras i'r deyrnas sydd ar daen
    Obry, pe gwyddwn gaffael yno'r nwyf
Oedd im pan arglwyddiaethwn yma o'r blaen.

Yna mae Prichard yn defnyddio ffigur ymadrodd anghyffredin wrth gymharu cân a ganwyd, hynny ydyw, y profiadau a gafwyd unwaith, i'r cen ar gefn brithyll sy'n pylu ar ôl ei dal;

Ond megis naid y brithyll bach i'w dranc
    Ar wâdd abwydyn y genweiriwr cudd
A phylni ei gen ar laswellt ar y banc
    Pan fflachiwyd arno danbaid wres y dydd,
Felly y daeth ei chân i galon llanc
O rith y llyn i fyw'n amddifad braidd.

Mae'n anodd dyfalu at bwy y cyfeiria 'ei' yn y llinell olaf ond un. Mae'r Athro W J Gruffudd yn ei feirniadaeth yn awgrymu y dylai Caradog Prichard ail-ysgrifennu'r pennill hwn i wneud y mater yn glir.[22] Er gwaethaf popeth, dywed yr hen ŵr nad yw am roi'r gorau i'w freuddwydion, 'ni ollyngaf delyn oes o'm llaw', meddai. Mae'n gweld dirgelwch y bywyd a fu, ei 'deyrnas rith', fel y'i gelwir, mor 'dragwyddol fud' â'r Sphinx.

Yna cyflwynir i'r bryddest ddwy riain, 'rianedd unwedd Mair', sy'n gweini arni, a gofynna'r hen ŵr iddynt ddatgan iddo 'ddirgelaf ddolur' eu harglwyddes, neu yr 'Anwylyd', fel y cyfeirir ati. Ymateb y rhianedd yw ei gynghori i roi ei 'delyn gyndyn heibio mwy'. Nid oes lle i'w gân mwyach; mae wedi mynd heibio fel y mae profiadau'r Anwylyd wedi mynd heibio. Yna mewn cymysgedd rhyfedd o'r byd a'r betws mae'r Anwylyd yn cael ei chyflwyno fel y dduwies a greodd y ddaear, ond ei bod wedi anghofio'r cwbl a greodd erbyn hyn.

---

22   *Cofnodion a Chyfansoddiadau Eisteddfod Genedlaethol 1929*, t. 62.

Yn y dechreuad un ofnadwy nos
        Oedd iddi'n rhan ac nid oedd Ei diddanu,
Anhysbys ydoedd gwrid persawrus ros,
        Ac nid oedd un aderyn bach yn canu,
Ac nid oedd llygad un afradlon dlos
        Yn dyfod ar lun seren i drywanu
Unnos ddihalog yr anwybod mawr,
Nes cronni nwydau'r oesoedd i ryw awr.

Ond mae ymwybod yn dychwelyd i'r Anwylyd, pan glyw y rhianedd yn wylo.

Gollyngodd nos ei gafael ar bob caeth,
        A'r dydd a'u troes yn 'fyrdd o ryfeddodau',
Yn dafod pob digrifwch, ac yn fant
Pob awel finfel a gusanodd dant.

Eithr byrhoedlog yw'r cyflwr hwn; mae'r rhianedd yn gofidio nad arhosai'r atgofion melys 'yn nydd ysblenydd Ei hymenydd iach', yn hytrach na mynd i ebargofiant:

Drosti daeth tristwch parlys mud, a ffoes
        O ŵydd yr harddwch oedd yn gwawdio'i chlwy'
I hedd y fro nas cyfaneddodd cnawd
Lle dychwel nodau'r gân pan ddarffo'n rhawd.

Serch hynny, dychwelyd yn lluddedig wnaeth yr atgofion a chyngor terfynol y rhianned i'r hen ŵr yw:

Ofer yw geiriau; rhaid yw i ni ddarparu
        I'w llywio'n ôl i'w thud er llawenhau
Bron yr Anwylyd yn Ei hawddfyd hir
Mewn gwerddon draw ar gyrrau'r anial dir.

Er bod y bardd yn ymdrin â chymeriad mytholegol, y Fam Ddaear, mae'n priodoli nodweddion merch o gig a gwaed iddi; mae hi'n anghofio, fel y mae meidrolion yn anghofio, ac mae arni angen ei chysuro, fel y mae pob un ohonom ni angen ein cysuro. Yn ogystal â'r cymysgedd hwn o'r haniaethol a'r diriaethol, gwelir naws beiblaidd ar yr iaith y mae'r bardd yn ei defnyddio i ddisgrifio hynt y dduwies: yr enw a rydd arni, sef yr Anwylyd, ymadroddion fel 'yn y dechreuad' a 'myrdd o ryfeddodau' a galw ei chartref yn yr anialwch yn 'anial dir', sydd yn dwyn i gof emyn Williams Pantycelyn, 'Pererin wyf mewn anial dir'.

Yn y darn olaf mae'r sefyllfa yn cael ei gwyrdroi a'r bardd yn gweld ei brofiadau ei hun yng ngweledigaethau'r hen ŵr. Dywed fod yr hen ŵr yn ei watwar ef am ganu cân 'lle nad oedd cân i'w chanu' ac am iddo

> Weld y Goruchaf ar lun
> Gwallgofrwydd arglwyddes hardd,
> A'm deffro i ganfod mai ffŵl
> Oedd yn gweld ei wallgofrwydd ei hun.

Gwallgofrwydd ei fam oedd ym meddwl y bardd pan luniodd y llinellau uchod, bid sicr. Dywed Menna Baines fod y darlun o'r Anwylyd fel mam yn gyson â'r weledigaeth o'r weddw yn ei bryddest 'Penyd', a'r diffaethwch wedi cymryd lle'r gwallgofdy.[23]

Gwelir llawer o ddylanwadau gwahanol ar 'Y Gân ni Chanwyd': profiadau personol y bardd, mytholeg a'r Beibl. Mae'r elfennau paganaidd a'r crefyddol wedi eu huniaethu mewn ffordd mor annatod fel na ellir eu gwahanu. Mae'r iaith a ddefnyddir i sôn am greadigaeth y Fam Ddaear yn debyg iawn i'r iaith a ddefnyddir i ddisgrifio'r creu yn yr Hen Destament ac mae'r term 'Anwylyd' a ddefnyddir i gyfeirio at yr arglwyddes hefyd yn adlais o'r Beibl. Wrth egluro beth oedd y cymhelliad i gyfansoddi 'Y Gân ni Chanwyd', dywedodd Caradog Prichard, 'Ni allwn, hyd yn oed ar ôl sgrifennu'r gerdd 'Penyd', ymguddio

---

23   *Yng Ngolau'r Lleuad*, 304.

rhag wyneb y sarff. Ond y drydedd waith, yn lle sôn am greadures o gnawd a gwaed, mynnwn dwyfoli'r fam a'i throi'n Fatriarch'.[24] Cyfeirio y mae'r bardd at y sarff yn un o weledigaethau Ioan yn Llyfr y Datguddiad 12:14, adnod y syrthiodd ei lygaid arni'n ddamweiniol ryw ddydd. Ni wyddys a ddarllenodd y bennod i gyd, ac er nad yw'r sarff yn digwydd fel delwedd benodol yn 'Y Gân ni Chanwyd' mae ei chysgod i'w gweld arni. Yn Datguddiad 12 mae Ioan yn gweld mam yn esgor ar blentyn a draig/sarff anferth yn disgwyl i'w ddifetha yn syth wedi iddo ddod allan o'r groth, ond achubir y plentyn rhag y sarff drwy ei gipio at Dduw a'r fam yn ffoi i'r anialwch, lle caiff ei chynnal gan Dduw am ddeuddeg cant a thrigain o ddyddiau. Yn 'Penyd' ceir awgrym fod y fam yn ei galar wedi ymwrthod â'i phlant a hithau yn cael ei danfon i ddiogelwch y gwallgofdy. Yn 'Y Gân ni Chanwyd', yng ngweledigaeth yr hen ŵr, mae'r Anwylyd yn cael ei gwasanaethu gan y ddwy riain a'i sefydlu yn yr anialwch. Yn ei hymdriniaeth feistrolgar ar waith Caradog Prichard a'r ffordd y mae amgylchiadau ei fywyd wedi effeithio ar ei waith llenyddol, dywed Menna Baines y gellid edrych ar 'Penyd' a'r adran am yr anwylyd sy'n ffurfio craidd 'Y Gân ni Chanwyd' fel ymdrechion ar ran y bardd i wneud rhyw fath o synnwyr o arhosiad ei fam yn y 'seilam',[25] fel y cyfeiriai'r bardd yn aml at y lle. Mewn geiriau eraill, mae diogelwch y diffaethwch yn gyfystyr â diogelwch y gwallgofdy ym meddylfryd y bardd.

Mae'r bryddest hon yn feiddgar o ddychmygus a'r ystyr yn dywyll ar adegau. Mae angen ei darllen fwy nag unwaith ac ni ellir ei deall heb fyfyrio hir uwch ei phen, ond er ei dirgelwch a'i hanhawster, mae hi'n gerdd sydd yn gwneud i'r darllenydd feddwl yn ddwys dros yr hyn a ddarllena ac mae'r ymdrech o geisio gwneud synnwyr ohoni yn brofiad gwerthfawr. Fel yn achos yr awdlau, nid yw'r pryddestau hyn at ddant yr oes bresennol, ond maent yn rhan bwysig o draddodiad llenyddol Cymru ac o'r herwydd maent yn werth ein sylw.

---

24 Caradog Prichard, *Afal Drwg Adda* (Dinbych 1973), 105.

25 *Yng Ngolau'r Lleuad*, 306.

Cynlluniwyd y gwaith hwn ac
argraffwyd gan

Gwasg Melita, Ynys Malta a chyhoeddwyd
gan Dr. D. Ben Rees,
Cyfarwyddwr Cwmni Cyhoeddiadau Modern Cymreig,
32 Garth Drive, Allerton, Lerpwl / L18 6HW